T0199246

Algebraic Structures in Natural Language

Algebraic Structures in Natural Language addresses a central problem in cognitive science concerning the learning procedures through which humans acquire and represent natural language. Until recently algebraic systems have dominated the study of natural language in formal and computational linguistics, AI, and the psychology of language, with linguistic knowledge seen as encoded in formal grammars, model theories, proof theories, and other rule-driven devices. Recent work on deep learning has produced an increasingly powerful set of general learning mechanisms which do not apply rule-based algebraic models of representation. The success of deep learning in NLP has led some researchers to question the role of algebraic models in the study of human language acquisition and linguistic representation. Psychologists and cognitive scientists have also been exploring explanations of language evolution and language acquisition that rely on probabilistic methods, social interaction, and information theory, rather than on formal models of grammar induction.

This book addresses the learning procedures through which humans acquire natural language, and the way in which they represent its properties. It brings together leading researchers from computational linguistics, psychology, behavioural science, and mathematical linguistics to consider the significance of non-algebraic methods for the study of natural language. The text represents a wide spectrum of views, from the claim that algebraic systems are largely irrelevant, to the contrary position that non-algebraic learning methods are engineering devices for efficiently identifying the patterns that underlying grammars and semantic models generate for natural language input. There are interesting and important perspectives that fall at intermediate points between these opposing approaches, and they may combine elements of both. The text will appeal to researchers and advanced students in each of these fields, as well as to anyone who wants to learn more about the relationship between computational models and natural language.

About the Editors

Shalom Lappin is a professor of computational linguistics at the University of Gothenburg, professor of natural language processing at Queen Mary University of London, and emeritus professor of computational linguistics at King's College London. His research focuses on the application of machine learning and probabilistic models to the representation and acquisition of linguistic knowledge.

Jean-Philippe Bernardy is a researcher at the University of Gothenburg. His main research interest is in interpretable linguistic models, in particular, those built from first principles of algebra, probability, and geometry.

Algebraic Structures in Natural Language

Edited by
Shalom Lappin
University of Gothenburg, Queen
Mary University of London, and
King's College London

Jean-Philippe Bernardy
University of Gothenburg

CRC Press
Taylor & Francis Group
Boca Raton London New York

CRC Press is an imprint of the
Taylor & Francis Group, an **informa** business

First edition published 2023
by CRC Press
6000 Broken Sound Parkway NW, Suite 300, Boca Raton, FL 33487-2742

and by CRC Press
4 Park Square, Milton Park, Abingdon, Oxon, OX14 4RN

CRC Press is an imprint of Taylor & Francis Group, LLC

Library of Congress Cataloging-in-Publication Data

Names: Lappin, Shalom, editor. | Bernardy, Jean-Philippe, editor.
Title: Algebraic structures in natural language / edited by Shalom Lappin, Queen Mary University of London ; Jean-Philippe Bernardy, University of Gothenburg.
Description: First edition. | Boca Raton : CRC Press, 2023. | Includes bibliographical references and index.
Identifiers: LCCN 2022031217 (print) | LCCN 2022031218 (ebook) | ISBN 9781032066547 (hardback) | ISBN 9781032071046 (paperback) | ISBN 9781003205388 (ebook)
Subjects: LCSH: Language acquisition. | Mathematical linguistics. | Deep learning (Machine learning) | LCGFT: Essays.
Classification: LCC P118 .A396 2023 (print) | LCC P118 (ebook) | DDC 401/.93--dc23/eng/2020920
LC record available at https://lccn.loc.gov/2022031217
LC ebook record available at https://lccn.loc.gov/2022031218

ISBN: 978-1-032-06654-7 (hbk)
ISBN: 978-1-032-07104-6 (pbk)
ISBN: 978-1-003-20538-8 (ebk)

DOI: 10.1201/9781003205388

Typeset in Latin Roman
by KnowledgeWorks Global Ltd

Publisher's note: This book has been prepared from camera-ready copy provided by the authors.

לנכדים, זוהר, אלה, עמרי, גליה, נועם, ועידו. באהבה מסבא

To my children, Miranda, and Irmeli.

Contents

Preface

Assembling this volume has given us a unique opportunity to encounter some of our colleagues' current research on issues in computational linguistics and machine learning that are central to our own work. It has been a privilege to edit their chapters, and to work with them on this collection. We very much appreciate their cooperation and their support in this enterprise.

Our work on the book was supported by grant 2014-39 from the Swedish Research Council, which funds the Centre for Linguistic Theory and Studies in Probability (CLASP) in the Department of Philosophy, Linguistics, and Theory of Science at the University of Gothenburg.

We are deeply grateful to Stergios Chatzikyriakidis, Alex Clark, Stephen Clark, Edward Gibson, Chris Howes, Joakim Nivre, Stephen Pulman, Asad Sayeed, and Richard Sproat for providing external reviews of the chapters. Their suggestions have been exceedingly useful to the contributors in revising their drafts.

We thank Elliot Morsia, our editor at Taylor & Francis, Simran Kaur, our editorial assistant, and Shashi Kumar, our Latex support person, for the help and encouragement that they provided during the compilation of this volume.

Finally, we are grateful to our families for being there for us during the long hours of work that we devoted to this project. We appreciate their patience and good humour.

Shalom Lappin and Jean-Philippe Bernardy
London and Gothenburg
June 2022

Contributors

Ben Ambridge is professor of psychology at the University of Manchester, and a member of the ESRC International Centre for Language and Communicative Development (LuCiD). His research focuses on how children learn the grammar and morphology of their languages.

Marco Baroni is an ICREA research professor in the Department of Translation and Language Sciences of the Universitat Pompeu Fabra in Barcelona. His current research focuses on the implications of deep-learning-based language models for linguistic theory, and on the idea of non-human-controlled machine-to-machine communication.

Jean-Philippe Bernardy is a researcher at the University of Gothenburg. His main research interest is in interpretable linguistic models, in particular those built from the first principles of algebra, probability, and geometry.

Samuel R. Bowman is a newly tenured faculty member at NYU, working in the Center for Data Science, the Department of Linguistics, and the Courant Institute's Department of Computer Science. His research focuses primarily on developing techniques and datasets for use in controlling and evaluating large language models, and additionally on applications of machine learning to scientific questions in linguistic syntax and semantics.

Nick Chater is professor of behavioural science at Warwick Business School. He is interested in the cognitive and social foundations of language and rationality.

Morten H. Christiansen is the William R. Kenan, Jr. Professor of Psychology at Cornell University, professor of cognitive science of language at the School of Communication and Culture as well as the Interacting Minds Centre at Aarhus University, Denmark, and a senior scientist at the Haskins Labs. His research focuses on the interaction of biological and environmental constraints in the evolution, acquisition, and processing of language.

Gabriella Chronis is a PhD student in the department of linguistics at the University of Texas at Austin who studies lexical semantics and figurative language through a computational lens.

Eve V. Clark is professor emerita of linguistics and symbolic systems at Stanford University. She has published extensively on semantics, pragmatics, and cross-linguistic comparisons in first language acquisition.

Katrin Erk is a professor in the Linguistics Department at the University of Texas at Austin. Her research is in computational semantics, in particular flexible computational representations for word meaning.

Jon Gauthier is a PhD candidate in the Department of Brain and Cognitive Sciences at Massachusetts Institute of Technology (MIT). His research uses computational modelling to study the representational and neural mechanisms that support language acquisition and comprehension.

Jennifer Hu is a PhD student at MIT in the Department of Brain and Cognitive Sciences. Her research focuses on the computational and cognitive principles that underlie human language, with dual goals of understanding the human mind and building better systems of artificial intelligence.

Anna Korhonen is a professor of natural language processing and a co-director of the Language Technology Laboratory (LTL) at the University of Cambridge. Her research focuses on natural language processing. Her work is centred around natural language understanding within and across languages and on how to develop, adapt, and apply fundamental techniques to meet real life needs.

Shalom Lappin is a professor of computational linguistics at the University of Gothenburg, professor of natural language processing at Queen Mary University of London, and emeritus professor of computational linguistics at King's College London. His research focuses on the application of machine learning and probabilistic models to the representation and the acquisition of linguistic knowledge.

Roger Levy is a professor of brain and cognitive sciences at MIT. His research focuses on the foundational architecture of natural language knowledge, processing, and acquisition.

Sharid Loáiciga is a computational linguist working at CLASP, University of Gothenburg. Her research focuses on document-level NLP, in particular on human and machine interpretation of referring expressions regarding entities vs events. She is also interested in multilingual NLP, resource annotation, and psycholinguistic methods.

Olga Majewska is an affiliated researcher in the Language Technology Laboratory at the University of Cambridge, currently working on developing multilingual dialogue systems at Amazon Alexa AI. Her research interests span multilingual lexical semantics, lexical typology, and task-oriented dialogue systems, with a focus on their large-scale multilingual expansion.

Lawrence S. Moss is professor of mathematics at Indiana University, and adjunct professor of computer science, linguistics, and philosophy. He is president of the Association for Logic, Language and Information, and editor-in-chief of the *Journal of Logic, Language and Information*.

Peng Qian is a PhD student in the Department of Brain and Cognitive Sciences at MIT and a member of the Computational Psycholinguistics Laboratory, advised by Roger Levy. His research combines behavioural experiments and computational models to study language and cognition.

Ivan Vulić is a senior research associate in the Language Technology Laboratory at the University of Cambridge. His research is focused on (but not limited to) multilingual and low-resource NLP, dialogue systems, and multi-modal semantics.

Alex Warstadt is a PhD student in linguistics at New York University working with Sam Bowman. He studies the learnability of grammar using artificial neural networks.

Ethan Gotlieb Wilcox is a PhD student at Harvard University in the Linguistics Department. His research uses experimental methods and contemporary neural network models to investigate how people learn and process language.

Introduction

For the past sixty years, most linguists have encoded knowledge of language within symbolic algebraic frameworks as formal grammars, type theories, and model theories. Until the end of the last century, most AI researchers, particularly those working in natural language processing, implemented algebraic rule-based systems of these kinds to handle the tasks in reasoning and analysis that they sought to solve. In recent years deep learning has largely displaced these systems within AI, even as grammars remain dominant among theoretical linguists.

Deep neural networks (DNNs) have matured to the point that they achieve impressive results across a wide range of NLP tasks. In some cases, they exceed human performance on these applications. For the most part, DNNs do not use symbolic rules, although they may incorporate rule-like learning biases in their design. They can also be trained on data annotated with symbolic labelling that implies rule-based representations.

Deep learning has demonstrated robustly wide coverage in many domains of NLP, where classical algebraic rule-based systems have yielded brittle performance for far more limited ranges of data. These results raise a number of important questions. First, what is the cognitive significance of deep learning? Most DNNs were designed as engineering systems to solve problems in machine learning and data processing. Can they yield insight into the limits of human learning and representation? Can they illuminate the way in which people actually acquire and encode knowledge, in particular, linguistic knowledge?

Second, what sort of learning and representational biases are required for efficient learning, particularly natural language? Determining the answer to this question could shed light on the learning biases we need to posit for human language acquisition. It would go some way to clarifying whether domain-general data-driven models, with weak domain-specific biases are sufficient for acquiring natural language.

Finally, to what extent do the distributed vector and matrix representations that DNNs use to process data correspond to the structures through which humans encode linguistic knowledge? By exploring this question, we can better understand the limits and possibilities of symbolic algebraic models of human reasoning and natural language.

A major obstacle to pursuing these three research questions is the opacity of DNNs. Most deep learning systems apply non-linear functions (such as sigmoid, tanh, and ReLU) to map one state of the system into its successor. These functions cause the operations through which a DNN combines vectors to be non-compositional in the sense that the output vectors are not consistently determined by a single set of functions that operate in a uniform way. The increasing reliance on large non-sequential transformers, like BERT and XLNet, has intensified the problem. These consist primarily of layers of attentional heads, which apply sets of such functions to input vectors. As a result, it is difficult to discern the patterns that DNNs identify, and the way in which they arrive at the generalisations that they extract from input data.

This volume brings together chapters by leading researchers in computational linguistics, natural language processing, cognitive science, psycholinguistics, and mathematical linguistics. They address different aspects of these three questions and issues that follow from them. Taken together, they offer a view of some of the major themes in contemporary work on the cognitive foundations of natural language, from both a computational and psychological perspective.

In Chapter 1, Marco Baroni proposes that DNNs can be taken as models of linguistic knowledge, and fruitfully compared to traditional algebraic linguistic theories. He points out that theoretical linguists have, for the most part, not taken account of work in deep learning for NLP, while a small but growing group of computational linguists is exploring the theoretical linguistic significance of DNNs. He envisages the benefits of closer cooperation between theoretical linguists and NLP researchers in assessing the comparative strengths and weaknesses of symbolic algebraic systems and DNNs for explaining human acquisition and representation of linguistic knowledge.

Alex Warstadt and Samuel R. Bowman consider the plausibility of DNNs as models of human language acquisition in Chapter 2. They argue that one of the main obstacles to using deep learning results to motivate claims about how much domain specific knowledge is required for successful language learning is the fact that current DNNs have access to far more data than children do during the learning process. They are also designed in a way that makes meaningful comparisons difficult. Warstadt and Bowman propose constructing deep learning models that do not have advantages over human learners, in order to render these models useful for language acquisition studies. They suggest that when constrained in this way, machine learning can yield important insights into the nature of prior learning biases required for efficient language acquisition.

In Chapter 3, Nick Chater and Morten H. Christiansen argue for a non-representationalist view of algebraic structure in natural language. In opposition to nativist notions of universal grammar, they advocate a view according to which algebraic structure emerges in languages as a case of spontaneous order in a complex social system. This system is built up through accretion, forming layers of communicative precedents. It evolves over time to resolve internal conflicts, and to optimise local solutions to challenges posed by the need to transfer and receive information. The patterns that govern linguistic communication are not internally represented by language users. They are properties of a culturally evolved system, rather than of the organisms that use and develop it.

Eve V. Clark presents a synchronic account of language acquisition in Chapter 4, which, in broad outline, accords with Chater and Christiansen's diachronic view of language evolution. She regards child-adult interaction and adult correction as the primary drivers of language learning. On this view children achieve linguistic competence by learning to use constructions in communication with adults. The feedback that they receive shapes their ability to use these constructions with increasing precision, and to combine them into more complex linguistic structures.

In Chapter 5, Ben Ambridge offers extensive experimental evidence, from a variety of languages, to argue for the conclusion that the passive construction is not generated by a formal syntactic rule specified independently of semantic content. Instead, it is conditioned by interpretational properties involving an affectedness constraint on thematic relations, in the event that the passivised verb indicates. This view implies that syntactic rules are defeasible and probabilistic in nature, with semantic and pragmatic factors playing a significant role in determining their scope of application.

Ethan Wilcox, Jon Gauthier, Jennifer Hu, Peng Qian, and Roger Levy consider the GPT-2 transformer as a model of syntactic learning, in Chapter 6. They discuss experiments on a variety of structures, including sentential complements, filler-gap dependencies, reflexives, and negative polarity items. They report that the model performs well on many of the tasks, but less so on others. Wilcox et al. discuss the implications of these results for previous claims on the need for domain-specific learning biases to support human language acquisition. Their work connects directly with that described by Warstadt and Bowman in Chapter 2.

In Chapter 7 Sharid Loáiciga takes up the question of how to use DNNs to extend the scope of small scale psycholinguistic experiments on discourse structure. She considers both discourse deixis and discourse entity representation. Loáiciga explores how probing techniques can be applied to illuminate the ways in which DNNs encode discourse structure in their processing of text. This approach offers the prospect of greatly expanding the range of work on the acquisition and representation of discourse information implicit in raw text. This work can contribute to our understanding of how humans learn discourse structure. It can also facilitate the development of more powerful text understanding and dialogue management systems.

Olga Majewska, Ivan Vulić, and Anna Korhonen consider in Chapter 8 how DNNs can be trained to achieve the linguistic knowledge required for complex NLP tasks with under-resourced languages for which limited amounts of online data are available. They suggest that using linguistically motivated labelling on small data sets, as well as other methods of introducing biases into the learning process, allows deep learning systems to achieve wide coverage through training with much less data than is used for well-represented languages. This approach combines deep learning with elements of rule-based algebraic models of linguistic theory. It employs knowledge distillation techniques for incorporating syntactic parsing and other biases into DNNs.

In Chapter 9, Katrin Erk and Gabriella Chronis explore properties of word embeddings with which DNNs are pretrained. They identify clustering patterns for these embeddings that correspond to story-like narratives. These reflect judgements and associations woven into the texts from which the embeddings are extracted. They observe that these stories are particularly pronounced in the word embeddings of transformers like BERT, which use word contexts to train the DNN to predict the occurrence of lexical items. Erk and Chronis point out that the story narratives encoded in word embeddings contain valuable semantic and discourse information that can be used to improve the performance of deep learning systems in certain NLP tasks. This information must also be identified and manipulated when controlling for cultural bias in DNNs.

Lawrence S. Moss compares symbolic algebraic and deep learning models, with application to natural language inference in Chapter 10. He notes that DNNs are outperforming rule-based systems in coverage and scope of data. He observes that the latter do not offer a theory of learning. However, the classical models capture inference patterns and semantic generalisations that are inaccessible to machine learning. He envisages a creative interaction between both sets of methods in the future development of computational approaches to natural language inference and semantics.

In Chapter 11, Jean-Philippe Bernardy and Shalom Lappin propose Unitary-Evolution RNNs (URNs) as an alternative deep learning model for NLP. These systems use unitary matrices as word embeddings and apply only the operations of linear algebra, specifically matrix multiplication to combine embeddings. No non-linear functions are included. As a result, the embedding of a compound is the multiplication of the embeddings of its parts. This means that they achieve compositionality in contrast to LSTMs and transformers. Consequently, the embeddings can be analysed out of context, and in this sense, the RNN is transparent. Bernardy and Lappin show that URNs achieve promising precision, and relatively stable learning patterns, on three NLP tasks involving long distance dependencies. They use unitary matrices and linear algebraic operations on them, rather than grammars, to encode linguistic information.

The contributions to this volume indicate the diversity of computational approaches to the foundational cognitive issues that are increasingly central to work in natural language processing. They also exhibit the vitality and innovation that characterises this part of the field. If the volume stimulates discussion and further research on the questions that are addressed, then it will have fulfilled its purpose.

CHAPTER 1

On the Proper Role of Linguistically Oriented Deep Net Analysis in Linguistic Theorising

Marco Baroni

Catalan Institute for Research and Advanced Studies (ICREA) / Universitat Pompeu Fabra

CONTENTS

ABSTRACT

A lively research field has recently emerged that uses experimental methods to probe the linguistic behaviour of modern deep networks. While work in this tradition often reports intriguing results about the grammatical skills of deep nets, it is not clear what their implications for linguistic theorising should be. As a consequence, linguistically oriented deep net analysis has had very little impact on linguistics at large. In this chapter, I suggest that deep networks should be treated as theories making explicit predictions about the acceptability of linguistic utterances. I argue that if we overcome some obstacles standing in the way of seriously pursuing this idea, we will gain a powerful new theoretical tool, complementary to mainstream algebraic approaches.

1.1 INTRODUCTION

During the last decade, deep neural networks have come to dominate the field of natural language processing (NLP) (Devlin et al., 2019; Sutskever et al., 2014; Vaswani et al., 2017). While earlier approaches to NLP relied on tools, such as part-of-speech taggers and parsers, that extracted linguistic knowledge from explicit manual annotation of text corpora (Jurafsky and Martin, 2008), deep-learning-based methods typically adopt an "end-to-end" approach: A deep net is directly trained to associate some form of natural linguistic input (e.g., text in a language) to a corresponding linguistic output (e.g., the same text in a different language), dispensing with the traditional pipeline of intermediate linguistic modules and the related annotation of latent linguistic structure (e.g., syntactic parses of source and target sentences) (Goldberg, 2017; Lappin, 2021).

This paradigm shift has important implications for the relation between theoretical and computational linguistics. The issue of which linguistic formalisms might provide the best annotation schemes to develop effective NLP tools is no longer relevant. Instead, in the last few years we have seen the rise of a new field of investigation consisting of the experimental analysis of the grammatical skills of deep nets trained without the injection of any explicit linguistic knowledge. For the remainder of the chapter, I will refer to this research area as LODNA, for *linguistically oriented deep net analysis*. LODNA takes the perspective of a psycholinguist (Futrell et al., 2019), or perhaps more accurately that of an ethologist (McCloskey, 1991; Scholte, 2016), designing sophisticated experiments to "probe" the knowledge implicit in a species' behaviour.

LODNA is currently a very active research field, with many papers focusing on whether neural networks have correctly induced specific kinds of grammatical generalisation (**Chaves:2020**; e.g., Chowdhury and Zamparelli, 2018; Futrell et al., 2019; Linzen, Dupoux, et al., 2016), as well as benchmarks attempting to probe their linguistic competence at multiple levels (Conneau, Kruszewski, et al., 2018; Warstadt et al., 2019). LODNA papers account for a significant proportion of the work presented at annual events such as the Society for Computation in Linguistics conference and the BlackBox NLP workshop.

LODNA is well-motivated from a machine-learning perspective. Understanding how a system behaves is a prerequisite to improving it, and it is important in the perspective of AI safety and explainability (Belinkov and Glass, 2019; Xie et al., 2020). However, there is no doubt that the grammatical performance of deep nets is also extremely intriguing from a linguistic perspective, particularly because the architectural primitives of these models (such as distributed representations and structures that linearly propagate information across time) are profoundly different from those postulated in linguistics (such as categorical labels and tree structures). Still, as we will see below, for all the enthusiasm for LODNA within NLP, this line of work is hardly having any impact on the current debate in theoretical linguistics.

In this chapter, after introducing, as an example of LODNA, the by-now "classic" domain of long-distance agreement probing (Section 1.2), I will present evidence for the claim that this sort of research, despite the intriguing patterns it uncovers, is hardly affecting contemporary linguistics (Section 1.3). I will then argue that this gap stems from lack of clarity about its theoretical significance (Section 1.4). In particular, I will show that modern deep networks cannot be treated as blank slates meant to falsify innateness claims. They should rather be seen as algorithmic linguistic theories making predictions about utterance acceptability. I will, however, outline several issues that are currently standing in the way of taking deep nets seriously as linguistic theories. I will conclude in Section 11.7 by briefly discussing why taking this stance might be beneficial to computational and theoretical linguistics, and by sketching two possible ways to pursue LODNA-based linguistic theorising.

1.2 LINGUISTICALLY ORIENTED ANALYSIS OF DEEP NETS: THE CASE OF LONG-DISTANCE AGREEMENT

Linguists identify sensitivity to syntactic structure that is not directly observable in the signal as one of the core properties of human grammatical competence (Everaert et al., 2015). A paradigmatic test for structure sensitivity comes from agreement phenomena. For example, subject-verb number agreement in an English clause depends on the c-command relation between the subject noun phrase and the corresponding verb, and it is not affected by nouns intervening between the NP head and the verb:

(1)   [The **kid** [near the *toys* in the *boxes*]] **is** tired.

In (1), an example of *long-distance agreement*, the fact that two plural nouns (*toys* and *boxes*) directly precede the main verb *is* does not affect its number, as the only noun that entertains the right relation with the verb is *kid*. As Everaert and colleagues' (2015) motto goes, it's all about *structures*, not strings!

Current deep network architectures, such as long short-term memory networks (LSTMs, Hochreiter and Schmidhuber, 1997), convolutional networks (CNNs, Kalchbrenner et al., 2014) or Transformers (Vaswani et al., 2017), do not encode (at least, by conscious designer decision) any prior favouring a structural analysis of their input over a sequential one. It is natural then to ask whether they are able to correctly handle structure-dependent phenomena, such as long-distance agreement. Consequently, starting with the influential work of Linzen, Dupoux, et al. (2016), long-distance agreement has become a standard test to probe their linguistic abilities.

Probably the most thorough analysis of long-distance number agreement in deep networks was the one carried out by Gulordava et al. (2018). We focused on LSTMs trained as *language models*. That is, networks were trained by exposing them to large amounts of textual data (samples from the Wikipedia of the relevant languages), with the task of predicting the next word given the context. No special tuning for the long-distance agreement challenge was applied. After this generic training, the networks were presented with sentence prefixes up to and excluding the second item in an agreement relation (e.g., *The kid near the toys in the boxes. . .*), and the probability they assigned to continuations with the right or wrong agreement (*is/are*) was measured. The experiment was conduced with a test set of genuine corpus examples in four languages (English, Hebrew, Italian, and Russian), and considering various agreement relations (not only noun-verb but, also, for example, verb-verb and adjective-noun). The networks got the right agreement with high accuracy in all languages and for all constructions.

Even more impressively, networks were also able to get agreement right when tested with nonsense sentences such as the one in (2), showing that they must extract syntactic rules at a rather abstract level.

(2)   The **carrot** around the *lions* for the *disasters*. . . **sings/*sing**.

Finally, we compared the agreement accuracy of the Italian network with that of native speakers (both on corpus-extracted and nonsense sentences), finding that the network is only marginally lagging behind human performance.

Other studies tested different deep architectures, such as CNNs (Bernardy and Lappin, 2017) and Transformers (Y. Goldberg, 2019), confirming that they also largely succeed at long-distance agreement.

Deep nets have been tested for a number of other linguistic generalisations, such as those pertaining to filler-gap constructions, auxiliary fronting and case assignment. See Linzen and Baroni (2021) for a recent survey of LODNA specifically aimed at linguists.[1] In pretty much all cases, while they departed here and there from human intuition, deep nets captured at least the general gist of the phenomena being investigated.

1.3   THE GAP

Results such as the ones on the long-distance agreement I briefly reviewed should provide food for thought to theoretical linguists, since, as already mentioned, deep nets ostensibly possess very different priors from those postulated by linguists as part of the universal language faculty, such as a predisposition for hierarchical structures (Adger, 2019; Berwick and Chomsky, 2016; Hauser et al., 2002). In reality, however, the growing body of work on LODNA is almost completely ignored in the current theoretical linguistics debate.

To sustain this claim with quantitative evidence, I looked at the impact of Tal Linzen's original paper on the long-distance agreement in deep nets (Linzen, Dupoux, et al., 2016). This is a highly cited paper, having amassed 514 Google Scholar citations in less than five years.[2] I sifted through these citations, keeping track of how many came from theoretical linguistics (under a very broad notion of what counts as theoretical linguistics). I found that only six citations qualified. Of these, three were opinion pieces, one of them written by Linzen himself. Note that the article does not lack general interdisciplinary appeal, as shown by many citations from psycho- and neuro-linguistics, and even four citations from the field of computational agricultural studies!

Perhaps Google Scholar does a poor job at tracking theoretical linguistic work. Indeed, David Adger's recent *Language Unlimited* volume (Adger, 2019) does extensively discuss Linzen's article, but I did not find it among the studies citing it according to Scholar. Thus, as a supplementary source of evidence, I also downloaded

---

[1]Lappin (2021) also provides a review of some of the relevant work, as part of a book-length treatment of the linguistic and cognitive implications of deep learning models.

[2]Google Scholar queried on May 27th, 2021.

all papers from the front page of LingBuzz, a popular linguistics preprint archive.[3] I filtered out papers that do not qualify as theoretical linguistics. Again, I tried to be inclusive: I excluded, for example, one paper about the aftermath of the "Pinker LSA letter" controversy (Kastner et al., 2021), but I did include one about phonosymbolysm in Pokémon character names (Kawahara et al., 2021). This left me with a corpus of 37 papers. I then went through their bibliographies, looking for references to deep learning work, and finding...none![4]

It is not fair to impute this lack of references to a putative endogamous bent of theoretical linguistics. To the contrary, papers in my mini-corpus reveal considerable interdisciplinary breadth, with frequent references to neuroscience, ethology, psycholinguistics, and sociolinguistics; they include statistical treatments of experimental and corpus data; and they use sophisticated computational tools, such as graph-theoretical methods. It is really NLP, and in particular deep-learning-based NLP, that is missing from the party.

To understand this gap, we need to ask: why should linguists care about the grammatical analysis of deep networks? What is it supposed to tell us about human linguistic competence? In other words, what is the theoretical significance of LODNA?

1.4 THE THEORETICAL SIGNIFICANCE OF LINGUISTICALLY ORIENTED DEEP NET ANALYSIS

When LODNA researchers situate their work within a broader theoretical context, it is invariably in terms of nature-or-nurture arguments resting on a view of deep nets as blank slates. For example, when asked about the significance of his work for theoretical linguistics, Tal Linzen told me that deep-net simulations "can help linguists focus on the aspects [...] that truly require explanation in terms of innate constraints. If the simulation shows that there is plenty of data for the learner to acquire a particular phenomenon, maybe there's nothing to explain!" (Tal Linzen, p.c.).

Similar claims are sprinkled throughout LODNA papers. Here are just a few examples (from otherwise excellent papers): "Our results also contribute to the long-running nature-nurture debate in language acquisition: whether the success of neural models implies that unbiased learners can learn natural languages with enough data, or whether human abilities to acquire language given sparse stimulus implies a strong innate human learning bias" (Papadimitriou and Jurafsky, 2020). "The APS [(argument from the poverty of the stimulus)] predicts that any artificial learner trained with no prior knowledge of the principles of syntax [...] must fail to make acceptability judgements with human-level accuracy. [...] If linguistically uninformed neural network models achieve human-level performance on specific phenomena [...], this

---

[3]Papers downloaded from `https://ling.auf.net/lingbuzz` on May 27th, 2021. I downloaded all *freshly changed* and *new* papers, as well as all the papers in the *Top Recent Downloads* and *Last 6 months* sections of the front page.

[4]I had performed a similar experiment in March 2021, by collecting papers from the latest issues of *Linguistic Inquiry*, *Natural Language and Linguistic Theory* and *Syntax*, with the very same outcome (no reference whatsoever to deep learning work).

would be clear evidence limiting the scope of phenomena for which the APS can hold" (Warstadt et al., 2019). "[I]f such a device [(a neural network)] could manage to replicate fine-grained human intuitions inducing them from the raw training input this would be evidence that exposure to language structures [...] should in principle be sufficient to derive a syntactic competence, against the innatist hypothesis" (Chowdhury and Zamparelli, 2018).

Deep nets are linguistic theories, not blank slates

If blank slate arguments were (perhaps) valid when looking at the simple connectionist models of the eighties (Churchland, 1989; Clark, 1989; Rumelhart et al., 1986), all modern deep networks possess highly structured innate architectures that considerably weaken them. Consider, for example, the Transformer (Vaswani et al., 2017), the current darling of NLP. A Transformer network is structured into a number of layered modules, each involving a complex bank of linear and non-linear transformations. These, in turn, differ in profound ways from the innate structure of an LSTM (Hochreiter and Schmidhuber, 1997). For example, an LSTM will read a sentence one token at a time and will use a recurrent function to preserve information across time, whereas the Transformer will read the whole sentence at once, and use an extended backward and forward attention systems to incorporate contextual information.

Even more importantly, as demonstrated by the widespread interest of NLP and machine learning researchers in proposing new architectures, differences in the supposedly "weak" and "general" biases of different deep nets lead them to behave very differently, given the same input data.

A striking illustration of this was recently provided by Kharitonov and Chaabouni (2021) in a study of so-called *seq2seq* deep nets, that is, networks trained to associate input and output sequences (as in, e.g., a translation task).

Kharitonov and Chaabouni trained such networks on really tiny corpora that severely underspecify the input-output relation. The test-time behaviour of the network in cases where different generalisations lead to different outputs was then inspected, to reveal which innate preferences the networks brought to the task.

In one of their experiments, the whole training corpus consists of the following *input → output* examples.

(3)   aabaa → b
        bbabb → a
        aaaaa → a
        bbbbb → b

The mini-corpus in (3) is compatible with (at least) two rules: a "hierarchical" one, stating that the output is generated by taking the character in the middle of the input; and a "linear" generalisation, stating that the output is the third character in the input sequence.[5]

---

[5]This can be seen as a schematic reproduction of classic poverty-of-the-stimulus thought experiments, such as the one built around English auxiliary fronting by Chomsky (1968).

After training it with just the examples in (3), a network is exposed to a new input where the two rules lead to different predictions, e.g., *aaabaaa*, where the hierarchical generalisation would pick *b* and the linear one *a*.

Of four widely used seq2seq models tested by Kharitonov and Chaabouni, two (LSTMs with attention and Transformers) show a strong preference for the hierarchical generalisation, and two (LSTMs without attention and CNNs) show a strong preference for the linear generalisation.

Studies such as this invalidate any blank-slate claim about deep nets. It is more appropriate, instead, to look at deep nets as *linguistic theories*, encoding non-trivial structural priors facilitating language acquisition and processing. More precisely, we can think of a deep net architecture, before any language-specific training, as a general theory defining a space of possible grammars, and of the same network trained on data from a specific language as a *grammar*, that is, a computational system that, given an input utterance in a language, can predict whether the sequence is acceptable to an idealised speaker of the language (e.g., Chomsky, 1986; Müller, 2020; Sag et al., 2003).[6]

It is undoubtedly easier to inspect the inner workings of a symbolic linguistic theory than those of a trained deep net, and indeed, a classic objection against artificial neural networks as cognitive theories is that they are unopenable black boxes (e.g., McCloskey, 1991). However, going hand in hand with the development of more complex models, the field has also made extensive progress in the development of methods to analyse their states and behaviours (Belinkov and Glass, 2019), providing strong methodological support for a systematic analysis of deep nets.

Why don't we see, then, many articles positioning deep nets as alternative or complementary theories to traditional grammatical formalism? I believe that two crucial ingredients are still missing, before deep nets can seriously contribute to contemporary linguistic theorising.

The problem of low commitment to models

Differences between deep nets, as we have discussed above, are huge. *Mutatis mutandis*, the difference between an LSTM, reading an input token at a time and building a joint representation through its recurrent state, and a Transformer, processing all input tokens in parallel to create multiple context-weighted representations, might be as large as that between a derivational and a constraint-based theory in formal linguistics.[7]

---

[6] Just like in linguistics (e.g., Lau et al., 2017; Murphy, 2007; Sprouse and Schütze, 2019), there is considerable debate on the best way to elicit acceptability judgements from trained deep net models in order to compare them to human data, and on whether such judgements should be probabilistic or categorical (e.g., Chowdhury and Zamparelli, 2018; Linzen, Dupoux, et al., 2016; Niu and Penn, 2020; Warstadt et al., 2019).

[7] At a deep mathematical level, recurrent networks (such as LSTMs) and Transformers might be more related than what a superficial comparison might suggest (see, e.g., Katharopoulos et al., 2020), just like some differences between derivational and constraint-based grammars might be more apparent than substantive (Hunter, 2019).

And, yet, researchers investigating the linguistic behaviour of these architectures almost never provide a theoretically grounded motivation for why they focused on one architecture or the other. Interest tends to shift with the state of the art in applied tasks such as machine translation or natural language inference. So, if nearly all early LODNA papers focused on recurrent LSTM networks, nowadays the field has nearly entirely shifted to analysing Transformer networks, not because the latter were found to be more plausible models of human language processing (if anything, their ability to read and process massive windows of text in parallel makes them *less* plausible models than recurrent networks), but because they became the mainstream approach in applied NLP, thanks to their astounding performance in applied tasks.

As a concrete illustration of this phenomenon, we can compare the LODNA papers from the first (2018) and third (2020) editions of the BlackBox NLP workshop (one of the core events in the area).[8] In the 2018 edition, I found 13 full papers that broadly qualify as LODNA. Of them, twelve focus on LSTM analysis, with the remaining one already looking at the Transformer. In two years, the balance has completely shifted. All nine relevant papers in the 2020 editions analyse some variant of the Transformer, with two also including LSTM variants among the comparison models. Importantly, in none of these papers there is a linguistically oriented (or even engineering-oriented) discussion of *why* the Transformer was picked over the LSTM or other architectures. Indeed, in a few cases, earlier work that was based on LSTMs is cited as corroborating evidence, only mentioning in passing that it was based on a (profoundly) different architecture.

The problem is mostly sociological: NLP puts a strong (and reasonable) emphasis on whichever models work best in applications, and consequently analytical work will also tend to concentrate on such models. However, if radical changes in the underlying architecture are not motivated by linguistic considerations, and indeed they tend to be completely glossed over, it is hard to take this work seriously from the perspective of linguistic theorising.[9]

Lack of mechanistic understanding

A good linguistic theory should not only fit what is already known about a language, but also make predictions about previously unexplored patterns. This is the typical *modus operandi* in formal syntax, where, for example, hypotheses about possible syntactic configurations lead to strong typological predictions about acceptable adverb and adjective orders (e.g., Cinque, 1999, 2010).

The standard approach in LODNA, instead, is to check whether pre-trained models capture well-known patterns, such as vanilla English subject-verb number agreement. The occasional focus on cases outside the standard paradigm is typically meant to highlight obviously *wrong* predictions made by the model (e.g., Kuncoro, Dyer,

---

[8]https://www.aclweb.org/anthology/volumes/W18-54/;
https://www.aclweb.org/anthology/volumes/2020.blackboxnlp-1/

[9]There are important exceptions. Work that does put an emphasis on the linguistic motivation of architectural choices includes that of Chris Dyer and colleagues on recurrent neural network grammars (e.g., Kuncoro, Dyer, Hale, Yogatama, et al., 2018), and that of Paul Smolensky and colleagues on tensor product decomposition networks (e.g., McCoy et al., 2019).

Hale, and Blunsom, 2018, show that, in some syntactic configurations, LSTMs let the verb agree with the first noun in a sentence even if it is not its subject).

What we are doing, then, is an extensive (and important!) sanity check of our systems, rather than using them to widen the coverage of linguistic phenomena we are able to explain through computational modelling.

In order to move from sanity checks to prediction generation, we need, however, to have a good-enough understanding of how the underlying mechanisms implemented in a network cause their linguistic behaviour. The large majority of LODNA studies focuses on the behavioural level. We need to shift the focus to a mechanistic *neural* level, so to speak.

As an example of the kind of study combining a granular understanding of a model's inner workings with a non-trivial prediction tested in humans, I will briefly summarise the detailed analysis of deep net long-distance number agreement that we reported in Lakretz, Hupkes, et al. (2021) and Lakretz, Kruszewski, et al. (2019).

In the first of these studies, a cell-by-cell analysis of pre-trained LSTMs performing the subject-verb agreement task revealed that they develop a sparse mechanism to store and propagate a single number feature between subject and verb. This sparse grammar-aware circuit is complemented by a distributed system that can fill in the number feature based on purely sequential heuristics.

This leads to an interesting prediction for sentences with two embedded long-distance dependencies, such as:

(4)   The **kid**$_1$ that the **dogs**$_2$ near the *toy* **like**$_2$/***likes**$_2$ **is**$_1$/***are**$_1$ tired.

Here, the sparse grammar-aware mechanism will be activated when *kid* is encountered, and, due to its sparsity, it will not be able to also record the number of *dogs*. Consequently, once *like(s)* is encountered, the heuristic distributed system will take over, and it will wrongly predict the singular form, since the sequentially closer noun is *toy*. On the other hand, once *is/are* is reached, the feature stored in the sparse long-distance circuit can be released, correctly predicting a preference for singular *is*. This is an interesting prediction because, intuitively but contrary to it, the longer-distance *kid-is* relation should be harder to track than the shorter-distance one connecting *dogs* and *like*.

In Lakretz, Hupkes, et al. (2021), we proceeded to test the prediction both in LSTMs and with human subjects. We did indeed find the predicted inner/outer agreement asymmetry both in machines and (more weakly) in humans. This suggests that agreement might be implemented by means of sparse feature-carrying mechanisms in humans as well.

Lakretz' study took about four years to run. By the time it was completed, it presented a detailed analysis of a model, the LSTM, that many in NLP would find obsolete. Its focus on a single grammatical construction might look quaint, now that the field has moved towards large-scale evaluation suites probing models on a variety of phenomena and tasks (e.g., Conneau and Kiela, 2018; Conneau, Kruszewski, et al., 2018; Marvin and Linzen, 2018; Wang et al., 2019; Warstadt et al., 2019). Yet, if we want to reach the sort of understanding of a deep model's inner working that can be useful to gain new insights on human linguistic competence and behaviour, I argue that we should have more studies running at the same slow, thorough, narrow-focused pace of this project.[10]

1.5   CONCLUSION

Language models based on deep network architectures such as the LSTM and the Transformer are computational devices that, by being exposed to large amounts of natural text, learn to assign probabilities to arbitrary word sequences. In the last five years or so, a rich tradition of studies has emerged that analyses such models in order to understand what kind of "grammatical competence" they possess.

The results of these studies are often intriguing, revealing the sophisticated linguistic skills of deep nets, as well as interesting error patterns. However, such studies have had very little impact on theoretical linguistics.

I attributed this gap to the fact that these studies tend to lack a clear theoretical standing and, when they do, it is one based on the wrong idea that we should treat modern deep nets as *tabulae rasae* without strong innate priors. Deep nets do possess such innate priors, as shown by the fact that different models trained on the same data can extract dramatically different generalisations. I proposed that a more solid theoretical standing for the linguistic analysis of deep nets can be achieved by treating them as *algorithmic linguistic theories*.

I discussed above some concrete roadblocks we must overcome if we want to seriously adopt this stance. I will conclude by briefly explaining why I think that such a stance is beneficial for both computational and theoretical linguists, and by providing quick sketches of what deep-net-based linguistic theorising could look like.

Why should computational linguists care?

The incredible progress in deep learning for NLP we've seen in the last few years must be entirely credited to NLP and machine-learning practitioners interested in solving concrete challenges such as machine translation. Ideas from theoretical linguistics have played no role in the area (Lappin, 2021), and there is no clear reason, in turn, why computational linguists interested in practical NLP technologies should care about the implications of their work for linguistics.

However, the success of events such as the already mentioned Society for Computation in Linguistics conference and BlackBox NLP workshop, as well as the fact that all major NLP conferences now feature special tracks on linguistic analysis of computational models, suggest that there is a significant sub-community of computational linguists who *are* interested in the linguistic implications of deep learning models.

These researchers should be bothered by the fact that their work is not having an impact on mainstream theoretical linguistics. Clarifying the theoretical status of deep

---

[10]Independent progress in causal intervention methods applied to modern language models (e.g., Meng et al., 2022) will hopefully speed up and generalise the process of understanding the mechanics of these deep nets.

net simulations, and in particular, boldly presenting them as alternative linguistic theories, might finally attract due attention from the linguistics community.

Why should theoretical linguists care?

Deep nets attained incredible empirical results in tasks that heavily depend on linguistic knowledge, such as machine translation (Edunov et al., 2018), well beyond what was ever achieved by symbolic or hybrid systems. While it is possible that deep nets are relying on a completely different approach to language processing than the one encoded in human linguistic competence, theoretical linguists should investigate what are the building blocks making these systems so effective: if not for other reasons, at least in order to explain why a model that is supposedly encoding completely different priors than those programmed into the human brain should be so good at handling tasks, such as translating from a language into another, that should presuppose sophisticated linguistic knowledge.

I conjecture however that deep nets and traditional symbolic theories are both valid algorithmic approaches to modelling human linguistic competence, and that they are complementary in the aspects they best explain. The more algebraic features of language, such as recursive structures, are elegantly handled by traditional linguistic formalisms such as generative syntax (Müller, 2020) and formal semantics (Heim and Kratzer, 1998). However, language has other facets, in particular those where the fuzzy, large-scale knowledge that characterises the lexicon is involved, where such theories struggle. Neural language models, by inducing a large set of context-dependent and fuzzy patterns from natural input, and by being inherently able to probabilistically generate and process text, should be better equipped to handle phenomena such as polysemy, the partial productivity of morphological derivation, non-fully-compositional phrase formation and diachronic shift (e.g., Boleda, 2020; Lenci, 2018; Marelli and Baroni, 2015; Vecchi et al., 2017).[11]

From this angle, the current emphasis of LODNA on exactly those phenomena (such as long-distance agreement) that are already satisfactorily captured by traditional algebraic models might be misguided. Curiously, even staying within the domain of syntax, there is no work I am aware of focusing instead on those patterns, such as partially lexicalised constructions (e.g., A. Goldberg, 2005, 2019), where the fuzzier rules typically learned by neural networks might give us novel insights into human generalisation.

Do neural network theories require a switch from algebraic to distributed models of linguistic competence?

The main topic of this volume is the role of algebraic systems in the representation of linguistic knowledge. By proposing a trained Transformer, with its billions of weights and its continuous activation vectors, as a "linguistic grammar", I am *de facto* implying that the appropriate level to represent linguistic knowledge is not algebraic

---

[11] These references mostly discuss a precursor of neural language models known as *distributional semantics*, but the same accounts could be replicated and extended using latest-generation neural language models.

but massively distributed. This requires a radical methodological shift in the way linguistic models are studied. Standard rule- or constraint-based systems can easily be probed by direct inspection. With deep networks, model probing requires sophisticated experiments, of the kind that the LODNA literature has only partially started designing, especially in terms of understanding the causal mechanisms underlying a model's linguistic behaviour.

However, I would like to leave the issue of the right level for deep-net-based linguistic theorising open. Optimality Theory (Prince and Smolensky, 2004) was the most fruitful outcome of early attempts to bring together linguistics and connectionism. Optimality theory is an algebraic approach whose principles are inspired by how linguistic constraints might be implemented by a traditional neural network. Could the way in which LSTMs or Transformers process linguistic information similarly inspire a symbolic theory of language? Perhaps, one that is not based on tree structures but on storage and retrieval mechanisms akin to gating and attention?

To conclude, despite the criticism I vented to some aspects of the field, I think that LODNA is one of the most exciting things that has happened to cognitive science in the last six years. I hope that, once we clarify its theoretical standing, and as we deepen our understanding of how deep networks accomplish linguistic tasks, the body of evidence assembled in this area will finally have the impact it deserves on linguistics at large.

ACKNOWLEDGMENTS

I would like to thank the anonymous reviewer, Jelke Bloem, Grzegorz Chrupała, Ido Dagan, Roberto Dessì, Emmanuel Dupoux, Dieuwke Hupkes, Shalom Lappin, Yair Lakretz, Paola Merlo, the members of the UPF Computational Linguistics and Linguistic Theory group, the participants in the EACL 2021 Birds-of-a-Feather Meetup on Linguistic Theories, the audience at EACL 2021 and, especially, David Adger, Gemma Boleda, Roberta D'Alessandro, Chris Dyer, Tal Linzen, Louise McNally, Tom McCoy, Paul Smolensky, and Adina Williams for a mixture of advice, stimulating discussion, and constructive feedback.

BIBLIOGRAPHY

Adger, David (2019). *Language Unlimited: The Science Behind Our Most Creative Power*. Oxford, UK: Oxford University Press.

Belinkov, Yonatan and James Glass (2019). "Analysis methods in neural language processing: A survey". In: *Transactions of the Association for Computational Linguistics* 7, pp. 49–72.

Bernardy, Jean-Philippe and Shalom Lappin (2017). "Using deep neural networks to learn syntactic agreement". In: *Linguistic Issues in Language Technology* 15.2, pp. 1–15.

Berwick, Robert and Noam Chomsky (2016). *Why Only Us: Language and Evolution*. Cambridge, MA: MIT Press.

Boleda, Gemma (2020). "Distributional semantics and linguistic theory". In: *Annual Review of Linguistics* 6, pp. 213–234.

Chaves, Rui (Jan. 2020). "What Don't RNN language models learn about filler-gap dependencies?" In: *Proceedings of the Society for Computation in Linguistics 2020*. New York, New York: Association for Computational Linguistics, pp. 1–11. URL: https://aclanthology.org/2020.scil-1.1.

Chomsky, Noam (1968). *Language and Mind*. Cambridge, UK: Cambridge University Press.

— (1986). *Knowledge of Language: Its Nature, Origin, and Use*. Wesport, CT: Praeger.

Chowdhury, Shammur and Roberto Zamparelli (2018). "RNN simulations of grammaticality judgments on long-distance dependencies". In: *Proceedings of COLING*. Santa Fe, NM, pp. 133–144.

Churchland, Paul (1989). *A Neurocomputational Perspective: The Nature of Mind and the Structure of Science*. Cambridge, MA: MIT Press.

Cinque, Guglielmo (1999). *Title Adverbs and Functional Heads: A Cross-Linguistic Perspective*. Oxford, UK: Oxford University Press.

— (2010). *The Syntax of Adjectives*. Cambridge, MA: MIT Press.

Clark, Andy (1989). *Microcognition: Philosophy, Cognitive Science, and Parallel Distributed Processing*. Cambridge, MA: MIT Press.

Conneau, Alexis and Douwe Kiela (2018). "SentEval: An evaluation toolkit for universal sentence representations". In: *Proceedings of LREC*. Miyazaki, Japan, pp. 1699–1704.

Conneau, Alexis, Germán Kruszewski, Guillaume Lample, Loïc Barrault, and Marco Baroni (2018). "What you can cram into a single $&!#* vector: Probing sentence embeddings for linguistic properties". In: *Proceedings ACL*. Melbourne, Australia, pp. 2126–2136.

Devlin, Jacob, Ming-Wei Chang, Kenton Lee, and Kristina Toutanova (2019). "BERT: Pre-training of deep bidirectional transformers for language understanding". In: *Proceedings of NAACL*. Minneapolis, MN, pp. 4171–4186.

Edunov, Sergey, Myle Ott, Michael Auli, and David Grangier (2018). "Understanding back-translation at scale". In: *Proceedings of EMNLP*. Brussels, Belgium, pp. 489–500.

Everaert, Martin, Marinus Huybregts, Noam Chomsky, Robert Berwick, and Johan Bolhuis (2015). "Structures, not strings: Linguistics as part of the cognitive sciences". In: *Trends in Cognitive Sciences* 19.12, pp. 729–743.

Futrell, Richard, Ethan Wilcox, Takashi Morita, Peng Qian, Miguel Ballesteros, and Roger Levy (2019). "Neural language models as psycholinguistic subjects: Representations of syntactic state". In: *Proceedings of NAACL*. Minneapolis, MN, pp. 32–42.

Goldberg, Adele (2005). *Constructions at Work: The Nature of Generalization in Language*. Oxford, UK: Oxford University Press.

— (2019). *Explain Me This: Creativity, Competition, and the Partial Productivity of Constructions*. Princeton, NJ: Princeton University Press.

Goldberg, Yoav (2017). *Neural Network Methods for Natural Language Processing.* San Francisco, CA: Morgan & Claypool.

— (2019). *Assessing BERT's Syntactic Abilities.* `https://arxiv.org/abs/1901.05287`.

Gulordava, Kristina, Piotr Bojanowski, Edouard Grave, Tal Linzen, and Marco Baroni (2018). "Colorless green recurrent networks dream hierarchically". In: *Proceedings of NAACL.* New Orleans, LA, pp. 1195–1205.

Hauser, Marc, Noam Chomsky, and Tecumseh Fitch (Nov. 2002). "The Faculty of language: What is it, who has it, and how did it evolve?" In: *Science* 298.5598, pp. 1569–1579.

Heim, Irene and Angelika Kratzer (1998). *Semantics in Generative Grammar.* Malden, MA: Blackwell.

Hochreiter, Sepp and Jürgen Schmidhuber (1997). "Long short-term memory". In: *Neural Computation* 9.8, pp. 1735–1780.

Hunter, Tim (2019). "What sort of cognitive hypothesis is a derivational theory of grammar?" In: *Catalan Journal of Linguistics* 2019 Special Issue, pp. 89–138.

Jurafsky, Dan and James Martin (2008). *Speech and Language Processing, 2nd ed.* Upper Saddle River: Prentice Hall.

Kalchbrenner, Nal, Edward Grefenstette, and Phil Blunsom (2014). "A convolutional neural network for modelling sentences". In: *Proceedings of ACL.* Baltimore, MD, pp. 655–665.

Kastner, Itamar, Hadas Kotek, Anonymous Anonymous, Rikker Dockum, Michael Dow, Maria Esipova, Caitlin Green, and Todd Snider (2021). *Who speaks for us? Lessons from the Pinker letter.* `https://ling.auf.net/lingbuzz/005381`.

Katharopoulos, Angelos, Apoorv Vyas, Nikolaos Pappas, and François Fleuret (2020). "Transformers are RNNs: Fast autoregressive transformers with linear attention". In: *Proceedings of ICML.* virtual conference, pp. 5156–5165.

Kawahara, Shigeto, Gakuji Kumagai, and Mahayana Godoy (2021). *English speakers can infer Pokémon types using sound symbolism.* `https://ling.auf.net/lingbuzz/005129`.

Kharitonov, Eugene and Rahma Chaabouni (2021). "What they do when in doubt: A study of inductive biases in seq2seq learners". In: *Proceedings of ICLR.* Proceedings at: `https://openreview.net/group?id=ICLR.cc/2021/Conference`. Online event.

Kuncoro, Adhiguna, Chris Dyer, John Hale, and Phil Blunsom (2018). *The perils of natural behavioral tests for unnatural models: The case of number agreement.* Poster presented at the Learning Language in Humans and in Machines conference, online at: `https://osf.io/view/L2HM/`. Paris, France.

Kuncoro, Adhiguna, Chris Dyer, John Hale, Dani Yogatama, Stephen Clark, and Phil Blunsom (2018). "LSTMs can learn syntax-sensitive dependencies well, but modeling structure makes them better". In: *Proceedings of ACL.* Melbourne, Australia, pp. 1426–1436.

Lakretz, Yair, Dieuwke Hupkes, Alessandra Vergallito, Marco Marelli, Marco Baroni, and Stanislas Dehaene (2021). "Mechanisms for handling nested dependencies in neural-network language models and humans". In: *Cognition.* In press.

Lakretz, Yair, Germán Kruszewski, Theo Desbordes, Dieuwke Hupkes, Stanislas Dehaene, and Marco Baroni (2019). "The emergence of number and syntax units in LSTM language models". In: *Proceedings of NAACL*. Minneapolis, MN, pp. 11–20.

Lappin, Shalom (2021). *Deep learning and linguistic representation*. Boca Raton, FL: CRC Press.

Lau, Jey Han, Alexander Clark, and Shalom Lappin (2017). "Grammaticality, acceptability, and probability: A probabilistic view of linguistic knowledge". In: *Cognitive Science* 41.5, pp. 1202–1241.

Lenci, Alessandro (2018). "Distributional models of word meaning". In: *Annual Review of Linguistics* 4.14, pp. 1–21.

Linzen, Tal and Marco Baroni (2021). "Syntactic structure from deep learning". In: *Annual Review of Linguistics* 7, pp. 195–212.

Linzen, Tal, Emmanuel Dupoux, and Yoav Goldberg (2016). "Assessing the ability of LSTMs to learn syntax-sensitive dependencies". In: *Transactions of the Association for Computational Linguistics* 4, pp. 521–535.

Marelli, Marco and Marco Baroni (2015). "Affixation in semantic space: Modeling morpheme meanings with compositional distributional semantics". In: *Psychological Review* 122.3, pp. 485–515.

Marvin, Rebecca and Tal Linzen (2018). "Targeted syntactic evaluation of language models". In: *Proceedings of EMNLP*. Brussels, Belgium, pp. 1192–1202.

McCloskey, Michael (1991). "Networks and theories: The place of connectionism in cognitive science". In: *Psychological Science* 2.6, pp. 387–395.

McCoy, Thomas, Tal Linzen, Ewan Dunbar, and Paul Smolensky (2019). "RNNs implicitly implement tensor-product representations". In: *Proceedings of ICLR*. Published online: `https://openreview.net/group?id=ICLR.cc/2019/conference`. New Orleans, LA.

Meng, Kevin, David Bau, Alex Andonian, and Yonatan Belinkov (2022). *Locating and Editing Factual Knowledge in GPT*. `https://arxiv.org/abs/2202.05262`.

Müller, Stefan (2020). *Grammatical Theory: From Transformational Grammar to Constraint-Based Approaches, 4th ed.* Berlin, Germany: Language Science Press.

Murphy, Brian (2007). "A Study of Notions of Participation and Discourse in Argument Structure Realisation". Dissertation. Trinity College Dublin.

Niu, Jingcheng and Gerald Penn (2020). "Grammaticality and language modelling". In: *Proceedings of the EMNLP Eval4NLP Workshop*. Online event, pp. 110–119.

Papadimitriou, Isabel and Dan Jurafsky (2020). "Learning music helps you read: Using transfer to study linguistic structure in language models". In: *Proceedings EMNLP*. Online event, pp. 6829–6839.

Prince, Alan and Paul Smolensky (2004). *Optimality Theory*. Malden, MA: Blackwell.

Rumelhart, David, James McClelland, and PDP Research Group, eds. (1986). *Parallel Distributed Processing: Explorations in the Microstructure of Cognition, Vol. 1: Foundations*. Cambridge, MA: MIT Press.

Sag, Ivan, Thomas Wasow, and Emily Bender (2003). *Syntactic Theory: A Formal Introduction*. Stanford, CA: CSLI.

Scholte, Steven (2016). "Fantastic DNimals and where to find them". In: *NeuroImage* 180, pp. 112–113.

Sprouse, Jon and Carson Schütze (2019). "Grammar and the use of data". In: *The Oxford Handbook of English Grammar*. Ed. by Bas Aarts, Jill Bowie, and Gergana Popova. Oxford, UK: Oxford University Press, pp. 40–58.

Sutskever, Ilya, Oriol Vinyals, and Quoc Le (2014). "Sequence to sequence learning with neural networks". In: *Proceedings of NIPS*. Montreal, Canada, pp. 3104–3112.

Vaswani, Ashish, Noam Shazeer, Niki Parmar, Jakob Uszkoreit, Llion Jones, Aidan Gomez, Łukasz Kaiser, and Illia Polosukhin (2017). "Attention is all you need". In: *Proceedings of NIPS*. Long Beach, CA, pp. 5998–6008.

Vecchi, Eva Maria, Marco Marelli, Roberto Zamparelli, and Marco Baroni (2017). "Spicy adjectives and nominal donkeys: Capturing semantic deviance using compositionality in distributional spaces". In: *Cognitive Science* 41.1, pp. 102–136.

Wang, Alex, Amanpreet Singh, Julian Michael, Felix Hill, Omer Levy, and Samuel R. Bowman (2019). "GLUE: A multi-task benchmark and analysis platform for natural language understanding". In: *Proceedings of ICLR*. Published online: `https://openreview.net/group?id=ICLR.cc/2019/conference`. New Orleans, LA.

Warstadt, Alex, Amanpreet Singh, and Samuel R. Bowman (2019). "Neural network acceptability judgments". In: *Transactions of the Association for Computational Linguistics* 7, pp. 625–641.

Xie, Ning, Gabrielle Ras, Marcel van Gerven, and Derek Doran (2020). *Explainable deep learning: A field guide for the uninitiated*. `https://arxiv.org/abs/2004.14545`.

CHAPTER 2

What Artificial Neural Networks Can Tell Us about Human Language Acquisition

Alex Warstadt

New York University, Department of Linguistics

Samuel R. Bowman

New York University, Department of Linguistics, Department of Computer Science, Center for Data Science

CONTENTS

DOI: 10.1201/9781003205388-2

ABSTRACT

Rapid progress in machine learning for natural language processing has the potential to transform debates about how humans learn language. However, the learning environments and biases of current artificial learners and humans diverge in ways that weaken the impact of the evidence gleaned from learning simulations. Today's most effective neural language models are trained on roughly one thousand times the amount of linguistic data available to a typical child. To increase the relevance of learnability results from computational models, we need to train model learners without significant advantages over humans. If an appropriate model successfully acquires some target linguistic knowledge, it can provide a proof of concept that the target is learnable in a hypothesised human learning scenario. Plausible model learners will enable us to carry out experimental manipulations to make causal inferences about variables in the learning environment, and to rigorously test poverty-of-the-stimulus-style claims arguing for innate linguistic knowledge in humans on the basis of speculations about learnability. Comparable experiments will never be possible with human subjects due to practical and ethical considerations, making model learners an indispensable resource. So far, attempts to deprive current models of unfair advantages obtain sub-human results for key grammatical behaviours such as acceptability judgements. But before we can justifiably conclude that language learning requires more prior domain-specific knowledge than current models possess, we must first explore non-linguistic inputs in the form of multimodal stimuli and multi-agent interaction as ways to make our learners more efficient at learning from limited linguistic input.

2.1 INTRODUCTION

In the thirteenth century, the Holy Roman Emperor Frederick II conducted a troubling experiment. He arranged for children to be raised from infancy without any human language in order to answer the following question: Which language do children know from birth – Hebrew, Latin, Greek or their mother's native tongue (Coulton, 1972)? Similar experiments were reportedly conducted by the Pharaoh Psamtik and Scotland's King James IV (Fromkin et al., 1974). Despite obvious ethical reasons not to conduct more experiments like this, it is clear that they get at long-standing

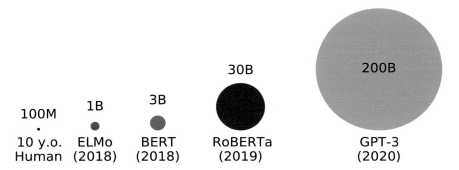

Figure 2.1   Comparison of human and model linguistic input (# of word tokens).

questions in the acquisition and origins of language that we have few other viable methods of addressing.

In the last decade, this possibility has begun to come within reach – without any of the ethical baggage – through the study of artificial neural networks (ANNs). Since the overwhelming success of deep learning methods in natural language processing (LeCun et al., 2015; Manning, 2015), we have gained access to ANNs that learn to compose high-quality multi-paragraph prose, to answer high school-level reading-comprehension questions, and to make human-like grammatical acceptability judgements (Brown et al., 2020; Chowdhery et al., 2022; Devlin et al., 2019; He et al., 2021; Liu et al., 2019; Rae et al., 2021). These models are all kinds of *language models* (LMs), which learn from unlabelled, naturally occurring text.

In this time, the active research area of *neural network probing* has begun to investigate the grammatical knowledge of LMs (Chaves, 2020; Choshen et al., 2021; Chowdhury and Zamparelli, 2018; Gulordava et al., 2019; Hu et al., 2020; Linzen, Dupoux, et al., 2016; Papadimitriou et al., 2021; Warstadt and Bowman, 2019, 2020; Warstadt, et al., 2020; Wilcox, Levy, et al., 2018). While these studies collectively find that LMs do not always show human-like language understanding and grammatical intuitions, there has been massive progress in this direction due to both technical innovations and increases in scale over the last few years (Linzen and Baroni, 2021; Manning et al., 2020).

Many authors of probing studies suggest that, to the extent that models succeed, this can provide evidence to inform debates about human language acquisition (Chowdhury and Zamparelli, 2018; Lau et al., 2017; Linzen, 2019; Pater, 2019; Warstadt and Bowman, 2020; Warstadt, Singh, et al., 2019). However, most studies in this vein focus on convenient but unrealistic learning scenarios, such as large LMs trained on massive corpora scraped from the internet (see Figure 2.1). As a result, these studies are not well suited to answer questions about *human* language learning, though their methodologies might be a useful stepping stone. At the same time, others have questioned the value of using neural networks to study human language acquisition at all, arguing that their inductive biases are too strong for this to be successful (Baroni, 2022, Chapter 1 of this volume).[1]

---

[1]In another piece sceptical about the relevance of LMs to linguistics, Dupre argues that research on LMs is unlikely to provide evidence for discriminating between competing theories of

TABLE 2.1 A *learning scenario* is characterised by the learner and its innate induc-tive bias on the one hand, and the learning environment on the other. These two factors can be broken down further into several variables, listed non-exhaustively here.

Learner Inductive Bias	Learning Environment
Architecture	Modality of input
Learning algorithm	Quantity of data
Hyperparameters	Data distribution (domain)
Order of presentation	Memory

The goal of this chapter is to characterise what we can (and cannot) hope to learn about human language acquisition from studying artificial learners, and how best to maximise the relevance of studies on ANNs to questions of human learning. We agree with many others who contend that artificial neural networks are especially well suited to provide proofs of concept for the possibilities of low-bias learning (Chowdhury and Zamparelli, 2018; Lau et al., 2017; Linzen, 2019; Pater, 2019; Warstadt and Bowman, 2020; Warstadt, Singh, et al., 2019). We make this claim more precise by arguing that computational modelling results can be made stronger under certain conditions, and that the most easily achievable conditions are the ones for showing that some hypothesised *advantage* (i.e., an innate bias or environmental stimulus) is *not* necessary for acquiring some target linguistic knowledge T.

The way to accomplish this is through an *ablation study* (or deprivation exper-iment) of a learning scenario which lacks the hypothesised advantage A. For our purposes, a *learning scenario* is determined by two main variables – the innate in-ductive bias of the learner, and the learning environment (see Table 2.1) – and aspects of either can be ablated. If the model succeeds after ablating A, it provides a proof of concept that the target is learnable without A. If the model, furthermore, does not enjoy any substantive advantages over humans, then we can conclude the result is likely to generalise to humans, and considerations from learnability do not justify the claim that humans require A.

---

linguistic competence (Dupre, 2021). He suggests this is because LMs are trained to simulate hu-man performance, and performance and competence may differ in systematic ways. However, as Dupre himself notes, this argument is "consistent with recent work...that has argued that [deep learning] may provide insight into the mechanisms by which linguistic competence is acquired." His argument does not rule out the possibility of inferring the linguistic competence of LMs. While this may currently differ from human linguistic competence too much to provide a testing ground for linguistic theories, we can still use comparisons between LM and human competence to test learnability claims.

> **Example: A toy ablation study**
>
> Goal: To test whether learners need to see triply embedded clauses are necessary to judge their acceptability under an assumption (which may or may not be correct) that humans learn in a grounded environment without a hierarchical bias. In the terminology of this paper, we test whether A is necessary to learn T under the hypothesis that S_H is the human learning scenario. To do so, we ablate A by removing from the input all examples like (1) and evaluate for knowledge of T.
>
> - **Hypothesised Advantage** A: Direct exposure to triply embedded clauses (1):
>
>   (1) I think you know that John told the lawyer where <u>the girl lives</u>.
>
> - **Target Knowledge** T: The ability to identify agreement errors of triply embedded verbs, e.g., *live* vs. *lives* in (1).
>
> - **Hypothetical Human Scenario** S_H:
>
>   a. Humans have grounding.
>
>   b. Humans lack a hierarchical bias.
>
>   c. ...

Consequently, positive results from model learners are more meaningful than negative results. The example above clarifies why: Supposing we tested a model and found that it acquired the T after ablating A. This result is likely to generalise from the model to the hypothesised human scenario as long as the model does not have any additional advantage over human learners, i.e., as long as the model also lacks a hierarchical bias. The result is generalisable whether or not the model has grounding.[2] By contrast, to infer that A *is* likely necessary for humans, the model must fail in a scenario that has at least as many advantages as a human, i.e., it must also have grounding. Otherwise, a lack of grounding would be a potential confound (perhaps exposure to the semantics of number accelerates morphological category learning). While this example is idealised, we believe it is generally far more practical to aim for model learners that lack any unfair advantages over humans, than to try to equip models with the full richness of the hypothesised human learning scenario.

Ablation experiments can provide a rigorous test for claims common in the language acquisition literature that the input to the learner lacks key evidence for acquiring certain forms of linguistic knowledge (Berwick et al., 2011; Chomsky, 1972; Legate and Yang, 2002; Lidz et al., 2003; Rasin and Aravind, 2021). They can also refute long-standing hypotheses that certain innate language-specific biases are necessary to explain human language learning (Chomsky, 1965; Chomsky and Lasnik, 1993). The implications for human learning have some limits, though. Showing that some bias is not necessary does not entail it is not present. Some things which are learnable in principle might be innate because individuals that do not have to acquire crucial knowledge have an advantage.

---

[2]For the sake of illustration, we assume in this example that the only advantages besides A where the model can differ from humans are grounding and a hierarchical bias.

To maximise the probability of obtaining generalisable results from model learners, we need to make models weaker in some ways and stronger in others. For example, state-of-the-art language models have a huge advantage over humans in terms of the quantity of linguistic input (see Figure 2.1). However, when researchers have attempted to deprive models of this advantage (Schijndel et al., 2019; Warstadt, et al., 2020; Zhang et al., 2021), the performance of the models suffers. The most practical course of action to close the data-efficiency gap between neural networks and humans is to exchange some of the massive amounts of text-only input that current LMs learn from with some of the non-linguistic advantages humans enjoy. These include multimodal inputs such as images and video, as well as input from interaction with other agents with adult grammars.

This paper begins with a theoretical discussion of how to apply the evidence from model learners to humans (Section 2.2), before turning to more practical considerations. It surveys existing benchmarks and evaluation methods that can be used to test for human-like linguistic performance (Section 2.3). It then reviews ways in which the learning environment and the learner can be (and have been) adapted to improve the relevance of results from model learners to humans (Sections 2.4 and 2.5). The discussion (Section 6.5) argues the case for using artificial neural networks as model learners and lays out a path towards building even more relevant models.

2.2   EVIDENCE FROM MODEL LEARNERS

Models in science are imperfect. The benefit of studying a model is to generalise results from a tractable or observable setting to a more fundamentally interesting setting. Thus, the most useful learnability results from models learners are ones that are likely to imply similar conclusions about humans. From this perspective, not all models or results are created equal. We recommend a strategy in which relatively impoverished model learners are used to obtain proofs of concept for learnability. We justify this recommendation through theoretical considerations about the conditions under which results generalise from models to humans.

2.2.1   Generalising Learnability Results from Models to Humans

One goal of the study of language acquisition is to determine the necessary and sufficient conditions for language learning in humans. However, there are some things we cannot easily learn just by observing humans. Observing an advantage in the human learning environment does not tell us whether it is *necessary* for language learning. For example, some children will receive explicit instruction in grammar, including negative evidence, but it is a matter of debate whether such an advantage is necessary or even useful (Chouinard and Clark, 2003; Marcus, 1993). Furthermore, significant advances in neuroscience are needed before we can directly and confidently observe whether the specific mechanisms in a hypothesised innate language acquisition device are present in the brain.

Learnability results from a model can inform all of these questions. We can gain evidence about whether negative evidence is necessary to learn some target T by observing whether or not a model learner learns T without it. Similarly, we can test whether some hypothesised inductive bias (e.g., a bias towards hierarchical syntax) is necessary to learn T by evaluating a model without that bias for knowledge of T. However, such results only tell us directly whether these advantages are necessary in the model learning scenario, leaving uncertainty about the relevance for humans.

Unfortunately, there may be significant differences between the learning scenarios of models and humans that make this inductive leap challenging. One solution is to try to reverse-engineer the human learning scenario, as advocated by Dupoux (Dupoux, 2018). As differences between the model and human scenario decrease, there is greater overlap between what is and is not learnable for the model and for humans. This means that as the model becomes more realistic, an arbitrary learnability result from that model is more likely to generalise to humans.

Thus, even imperfect models can provide useful evidence about human language learning. In fact, it is even possible to construct hypothetical scenarios where the success of an imperfect model learner is certain to generalise to a (hypothesised) human scenario. The example below illustrates a difference between model and human learning scenarios that has no effect on the generalisation of results:

> **Example: A difference that is irrelevant to the generalisability of the result**
>
> Let the model M be a perfect simulation of a human, with one exception: When M encounters a sentence surrounded by the tags `<bigram>...</bigram>`, it outputs the probability of the sentence under a bigram model. Any results from studying M generalise with full confidence to humans, as long as sequences with the `<bigram>...</bigram>` tags are irrelevant to our evaluation of the model's behaviour.

More interestingly, some differences do not interfere with the intended conclusion because they make the result even stronger. There are two ways this can happen: First, if the model is at a strict disadvantage relative to the hypothesised human scenario, and the model succeeds, then the hypothesised human scenario must also be sufficient for learning the target. Second (and less practical), if the model is at a strict advantage and fails, then the hypothesised human scenario must be insufficient.

> **Example: A difference that strengthens the generalisability of the result**
>
> Let M be a model learner that is identical to a hypothetical human. Suppose we are testing the hypothesis that humans need at least 50 examples of a noun with irregular plural marking to learn (up to some threshold for success) whether it is singular or plural. Take a set of irregular plurals which the model learns, and for which the frequency in a typical learning environment is about 50, and remove or replace instances until there are fewer than 50 tokens of each noun. Further, suppose the model environment has another unintended disadvantage: There is an implausibly high rate of subject-verb agreement errors for irregular plurals. If the model succeeds in the ablated setting despite an (unrelated) disadvantage, then humans must also succeed.

When such differences are present, the generalisability of the result depends on whether the model succeeds or fails. If the intervention of removing irregular plurals causes the model to fail, the added disadvantage of agreement errors is a confound: Would humans also fail, given the same intervention but without agreement errors?

2.2.2 Why Positive Results are More Relevant

In practice, the model learners that we will have access to will be imperfect in many ways. But the example above shows that to answer questions about learnability, it is not necessary to aim for perfect models: It is enough to *undershoot* the advantages of human learners. This alone does not explain why positive results are more relevant, because there is a symmetric case: If our models *overshoot* the advantages of human learners, then their failures are likely to generalise to humans.

The reason why positive results are more generalisable is simply that it is easier to build models that undershoot the advantages of humans. Table 2.2 gives a rough overview of the relative advantages of humans and models. While neither has a strict advantage or disadvantage, it is obvious that it will be easier to deprive our models of their current advantages than to equip them with all the advantages of humans. This is especially true of environmental advantages, as we discuss in Section 2.4.

TABLE 2.2   Relative advantages of humans and typical LMs.

	Human Advantages	**Model Advantages**
Environmental	Sensorimotor stimuli Inter-agent interaction Environmental interaction Prosody	Quantity of text Text domain (edited writing) Punctuation
Innate	Number of parameters Domain-general bias Language-specific bias (?)	Numerical precision Working memory capacity

This suggests that one strategy for obtaining strongly generalisable learnability results is to severely impoverish model learners. The problem with this strategy is that we are unlikely to observe positive results from very weak learners. If we find that our impoverished models fail, the next course of action is to test whether this is really due to the ablation by enriching the model scenario in innocent ways. This could involve adding to the model scenario sensorimotor input, interaction, and other advantages that humans enjoy.

2.2.3 Applying Ablations to Debates in Language Acquisition

The literature on language acquisition has centred around the necessity and sufficiency of innate and environmental advantages. Nativist arguments in favour of a richer set of innate advantages for humans tend to be supported by claims of the insufficiency of certain aspects of the environment, often under the rubric of *poverty of the stimulus arguments* (Baker, 1978; Chomsky, 1965, 1972; Crain and Nakayama, 1987; Fodor and Crowther, 2002; Legate and Yang, 2002, i.a.). Empiricist rebuttals to this position usually try to argue that known advantages in the human learning environment are sufficient to explain learning given domain-general innate bias (Landauer and Dutnais, 1997; Perfors et al., 2011; Reali and Christiansen, 2005, i.a.).

Ablation studies with model learners are best suited to supporting empiricist claims and refuting nativist claims. This is simply because, for reasons discussed above, positive results or proofs of concepts are more practically generalisable than negative results. To get strong evidence for a nativist claim, one would have to show that an ablation leads to failure in a model scenario without significant disadvantages relative to a typical human.

There are many specific phenomena where the input to learners has been argued to be too impoverished to acquire the observed linguistic behaviour without some innate language-specific bias. An exhaustive survey of such claims is beyond the scope of this paper, but some examples (mostly discussed in, but not necessarily limited to, English) include subject auxiliary inversion (Chomsky, 1972; Crain and Nakayama, 1987; Legate and Yang, 2002), other structure dependent transformations (Berwick et al., 2011), plurals in noun-noun compounds (Gordon, 1985), auxiliary sequence ordering (Kimball, 1973), anaphoric "one" (Baker, 1978; Lidz et al., 2003), the denotation of "every" (Rasin and Aravind, 2021), epistemic meanings of modals (Dooren et al., 2022), binding (Reuland, 2017), and verb position in Korean (Han et al., 2016).

2.3 TESTS OF HUMAN-LIKE LINGUISTIC KNOWLEDGE

Ablation experiments require subjecting the model learner to some test of whether it acquires some target human-like linguistic ability. In this section, we discuss in theory what it means to test an artificial learner for human-like linguistic ability in light of the competence/performance distinction, before surveying existing resources that can be used as tests of linguistic performance.

2.3.1 Testing for Competence vs. Performance

In principle, the target linguistic ability we are interested in could be an aspect of human linguistic competence or performance.[3] In practice, however, most tests are behavioural, and therefore target performance. Performance has the advantages of being easily observable and more theory-neutral than competence. By contrast, competence is a theoretical construct even for humans, so a test of competence would always be subject to our degree of belief in the theory.

---

[3]Dupre discusses the relation between ANNs and competence at length (Dupre, 2021), and suggests that ANNs are better viewed as models of human performance rather than competence because they are trained on the output of human performance. We broadly agree with this view, and note that it does not contradict our claim that competence for ANNs may still be well-defined and testable.

We can also study performance to make inferences about competence. We can construe performance very broadly to include many aspects of behaviour, ranging from acceptability judgements to order of acquisition and reading time. Although this has its limitations – two systems that have identical behaviour in some respects could have very different internal functioning – the more behavioural similarities we observe between two systems, the greater the evidence that they share an underlying mechanism.

Due in part to a massive growth in NLP research focused on LM evaluation and probing, there are now numerous well-motivated, controlled, and challenging tests for different aspects of neural networks' grammatical knowledge. These tests fall roughly into two main categories: supervised and unsupervised. Unsupervised tests do not rely on labelled training data or any task-specific training beyond a self-supervised training objective such as language modelling. Thus any linguistic knowledge revealed by these methods can only have been acquired through self-supervised exposure to the learning environment, or to innate abilities in the learner. Supervised tests play a complementary role. While they give models to task-specific instruction not available to humans, supervised tasks can be constructed much like artificial language learning experiments on humans (Gómez and Gerken, 2000) to answer a different set of questions.

2.3.2 Unsupervised Tests

Unsupervised tests of LMs take advantage of the fact that autoregressive LMs are already trained to estimate the likelihood of an element of sequence w_i from the preceding elements $W_{<i}$, and that these predictions can be used to estimate the likelihood of the entire sequence W as a whole:[4]

$$P_{LM}(W) = \prod_{i=1}^{|W|} P_{LM}(w_i|W_{<i})$$

We survey three tasks that use LM likelihood scores to evaluate grammatical knowledge of LMs without additional supervision: acceptability judgements, reading time prediction, and age-of-acquisition prediction.

2.3.2.1 *Acceptability Judgements, Minimal Pairs, BLiMP*

Acceptability judgements provide a rich behavioural test for grammatical knowledge. They are the main empirical test for many theories of syntax (Schütze, 1996), and a vast array of subtle human acceptability judgements have been documented by

---

[4]This method has been extended to masked language models like BERT (Devlin et al., 2019) by computing the *pseudo likelihood* of a sequence (Salazar et al., 2020; Wang and Cho, 2019) by sequentially masking one word of the sequence:

$$P_{MLM}(W) = \prod_{i=1}^{|W|} P_{LM}(w_i|W_{\setminus i})$$

TABLE 2.3 Minimal pairs from each of the twelve categories covered by BLiMP. Differences between sentences are underlined. N is the number of minimal pair types within each broad category. (Table from Warstadt, et al. (2020) reprinted with permission.)

Phenomenon	N	Acceptable Example	Unacceptable Example
Anaphor agr.	2	*Many girls insulted <u>themselves</u>.*	*Many girls insulted <u>herself</u>.*
Arg. structure	9	*Rose wasn't <u>disturbing</u> Mark.*	*Rose wasn't <u>boasting</u> Mark.*
Binding	7	*Carlos said that Lori helped <u>him</u>.*	*Carlos said that Lori helped <u>himself</u>.*
Control/raising	5	*There was <u>bound</u> to be a fish escaping.*	*There was <u>unable</u> to be a fish escaping.*
Det.-noun agr.	8	*Rachelle had bought that <u>chair</u>.*	*Rachelle had bought that <u>chairs</u>.*
Ellipsis	2	*Anne's doctor cleans one <u>important book</u> and Stacey cleans a few.*	*Anne's doctor cleans one book and Stacey cleans a few <u>important</u>.*
Filler-gap	7	*Brett knew <u>what</u> many waiters find.*	*Brett knew <u>that</u> many waiters find.*
Irregular forms	2	*Aaron <u>broke</u> the unicycle.*	*Aaron <u>broken</u> the unicycle.*
Island effects	8	*Which <u>bikes</u> is John fixing?*	*Which is John fixing <u>bikes</u>?*
NPI licensing	7	*The truck has <u>clearly</u> tipped over.*	*The truck has <u>ever</u> tipped over.*
Quantifiers	4	*No boy knew <u>fewer than</u> six guys.*	*No boy knew <u>at most</u> six guys.*
Subj.-verb agr.	6	*These casseroles <u>disgust</u> Kayla.*	*These casseroles <u>disgusts</u> Kayla.*

linguists. Furthermore, for native speakers of a language, knowledge of acceptability is both implicit – i.e., not learned through instruction – and widely shared.

Unsupervised acceptability judgements over minimal pairs (sometimes called *targeted syntactic evaluation*) have become a widespread evaluation method since their first application to LM probing several years ago (Linzen, Dupoux, et al., 2016; Marvin and Linzen, 2018). This method relies on the assumption that a grammatical sentence W_{good} should have greater probability than a minimally different ungrammatical sentence W_{bad}, in order to say that the LM correctly predicts the contrast in acceptability if and only if

$$P_{LM}(W_{good}) > P_{LM}(W_{bad}).$$

Minimal pairs present several advantages. First, they zoom in on the decision boundary between acceptable and unacceptable sentences. Second, they make it possible to evaluate the ability of models to predict gradient differences in acceptability: Even when Boolean acceptability judgements are difficult, such forced-choice preference judgements are highly reproducible (Sprouse et al., 2013). Third, the sentences comprising a minimal pair are generally closely matched in length and unigram probability, which are two determinants of a sequence's likelihood orthogonal to acceptability (Lau et al., 2017).

BLiMP (The Benchmark of Linguistic Minimal Pairs; Warstadt, et al., 2020) is the largest-scale resource for language model scoring. It tests 67 minimal pair types in English, each consisting of 1k pairs, organised into 12 broad categories. These categories cover morphology (e.g., subject-verb agreement and determiner-noun agreement), syntax (e.g., argument structure, island effects, and binding), and semantics phenomena (e.g., quantification and negative polarity items). Table 2.3

shows examples from BLiMP of one minimal pair type for each of these categories. Closely related is SyntaxGym (Gauthier et al., 2020; Hu et al., 2020), which adopts a version of the LM scoring paradigm in which the model's predictions must conform to more than one hypothesised inequality over a set of sentences, rather than just a minimal pair.

2.3.2.2 Other Behavioural Predictions: Reading Time, Age-of-Acquisition

Language model scores can be used to predict other aspects of human linguistic performance. Reading times is a prime example. For example, Wilcox, Vani, et al. (2021) test LMs' predictions against humans' online processing difficulty using SyntaxGym. Under the theoretically motivated assumption that there should be a log-linear relationship between a word's online processing time in humans and an LM's predicted probability for the word in context (Hale, 2001; Levy, 2008), it is possible to test the conditions under which human-like processing can be acquired. Related is the Natural Stories corpus (Futrell et al., 2021), which is a benchmark that provides human reading times for a diverse set of sentence types in naturalistic contexts.

Predicting age-of-acquisition is another possible point of comparison between humans and models. Through databases like Wordbank (Frank et al., 2017), we have large-scale multilingual parent-reported data on vocabulary development in a large number of individuals. This data can be used to construct item-level learning trajectories for humans, to which we can compare the learning trajectories of LMs (Chang and Bergen, 2022).

2.3.3 Supervised Tests

Supervised classification tasks such as part-of-speech tagging, dependency arc labelling, and coreference resolution have been used as *probing tasks* for model evaluation in NLP (Adi et al., 2017; Belinkov and Glass, 2019; Ettinger et al., 2016; Hewitt and Manning, 2019; Shi et al., 2016; Tenney et al., 2019). Recently, these methods have been widely criticised because the use of supervision makes it difficult to distinguish knowledge acquired through pretraining from knowledge acquired through task-specific training (Hewitt and Liang, 2019; Pimentel et al., 2020; Voita and Titov, 2020). In this section, we survey a family of evaluation tasks that use constrained supervision to probe how neural networks generalise. In this approach, what is under investigation is not knowledge of a particular phenomenon in the training data, but whether models extend knowledge to unseen cases in ways that we expect humans to.

This approach can tell us the extent to which models form generalisations governed by consistent, high-level rules. For example, COGS (Compositional Generalisation Challenge based on Semantic Interpretation; Kim and Linzen, 2020) is a semantic parsing dataset in which certain semantic configurations in the test data are systematically held-out from the training data. If a model is able to learn that semantics, syntax, and surface form are related by a set of general compositional and phrase-structure rules, then it should correctly parse a noun in any syntactic position, even if it has only seen that noun in object position during training.

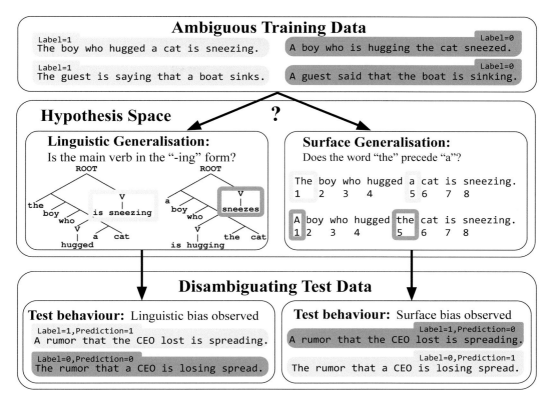

Figure 2.2   Example of an experiment following the Poverty of the Stimulus design from the MSGS dataset (reprinted from Warstadt, et al. (2020) with permission). A model is trained on ambiguous data whose labels are consistent with either a linguistic or a surface generalisation, and tested on disambiguating data whose labels support only the linguistic generalisation. Light green and darker red shading represents data or features associated with the positive and negative labels/predictions, respectively.

Constrained supervision is also useful for probing the inductive biases of neural networks. The Poverty of the Stimulus experimental design (Wilson, 2006) provides a paradigm for doing so. Figure 2.2 gives an example from Warstadt, et al. (2020) of an experiment following this design. A learner is trained to perform a task given data that is ambiguous between (at least) two hypotheses, and tested on data where the hypotheses make divergent predictions. For example, numerous studies have used this design to test whether ANNs prefer a generalisation based on syntactic structure or one based on linear order for subject auxiliary inversion (Frank and Mathis, 2007; McCoy et al., 2018, 2020; Warstadt and Bowman, 2020).

One large-scale dataset making use of this design is MSGS (The Mixed Signals Generalisation Set) (Warstadt, et al., 2020), which tests whether a learner has a bias towards linguistic or surface generalisations. MSGS consists of 20 ambiguous tasks, each pairing one of four linguistic generalisations (e.g., *labels indicate whether the main verb of the sentence is in the progressive form*) with one of five surface generalisations (e.g., *labels indicate whether the sentence is longer than 10 words*). In concurrent work, Lovering et al. (2021) introduced a similar dataset in which linguistic generalisations do not apply linguistic features in arbitrary ways, but correspond to acceptability judgements.

2.3.3.1 What Do Out-of-Domain Tests Tell Us about Learnability?

Although humans do not learn language from labelled data, training and testing models on a supervised task with labelled data can still provide useful evidence about human learning. The key is to use LMs to provide task-specific models with linguistic features acquired from a general pretraining setting. This could be an application of the popular pretrain-and-fine-tune paradigm in NLP (Dai and Le, 2015; Devlin et al., 2019; Howard and Ruder, 2018; Radford, Narasimhan, et al., 2018), or the prompt-based few-shot learning paradigm (Brown et al., 2020).

Following this setup, the experiment can tell us whether an inductive bias, such as a hierarchical bias or a compositionality bias, can be *acquired* through exposure to the unstructured learning environment (Warstadt and Bowman, 2020; Warstadt, et al., 2020). An acquired inductive bias, though not present innately in the learner, can still influence how the learner forms generalisations about sub-problems encountered during the learning process.

2.4 THE LEARNING ENVIRONMENT

The learning environment of typical, present-day ANNs diverges from the human learning environment in ways that give both advantages and disadvantages. On the one hand, LMs are exposed to hundreds or thousands of times more words than a child, and much of that text is written or edited. On the other hand, children learn in a grounded environment through interaction with other agents. These are just the most obvious of a long list of differences in the learning environment that are likely to affect language learning.

The presence of these differences substantially weakens our ability to generalise results from model learners to humans. To achieve strong positive evidence that something is learnable for humans, it is necessary to create a learning environment for the artificial learner that represents a lower bound on the richness of the input for human learners. The learner's environment should not exceed the quantity or quality of data available to humans. Of course, if a model successfully learns some target knowledge in an environment that is *far poorer* than a human's – for instance, one containing only a few thousand words – this result would be highly likely to generalise to humans. However, initial experiments attempting this by limiting text data quantity to LMs have found that they fail to acquire key linguistic abilities (Schijndel et al., 2019; Zhang et al., 2021). Fortunately, there is ample room to enrich the learning environment of LMs using multimodal inputs and interactive objectives all without exceeding the richness of the input to humans.

2.4.1 Data Quantity

The most popular ANNs for NLP have been trained on far more words than a human learner. While this was not the case only a few years ago, this trend has only been increasing. Thus, researchers interested in questions about human language acquisition have already begun to intentionally shift their focus to evaluating models trained on more human-scale datasets (Hu et al., 2020; Pannitto and Herbelot, 2020; Pérez-Mayos et al., 2021; Schijndel et al., 2019; Warstadt, et al., 2020; Zhang et al., 2021).

However, it is not trivial to determine how many words a typical human learner is exposed to. The best-known figures come from Hart and Risley's study on American English-speaking children's linguistic exposure in the home (Hart and Risley, 1992). They find that children are exposed to anywhere from 11M words per year to as little as 3M words. These figures include all speech in the home environment, not just child-directed speech. More recent work by Gilkerson et al. (2017) places this estimate between approximately 2M and 7M words per year (extrapolated from mean daily words ± 1 standard deviation). Choosing the beginning of puberty as a rough cutoff point for language acquisition and assuming that these rates are consistent across childhood, a child will acquire language with anywhere from tens of millions of words to as much as a hundred million words.

By comparison, popular neural language models are trained on corpora consisting of far more data (see Figure 2.1): ELMo (Peters et al., 2018) is trained on one billion words, BERT (Devlin et al., 2019) is trained on about 3.3 billion words, RoBERTa (Liu et al., 2019) is trained on about 30 billion, and GPT-3 (Brown et al., 2020) is trained on about 200 billion. Thus, the most impoverished of these models has linguistic experience equivalent to about 300 human years, and the most enriched is at 20,000 human years.

We can already begin to draw some conclusions about how linguistic performance of LMs scales with the quantity of available data. One study by Zhang et al. (2021) uses BLiMP to evaluate models trained in the style of RoBERTa on datasets ranging from 1M words to 1B words. Figure 2.3 summarises their results, showing the growth in sensitivity to acceptability contrasts as a function of the amount of training data available to an LM. They find that language models do learn many human-like generalisations given abundant data when tested using unsupervised LM scoring. RoBERTa$_{\text{BASE}}$ which is trained on about 30B words (Liu et al., 2019) achieves near-human performance (which we define as accuracy within 2% points of humans or better) on 6 out 12 BLiMP categories. Among these categories are phenomena involving long-distance syntactic dependencies such as filler-gap dependencies and island effects, which have been previously found to be challenging for LMs (Warstadt, et al., 2020).

On the other hand, language models generally fail to reach human-level accuracy when restricted to human-scale data quantities. According to the same study, RoBERTa models trained at human scale on 100M words only achieve near-human performance in at most two BLiMP categories (Figure 2.4). Models trained on 10M words are unsurprisingly even worse, reaching near-human performance in only a single BLiMP category.

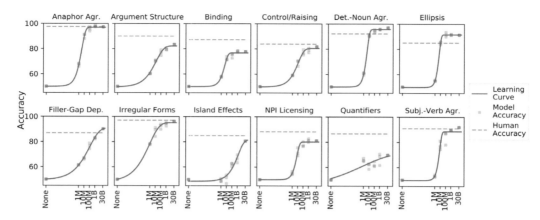

Figure 2.3 Learning curves adapted from Zhang et al. (2021) (printed here with permission) showing LM improvement in BLiMP performance as a function of the number of words of training data available to the model. Human task agreement was originally reported in the release of BLiMP (Warstadt, et al., 2020).

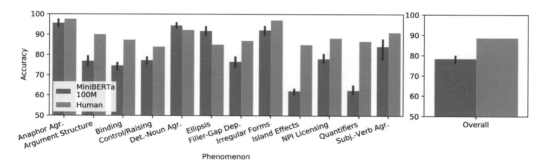

Figure 2.4 Comparison of BLiMP performance between adult humans and human-scale LMs. Model results are averages over three 100M word miniBERTas reported by Zhang et al. (2021).

Zhang et al. also find that most improvement in language models on BLiMP occurs as training corpus volume increases from 1M to 10M words. This can be seen in many phenomenon-specific learning curves in Figure 2.3. Substantial improvements are still possible between 10M and 100M words, but after this point, performance starts to plateau. This finding is corroborated by several other studies that report results from LMs with different architectures trained at similar data scales (Schijndel et al., 2019; Warstadt, et al., 2020).

2.4.2 Data Source

Another point of divergence between human and model learning environments is the source of language data. One of the main distributional differences is that all the linguistic input to a pre-literate child is spoken or signed. Ideally, the model learner's environment should consist of unstructured audio or video of real-life communication.

While there have been some first steps towards training LMs on such data (Lakhotia et al., 2021; Lavechin et al., 2022; Nguyen et al., 2020), these models are not yet advanced enough to learn complex syntax.[5]

As long as text-based training remains the main viable option for training effective LMs, the most ecologically valid text domain is transcribed speech. One source of such data is CHILDES, a database of transcribed parent-child discourse (MacWhinney, 2014). Indeed, such infant-directed speech is a major source of input to many child learners, and some go so far as to train model learners exclusively on child-directed speech (Perfors et al., 2011; Reali and Christiansen, 2005). This is probably overkill: Child-directed speech makes up only a part of the linguistic input to child learners, and in some communities it is vanishingly rare (Cristia et al., 2019). An additional barrier at the present moment is the volume of CHILDES, whose American English portion contains only about 5M words (Huebner et al., 2021).

Another large-scale source of transcribed speech is COCA (Davies, 2009), which includes 83M words of transcribed speech from unscripted radio and TV programs. One step down in terms of ecological validity is OpenSubtitles (Lison and Tiedemann, 2016), which contains over 2B words of English subtitles from scripted and unscripted television and radio, as well as over 100M words of subtitles in numerous other languages. While these datasets are ultimately not what is needed to obtain the most generalisable proofs of concept, they can give more compelling evidence than training datasets currently used to train popular language models such as Wikipedia, news, and web data.

2.4.3 Prosody

There is substantial linguistic information in speech not present in text, especially prosody. Prosodic bootstrapping is thought to play a major role in syntactic acquisition (Gleitman and Wanner, 1982; Soderstrom et al., 2003), so LMs are at a distinct disadvantage in this respect. On the other hand, text data has punctuation and white space, and is tokenised prior to input into an LM, which provides an *advantage* to models when it comes to detecting word, phrase, and sentence boundaries. Again, if practical limitations are not an issue, it is best to study models trained mostly on audio. But since this is not totally practical at the moment, there is still a lot to learn from LMs trained on text. Text exceeds the richness of speech in fairly limited ways, meaning that results from text-trained LMs still give suggestive evidence about humans.

2.4.4 Non-Linguistic Input

Despite some advantages in the linguistic environments of typically studied ANNs, they have severe non-linguistic disadvantages compared to humans. Whereas most ANNs studied in this literature learn in a text-only environment with a simple LM

---

[5]For example, current state-of-the-art performance of audio-trained LMs on a modified audio version of BLiMP is only 58% accuracy – just 8% points above chance – compared to over 79% accuracy for RoBERTa models trained on 100M words.

training objective, humans learn in a multifaceted environment with many forms of sensory input, other agents to interact with, and complex risks and rewards. The effects of these differences in non-linguistic input on grammar learning are likely to be more indirect than changes in linguistic input. Still, they may turn out to be substantial, especially when it comes to the quantity of linguistic input the learner requires.

2.4.4.1 Multimodal Input

Theories of language acquisition have long hypothesised a substantial role for sensorimotor input. The presence of a conceptual scaffolding acquired through sensorimotor input has been suggested to accelerate or improve grammar learning (Howell et al., 2005). This is one explanation for the well-known noun bias in early word learning: Concepts for objects may be learned earlier than concepts for *relations* or *properties* of objects (Gentner, 1982).

Any conceptual scaffolding that typical language models possess must be acquired from text alone. Consequently, conceptual knowledge is not available to facilitate the early stages of language learning in LMs. Indeed, these models can eventually acquire some semblance of world knowledge. Pretrained models can function as knowledge bases for retrieval of encyclopedic knowledge, accurately completing factual statements like *iPod Touch is produced by* ____ (Petroni et al., 2019), and they achieve strong performance on challenge sets focusing on physical and social common sense (Huang et al., 2019; Sakaguchi et al., 2020; Zellers et al., 2018). But the same models that pass these benchmarks still show signs of inconsistent or contradictory knowledge (Elazar, Kassner, et al., 2021). Furthermore, the quantity of training data needed to achieve strong performance on even these limited benchmarks is on the order of billions of words (Zhang et al., 2021). Thus, whatever limited world knowledge language models can acquire is not likely to be useful for language acquisition from human-scale data.

An ideal model learner would experience sensorimotor input that is indistinguishable from a typical child's. If we focus on just the audiovisual domain, the closest usable learning environment to this ideal is the SAYCam dataset (Sullivan et al., 2021), which consists of first-person perspective audio and video from head-mounted cameras worn by children under three years. While this data has been used for training computer vision models (Orhan et al., 2020), with only an estimated 1-2M words in its audio recordings, it contains too little linguistic data at present to be used to model anything beyond the first few months of language learning.

At the practical end of the spectrum, there is a growing inventory of ANNs trained jointly on vision and language data (Y.-C. Chen et al., 2020; Kamath et al., 2021; Lazaridou, Pham, et al., 2015; Lu et al., 2019; Radford, J. W. Kim, et al., 2021; Singh et al., 2022; Su et al., 2020; Tan and Bansal, 2019). Transformer-based multimodal models accept inputs as text-image pairs, which are passed into a shared multimodal encoder (possibly after passing through separate unimodal encoders). Most are pretrained using self-supervised objectives similar to language modelling. We summarise three representative objectives:

1. Masked multimodal modelling: The objective is to reconstruct masked text or image regions from an image-text pair (Tan and Bansal, 2019). Approaches vary as to whether masking occurs only in the text, only in the image or both.

2. Image-text matching: The objective is to classify an image-text pair as matched (e.g., an image and its caption) or unmatched (i.e., randomly aligned).

3. Contrastive: Given N matched image-text pairs, the objective is to jointly maximise the representational similarity of all N matched pairs and minimise the similarity of all $N(N-1)$ mismatched pairs in a shared embedding space (Radford, J. W. Kim, et al., 2021).

Despite rapid progress in this area, hardly any results so far show that enriching the visual environment of neural networks leads to better language learning. The language encoder of multimodal models is often initialised with weights from a pretrained language-only model, but these multimodal models consistently perform *worse* on linguistic evaluations than the original language-only model (Iki and Aizawa, 2021). Similarly, models trained end-to-end on a multimodal corpus failed to significantly outperform models trained on the text-only portion of the corpus (Yun et al., 2021).

These results may reflect limitations of current multimodal models rather than fundamental limitations of the utility of multimodal input. For example, the linguistic input of typical multimodal models is even farther from that of human learners than language-only models. Most are trained entirely on image caption datasets such as MS COCO or Visual Genome (X. Chen et al., 2015; Krishna et al., 2017), which lack extended discourses and dialogues, and contain a non-representative sample of sentence types. Furthermore, visual input to humans is continuous and moving, and thus richer than still images. Video and language models do not achieve a more realistic training environment. For example, VideoBERT is trained on YouTube cooking videos and text from automatic speech recognition (Sun et al., 2019).

2.4.4.2 Interactive Learning

Another ingredient missing from the input to most available model learners is interaction with an environment containing other conversational agents. While the objective of LMs is to reproduce the distribution of words and phrases in the language as faithfully as possible, human learners have a much more complex and varied objective function. We use language to share information, to make queries, and to issue and comprehend directives (Austin, 1962; Searle, 1969). The incentive for acquiring grammar in humans is that it leads to communicative success in these kinds of interactions, helping us achieve our non-linguistic goals.

The artificial learning paradigm that comes closest to reproducing this aspect of the human learning environment is multiagent reinforcement learning (Lazaridou, Peysakhovich, et al., 2017). In this framework, multiple artificial agents must develop a mode of communication to meet a cooperative goal, such as solving a reference game. However, the goal of this research, rather than to build more cognitively plausible or efficient model learners, is generally to study language emergence, as the emergent modes of communication differ greatly from human language (Bouchacourt and Baroni, 2018; Kottur et al., 2017; Lazaridou and Baroni, 2020). A good deal of work has gone into engineering agents, environments, and populations (Chaabouni, Strub, et al., 2022; Mankewitz et al., 2021) that derive basic properties of human language, such as compositionality (Lazaridou, Hermann, et al., 2018; Ren et al., 2019; Resnick et al., 2020), communicative efficiency (Chaabouni, Kharitonov, et al., 2019; Rita et al., 2020), and learnability (Chaabouni, Strub, et al., 2022; Li and Bowling, 2019).

Still, efforts to incorporate multi-agent interaction and language modelling have been limited. Lazaridou, Potapenko, et al. (2020) explore several ways of doing so, by initialising agents with LMs pretrained on natural language, or by training agents on the language modelling and interactive objectives in a multi-task setting. However, these approaches are susceptible to language drift, resulting in communication protocols that are no longer understandable by humans. Thus, more progress needs to be made in combining these objectives before we should expect to see interactive learning close the data-efficiency gap between model and human learners.

2.5 THE LEARNER

In this section we consider the final condition on strong evidence of learnability: an appropriate model learner. At the theoretical level, the considerations are the same as with the learning environment. Namely, the less the model learner has an advantage over humans (independent of the experimental manipulation), the greater the chance a positive result from an ablation will generalise to humans. In this case, the relevant advantages are properties that are built into the learner, via its architecture or learning algorithm.

However, the path towards building an ideal model learner is far from clear. This contrasts sharply with the situation in learning environments. Determining what constitutes an innate advantage raises theoretical questions about the nature of inductive bias. The task of probing the inductive bias of models is itself a challenging empirical problem. Our ability to control the inductive bias of our model learners is extremely limited. But most worrying, to compare the inductive bias of a model learner to that of a human, we need a certain understanding of the innate advantages of humans. Not only is this one of the most hotly debated issues in language acquisition, it is one of the questions where we hope that evidence from model learners will be of greatest value.

2.5.1 Formalising Innate Advantage

Before tackling these issues, we need a way to quantify and compare innate advantages across humans and models. We can reinterpret the notion of an innate advantage in terms of inductive bias. The inductive bias of a learner determines how it arrives at a generalisation from a finite set of examples; in other words, how it makes an inductive leap. Roughly, a learner has an innate advantage if its inductive bias favours the "right" kind of generalisation.

We can make this intuition more precise. Suppose we are subjecting the learner to a particular evaluation task, in which the objective is to learn a binary classification function for a target concept C over some instance space X. For instance, X might be the set of all strings, and C the set containing all and only the acceptable sentences of X. Or X might be the set of all ordered pairs of sentences (s_1, s_2), and C is the set of all pairs where s_1 is more acceptable than s_2. The hypothesis space $\mathbf{H}$ is the set of all binary classification functions h defined over X, i.e., the set containing the characteristic function for each element of $\mathcal{P}(X)$.

Recall our goal: to quantify how strongly a learner favours the right kind of generalisation such that we can make comparisons between learners. Intuitively, this corresponds to how much prior probability the learner assigns to the classification function h^* that characterises the target concept C:

$$A(L, h^*) := P_L(H = h^*)$$

The learner's prior $P_L(H)$ can be better understood by specifying a prior over the sorts of learning environments e that we expect the learner to be exposed to:[6]

$$P_L(H) = \sum_{e \in E} P_L(H, e)$$
$$= \sum_{e \in E} P_L(H|e) \cdot P(e)$$

If we assume that L learns by a deterministic algorithm, then $P_L(H|e) = 1$ for a single hypothesis $h \in H$, and 0 for all others, i.e., L is a function from a learning environment e to a hypothesis, which we denote $L(e)$. Thus, we can express the learner's innate advantage as follows:

$$A(L, h^*) := P_L(H = h^*)$$
$$= \sum_{e \in E} P_L(H = h^*|e) \cdot P(e)$$
$$= \sum_{\substack{e \in E \\ s.t. L(e) = h^*}} P(e)$$

In other words, the learner's innate advantage is the total probability that it will converge on the target hypotheses, assuming a particular distribution over learning environments. Relativising advantage to the distribution over environments is motivated by the intuition that some learning environments are more typical than others. A learner does not have an advantage if it assigns higher weight to the correct generalisation in certain highly contrived environments, but rarely in typical ones. This means that to assess whether one learner has an advantage over another, we must compare advantages using the same prior over learning environments.

---

[6]It is not totally clear what kind of distribution to use in realistic experiments, and furthermore, the choice of the distribution can have a large impact on this quantity. However, a useful notion of a prior over hypotheses should be based on environments that support many types of hypotheses related to but not necessarily identical to the target hypotheses. Furthermore, adversarial environments (like the ones considered by Gold (1967)) should have low or zero probability.

One more refinement to the naive notion of innate advantage is justified: There is generally not one classification function h^* that we would accept as human-like, but a whole set of functions $\mathbf{H}^*$. This set could be defined in the probably approximately correct learning framework (Haussler, 1990; Valiant, 1984) as the set of generalisations which have generalisation error (compared to h^*) less than some *error tolerance* ϵ. Or, recognising the existence of individual variation in adult human grammars, it can be the set of generalisations consistent with being a typical native speaker of the language.

These ingredients allow us to quantify the innate advantage A of learner L relative to the class of target generalisations $\mathbf{H}^*$ as follows:

$$A(L, \mathbf{H}^*) := \sum_{\substack{e \in E \\ L(e) \in \mathbf{H}^*}} P(E = e).$$

This quantity is quite simply the total probability that L will converge to an acceptable generalisation in a typical learning environment (as defined by the prior over environments).

2.5.2 A Lower Bound on Human Inductive Bias

The benefit of a formal definition of innate advantage is that it can provide a rough guideline for determining an appropriate model learner. It does not provide a usable criterion for guaranteeing that the model is suitable, for the simple reason that it is impractical to measure in models and in humans. It also does little to clear the path towards building better model learners. Our ability to control the inductive bias of model learners is limited. We are limited by the available set of learners, and developing effective new artificial learners is a large and mature field of research in its own right. Thus, while the theoretical considerations around idea model learners and much like those we considered for model environments, there is far less we can do in practice to guarantee or achieve a tight lower bound on human innate advantage than on the human learning environment.

Comparing the inductive bias of neural networks and humans may require substantial empirical work that is more intensive than conducting an experimental manipulation like an ablation. For a model learner, the naive approach to estimating $A(L, H^*)$ is a Monte Carlo approximation (Wilson and Izmailov, 2020), to train the learner repeatedly in sampled learning environments and test on the target evaluation. But this can hardly be a *precondition* for doing an experiment on a model learner since it entails doing the entire experiment repeatedly. The situation is even worse for measuring human inductive bias. In order for the argument from an ablation to go through, we must convince ourselves that humans have at least as strong an advantage in the ablated environment. To determine this, we would need to estimate a human's prior distribution over generalisations *in the ablated environment*. But if we already had this information, this would eliminate much of the need to study model learners in the first place. The only convincing solution to this problem would be to develop techniques to compare inductive bias in models and humans without relying on observations of how each generalises in typical environments.

2.5.2.1   Misconception 1: A Good Model Learner Must be Unbiased

One possible misconception is that a model learner must be an unbiased *tabula rasa* in order to prove some innate bias unnecessary for language acquisition. First, this would be an impossible standard to meet since all learners have some inductive bias. An inductive bias is just a prior over the hypothesis space, and thus a necessary property of any learner that can converge (Mitchell, 1980). Second, we know of no claims that humans are totally unbiased learners. Many do argue that *language-specific* biases are not necessary to explain language acquisition (Christiansen et al., 2016; A. Clark and Lappin, 2010; Kirby, 1999; Reali and Christiansen, 2005). They suggest that we may instead have innate *domain-general* biases that aid us in language acquisition. For an existence proof of this claim, the model learner only needs to lack language-specific bias and can possess domain-general bias as long as it is no stronger than a human's.

What does it mean for a bias to be language-specific? It is not clear that this is even a precise notion. An example of the subtlety of this issue is hierarchical bias. Chomsky famously argues that humans have a bias towards forming generalisations based on syntactic structures when acquiring grammatical operations like subject-auxiliary inversion, when linear generalisations would adequately describe most of the data (Chomsky, 1965). However, it is possible to question how language-specific even this bias is, since non-linguistic aspects of human cognition also make use of hierarchical structures, such as music (Lerdahl and Jackendoff, 1983) and categorisation. More recently, Chomsky has claimed that the primary innate endowment that enables language learning is unbounded Merge, or the ability to form recursive concepts (Chomsky, 2007). Merge in this view emerged prior to language as we know it: It would have evolved mainly to facilitate abstract thought, with language later co-opting this operation. While Chomsky suggests that Merge in this incarnation is implicated in the language of thought, whether it can be claimed to be truly language-specific seems to be a matter more of terminology than of actual substantive debate. Ultimately, it may be misguided to think of inductive bias as language-specific or not. Instead, learners that place more prior probability on linguistic generalisations have a stronger linguistic bias.

2.5.2.2   Misconception 2: More Expressive Models Have an Advantage

Another possible misconception is that a learner with greater expressive capacity has an advantage compared to a less expressive one. Of course, this is often the case: There are many examples of more expressive models having an advantage over less expressive ones. For example, a unigram LM is less expressive than a bigram LM with backoff (Katz, 1987), and it clearly has a disadvantage when it comes to modelling some domains of grammar, such as local subject-verb agreement in strings like *The cats purr / *The cat purr*. But this is due to the fact that the bigram LM, but not the unigram LM, reasons over a hypothesis space that overlaps with the set of target generalisation $\mathbf{H}^*$, while the unigram model does not. In other words, $A(unigram, \mathbf{H}^*) = 0$, and $A(bigram, \mathbf{H}^*) \geq 0$. We get the impression that less expressive models may be generally at a disadvantage simply because a smaller hypothesis space often has less overlap with $\mathbf{H}^*$.

But in fact, a learner can sometimes become more advantaged by becoming less expressive. This happens when the learner's hypothesis space shrinks in a highly specific way to exclude incorrect hypotheses, and some of the freed probability mass is placed on $\mathbf{H}^*$. This is precisely the nature of the innate advantages hypothesised in nativist theories of language acquisition.

A similar kind of innate advantage is often built into Bayesian models of language acquisition (Abend et al., 2017; Perfors et al., 2011; Yang and Piantadosi, 2022). To focus on one example, Perfors et al. study a Bayesian grammar induction system that reasons over a hypothesis space consisting only of a few types of formal systems, including a (limited) set of context-free grammars and finite-state grammars. Compared to a typical LSTM or Transformer language model, this learner has a highly restrictive and peaked prior. While this would be a disadvantage for many kinds of tasks, it is an advantage when it comes to learning specific rules of English syntax, because the learner's inductive bias places relatively great weight on English-like grammars.

2.5.3 Achieving a Lower Bound on Human Inductive Bias in Practice

Practically, our ability to choose appropriate model learners is constrained by the available models. In recent years, our understanding of these models' inductive biases has grown substantially thanks to much empirical work.

2.5.3.1 Available Models

Most research in contemporary natural language processing makes use of a small number of neural architectures. Recurrent neural networks (RNNs) (Elman, 1990) such as LSTMs (Hochreiter and Schmidhuber, 1997) and GRUs (Chung et al., 2014) remain widely studied in LM probing, but Transformers (Vaswani et al., 2017) are dominant in modern NLP applications.

2.5.3.2 The Inductive Biases of Neural Network Architectures

Do any of these models represent a strict lower bound on humans' innate inductive bias? Strictly speaking, the answer is probably "no". It would be extremely surprising if their inductive biases gave them no advantages over humans, as these models have become widely used due to their empirical success in NLP applications rather than a strict adherence to not exceeding humans' advantage.

So what do we know about the inductive bias of these models, and are learnability results from them likely to generalise to humans? A growing body of work helps to address these questions by evaluating neural networks for a variety of human-like inductive biases.

Numerous studies have found that ANNs lack a variety of human-like inductive biases prior to self-supervised training. One striking example is that humans, but not ANNs, show a strong *compositionality bias*. A key property of language is that words and phrases in language make stable compositional contributions to the semantics of larger constituents (Fodor and Pylyshyn, 1988; Montague, 1973). One consequence of this is that humans can understand the compositional semantic contribution of a newly learned word in any appropriate context (Lake et al., 2019). However, ANNs at human-like data scales have shown a general inability to make compositional generalisations (Keysers et al., 2020; Kim and Linzen, 2020; Lake and Baroni, 2018).

ANNs also generally lack a bias towards adopting hierarchical generalisations. McCoy et al. (2020) test several varieties of RNNs without any pretraining using the Poverty of the Stimulus method on an ambiguous subject auxiliary inversion task, and find that none converge on a systematic hierarchical generalisation. Subsequently, Petty and R. Frank (2021) have shown a similar result for Transformers.

The fact that ANNs appear to lack these human-like biases might make them more appropriate model learners for two reasons. First, it means they probably do not have any special innate advantage over humans in these respects. Second, if the goal of the study is to establish, for example, whether an innate structural bias is necessary for learning some target, then an off-the-shelf ANN is already a relatively appropriate test subject without any special modification to remove the bias in question. However, much stronger evidence about their inductive biases is needed for strong existence proofs.

One practical question is whether there is an advantage to using RNNs or Transformers as model learners. RNNs have a strong locality bias (Dhingra et al., 2018; Ravfogel, Goldberg, et al., 2019), which Transformers lack. This is a consequence of the models' architectures: RNNs have the notion of linear order built-in, since they get information about the rest of the sequence only from the previous token's output. Transformers on the other hand, only receive information about linear order through a set of dedicated *positional embeddings* added to the input. As a result, Transformers must learn the semantics of positional embeddings, including notions like locality, from scratch.

On the other hand, the differences between the biases of LSTMs and Transformers may be weaker than one might expect when it comes to grammar learning. For example, Warstadt, et al. (2020) compute the correlation between the accuracy scores of pairs of LMs on BLiMP. Among a population of models including an n-gram model, an LSTM, and two Transformers, they found that the most strongly correlated models were the LSTM and one of the Transformers.

2.6 DISCUSSION

We set out to determine what artificial neural networks can teach us about human language learning. We have shown that in the best-case scenario, model learners will be able to prove that specific linguistic behaviours are learnable under impoverished conditions, and thereby help to establish the causal roles of hypothesised advantages in the learning environment and the learner. We have also outlined the path leading up to this best-case scenario. However, we are still far from the best-case scenario. What does this mean for work that is already being done in this area?

2.6.1 The Case for Model Learners

At present, the strongest justifications for studying neural networks as models of human learners involve expense, ethics, and the potential for new experimental paradigms. Research on artificial learners is more scalable than research on children. With current language model architectures and hardware, a full simulation of the entire language acquisition period of a human learner takes on the order of one week on a single computer.[7] Parallelisation can make this even faster. Very little hands-on work is required during this training period.

Experimentation on artificial learners comes with few ethical restrictions. This is in contrast to experiments on human subjects – and especially infants – which must present minimal risk of harm to the subject. By design, ablations are often very harmful to learning outcomes, meaning we can never do an ablation on L1 acquisition in humans. Aside from experimentation on artificial language learning in humans, the only acquisition ablations we can do on language acquisition is in model learners.

Finally, the use of model learners unlocks many novel experimental paradigms which are infeasible with human subjects for a number of reasons. With simulations, we have access to all aspects of the learning algorithm, the learner, and the learning environment. Machine learning methods provide many ways to manipulate the learning algorithm, offering choices from training objectives and regularisation to curricula and multitask training. We can manipulate the learner's internal structure through simply changing neural architectures or hyperparameters such as depth, or making causal interventions such as changes to individual neurons (Finlayson et al., 2021; Vig et al., 2020) or interpretable linguistic features (Elazar, Ravfogel, et al., 2021; Ravfogel, Elazar, et al., 2020). But arguably the greatest potential is in our ability to manipulate the learning environment. We are not limited to manipulating the size or source of the training data. Starting with a naturalistic corpus, we can manipulate the distribution of syntactic phenomena and word types, add noise or inject counterfactual phenomena.

2.6.2 The Future of Model Learners

One thing is clear: Machine learning and NLP are advancing at an unprecedented rate. This makes the prospect of using artificial learners as models of human language acquisition an especially salient possibility. In the last decade, there has been remarkable progress in the abilities of artificial learners to process human language and our ability to access these models. It is only natural that such a shift in our understanding of the learnability of language learning should have some real impact on debates about human language acquisition.

To deliver on this goal, we must make conscious choices to build more ecologically valid learners and learning environments. While the NLP community could make substantial progress on this problem, the focus is more often on improving the state of the art on well-known NLP tasks at whatever cost. Similarly, while language model probing and "BERTology" have become substantial subfields in recent years (Rogers

---

[7]This estimate is based on a reproduction of the pretraining procedure of Warstadt, et al. (2020).

et al., 2020), this work often focuses on landmark models like BERT or the state of the art at the time. To obtain more useful cognitive models, cognitive scientists need to deliberately cultivate a model-building research agenda that builds on NLP, but with separate objectives. Benchmarks and competitions that set strict upper bounds on the quantity and nature of pretraining data could focus attention on this objective. Having a population of more plausible model learners will enable researchers to use existing LM probing methods to accelerate progress on questions in human language acquisition.

While work on artificial learners in the near future is unlikely to yield incontrovertible proof about human learnability, we do not consider this cause for despair. A model learner that does not meet the stringent conditions of having no advantage over humans can still contribute converging evidence about human learnability. The evidence becomes stronger as we construct more plausible learning environments and learners.

ACKNOWLEDGMENTS

We are grateful to Ailis Cournane, Michael C. Frank, Najoung Kim, Tal Linzen, Will Merrill, and Grusha Prasad for comments on this chapter. This work was improved by discussions with audiences at the Machine Learning for Language group at NYU, the Computational and Pyscholinguistics Lab at NYU and Johns Hopkins, the Stanford Language and Cognition Lab, RyCoLab at ETH Zurich, and the Cognitive Machine Learning group at Ecole Normale Superieure, and with Roger Levy and Ellie Pavlick. We also thank the editors Shalom Lappin and Jean-Philippe Bernardy, and an anonymous reviewer for helpful comments.

This project has benefited from financial support to SB by Eric and Wendy Schmidt (made by recommendation of the Schmidt Futures program), Samsung Research (under the project *Improving Deep Learning using Latent Structure*), Apple, and Intuit. This material is based upon work supported by the National Science Foundation under Grant No. 1850208. Any opinions, findings, and conclusions or recommendations expressed in this material are those of the author(s) and do not necessarily reflect the views of the National Science Foundation.

BIBLIOGRAPHY

Abend, Omri, Tom Kwiatkowski, Nathaniel J. Smith, Sharon Goldwater, and Mark Steedman (July 2017). "Bootstrapping language acquisition". en. In: *Cognition* 164, pp. 116–143. ISSN: 00100277. DOI: 10.1016/j.cognition.2017.02.009. URL: https://linkinghub.elsevier.com/retrieve/pii/S0010027717300495 (visited on 03/14/2022).

Adi, Yossi, Einat Kermany, Yonatan Belinkov, Ofer Lavi, and Yoav Goldberg (2017). "Fine-grained analysis of sentence embeddings using auxiliary prediction tasks". In: *Proceedings of ICLR Conference Track. Toulon, France*. URL: https://arxiv.org/pdf/1608.04207v3.pdf.

Austin, JL (1962). *How to Do Things With Words*. Oxford University Press.

Baker, Carl Lee (1978). *Introduction to Generative-Transformational Synta*. Englewood Cliffs, NJ: Prentice-Hall.

Baroni, Marco (2022). "On the proper role of linguistically-oriented deep net analysis in linguistic theorizing". In: *Algebraic Structures in Natural Language*. Ed. by Shalom Lappin and Jean-Philippe Bernardy. Taylor and Francis.

Belinkov, Yonatan and James R. Glass (2019). "Analysis methods in neural language processing: A survey". In: *Transactions of the Association for Computational Linguistics* 7, pp. 49–72. URL: https://www.aclweb.org/anthology/Q19-1004.pdf.

Berwick, Robert C, Paul Pietroski, Beracah Yankama, and Noam Chomsky (2011). "Poverty of the stimulus revisited". In: *Cognitive Science* 35.7. Publisher: Wiley Online Library, pp. 1207–1242.

Bouchacourt, Diane and Marco Baroni (2018). "How agents see things: On visual representations in an emergent language game". In: *Proceedings of the 2018 conference on empirical methods in natural language processing*. Brussels, Belgium: Association for Computational Linguistics, pp. 981–985. DOI: 10.18653/v1/D18-1119. URL: https://aclanthology.org/D18-1119.

Brown, Tom B., Benjamin Mann, Nick Ryder, Melanie Subbiah, Jared Kaplan, Prafulla Dhariwal, Arvind Neelakantan, Pranav Shyam, Girish Sastry, Amanda Askell, Sandhini Agarwal, Ariel Herbert-Voss, Gretchen Krueger, Tom Henighan, Rewon Child, Aditya Ramesh, Daniel M. Ziegler, Jeffrey Wu, Clemens Winter, Christopher Hesse, Mark Chen, Eric Sigler, Mateusz Litwin, Scott Gray, Benjamin Chess, Jack Clark, Christopher Berner, Sam McCandlish, Alec Radford, Ilya Sutskever, and Dario Amodei (2020). "Language models are few-shot learners". In: *Advances in Neural Information Processing Systems*. URL: https://papers.nips.cc/paper/2020/file/1457c0d6bfcb4967418bfb8ac142f64a-Paper.pdf.

Chaabouni, Rahma, Eugene Kharitonov, Emmanuel Dupoux, and Marco Baroni (2019). "Anti-efficient encoding in emergent communication". In: *Advances in Neural Information Processing Systems* 32.

Chaabouni, Rahma, Florian Strub, Florent Altché, Eugene Tarassov, Corentin Tallec, Elnaz Davoodi, Kory Wallace Mathewson, Olivier Tieleman, Angeliki Lazaridou, and Bilal Piot (2022). "Emergent Communication at Scale". In: *International Conference on Learning Representations*. URL: https://openreview.net/forum?id=AUGBfDIV9rL.

Chang, Tyler A. and Benjamin K. Bergen (Jan. 2022). "Word acquisition in neural language models". en. In: *Transactions of the Association for Computational Linguistics* 10, pp. 1–16. ISSN: 2307-387X. DOI: 10.1162/tacl_a_00444. URL: https://direct.mit.edu/tacl/article/doi/10.1162/tacl_a_00444/109271/Word-Acquisition-in-Neural-Language-Models (visited on 03/15/2022).

Chaves, Rui (Jan. 2020). "What Don't RNN Language Models Learn About Filler-Gap Dependencies?" In: *Proceedings of the Society for Computation in Linguistics 2020*. New York, New York: Association for Computational Linguistics, pp. 1–11. URL: https://aclanthology.org/2020.scil-1.1.

Chen, Xinlei, Hao Fang, Tsung-Yi Lin, Ramakrishna Vedantam, Saurabh Gupta, Piotr Dollar, and C. Lawrence Zitnick (Apr. 2015). "Microsoft COCO captions: data collection and evaluation server". en. In: *European conference on computer vision*. arXiv: 1504.00325. Springer, pp. 740–755. URL: http://arxiv.org/abs/1504.00325 (visited on 09/29/2021).

Chen, Yen-Chun, Linjie Li, Licheng Yu, Ahmed El Kholy, Faisal Ahmed, Zhe Gan, Yu Cheng, and Jingjing Liu (2020). "UNITER: UNiversal image-text representation learning". In: *Computer vision – ECCV 2020*. Ed. by Andrea Vedaldi, Horst Bischof, Thomas Brox, and Jan-Michael Frahm. Cham: Springer International Publishing, pp. 104–120. ISBN: 978-3-030-58577-8.

Chomsky, Noam (1965). *Aspects of the Theory of Syntax*. MIT Press.

— (1972). *Problems of knowledge and freedom: The Russell lectures / Noam Chomsky*. English. Fontana/Collins London, 95 pages. URL: https://nla.gov.au/nla.cat-vn4983825.

— (Jan. 2007). "Biolinguistic explorations: Design, development, evolution". en. In: *International Journal of Philosophical Studies* 15.1, pp. 1–21. ISSN: 0967-2559, 1466-4542. DOI: 10.1080/09672550601143078. URL: http://www.tandfonline.com/doi/abs/10.1080/09672550601143078 (visited on 09/09/2021).

Chomsky, Noam and Howard Lasnik (1993). "The theory of principles and parameters". In: *Syntax: An international handbook of contemporary research*. Ed. by Joachim Jacobs, Arnim von Stechow, Wolfgang Sternefeld, and Theo Vennemann, 506-569. Berlin: de Gruyter. Reprinted in Noam Chomsky, The Minimalist Program, Cambridge, Mass.: MIT Press.

Choshen, Leshem, Guy Hacohen, Daphna Weinshall, and Omri Abend (2021). "The grammar-learning trajectories of neural language models". In: *arXiv preprint arXiv:2109.06096*.

Chouinard, Michelle M and Eve V Clark (2003). "Adult reformulations of child errors as negative evidence". In: *Journal of child language* 30.3. Publisher: Cambridge University Press, pp. 637–669.

Chowdhery, Aakanksha, Sharan Narang, Jacob Devlin, Maarten Bosma, Gaurav Mishra, Adam Roberts, Paul Barham, Hyung Won Chung, Charles Sutton, Sebastian Gehrmann, Parker Schuh, Kensen Shi, Sasha Tsvyashchenko, Joshua Maynez, Abhishek Rao, Parker Barnes, Yi Tay, Noam Shazeer, Vinodkumar Prabhakaran, Emily Reif, Nan Du, Ben Hutchinson, Reiner Pope, James Bradbury, Jacob Austin, Michael Isard, Guy Gur-Ari, Pengcheng Yin, Toju Duke, Anselm Levskaya, Sanjay Ghemawat, Sunipa Dev, Henryk Michalewski, Xavier Garcia, Vedant Misra, Kevin Robinson, Liam Fedus, Denny Zhou, Daphne Ippolito, David Luan, Hyeontaek Lim, Barret Zoph, Alexander Spiridonov, Ryan Sepassi, David Dohan, Shivani Agrawal, Mark Omernick, Andrew M. Dai, Thanumalayan Sankaranarayana Pillai, Marie Pellat, Aitor Lewkowycz, Erica Moreira, Rewon Child, Oleksandr Polozov, Katherine Lee, Zongwei Zhou, Xuezhi Wang, Brennan Saeta, Mark Diaz, Orhan Firat, Michele Catasta, Jason Wei, Kathy Meier-Hellstern, Douglas Eck, Jeff Dean, Slav Petrov, and Noah Fiedel (2022). "PaLM: Scaling Language Modeling with Pathways". In: DOI: 10.48550/ARXIV.2204.02311. URL: https://arxiv.org/abs/2204.02311.

Chowdhury, Shammur Absar and Roberto Zamparelli (2018). "RNN simulations of grammaticality judgments on long-distance dependencies". In: *Proceedings of the 27th international conference on computational linguistics*, pp. 133–144.

Christiansen, Morten H., Nick Chater, and Peter W. Culicover (Apr. 2016). *Creating Language: Integrating Evolution, Acquisition, and Processing*. The MIT Press. ISBN: 9780262034319. DOI: 10.7551/mitpress/9780262034319.001.0001. URL: https://doi.org/10.7551/mitpress/9780262034319.001.0001.

Chung, Junyoung, Caglar Gulcehre, KyungHyun Cho, and Yoshua Bengio (Dec. 2014). "Empirical evaluation of gated recurrent neural networks on sequence modeling". en. In: *arXiv:1412.3555 [cs]*. arXiv: 1412.3555. URL: http://arxiv.org/abs/1412.3555 (visited on 09/15/2021).

Clark, Alexander and Shalom Lappin (2010). *Linguistic nativism and the poverty of the stimulus*. John Wiley & Sons.

Coulton, G. G. (1972). "The Princes of the World". In: *From St. Francis to Dante*. 2nd ed. Translations from the Chronicle of the Franciscan Salimbene, 1221-1288. University of Pennsylvania Press, pp. 239–256. ISBN: 978-0-8122-7672-5. URL: https://www.jstor.org/stable/j.ctv4t8279.25 (visited on 09/26/2021).

Crain, Stephen and Mineharu Nakayama (1987). "Structure dependence in grammar formation". In: *Language*. Publisher: JSTOR, pp. 522–543.

Cristia, Alejandrina, Emmanuel Dupoux, Michael Gurven, and Jonathan Stieglitz (May 2019). "Child-directed speech is infrequent in a Forager-Farmer population: A time allocation study". en. In: *Child Development* 90.3, pp. 759–773. ISSN: 0009-3920, 1467-8624. DOI: 10.1111/cdev.12974. URL: https://onlinelibrary.wiley.com/doi/10.1111/cdev.12974 (visited on 09/21/2021).

Dai, Andrew M and Quoc V Le (2015). "Semi-supervised sequence learning". In: *Advances in neural information processing systems*. Ed. by C. Cortes, N. Lawrence, D. Lee, M. Sugiyama, and R. Garnett. Vol. 28. Curran Associates, Inc. URL: https://proceedings.neurips.cc/paper/2015/file/7137debd45ae4d0ab9aa953017286b20-Paper.pdf.

Davies, Mark (2009). "The 385+ million word corpus of contemporary American English (1990–2008+): Design, architecture, and linguistic insights". In: *International journal of corpus linguistics* 14.2. Publisher: John Benjamins, pp. 159–190.

Devlin, Jacob, Ming-Wei Chang, Kenton Lee, and Kristina Toutanova (2019). "BERT: Pre-training of deep bidirectional transformers for language understanding". In: *Proceedings of the 2019 Conference of the North American Chapter of the Association for Computational Linguistics: Human Language Technologies, Volume 1 (Long and Short Papers)*, pp. 4171–4186. URL: https://www.aclweb.org/anthology/N19-1423.

Dhingra, Bhuwan, Qiao Jin, Zhilin Yang, William Cohen, and Ruslan Salakhutdinov (2018). "Neural models for reasoning over multiple mentions using coreference". In: *Proceedings of the 2018 Conference of the North American Chapter of the Association for Computational Linguistics: Human Language Technologies, Volume 2 (Short Papers)*, pp. 42–48.

Dupoux, Emmanuel (Apr. 2018). "Cognitive Science in the era of Artificial Intelligence: A roadmap for reverse-engineering the infant language-learner". In: *Cognition* 173. arXiv: 1607.08723, pp. 43–59. ISSN: 00100277. DOI: 10.1016/j.cognition.2017.11.008. URL: http://arxiv.org/abs/1607.08723 (visited on 09/26/2021).

Dupre, Gabe (Sept. 2021). "(What) Can Deep Learning Contribute to Theoretical Linguistics?" en. In: *Minds and Machines.* ISSN: 0924-6495, 1572-8641. DOI: 10.1007/s11023-021-09571-w. URL: https://link.springer.com/10.1007/s11023-021-09571-w (visited on 09/27/2021).

Elazar, Yanai, Nora Kassner, Shauli Ravfogel, Abhilasha Ravichander, Eduard Hovy, Hinrich Schütze, and Yoav Goldberg (2021). "Measuring and improving consistency in pretrained language models". In: *Transactions of the Association for Computational Linguistics* 9, pp. 1012–1031.

Elazar, Yanai, Shauli Ravfogel, Alon Jacovi, and Yoav Goldberg (2021). "Amnesic Probing: Behavioral Explanation with Amnesic Counterfactuals". en. In: *Transactions of the Association for Computational Linguistics* 9, pp. 160–175.

Elman, Jeffrey L (1990). "Finding structure in time". In: *Cognitive science* 14.2. Publisher: Wiley Online Library, pp. 179–211.

Ettinger, Allyson, Ahmed Elgohary, and Philip Resnik (2016). "Probing for semantic evidence of composition by means of simple classification tasks". In: *Proceedings of the 1st Workshop on Evaluating Vector-Space Representations for NLP*, pp. 134–139. URL: https://www.aclweb.org/anthology/W16-2524.

Finlayson, Matthew, Aaron Mueller, Sebastian Gehrmann, Stuart Shieber, Tal Linzen, and Yonatan Belinkov (2021). "Causal Analysis of Syntactic Agreement Mechanisms in Neural Language Models". en. In: *Proceedings of the 59th Annual Meeting of the Association for Computational Linguistics and the 11th International Joint Conference on Natural Language Processing (Volume 1: Long Papers).* Online: Association for Computational Linguistics, pp. 1828–1843. DOI: 10.18653/v1/2021.acl-long.144. URL: https://aclanthology.org/2021.acl-long.144 (visited on 03/13/2022).

Fodor, Janet Dean and Carrie Crowther (Jan. 2002). "Understanding stimulus poverty arguments". en. In: *The Linguistic Review* 18.1-2. ISSN: 0167-6318, 1613-3676. DOI: 10.1515/tlir.19.1-2.105. URL: https://www.degruyter.com/document/doi/10.1515/tlir.19.1-2.105/html (visited on 03/09/2022).

Fodor, Jerry A and Zenon W Pylyshyn (1988). "Connectionism and cognitive architecture: A critical analysis". In: *Cognition* 28.1-2. Publisher: Elsevier, pp. 3–71.

Frank, Michael C, Mika Braginsky, Daniel Yurovsky, and Virginia A. Marchman (May 2017). "Wordbank: an open repository for developmental vocabulary data". en. In: *Journal of Child Language* 44.3, pp. 677–694. ISSN: 0305-0009, 1469-7602. DOI: 10.1017/S0305000916000209. URL: https://www.cambridge.org/core/product/identifier/S0305000916000209/type/journal_article (visited on 03/15/2022).

Frank, Robert and Donald Mathis (2007). "Transformational networks". In: *Models of Human Language Acquisition*, p. 22.

Fromkin, Victoria, Stephen Krashen, Susan Curtiss, David Rigler, and Marilyn Rigler (1974). "The Development of Language in Genie: a Case of Language Acquisition beyond the Critical Period". In: *Brain and Language* 1, pp. 81–107.

Futrell, Richard, Edward Gibson, Harry J Tily, Idan Blank, Anastasia Vishnevetsky, Steven T Piantadosi, and Evelina Fedorenko (Mar. 2021). "The Natural Stories corpus: a reading-time corpus of English texts containing rare syntactic constructions". en. In: *Language Resources and Evaluation* 55.1, pp. 63–77. ISSN: 1574-020X, 1574-0218. DOI: 10.1007/s10579-020-09503-7. URL: https://link.springer.com/10.1007/s10579-020-09503-7 (visited on 03/15/2022).

Gauthier, Jon, Jennifer Hu, Ethan Wilcox, Peng Qian, and Roger Levy (July 2020). "SyntaxGym: An Online Platform for Targeted Evaluation of Language Models". In: *Proceedings of the 58th Annual Meeting of the Association for Computational Linguistics: System Demonstrations*. Online: Association for Computational Linguistics, pp. 70–76. DOI: 10.18653/v1/2020.acl-demos.10. URL: https://aclanthology.org/2020.acl-demos.10 (visited on 09/19/2021).

Gentner, Dedre (1982). "Why nouns are learned before verbs: Linguistic relativity versus natural partitioning". en. In: *Language development: Language cognition and culture*. Ed. by S Kuczaj, p. 48.

Gilkerson, Jill, Jeffrey A Richards, Steven F Warren, Judith K Montgomery, Charles R Greenwood, D Kimbrough Oller, John HL Hansen, and Terrance D Paul (2017). "Mapping the early language environment using all-day recordings and automated analysis". In: *American journal of speech-language pathology* 26.2. Publisher: ASHA, pp. 248–265.

Gleitman, Lila and Eric Wanner (1982). "Language Acquisition: The State of the Art". In: *Language Acquisition: The State of the Art*. Ed. by Lila Gleitman and Eric Wanner. Cambridge University Press.

Gold, E Mark (1967). "Language identification in the limit". In: *Information and control* 10.5. Publisher: Elsevier, pp. 447–474.

Gómez, Rebecca L and LouAnn Gerken (2000). "Infant artificial language learning and language acquisition". In: *Trends in cognitive sciences* 4.5. Publisher: Elsevier, pp. 178–186.

Gordon, Peter (1985). "Level-ordering in lexical development". In: *Cognition*, pp. 73–93.

Gulordava, Kristina, Piotr Bojanowski, Edouard Grave, Tal Linzen, and Marco Baroni (2019). "Colorless green recurrent networks dream hierarchically". In: *Proceedings of the Society for Computation in Linguistics* 2.1, pp. 363–364.

Hale, John (2001). "A Probabilistic Earley Parser as a Psycholinguistic Model". In: *Second Meeting of the North American Chapter of the Association for Computational Linguistics*. URL: https://aclanthology.org/N01-1021 (visited on 09/28/2021).

Han, Chung-hye, Julien Musolino, and Jeffrey Lidz (Jan. 2016). "Endogenous sources of variation in language acquisition". en. In: *Proceedings of the National Academy of Sciences* 113.4, pp. 942–947. ISSN: 0027-8424, 1091-6490. DOI: 10.1073/pnas.1517094113. URL: https://pnas.org/doi/full/10.1073/pnas.1517094113 (visited on 03/09/2022).

Hart, Betty and Todd R Risley (1992). "American parenting of language-learning children: Persisting differences in family-child interactions observed in natural home environments." In: *Developmental Psychology* 28.6. Publisher: American Psychological Association, p. 1096. URL: https://psycnet.apa.org/fulltext/1993-09151-001.pdf.

Haussler, David (1990). "Probably approximately correct learning". In: *Proceedings of the eighth national conference on artificial intelligence*. AAAI Press, pp. 1101–1108.

He, Pengcheng, Xiaodong Liu, Jianfeng Gao, and Weizhu Chen (2021). "DeBERTa: Decoding-enhanced BERT with disentangled attention". In: *International Conference on Learning Representations*. URL: https://openreview.net/forum?id=XPZIaotutsD.

Hewitt, John and Percy Liang (2019). "Designing and interpreting probes with control tasks". In: *Conference on Empirical Methods in Natural Language Processing*. event-place: Hong Kong. Association for Computational Linguistics. URL: https://www.aclweb.org/anthology/D19-1275.

Hewitt, John and Christopher D Manning (2019). "A structural probe for finding syntax in word representations". In: *Proceedings of the 2019 Conference of the North American Chapter of the Association for Computational Linguistics: Human Language Technologies, Volume 1 (Long and Short Papers)*, pp. 4129–4138. URL: https://www.aclweb.org/anthology/N19-1419.

Hochreiter, Sepp and Jürgen Schmidhuber (1997). "Long short-term memory". In: *Neural Computation* 9.8. Publisher: MIT Press, pp. 1735–1780.

Howard, Jeremy and Sebastian Ruder (2018). "Universal language model fine tuning for text classification". In: *Proceedings of the 56th Annual Meeting of the Association for Computational Linguistics (Volume 1: Long Papers)*, pp. 328–339.

Howell, Steve R, Damian Jankowicz, and Suzanna Becker (Aug. 2005). "A model of grounded language acquisition: Sensorimotor features improve lexical and grammatical learning". en. In: *Journal of Memory and Language* 53.2, pp. 258–276. ISSN: 0749596X. DOI: 10.1016/j.jml.2005.03.002. URL: https://linkinghub.elsevier.com/retrieve/pii/S0749596X05000495 (visited on 09/26/2021).

Hu, Jennifer, Jon Gauthier, Peng Qian, Ethan Wilcox, and Roger Levy (July 2020). "A Systematic Assessment of Syntactic Generalization in Neural Language Models". In: *Proceedings of the 58th Annual Meeting of the Association for Computational Linguistics*. Online: Association for Computational Linguistics, pp. 1725–1744. URL: https://www.aclweb.org/anthology/2020.acl-main.158.

Huang, Lifu, Ronan Le Bras, Chandra Bhagavatula, and Yejin Choi (Nov. 2019). "Cosmos QA: Machine reading comprehension with contextual commonsense reasoning". In: *Proceedings of the 2019 conference on empirical methods in natural language processing and the 9th international joint conference on natural language processing (EMNLP-IJCNLP)*. Hong Kong, China: Association for Computational Linguistics, pp. 2391–2401. DOI: 10.18653/v1/D19-1243. URL: https://aclanthology.org/D19-1243.

Huebner, Philip A, Elior Sulem, Fisher Cynthia, and Dan Roth (Nov. 2021). "BabyBERTa: Learning more grammar with small-scale child-directed language". In:

Proceedings of the 25th conference on computational natural language learning. Online: Association for Computational Linguistics, pp. 624–646. DOI: 10.18653/v1/2021.conll-1.49. URL: https://aclanthology.org/2021.conll-1.49.

Iki, Taichi and Akiko Aizawa (2021). "Effect of visual extensions on natural language understanding in vision-and-language models". en. In: *Proceedings of the 2021 Conference on Empirical Methods in Natural Language Processing.* Online and Punta Cana, Dominican Republic: Association for Computational Linguistics, pp. 2189–2196. DOI: 10.18653/v1/2021.emnlp-main.167. URL: https://aclanthology.org/2021.emnlp-main.167 (visited on 02/21/2022).

Kamath, Aishwarya, Mannat Singh, Yann LeCun, Gabriel Synnaeve, Ishan Misra, and Nicolas Carion (2021). "MDETR-modulated detection for end-to-end multi-modal understanding". In: *Proceedings of the IEEE/CVF International Conference on Computer Vision*, pp. 1780–1790.

Katz, Slava (1987). "Estimation of probabilities from sparse data for the language model component of a speech recognizer". In: *IEEE transactions on acoustics, speech, and signal processing* 35.3, pp. 400–401.

Keysers, Daniel, Nathanael Schärli, Nathan Scales, Hylke Buisman, Daniel Furrer, Sergii Kashubin, Nikola Momchev, Danila Sinopalnikov, Lukasz Stafiniak, Tibor Tihon, Dmitry Tsarkov, Xiao Wang, Marc van Zee, and Olivier Bousquet (June 2020). "Measuring compositional generalization: A comprehensive method on realistic data". In: *arXiv:1912.09713 [cs, stat].* arXiv: 1912.09713. URL: http://arxiv.org/abs/1912.09713 (visited on 09/29/2021).

Kim, Najoung and Tal Linzen (Nov. 2020). "COGS: A compositional generalization challenge based on semantic interpretation". In: *Proceedings of the 2020 Conference on Empirical Methods in Natural Language Processing (EMNLP).* Online: Association for Computational Linguistics, pp. 9087–9105. DOI: 10.18653/v1/2020.emnlp-main.731. URL: https://aclanthology.org/2020.emnlp-main.731 (visited on 09/19/2021).

Kimball, John P. (1973). *The Formal Theory of Grammar.* Englewood Cliffs, NJ: Prentice-Hall.

Kirby, Simon (1999). *Function, selection, and innateness: The emergence of language universals.* OUP Oxford.

Kottur, Satwik, José Moura, Stefan Lee, and Dhruv Batra (Sept. 2017). "Natural language does not emerge 'naturally' in multi-agent dialog". In: *Proceedings of the 2017 conference on empirical methods in natural language processing.* Copenhagen, Denmark: Association for Computational Linguistics, pp. 2962–2967. DOI: 10.18653/v1/D17-1321. URL: https://aclanthology.org/D17-1321.

Krishna, Ranjay, Yuke Zhu, Oliver Groth, Justin Johnson, Kenji Hata, Joshua Kravitz, Stephanie Chen, Yannis Kalantidis, Li-Jia Li, David A. Shamma, Michael S. Bernstein, and Li Fei-Fei (May 2017). "Visual genome: Connecting language and vision using crowdsourced Dense image annotations". en. In: *International Journal of Computer Vision* 123.1, pp. 32–73. ISSN: 0920-5691, 1573-1405. DOI: 10.1007/s11263-016-0981-7. URL: http://link.springer.com/10.1007/s11263-016-0981-7 (visited on 09/29/2021).

Lake, Brenden M, Tal Linzen, and Marco Baroni (May 2019). "Human few-shot learning of compositional instructions". In: *Proceedings of the 41st Annual Conference of the Cognitive Science Society.* (Visited on 09/29/2021).

Lake, Brenden and Marco Baroni (2018). "Generalization without systematicity: On the compositional skills of sequence-to-sequence recurrent networks". In: *International Conference on Machine Learning*, pp. 2879–2888.

Lakhotia, Kushal, Evgeny Kharitonov, Wei-Ning Hsu, Yossi Adi, Adam Polyak, Benjamin Bolte, Tu-Anh Nguyen, Jade Copet, Alexei Baevski, Adelrahman Mohamed, and Emmanuel Dupoux (Sept. 2021). "Generative spoken language modeling from raw audio". In: *arXiv:2102.01192 [cs]*. arXiv: 2102.01192. URL: `http://arxiv.org/abs/2102.01192` (visited on 09/21/2021).

Landauer, Thomas K and Susan T Dutnais (1997). "A solution to Plato's problem: The latent semantic analysis theory of acquisition, induction, and representation of knowledge". en. In: *Psychological Review* 104.2, pp. 211–240.

Lau, Jey Han, Alexander Clark, and Shalom Lappin (2017). "Grammaticality, acceptability, and probability: A probabilistic view of linguistic knowledge". In: *Cognitive Science* 41.5. Publisher: Wiley Online Library, pp. 1202–1241.

Lavechin, Marvin, Maureen de Seyssel, Marianne Métais, Florian Metze, Abdelrahman Mohamed, Hervé BREDIN, Emmanuel Dupoux, and Alejandrina Cristia (2022). "Early phonetic learning from ecological audio: domain-general versus domain-specific mechanisms". In: Publisher: PsyArXiv.

Lazaridou, Angeliki and Marco Baroni (July 2020). "Emergent Multi-Agent Communication in the Deep Learning Era". In: *arXiv:2006.02419 [cs]*. arXiv: 2006.02419. URL: `http://arxiv.org/abs/2006.02419` (visited on 09/29/2021).

Lazaridou, Angeliki, Karl Moritz Hermann, Karl Tuyls, and Stephen Clark (2018). "Emergence of linguistic communication from referential games with symbolic and pixel input". In: *International conference on learning representations*.

Lazaridou, Angeliki, Alexander Peysakhovich, and Marco Baroni (Mar. 2017). "Multi-Agent Cooperation and the Emergence of (Natural) Language". In: *International Conference on Learning Representations*. arXiv: 1612.07182. URL: `http://arxiv.org/abs/1612.07182` (visited on 09/29/2021).

Lazaridou, Angeliki, Nghia The Pham, and Marco Baroni (May 2015). "Combining Language and Vision with a Multimodal Skip-gram Model". In: *Proceedings of the 2015 Conference of the North American Chapter of the Association for Computational Linguistics: Human Language Technologies.* Denver, Colorado: Association for Computational Linguistics, pp. 153–163. DOI: `10.3115/v1/N15-1016`. URL: `https://aclanthology.org/N15-1016` (visited on 09/29/2021).

Lazaridou, Angeliki, Anna Potapenko, and Olivier Tieleman (July 2020). "Multi-agent Communication meets Natural Language: Synergies between Functional and Structural Language Learning". In: *Proceedings of the 58th Annual Meeting of the Association for Computational Linguistics.* Online: Association for Computational Linguistics, pp. 7663–7674. DOI: `10.18653/v1/2020.acl-main.685`. URL: `https://aclanthology.org/2020.acl-main.685` (visited on 09/29/2021).

LeCun, Yann, Yoshua Bengio, and Geoffrey Hinton (2015). "Deep learning". In: *Nature* 521.7553. Publisher: Nature Publishing Group, p. 436.

Legate, Julie Anne and Charles D Yang (2002). "Empirical re-assessment of stimulus poverty arguments". In: *The Linguistic Review* 18.1-2. Publisher: Walter de Gruyter, pp. 151–162.

Lerdahl, Fred and Ray Jackendoff (1983). *A Generative Theory of Tonal Music*. MIT Press.

Levy, Roger (Mar. 2008). "Expectation-based syntactic comprehension". en. In: *Cognition* 106.3, pp. 1126–1177. ISSN: 00100277. DOI: 10.1016/j.cognition.2007.05.006. URL: https://linkinghub.elsevier.com/retrieve/pii/S0010027707001436 (visited on 09/28/2021).

Li, Fushan and Michael Bowling (2019). "Ease-of-teaching and language structure from emergent communication". In: *Advances in neural information processing systems* 32.

Lidz, Jeffrey, Sandra Waxman, and Jennifer Freedman (Oct. 2003). "What infants know about syntax but couldn't have learned: experimental evidence for syntactic structure at 18 months". en. In: *Cognition* 89.3, pp. 295–303. ISSN: 00100277. DOI: 10.1016/S0010-0277(03)00116-1. URL: https://linkinghub.elsevier.com/retrieve/pii/S0010027703001161 (visited on 09/27/2021).

Linzen, Tal (2019). "What can linguistics and deep learning contribute to each other? Response to Pater". In: *Language* 95.1. Publisher: Linguistic Society of America, e99–e108.

Linzen, Tal and Marco Baroni (2021). "Syntactic Structure from Deep Learning". In: *Annual Review of Linguistics* 7.1, pp. 195–212. eprint: https://doi.org/10.1146/annurev-linguistics-032020-051035.

Linzen, Tal, Emmanuel Dupoux, and Yoav Goldberg (2016). "Assessing the Ability of LSTMs to Learn Syntax-Sensitive Dependencies". In: *Transactions of the Association for Computational Linguistics* 4, pp. 521–535.

Lison, Pierre and Jorg Tiedemann (2016). "OpenSubtitles2016: Extracting Large Parallel Corpora from Movie and TV Subtitles". en. In: *Proceedings of the 10th International Conference on Language Resources and Evaluation (LREC 2016)*, p. 7.

Liu, Yinhan, Myle Ott, Naman Goyal, Jingfei Du, Mandar Joshi, Danqi Chen, Omer Levy, Mike Lewis, Luke Zettlemoyer, and Veselin Stoyanov (2019). "RoBERTa: A robustly optimized BERT pretraining approach". In: *arXiv preprint arXiv:1907.11692*. URL: http://arxiv.org/abs/1907.11692.

Lovering, Charles, Rohan Jha, Tal Linzen, and Ellie Pavlick (2021). "Predicting Inductive Biases of Fine-tuned Models". In: *International Conference on Learning Representations*. URL: https://openreview.net/forum?id=mNtmhaDkAr.

Lu, Jiasen, Dhruv Batra, Devi Parikh, and Stefan Lee (2019). "ViLBERT: Pretraining Task-Agnostic Visiolinguistic Representations for Vision-and-Language Tasks". In: *Advances in Neural Information Processing Systems*. Vol. 32. Curran Associates, Inc. URL: https://proceedings.neurips.cc/paper/2019/hash/c74d97b01eae257e44aa9d5bade97baf-Abstract.html (visited on 09/29/2021).

MacWhinney, Brian (2014). *The CHILDES project: Tools for analyzing talk, Volume II: The database*. Psychology Press.

Mankewitz, Jessica, Veronica Boyce, B. Waldon, Georgia Loukatou, D. Yu, Jesse Mu, Noah D Goodman, and Michael C Frank (2021). "Multi-party referential communication in complex strategic games". In: *Meaning in Context Workshop at the 35th Conference on Neural Information Processing Systems (NeurIPS 2021)*. URL: `https://psyarxiv.com/tfb3d`.

Manning, Christopher D. (Dec. 2015). "Computational Linguistics and Deep Learning". en. In: *Computational Linguistics* 41.4, pp. 701–707. ISSN: 0891-2017, 1530-9312. DOI: `10.1162/COLI_a_00239`. URL: `https://direct.mit.edu/coli/article/41/4/701-707/1512` (visited on 09/06/2021).

Manning, Christopher D, Kevin Clark, John Hewitt, Urvashi Khandelwal, and Omer Levy (Dec. 2020). "Emergent linguistic structure in artificial neural networks trained by self-supervision". en. In: *Proceedings of the National Academy of Sciences* 117.48, pp. 30046–30054. ISSN: 0027-8424, 1091-6490. DOI: `10.1073/pnas.1907367117`. URL: `http://www.pnas.org/lookup/doi/10.1073/pnas.1907367117` (visited on 09/25/2021).

Marcus, Gary F. (1993). "Negative evidence in language acquisition". In: *Cognition* 46.1. Publisher: Elsevier, pp. 53–85.

Marvin, Rebecca and Tal Linzen (2018). "Targeted Syntactic Evaluation of Language Models". In: *Proceedings of the 2018 Conference on Empirical Methods in Natural Language Processing*, pp. 1192–1202.

McCoy, Richard Thomas, Robert Frank, and Tal Linzen (2018). "Revisiting the poverty of the stimulus: hierarchical generalization without a hierarchical bias in recurrent neural networks". In: *Proceedings of the 40th Annual Conference of the Cognitive Science Society*.

— (Dec. 2020). "Does Syntax Need to Grow on Trees? Sources of Hierarchical Inductive Bias in Sequence-to-Sequence Networks". en. In: *Transactions of the Association for Computational Linguistics* 8, pp. 125–140. ISSN: 2307-387X. DOI: `10.1162/tacl_a_00304`. URL: `https://direct.mit.edu/tacl/article/43542` (visited on 07/19/2021).

Mitchell, Tom M (1980). *The need for biases in learning generalizations*. Department of Computer Science, Laboratory for Computer Science Research ...

Montague, Richard (1973). "The proper treatment of quantification in ordinary English". In: *Approaches to natural language*. Springer, pp. 221–242.

Nguyen, Tu Anh, Maureen de Seyssel, Patricia Rozé, Morgane Rivière, Evgeny Kharitonov, Alexei Baevski, Ewan Dunbar, and Emmanuel Dupoux (Dec. 2020). "The Zero Resource Speech Benchmark 2021: Metrics and baselines for unsupervised spoken language modeling". In: *arXiv:2011.11588 [cs, eess]*. arXiv: 2011.11588. URL: `http://arxiv.org/abs/2011.11588` (visited on 09/21/2021).

Orhan, Emin, Vaibhav Gupta, and Brenden M Lake (2020). "Self-supervised learning through the eyes of a child". In: *Advances in Neural Information Processing Systems*. Ed. by H. Larochelle, M. Ranzato, R. Hadsell, M.F. Balcan, and H. Lin. Vol. 33. Curran Associates, Inc., pp. 9960–9971. URL: `https://proceedings.neurips.cc/paper/2020/file/7183145a2a3e0ce2b68cd3735186b1d5-Paper.pdf`.

Pannitto, Ludovica and Aurélie Herbelot (Nov. 2020). "Recurrent babbling: evaluating the acquisition of grammar from limited input data". In: *Proceedings of the 24th Conference on Computational Natural Language Learning*. Online: Association for Computational Linguistics, pp. 165–176. DOI: `10.18653/v1/2020.conll-1.13`. URL: `https://aclanthology.org/2020.conll-1.13` (visited on 09/17/2021).

Papadimitriou, Isabel, Ethan A. Chi, Richard Futrell, and Kyle Mahowald (Apr. 2021). "Deep subjecthood: Higher-order grammatical features in multilingual BERT". In: *Proceedings of the 16th conference of the european chapter of the association for computational linguistics: Main volume*. Online: Association for Computational Linguistics, pp. 2522–2532. DOI: `10.18653/v1/2021.eacl-main.215`. URL: `https://aclanthology.org/2021.eacl-main.215`.

Pater, Joe (2019). "Generative linguistics and neural networks at 60: Foundation, friction, and fusion". In: *Language* 95.1. Publisher: Linguistic Society of America, e41–e74.

Pérez-Mayos, Laura, Miguel Ballesteros, and Leo Wanner (Nov. 2021). "How much pretraining data do language models need to learn syntax?" In: *Proceedings of the 2021 Conference on Empirical Methods in Natural Language Processing*. Online and Punta Cana, Dominican Republic: Association for Computational Linguistics, pp. 1571–1582. DOI: `10.18653/v1/2021.emnlp-main.118`. URL: `https://aclanthology.org/2021.emnlp-main.118`.

Perfors, Andy, Joshua B Tenenbaum, and Terry Regier (2011). "The learnability of abstract syntactic principles". In: *Cognition* 118.3. Publisher: Elsevier, pp. 306–338.

Peters, Matthew, Mark Neumann, Mohit Iyyer, Matt Gardner, Christopher Clark, Kenton Lee, and Luke Zettlemoyer (2018). "Deep Contextualized Word Representations". In: *Proceedings of the 2018 Conference of the North American Chapter of the Association for Computational Linguistics: Human Language Technologies, Volume 1 (Long Papers)*. event-place: New Orleans, Louisiana. Association for Computational Linguistics, pp. 2227–2237. DOI: `10.18653/v1/N18-1202`. URL: `http://aclweb.org/anthology/N18-1202`.

Petroni, Fabio, Tim Rocktäschel, Sebastian Riedel, Patrick Lewis, Anton Bakhtin, Yuxiang Wu, and Alexander Miller (Nov. 2019). "Language Models as Knowledge Bases?" In: *Proceedings of the 2019 Conference on Empirical Methods in Natural Language Processing and the 9th International Joint Conference on Natural Language Processing (EMNLP-IJCNLP)*. Hong Kong, China: Association for Computational Linguistics, pp. 2463–2473. DOI: `10.18653/v1/D19-1250`. URL: `https://www.aclweb.org/anthology/D19-1250`.

Petty, Jackson and Robert Frank (2021). *Transformers Generalize Linearly*. DOI: `10.48550/ARXIV.2109.12036`. URL: `https://arxiv.org/abs/2109.12036`.

Pimentel, Tiago, Josef Valvoda, Rowan Hall Maudslay, Ran Zmigrod, Adina Williams, and Ryan Cotterell (July 2020). "Information-Theoretic Probing for Linguistic Structure". In: *Proceedings of the 58th Annual Meeting of the Association for Computational Linguistics*. Online: Association for Computational Linguistics, pp. 4609–4622. DOI: 10.18653/v1/2020.acl-main.420. URL: https://www.aclweb.org/anthology/2020.acl-main.420.

Radford, Alec, Jong Wook Kim, Chris Hallacy, Aditya Ramesh, Gabriel Goh, Sandhini Agarwal, Girish Sastry, Amanda Askell, Pamela Mishkin, Jack Clark, Gretchen Krueger, and Ilya Sutskever (18–24 Jul 2021). "Learning Transferable Visual Models From Natural Language Supervision". In: *Proceedings of the 38th International Conference on Machine Learning*. Ed. by Marina Meila and Tong Zhang. Vol. 139. Proceedings of Machine Learning Research. PMLR, pp. 8748–8763. URL: https://proceedings.mlr.press/v139/radford21a.html.

Radford, Alec, Karthik Narasimhan, Tim Salimans, and Ilya Sutskever (2018). *Improving language understanding with unsupervised learning*. Tech. rep. Technical report, OpenAI.

Rae, Jack W, Sebastian Borgeaud, Trevor Cai, Katie Millican, Jordan Hoffmann, Francis Song, John Aslanides, Sarah Henderson, Roman Ring, Susannah Young, et al. (2021). "Scaling language models: Methods, analysis & insights from training gopher". In: *arXiv preprint arXiv:2112.11446*.

Rasin, Ezer and Athulya Aravind (June 2021). "The nature of the semantic stimulus: the acquisition of every as a case study". en. In: *Natural Language Semantics* 29.2, pp. 339–375. ISSN: 0925-854X, 1572-865X. DOI: 10.1007/s11050-020-09168-6. URL: https://link.springer.com/10.1007/s11050-020-09168-6 (visited on 09/27/2021).

Ravfogel, Shauli, Yanai Elazar, Hila Gonen, Michael Twiton, and Yoav Goldberg (2020). "Null It Out: Guarding Protected Attributes by Iterative Nullspace Projection". en. In: *Proceedings of the 58th Annual Meeting of the Association for Computational Linguistics*. Online: Association for Computational Linguistics, pp. 7237–7256. DOI: 10.18653/v1/2020.acl-main.647. URL: https://www.aclweb.org/anthology/2020.acl-main.647 (visited on 03/13/2022).

Ravfogel, Shauli, Yoav Goldberg, and Tal Linzen (2019). "Studying the Inductive Biases of RNNs with Synthetic Variations of Natural Languages". In: *Proceedings of NAACL-HLT*, pp. 3532–3542.

Reali, Florencia and Morten H Christiansen (2005). "Uncovering the richness of the stimulus: Structure dependence and indirect statistical evidence". In: *Cognitive Science* 29.6. Publisher: Wiley Online Library, pp. 1007–1028.

Ren, Yi, Shangmin Guo, Matthieu Labeau, Shay B Cohen, and Simon Kirby (2019). "Compositional languages emerge in a neural iterated learning model". In: *International conference on learning representations*.

Resnick, Cinjon, Abhinav Gupta, Jakob Foerster, Andrew M Dai, and Kyunghyun Cho (2020). "Capacity, bandwidth, and compositionality in emergent language learning". In: *Proceedings of the 19th international conference on autonomous agents and MultiAgent systems*, pp. 1125–1133.

Reuland, Eric (Nov. 2017). "Grammar of binding in the languages of the world: Unity versus diversity". en. In: *Cognition* 168, pp. 370–379. ISSN: 00100277. DOI: 10.1016/j.cognition.2016.01.020. URL: https://linkinghub.elsevier.com/retrieve/pii/S0010027716300208 (visited on 03/11/2022).

Rita, Mathieu, Rahma Chaabouni, and Emmanuel Dupoux (Nov. 2020). "'LazImpa': Lazy and Impatient neural agents learn to communicate efficiently". In: *Proceedings of the 24th conference on computational natural language learning*. Online: Association for Computational Linguistics, pp. 335–343. URL: https://www.aclweb.org/anthology/2020.conll-1.26.

Rogers, Anna, Olga Kovaleva, and Anna Rumshisky (2020). "A Primer in BERTology: What we know about how BERT works". In: *Findings of EMNLP*. URL: https://www.aclweb.org/anthology/2020.tacl-1.54.

Sakaguchi, Keisuke, Ronan Le Bras, Chandra Bhagavatula, and Yejin Choi (2020). "WinoGrande: An Adversarial Winograd Schema Challenge at Scale". en. In: *Proceedings of the AAAI Conference on Artificial Intelligence*. Vol. 34(05), pp. 8732–8740. DOI: https://doi.org/10.1609/aaai.v34i05.6399.

Salazar, Julian, Davis Liang, Toan Q. Nguyen, and Katrin Kirchhoff (July 2020). "Masked Language Model Scoring". In: *Proceedings of the 58th Annual Meeting of the Association for Computational Linguistics*. Online: Association for Computational Linguistics, pp. 2699–2712. DOI: 10.18653/v1/2020.acl-main.240. URL: https://www.aclweb.org/anthology/2020.acl-main.240.

Schijndel, Marten van, Aaron Mueller, and Tal Linzen (Nov. 2019). "Quantity doesn't buy quality syntax with neural language models". In: *Proceedings of the 2019 Conference on Empirical Methods in Natural Language Processing and the 9th International Joint Conference on Natural Language Processing (EMNLP-IJCNLP)*. Hong Kong, China: Association for Computational Linguistics, pp. 5831–5837. DOI: 10.18653/v1/D19-1592. URL: https://www.aclweb.org/anthology/D19-1592.

Schütze, Carson T. (1996). *The Empirical Base of Linguistics: Grammaticality Judgments and Linguistic Methodology*. University of Chicago Press.

Searle, John R. (1969). *Speech Acts: An Essay in the Philosophy of Language*. Cambridge University Press. DOI: 10.1017/CBO9781139173438.

Shi, Xing, Inkit Padhi, and Kevin Knight (2016). "Does string-based neural MT learn source syntax?" In: *Proceedings of the 2016 Conference on Empirical Methods in Natural Language Processing*, pp. 1526–1534.

Singh, Amanpreet, Ronghang Hu, Vedanuj Goswami, Guillaume Couairon, Wojciech Galuba, Marcus Rohrbach, and Douwe Kiela (2022). "FLAVA: A Foundational Language And Vision Alignment Model". In: *CVPR*.

Soderstrom, Melanie, Amanda Seidl, Deborah G Kemler Nelson, and Peter W Jusczyk (2003). "The prosodic bootstrapping of phrases: Evidence from prelinguistic infants". In: *Journal of Memory and Language* 49.2. Publisher: Elsevier, pp. 249–267.

Sprouse, Jon, Carson T. Schütze, and Diogo Almeida (2013). "A comparison of informal and formal acceptability judgments using a random sample from Linguistic Inquiry 2001–2010". In: *Lingua* 134. Publisher: Elsevier, pp. 219–248.

Su, Weijie, Xizhou Zhu, Yue Cao, Bin Li, Lewei Lu, Furu Wei, and Jifeng Dai (2020). "VL-BERT: Pre-training of Generic Visual-Linguistic Representations". In: *International Conference on Learning Representations*. URL: https://openreview.net/forum?id=SygXPaEYvH.

Sullivan, Jessica, Michelle Mei, Andrew Perfors, Erica Wojcik, and Michael C. Frank (May 2021). "SAYCam: A Large, Longitudinal Audiovisual Dataset Recorded From the Infant's Perspective". en. In: *Open Mind* 5, pp. 20–29. ISSN: 2470-2986. DOI: 10.1162/opmi_a_00039. URL: https://direct.mit.edu/opmi/article/doi/10.1162/opmi_a_00039/97495/SAYCam-A-Large-Longitudinal-Audiovisual-Dataset (visited on 02/22/2022).

Sun, Chen, Austin Myers, Carl Vondrick, Kevin Murphy, and Cordelia Schmid (2019). "Videobert: A joint model for video and language representation learning". In: *Proceedings of the IEEE/CVF international conference on computer vision*, pp. 7464–7473.

Tan, Hao and Mohit Bansal (Nov. 2019). "LXMERT: Learning Cross-Modality Encoder Representations from Transformers". In: *Proceedings of the 2019 Conference on Empirical Methods in Natural Language Processing and the 9th International Joint Conference on Natural Language Processing (EMNLP-IJCNLP)*. Hong Kong, China: Association for Computational Linguistics, pp. 5100–5111. DOI: 10.18653/v1/D19-1514. URL: https://aclanthology.org/D19-1514 (visited on 09/29/2021).

Tenney, Ian, Patrick Xia, Berlin Chen, Alex Wang, Adam Poliak, Richard Thomas McCoy, Najoung Kim, Benjamin Van Durme, Samuel R. Bowman, Dipanjan Das, et al. (2019). "What do you learn from context? Probing for sentence structure in contextualized word representations". In: *Proceedings of ICLR*. URL: http://arxiv.org/abs/1905.06316.

Valiant, L. G. (Nov. 1984). "A theory of the learnable". en. In: *Communications of the ACM* 27.11, pp. 1134–1142. ISSN: 0001-0782, 1557-7317. DOI: 10.1145/1968.1972. URL: https://dl.acm.org/doi/10.1145/1968.1972 (visited on 02/28/2022).

Dooren, Annemarie van, Anouk Dieuleveut, Aílís Cournane, and Valentine Hacquard (Aug. 2022). "Figuring Out Root and Epistemic Uses of Modals: The Role of the Input". In: *Journal of Semantics*. ISSN: 0167-5133. DOI: 10.1093/jos/ffac010. eprint: https://academic.oup.com/jos/advance-article-pdf/doi/10.1093/jos/ffac010/45549153/ffac010.pdf. URL: https://doi.org/10.1093/jos/ffac010.

Vaswani, Ashish, Noam Shazeer, Niki Parmar, Jakob Uszkoreit, Llion Jones, Aidan N Gomez, Łukasz Kaiser, and Illia Polosukhin (2017). "Attention is All you Need". In: *Advances in Neural Information Processing Systems 30*. Ed. by I. Guyon, U. V. Luxburg, S. Bengio, H. Wallach, R. Fergus, S. Vishwanathan, and R. Garnett. Curran Associates, Inc., pp. 5998–6008. URL: http://papers.nips.cc/paper/7181-attention-is-all-you-need.pdf.

Vig, Jesse, Sebastian Gehrmann, Yonatan Belinkov, Sharon Qian, Daniel Nevo, Yaron Singer, and Stuart Shieber (2020). "Investigating gender bias in language models using causal mediation analysis". In: *Advances in neural information processing systems*. Ed. by H. Larochelle, M. Ranzato, R. Hadsell, M. F. Balcan, and H. Lin. Vol. 33. Curran Associates, Inc., pp. 12388–12401. URL: https://proceedings.neurips.cc/paper/2020/file/92650b2e92217715fe312e6fa7b90d82-Paper.pdf.

Voita, Elena and Ivan Titov (Nov. 2020). "Information-Theoretic Probing with Minimum Description Length". In: *Proceedings of the 2020 Conference on Empirical Methods in Natural Language Processing*. Punta Cana, Dominican Republic: Association for Computational Linguistics. URL: https://www.aclweb.org/anthology/2020.emnlp-main.14.pdf.

Wang, Alex and Kyunghyun Cho (June 2019). "BERT has a mouth, and it must speak: BERT as a Markov random field language model". In: *Proceedings of the workshop on methods for optimizing and evaluating neural language generation*. Minneapolis, Minnesota: Association for Computational Linguistics, pp. 30–36. DOI: 10.18653/v1/W19-2304. URL: https://aclanthology.org/W19-2304.

Warstadt, Alex and Samuel R. Bowman (2019). *Linguistic Analysis of Pretrained Sentence Encoders with Acceptability Judgments*. DOI: 10.48550/ARXIV.1901.03438. URL: https://arxiv.org/abs/1901.03438.

— (2020). "Can neural networks acquire a structural bias from raw linguistic data?" In: *Proceedings of the 42th annual conference of the Cognitive Science Society*.

Warstadt, Alex, Alicia, Haokun Liu, Anhad Mohananey, Wei Peng, Sheng-Fu Wang, and Samuel R. Bowman (2020). "BLiMP: The Benchmark of Linguistic Minimal Pairs for English". In: *Transactions of the Association for Computational Linguistics* 8. _eprint: https://doi.org/10.1162/tacl_a_00321, pp. 377–392. DOI: 10.1162/tacl_a_00321. URL: https://doi.org/10.1162/tacl_a_00321.

Warstadt, Alex, Amanpreet Singh, and Samuel R. Bowman (Sept. 2019). "Neural Network Acceptability Judgments". In: *Transactions of the Association for Computational Linguistics* 7, pp. 625–641. ISSN: 2307-387X. DOI: 10.1162/tacl_a_00290. URL: https://doi.org/10.1162/tacl%5C_a%5C_00290.

Warstadt, Alex, Yian, Haau-Sing Li, Haokun Liu, and Samuel R. Bowman (Nov. 2020). "Learning Which Features Matter: RoBERTa Acquires a Preference for Linguistic Generalizations (Eventually)". In: *Proceedings of the 2020 Conference on Empirical Methods in Natural Language Processing*. Punta Cana, Dominican Republic: Association for Computational Linguistics.

Wilcox, Ethan, Roger Levy, Takashi Morita, and Richard Futrell (2018). "What do RNN Language Models Learn about Filler–Gap Dependencies?" In: *Proceedings of the 2018 EMNLP Workshop BlackboxNLP: Analyzing and Interpreting Neural Networks for NLP*, pp. 211–221.

Wilcox, Ethan, Pranali Vani, and Roger Levy (Aug. 2021). "A Targeted Assessment of Incremental Processing in Neural Language Models and Humans". In: *Proceedings of the 59th Annual Meeting of the Association for Computational Linguistics and the 11th International Joint Conference on Natural Language Processing (Volume 1: Long Papers)*. Online: Association for Computational Linguistics, pp. 939–952. DOI: 10.18653/v1/2021.acl-long.76. URL: https://aclanthology.org/2021.acl-long.76 (visited on 09/28/2021).

Wilson, Andrew G and Pavel Izmailov (2020). "Bayesian deep learning and a probabilistic perspective of generalization". In: *Advances in neural information processing systems* 33, pp. 4697–4708.

Wilson, Colin (2006). "Learning phonology with substantive bias: An experimental and computational study of velar palatalization". In: *Cognitive science* 30.5. Publisher: Wiley Online Library, pp. 945–982.

Yang, Yuan and Steven T. Piantadosi (Feb. 2022). "One model for the learning of language". en. In: *Proceedings of the National Academy of Sciences* 119.5, e2021865119. ISSN: 0027-8424, 1091-6490. DOI: 10.1073/pnas.2021865119. URL: https://pnas.org/doi/full/10.1073/pnas.2021865119 (visited on 03/14/2022).

Yun, Tian, Chen Sun, and Ellie Pavlick (Sept. 2021). "Does Vision-and-Language Pretraining Improve Lexical Grounding?" en. In: *Proceedings of EMNLP*. arXiv: 2109.10246. (Visited on 09/29/2021).

Zellers, Rowan, Yonatan Bisk, Roy Schwartz, and Yejin Choi (2018). "SWAG: A large-scale adversarial dataset for grounded commonsense inference". In: *Proceedings of the 2018 conference on empirical methods in natural language processing*. Brussels, Belgium: Association for Computational Linguistics, pp. 93–104. DOI: 10.18653/v1/D18-1009. URL: https://aclanthology.org/D18-1009.

Zhang, Yian, Alex Warstadt, Xiaocheng Li, and Samuel R. Bowman (Aug. 2021). "When Do You Need Billions of Words of Pretraining Data?" In: *Proceedings of the 59th Annual Meeting of the Association for Computational Linguistics and the 11th International Joint Conference on Natural Language Processing (Volume 1: Long Papers)*. Online: Association for Computational Linguistics, pp. 1112–1125. DOI: 10.18653/v1/2021.acl-long.90. URL: https://aclanthology.org/2021.acl-long.90 (visited on 09/17/2021).

CHAPTER 3

Grammar through Spontaneous Order

Nick Chater
University of Warwick

Morten H. Christiansen
Cornell University, Aarhus University and Haskins Laboratories

CONTENTS

ABSTRACT

How do the algebraic regularities in natural language, described by generative grammar, emerge? One traditional viewpoint has been that these are encoded with a species-specific and innately specified universal grammar, which has somehow come to be part of the human biological endowment. From this point of view, the strange mix of regularities, subregularities, and downright exceptions observed across languages and levels in linguistic analysis are somewhat puzzling. An alternative perspective is that language begins through attempts to solve immediate communicative problems between specific people on specific occasions; but each new communicative exchange draws on precedents from past exchanges, and sets precedents for future exchanges. Over time, specific linguistic patterns will become entrenched, and layered upon each other, to create a complex spontaneously ordered system, analogous to case law. From this point of view, the algebraic patterns in language are always various, partial and subject to exceptions.

3.1 INTRODUCTION

Language, like so much else in the natural and cultural worlds, is a curious mix of order and disorder. Where does this order come from? And why is it mixed with

DOI: 10.1201/9781003205388-3

disorder – with collisions between rules and downright exceptions? In this chapter, we will argue that the answers to these questions may be related.[1]

In explaining any mixture of order and disorder, we can take either one or the other as basic. First, let us consider what we shall call the "order-first" viewpoint. According to this view, there are some underlying forces which initially create the orderly pattern in its "pure" form. For example, we might suppose that there is a purely logical "language of thought" built into the mind of each person (where the order of this logical language comes from, we will not enquire). This language of thought, having the form of something like predicate calculus or a more expressive logical language has an orderly, and in particular algebraic, structure. It has a well-defined set of syntactic rules (generating the familiar syntactic tree-structures or some equivalent), and a compositional semantics defined over those rules. But this orderly structure is then assumed to be disturbed by other more unruly forces, for example, concerning the practical challenges of communication. For example, it may be assumed, we somehow have to encode these purely logical structures into a convenient form that can be spoken or signed; and this must be done in the light of a myriad of practical constraints. Shortcuts and ad hoc devices may be useful to get particular messages across rapidly; cognitive limitations might have distorting impacts on how we convey ideas that have excessive logical complexity; ambiguities might be allowed, and even functionally appropriate, where context is sufficient to make it "obvious" what is meant and time is short (Piantadosi, Tily, & Gibson, 2012). More broadly, from this general standpoint, the mixture of orderly and disorderly aspects of languages arises from the multitude of "corrupting" influences of practical constraints on what is, at base, a perfectly orderly system.

This "order-first" picture can, of course, be filled out in a variety of ways. For example, Chomsky has proposed that sentences have a syntactic representation, LF, over which semantic interpretation is defined.[2] Chomsky's LF is not quite a conventional logical language, though it does have a "pure" algebraic structure and compositional semantics (Chomsky, 1995). According to the minimalist program, patterns in language then arise through the process of optimising the relationship between LF and phonological representations (or, more generally, optimising the mapping between conceptual representations and the sensorimotor system). This optimisation is not, perhaps surprisingly, presumed to be based on practical considerations, such as statistical regularities in what messages need to be conveyed, fine-details of the operation of the auditory system, the speech apparatus, or memory, but is viewed in much more abstract terms. Nonetheless, some of the irregularities and complexities of natural language, at least, can be seen as arising from the inherently messy task of mapping from LF to a sound-based representation.[3] Indeed, the minimalist program

---

[1] The ideas in this chapter are outlined more extensively in Christiansen and Chater (2022).

[2] In particular, LF is designed to resolve scope ambiguities: For example, the different meanings of every book published in English are stored in a well-known library – where this sentence might be taken to imply that there is a single such library (so that a natural question would be which one?), or only to say that every book is stored in some well-known or other (so that no library need be completely comprehensive). The relationship between LF and related ideas in linguistics and the traditional concept of logical form in the philosophy of language is debated (e.g., Stich, 1975).

[3] If language is primarily for thought, rather than communication, then the process of translating

proposes that many aspects of language can be explained on the assumption that this mapping will generate inevitable complexity – even if the mapping is as "perfect" as possible (Chomsky, 1995; Lasnik, 2002). Many of the quirks of individual languages are, though, viewed as relegated to the "periphery" rather than the "core" of language, and are viewed as being of rather little linguistic interest.[4] Another popular, although by no means essential, aspect of this type of view is that the most essential elements of the algebraic structure of language, captured in a so-called "universal grammar," arise not purely from domain-general principles of cognition but from a genetically encoded language faculty (e.g., Chomsky 1980). Thus, the orderly nature of language arises, this point of view, from a language faculty – a genetically specified, and language-specific set of biological constraints.[5] Quite what constraints the language faculty is presumed to contain is not at all clear, but it is generally assumed at least to include recursion, which may seem particularly central to the algebraic structure of language.

Other very different approaches to generative grammar and compositional semantics may have different theoretical presuppositions. But the order-first story is usually tacitly assumed across many areas of linguistics and the philosophy of language. Indeed, the order-first viewpoint is built into approaches to languages which assume that sentences have an underlying logical form (whether that logical form is cognitively represented or not), a viewpoint which can be traced back to the inception of analytic philosophy with the work of Frege (see Dummett, 1981) and Russell (1905). Similarly, to the degree that the compositional semantics of natural language is presumed to be patterned on the compositional semantics of formal logical languages, the "order-first" viewpoint is built into the view of language emerging from Tarski's theory of truth and Montague Semantics (e.g., Dowty, Wall, & Peters, 1981).

We have so far reviewed the idea that language is at root orderly, but made disorderly by contact with extra-linguistic factors of various kinds. But our objective in this chapter is to explore the opposite perspective. From this point of view, language

---

from LF to a phonological form seems to be entirely pointless. Indeed, it seems to be counterproductive, because surely reasoning is defined over logical, not phonological, representations. Moreover, if language were centrally involved in thought, then intelligent thought should be largely eliminated in global aphasics (with no language) and should show distinctive neural traces of covert natural language processing. Neither prediction appears to be correct (Fedorenko & Varley, 2016). Now, of course, it may be that the process of generating natural language helps us clarify and formulate our thoughts. Of course, one might wonder whether it is possible even to make sense of the very idea of thoughts, independent of their expression in a publicly accessible language, in the light, for example, of Wittgenstein's and Kripke's thoughts on rules and private languages (Kripke, 1982). But this would be to suggest that the process of communication is essential to thought, and hence language is useful for thinking not independently of its communicative function, but because of its communicative function.

[4]Chomsky is loath to see interesting aspects of language as arising from practical considerations of communication, in the light of his counterintuitive view that language is primarily for thought rather than communication mentioned above. (For opposite viewpoints, see, e.g., Christiansen & Chater, 2016; Gibson et al., 2019; Hahn, Jurafsky & Futrell, 2020; Hawkins, 1994).

[5]We have argued elsewhere that telling an evolutionarily credible story about the origin of such a language faculty is very difficult (Christiansen & Chater, 2008). Whether recursion is either language-specific rather than a general property of human cognition is also very much to open to challenge (e.g., Christiansen & Chater, 2015; Conway & Christiansen, 2001).

should be viewed as by the default ad hoc and disorderly; but order emerges, to an extent, through the pressures on different linguistic forms generated by their endless use and reuse, and crucially the interactions between them. That is, the patterns in language arise through a process of *spontaneous order*.

3.2 SPONTANEOUS ORDER: THE VERY IDEA

The idea of spontaneous order in social phenomena is imported, originally, from the natural sciences.[6] Polanyi (1941), a leading physical chemist early in his career, noted that coherence in the domains of ideas, culture, and social structure might potentially arise through the process of mutual balancing and interaction of forces analogous to that observed when ice forms intricate snowflakes, gas coheres in into spherical bubbles in a liquid, or water 'finds a level' a container. He initially termed this mutual balancing of the interactions between many independent elements with no central coordination 'dynamic order' later shifting to 'spontaneous order' (Polanyi, 1951). Polanyi viewed the processes by which the mind organises sensory input as operating according to such principles, attributing this viewpoint to the Gestalt psychologist Wolfgang Kohler (1929/1970). Moreover, he viewed science as having the same character being, in a sense, an extension of perception. In both domains, local scraps of information and insight are continually in tension – some mutually reinforcing each other, and others in competition. This process of alliance and jostling leads, from the bottom up, to a more or less coherent representation of the patterns in the external world.

In practice, the huge variety of representations created by the perceptual system are not fully coherent (Dennett, 1993; Svarverud, Gilson, & Glennerster, 2012). Similarly, our representations of the common-sense physical properties of the everyday world, our moral judgements, or our mathematical intuitions are inevitably partial and inconsistent. As far as possible, perceptual processing (or scientific theorising) attempts to piece together locally coherent models of aspects of reality (e.g., Kelso, 1995; Kugler & Turvey,1987; Thelen & Smith, 1996), but our understanding is full of gaps and contradictions (Chater, 2018; Chater & Oaksford, 2017; Rozenblit & Keil, 2002). Indeed, it has been argued that, even in physics, we have no more than a patchwork of loosely connected local models of different phenomena, which cannot be joined up to form a consistent global representation of the world (Cartwright, 1983, 1999). Still, the attempt to bring local insights into alignment where possible is the route by which our models and theories become increasingly, though inevitably partially, coherent.

The idea of spontaneous order has particularly been taken up in economics (Hayek, 1960; Krugman, 1996; Sugden, 1989), to help understand how the tenuous and largely myopic interactions of makers, buyers, and sellers in a hugely complex web somehow conspire to generate and produce goods and services, supply chains, and financial and legal machinery of a complexity far beyond the understanding of

---

[6]In the natural sciences, spontaneous order is usually known as self-organisation (e.g., Camazine, Deneubourg, Franks, Sneyd, Theraula & Bonabeau, 2001; Nicolis & Prigogine, 1977).

any individual market participant. But Polanyi (1941) intended the idea much more generally, to apply to culture broadly defined, including natural language:

> The social legacies of language, writing, literature and of the various arts, pictorial and musical; of practical crafts, including medicine, agriculture, manufacture and the technique of communications; of sets of conventional units and measures, and of customs of intercourse; of religious, social and political thought all these are systems of dynamic order which were developed by the method of direct individual adjustment, (Polanyi, 1941, p. 438)

And Hayek sees language as a particularly striking example on spontaneous order. As Schmidtz and Boettke (2021) explain, Hayek argued that:

> Just as no one had to invent natural selection, no one had to invent the process by which natural languages evolve. A language is a massively path-dependent process of unending mutual adjustment. Language evolves spontaneously. It would make no sense to call any language optimally efficient, but it does make sense to see languages as highly refined and effective adaptations to the evolving communication needs of particular populations. (Hayek. 1945, p. 528).

So much for the big picture. But how might a story of the spontaneous evolution of language work? And how might it explain the algebraic-style regularities that appear so prominent in language? How, indeed, can it explain the mixture of order and disorder that seems so typical across every aspect of language, from phonology to syntax and semantics?

3.3 FROM CHARADES TO GRAMMATICALISATION

In the party game of charades, people attempt to communicate through novel gestures, with the use of language being expressly forbidden. Inevitably, much of the work is done by iconicity – people attempt to mime particular actions, form shapes suggesting a particular object or mimic an individual person's characteristic gestures and movements. But as the game progresses, particular gestures can rapidly become conventionalised – a full scale re-enactment of a golf shot (initially part of a mime to indicate Tiger Woods) may become a little more than a swish of the forefinger. It may, moreover, be reused, perhaps with additional gestures, when attempting to convey the game of golf, the US Masters or even an actual tiger (see Christiansen and Chater, 2022, for extensive discussion of the charades metaphor for linguistic communication).

There is no algebraic structure here, of course. Instead, all the work is being done by loose and creative invention, and, crucially, the repurposing and gradual conventionalisation of previously used charades. But as each new charade is interpreted in the light of previous charades, we might expect that increasing standardisation of gestures and their deployment will arise. But where does the algebraic structure of grammar come from?

A natural answer is through processes of grammaticalisation identified in the study of language change. Grammaticalisation is "the development from lexical to grammatical forms and from grammatical to even more grammatical forms" (Heine and Kuteva, 2002, p. 377). It provides a mechanism from which a simple charade-like communication can be gradually transformed into a much more complex and systematic linguistic system. Heine and Kuteva (2007) attempt to reconstruct the broad patterns of such changes by looking at the historical language record – but they propose that the same general patterns of change will have operated long before writing systems were invented, and may run back to the very origin of language. From this perspective, language evolution is language change "writ large," rather than involving the biological evolution of a language faculty, or indeed, language-specific cognitive machinery of any kind, as assumed in many accounts of language evolution (e.g., Pinker & Bloom, 1990).

Grammaticalisation provides a mechanism for local changes to the language – but of course to create a linguistic system, requires the interaction, and mutual constraint, of many such changes. To generate spontaneous order, rather than merely independent threads of linguistic change, requires that an aspect of the language is under pressure to adjust to fit in with its neighbours. And such pressures are not only present but are many and varied. The fundamentally case-based and analogical nature of learning and memory will continually impose generalisation: gently tending to pull similar linguistic items to behave still more similarly. To take the simplest possible case, if the linguistic contexts in which *dog* and *cat* are used heavily overlap, it is likely that generalisation will tend to increase their overlap still further. Thus, while each lexical item might, initially, have distinct distributional behaviour, the distributions of similar items will tend to become more similar still, so that lexical items can, increasingly, be grouped by their distributional properties. In short, such a process will gradually group words into increasingly discrete syntactic categories. But the inherently partial and unsystematic nature of such generalisation does not guarantee the emergence of a small finite set of syntactic categories used by traditional grammarians, or in generative grammar. Instead, we should expect the processes of spontaneous order to be no more than partial. Indeed, Culicover (1999) persuasively argues that the distributional properties of words do not break neatly into distinct categories. To slightly adapt one of Culicover's examples (1999, p 47), we might imagine that *likely* and *probable* must have the same syntactic (and indeed semantic) properties. But there remain curious cases where the two do not have the parallel distributional properites, even though there is no difficulty semantically interpreting the anomalous sentence (1d):

(1) a. It is likely that John will be elected President next year

    b. It is probable that John will be elected President next year

    c. John is likely to be elected President next year

    d. *John is probable to be elected President next year

Culicover shows convincingly that these types of cases are ubiquitous throughout language – so much so, indeed, that he argues that it may be appropriate to see each individual word as having its own unique distributional characteristics and hence, in a sense, its own unique syntactic category. The forces of spontaneous order will, though, continually operate to bring innumerable conflicting local patterns into a more orderly form, while innovation to solve ever-changing communicative challenges will continually inject more variety, and hence disorder.

While a thorough-going construction-based perspective on language, such as Culicover's, sees abstract syntactic categories as abstractions from the diverse idiosyncratic behaviours of individual words, these abstractions nonetheless provide a useful when considering the process through which function words and morphological markers arise through the cultural evolution of language. It is easy enough to imagine how communication can be kick-started with, perhaps initially iconic, sounds or gestures to denote specific objects or actions. But it is less clear how markers for tense and aspects, case markings, determiners, conjunctions, and the like might form through processes of spontaneous change.

According to a grammaticalisation account, the puzzle is solved by observing that entrenchment and increasing conventionalisation can lead words in one syntactic category to shift into another – a process which typically flows only in one direction. A sketch of some of the key pathways is outlined in Figure 3.1 (based on Heine and Kutova, 2007), based on historically recorded language change (possibly only, of course, for written languages) and inevitably more speculative language reconstruction where there is no written record.

Languages can, of course, evolve in a wide variety of ways. From the perspective of spontaneous order, this is just what we should expect. Of course, there will be many overlapping patterns arising from any process of biological or cultural evolution, both through shared evolutionary history and process of coevolution. But there should be no "archetypal" languages or underlying "bauplan" for all languages, any more than there is an archetypal snow-flake. Indeed, the process of diversity ramifying in many and varied directions is the normal outcome in process of cultural and biological evolution alike. Religious traditions, agricultural technologies and institutions for managing common resources (e.g., Ostrom, 1990) are all remarkably diverse, and the spectacular variety of the biological world exemplifies the non-existence of any single optimal self-reproducing creature to which all life-forms are converging.

If an underlying bauplan for all languages could be uncovered, this would be strong evidence for the order-first viewpoint and against the spontaneous order perspective advocated here. The existence of such a bauplan is, we suggest, better viewed as a methodological assumption in the Chomskian tradition than an established fact. Indeed, exploration of the phonological, syntactic, and semantic properties of the world's languages seems continually to throw up astonishing variety, rather than revealing common underlying patterns (Evans & Levinson, 2007).

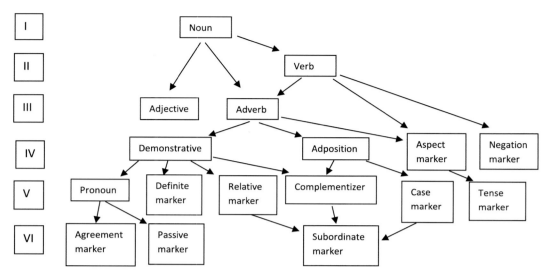

Figure 3.1 A reconstruction of historical transitions in syntactic categories through grammaticalisation (redrawn from Heine, Kaltenböck, & Kuteva, 2013).

3.4 THE EMERGENCE OF HIERARCHICAL STRUCTURE AND COMPOSITIONALITY

One of the most powerful communicative pressures on language is, of course, the ability to efficiently express a wide variety of meanings. In a game of charades, we may initially sequence our gestures in a rather haphazard way. But processes of grammaticalisation may naturally entrench particular orders as having particular semantic interpretation, so that word order may become increasingly stable. Indeed, this is also observed in the improvised gestural communicative systems sometimes created by deaf children and hearing parents. Such so-called "home sign" systems typically develop regularities in word order, usually adopted more thoroughly by child learners than their parents (Goldin-Meadow & Mylander, 1998).

Moreover, we should also expect the hierarchical structure of meaning to induce a degree of hierarchical structure at the level of syntax. So, for example, to pick out one object, we may need first to pick out another, so that noun phrases must be able be embedded within each other. Thus, it hard to imagine a useful language without at least a minimal hierarchical structure (e.g., [the woman [with [a hat]]]). And then we should expect that, by default at least, these larger units will operate syntactically roughly in the same way as phrases that pick out the same object directly (e.g., Gladys) – because we want to say the same types of things about people, however we pick them out (e.g., [the woman with a hat]/[Gladys] likes singing; does [the woman in a hat]/[Gladys] like singing?; and so on). More generally, we might reasonably expect something close to a phrase structure grammar spontaneously to emerge purely from these simple constraints.[7] Indeed, on the face of it, the ability of

---

[7] A hierarchical "chunked" structure to language may also be required where no compositional semantics is involved – purely to deal with the severe processing bottleneck in both production

small communities rapidly to create rich structured communicative systems over a few generations testifies that this is possible (as in the well-known cases of Nicaraguan sign language Kegl, Senghas, & Coppola, 1999).[8]

Compositionality also helps with learnability, of course. The simpler the mapping between meanings and linguistic forms, the more briefly that mapping can be encoded and the less linguistic input should be required to learn it (Hsu, Chater, & Vitányi, 2011). Compositional mappings are, of course, particularly simple. Moreover, a wide range of laboratory studies on the cultural evolution of artificial languages (e.g., Beckner, Pierrehumbert, & Hay 2017; Kirby, Cornish, & Smith 2008; Kirby, Tamariz, Cornish, & Smith 2015) have shown that sequential, meaningful units can spontaneously emerge from meaningless elementary units (e.g., morphs arise from the concatenation of phones), without explicit supervision or teaching, from a process of iterated learning (the input for each learner is the output of a previous learner). Recently, it has been shown that sensitivity to word order, and hierarchical structures can rapidly and spontaneously be generated in laboratory conditions (Saldana, Kirby, Truswell, & Smith, 2019).

But there will, of course, be many additional pressures on the cultural evolution of language, which will complicate this picture considerably. In broad terms, to modify Givón's well-known adage,[9] yesterday's pragmatics is today's syntax. Thus, the pragmatic drive to communicate briefly may lead to omissions and compressions of syntactic patterns. This line of thinking was developed by the philosopher and logician Hilary Putnam in an early critique of the nativist program in linguistics (Putnam, 1967). He points out that a standard phrase structure grammar for an artificial logical language would generate a structure with the form "That is $\exists!x(x$ is a lady and I saw you with x last night)"[10] which may be contracted to *That is the lady I saw you with last night* (traditionally explained in terms of a transformation, leaving a "gap" between *with* and *last*). Of course, the rules governing which such "abbreviations" are grammatically acceptable are subtle – but it seems entirely possible that these constraints may arise from ease-of-processing, rather than innately specified constraints on the structure of language itself.

In a rather different vein, Levinson (1987, 2000) argues persuasively that pragmatic factors may explain the origin of many interesting aspects of grammar, including the binding constraints (Chomsky, 1981). For example, standard pragmatic

---

and comprehension (Christiansen & Chater, 2016) – as is observed in the hierarchically chunking in music (Lerdahl & Jackendoff, 1983), in mnemonic strategies for recalling long sequences of digits (Ericsson, Chase, & Faloon, 1980), an in the hierarchical structure of actions and plans more broadly (Dezfouli, Lingawi, & Balleine, 2014).

[8]The rapid emergence of complex linguistic structure in Nicaraguan sign language is often taken as evidence for the innateness of such structure. We suggest the opposite: that it indicates how processes of spontaneous order can arise rapidly in the absence of language-specific constraints through the necessity to communicate. Of course, as with any aspect of cultural evolution, the outcome will depend on the cognitive machinery of the agents involved, but we see no compelling reason to believe that this machinery is language-specific.

[9]The original aphorism is: "today's morphology is yesterday's syntax," Givón, T. (1971, p.413).

[10]Here we use $\exists!x$ to denote "there exists a unique, such that..." rather than the less usual notation in Putnam's original quotation.

principles imply that the availability of the word *himself* leads to the presumption that in *John likes him* the pronoun *him* does not refer to John – otherwise the more precise *himself* would have been used. This type of pragmatic reasoning is very general and is, indeed, observed in communicative exchanges with entirely arbitrary non-linguistic signals (e.g., Misyak, Noguchi, & Chater, 2016). But when, through normal processes of grammaticalisation, this assumption of non-coreference becomes increasingly obligatory, it becomes more naturally viewed a part of syntax rather than pragmatics (although, according to the present perspective, the boundary between the two is graded, rather than all-or-nothing). Levinson develops similar arguments to create a comprehensive account of the origins of Chomsky's (1981) binding constraints, and putative exceptions to them, purely using pragmatic principles. Thus, syntactic phenomena that may seem highly abstract and arbitrary may be explicable through processes of spontaneous order, deriving from the gradual interaction, and conventionalisation, of regularities with pragmatic origins.

With any such explanations it is, of course, always possible to argue about the details – indeed, such argument is quite rightly the very essence of linguistic debate. But the existence of such historical explanations, even where partial and incomplete, strongly suggests that many apparently abstract principles of grammar result from processes of spontaneous order. At least if we presume the opposite, that they are arbitrary constraints built into a language-specific universal grammar (taking the standard order-first viewpoint), then the possibility of finding potential historical lines of explanation for such phenomena using pragmatic principles appears to be a remarkable and unexplained coincidence.

3.5 IS THE ALGEBRAIC STRUCTURE OF LANGUAGE MENTALLY REPRESENTED?

Nature is full of patterns. But typically, these patterns arise from complex sets of rules which are represented only in the mind (and by the mathematical tools) of the theorist. Thus, the elliptical orbits of the planets emerge from the "laws" of gravitation. But the planets are not, of course, representing those laws – or indeed, representing anything at all. The planets are *governed* by these rules but do not *follow* them – in the sense of consulting and conforming to a representation of those rules.

In the natural sciences, the spontaneous emergence of complexity always has this character: snowflakes form complex geometric patterns with rich symmetries but do not in any way represent those patterns (there is, of course, no blueprint that the freezing water molecules need consult to ensure that a snowflake grows appropriately). Similarly, the astonishing complexity of a wasp nest or an ant colony is not represented in the mind (or the genes) of any individual wasp or ant; rather, this complexity emerges, somehow, through the playing out of the presumably fairly simple local rules that govern the laying down and following of pheromone trails and the like.

According to advocates of spontaneous order in the social sciences, the story is the same for human culture. The remarkably complex structures in human societies, patterns of economic interaction, financial markets, and cultural products of all kinds, are not represented, and do not need to be represented, by the agents whose busy interactions somehow collectively create them. Indeed, the process of social scientific explanation seems naturally to fit with this perspective. Social scientists are typically trying to provide "rational reconstructions" (to borrow, and somewhat repurpose, a suggestive phrase of Lakatos [1970]) that explain why social and culture systems operate successfully. Thus, for example, theorists wonder about the underlying rationale that allows fiat money (not based on some good of intrinsic value such as gold) to serve as a reliable story of value and medium of exchange; what kind of logic underpins the value of intangible assets of a company, such as reputation, or what determines the allocation of capital to investment projects, the divergent structures of companies in different industries, or the allocation of rewards to workers with different skills (e.g., Cabral, 2017); or even, extending this style of explanation further and perhaps more controversially, the economic logic behind dowries, bride-prices, patterns of inheritance, even the nature and functioning of the family unit (e.g., Becker, 1991). Or consider the linguistic turn that has been distinctive of twentieth century philosophy. Here, a common view of the project of philosophy is to attempt to create a set of rational principles that can explain our diverse and apparently rather contradictory intuitions about causality, mind, morality or any other topic. But in none of these domains is there typically an assumption that the "true" theory is mentally represented in the minds of the people engaging in economic transactions, social interactions, or ethical thought. Indeed, from the spontaneous order viewpoint, this is as it should be: complex order arises from networks of the interactions of large numbers of units or agents and will not be represented in any individual unit.

Language seems to be an archetypical collective cultural construction, generated by the layering of countless conversational interactions, each focussed only on the communicative demands of the moment but gradually stretching and pulling the language in new directions. Curiously, though, an influential strand of linguistics in the order-first tradition we described above has adopted precisely the opposite perspective. Chomsky (1980) explicitly argues that language (or at least a somewhat idealised form of language as actually spoken) is fundamentally a property of each individual human; that the "interesting" structure of the language (the universal grammar) is represented in the mind of each individual; and, moreover, that these representations are innately specified in the genes, and ultimately the brain, of each child. From this perspective, the algebraic structure of language is built in.

There are many difficulties with this order-first nativist perspective on the algebraic structure of language, which we will not review here (e.g., Chater, Clark, Goldsmith, & Perfors, 2015; Clark & Lappin, 2010; Culicover, 1999; Evans & Levinson, 2009; Pullum & Scholz, 2002; Putnam, 1967; Tomasello, 1992). Here, we have primarily aimed to present and illustrate the viability of the opposite viewpoint, drawing especially on the theory of grammaticalisation. Moreover, drawing parallels with complex phenomena across the natural and social sciences, we have illustrated the possibility of rich algebraic patterns arising in language through a process of spontaneous order.[11] Thus, we hope to persuade the reader that the idea that patterns arise spontaneously from complex patterns of interactions between many agents over countless generations, while the agents do not in any way mentally represent those patterns, is plausible in the case of language.

Indeed, we hope the spontaneous order viewpoint can help shift researchers away from what has often been an order-first, nativist explanation as the default assumption in some areas of the science of language. The patterns observed in language are endlessly subtle and puzzling. But the right starting point from which to address such puzzles is, we believe, through exploring the variety of interacting forces operating on the development of language. Natural languages are shaped by the specifics of perception, motor control, memory, learning, pragmatic factors, and the relentless forces of grammaticalisation. There is both the relentless language-internal jostling to reconcile local, partially inconsistent constraints and the need for generalisation to deal with new communicative challenges. These processes have, over time, generated a continual flow of new linguistic innovation and a gradually and spontaneously emerging order, generating the vast range of regularities, sub-regularities, and outright exceptions that are characteristic of natural language (Christiansen & Chater, 2022).

BIBLIOGRAPHY

Becker, G. S. (1991). *A Treatise on the Family: Enlarged Edition.* Cambridge, MA: Harvard University Press.

Beckner, C., Pierrehumbert, J. B., & Hay, J. (2017). The emergence of linguistic structure in an online iterated learning task. *Journal of Language Evolution,* lzx001. doi: 10.1093/jole/lzx001

Benson, D. (2006). *Music: A Mathematical Offering.* Cambridge, UK: Cambridge University Press.

Cabral, L. M. (2017). *Introduction to Industrial Organisation.* Cambridge, MA: MIT press.

Camazine, S., Deneubourg, J. L., Franks, N. R., Sneyd, J., Theraula, G., & Bonabeau, E. (2001). *Self-organisation in biological systems.* Princeton, NJ: Princeton University Press.

Cartwright, N. (1983). *How the laws of physics lie.* Oxford, UK: Oxford University Press.

Cartwright, N. (1999). *The dappled world: A study of the boundaries of science.* Cambridge, UK: Cambridge University Press.

Chater, N. & Oaksford, M. (2017). Theories or fragments? (Commentary on Lake et al.) *Behavioural and Brain Sciences. 40,* e258.

Chater, N., Clark, A., Goldsmith, J. A., & Perfors, A. (2015). *Empiricism and Language Learnability.* Oxford, UK: Oxford University Press.

---

[11]Indeed, we could equally have considered the algebraic patterns, often modelled by rather sophisticated group theory, that arise in the patterns in the visuals arts (Weyl, 1952) and in music (Benson, 2006).

Chomsky, N. (1980). Rules and representations. *Behavioural and Brain Sciences*, *3*(1), 1–15.

Chomsky, N. (1981). *Lectures on government and binding: The Pisa lectures*. Dordrecht: Foris.

Chomsky, N. (1995) *The Minimalist Program*. Cambridge, MA: MIT Press

Christiansen, M. H., & Chater, N. (2008). Language as shaped by the brain. *Behavioural and Brain Sciences*, *31*(5), 489–509.

Christiansen, M. H., & Chater, N. (2015). The language faculty that wasn't: A usage-based account of natural language recursion. *Frontiers in Psychology*, *6*, 23–40.

Christiansen, M.H. & Chater, N. (2016). The Now-or-Never bottleneck: A fundamental constraint on language. *Behavioural and Brain Sciences*, *39*, 1–72.

Christiansen, M. H. & Chater, N. (2022). *The Language Game*. London, UK: Bantam Books/New York, NY: Basic Books.

Clark, A., & Lappin, S. (2010). *Linguistic Nativism and the Poverty of the Stimulus*. Oxford, UK: John Wiley & Sons.

Conway, C. M., & Christiansen, M. H. (2001). Sequential learning in non-human primates. *Trends in Cognitive Sciences*, *5*(12), 539–546.

Culicover, P. W., & Culicover, P. W. (1999). *Syntactic Nuts: Hard Cases, Syntactic Theory, and Language Acquisition*. Oxford, UK: Oxford University Press.

Dennett, D. C. (1993). *Consciousness Explained*. London, UK: Penguin.

Dezfouli, A., Lingawi, N. W., & Balleine, B. W. (2014). Habits as action sequences: hierarchical action control and changes in outcome value. *Philosophical Transactions of the Royal Society B: Biological Sciences*, *369*(1655), 20130482.

Dowty, D. R., Wall, R., & Peters, S. (1981). *Introduction to Montague Semantics*. Berlin: Springer Science & Business Media.

Dummett, M. (1981). *Frege: Philosophy of Language*. Cambridge, MA: Harvard University Press.

Ericsson, K. A., Chase, W. G., & Faloon, S. (1980). Acquisition of a memory skill. *Science*, *208*(4448), 1181–1182.

Evans, N., & Levinson, S. C. (2009). The myth of language universals: Language diversity and its importance for cognitive science. *Behavioural and Brain Sciences*, *32*(5), 429–448.

Fedorenko, E. & Varley, R. (2016). Language and thought are not the same thing: Evidence from neuroimaging and neurological patients. *Annals of the New York Academy of Sciences*, *1369*(1), 132–153.

Gibson, E., Futrell, R., Piantadosi, S.T., Dautriche, I., Mahowald, K., Bergen, L. & Levy, R. (2019). How Efficiency Shapes Human Language. *Trends in Cognitive Sciences*, *23*(5), 389–407.

Givón, T. (1971). Historical syntax and synchronic morphology: an archaeologist's field trip. *Chicago Linguistic Society*, *7*(1), 394–415,

Goldin-Meadow, S., & Mylander, C. (1998). Spontaneous sign systems created by deaf children in two cultures. *Nature*, *391*(6664), 279–281.

Hahn, M., Jurafsky, D., & Futrell, R. (2020). Universals of word order reflect optimization of grammars for efficient communication. *Proceedings of the National Academy of Sciences, 117*(5), 2347–2353.

Hawkins, J. A. (1994). *A Performance Theory of Order and Constituency*. Cambridge, UK: Cambridge University Press.

Hayek, F. A. (1945). The use of knowledge in society. *The American Economic Review, 35*(4), 519–530.

Heine, B., Kaltenböck, G., & Kuteva, T. (2013). "On the origin of grammar." In C. Lefebvre, B. Comrie, & H. Cohen, (Eds.). *New Perspectives on the Origins of Language* (pp. 379–405). Amsterdam: John Benjamins Publishing.

Heine, B., & Kuteva, T. (2002). On the evolution of grammatical forms. In. A. Wray (Ed.) *The Transition to Language* (pp. 376–397). Oxford, UK: Oxford University Press.

Heine, B., & Kuteva, T. (2007). *The Genesis of Grammar: A Reconstruction*. Oxford, UK: Oxford University Press.

Hsu, A. S., Chater, N., & Vitányi, P. M. (2011). The probabilistic analysis of language acquisition: Theoretical, computational, and experimental analysis. *Cognition, 120*(3), 380–390.

Kegl, J., Senghas, A., and Coppola, M. (1999). Creation through contact: Sign language emergence and sign language change in Nicaragua. In M. DeGraff (Ed.) *Language Creation and Language Change: Creolization, Diachrony, and Development* (pp. 179–237). Cambridge: MIT Press.

Kelso, J. S. (1995). *Dynamic Patterns: The Self-Organisation of Brain and Behaviour*. Cambridge, MA: MIT press.

Kirby, S., Cornish, H., & Smith, K. (2008). Cumulative cultural evolution in the laboratory: An experimental approach to the origins of structure in human language. *Proceedings of the National Academy of Sciences, 105*(31), 10681–10686. doi: 10.1073/pnas.0707835105

Kirby, S., Tamariz, M., Cornish, H., & Smith, K. (2015). Compression and communication in the cultural evolution of linguistic structure. *Cognition, 141*, 87–102. doi: 10.1016/j.cognition .2015.03.016

Kohler, W. (1929/1970). *Gestalt Psychology: An Introduction to New Concepts in Modern Psychology*. New York, NY: WW Norton & Company.

Kripke, S. A. (1982). *Wittgenstein on Rules and Private Language: An Elementary Exposition*. Cambridge, MA: Harvard University Press.

Krugman, P. R. (1996). *The Self-Organising Economy*. Oxford, UK: Blackwell.

Kugler, P. N., & Turvey, M. T. (1987). *Information, Natural Law, and the Self-Assembly of Rhythmic Movement*. Hillsdale, NJ: Erlbaum.

Lakatos, I. (1970). History of science and its rational reconstructions. *PSA: Proceedings of the Biennial Meeting of the Philosophy of Science Association* (pp. 91–136). Berlin: Springer.

Lasnik, H. (2002). The minimalist program in syntax. *Trends in Cognitive Sciences, 6*(10), 432–437.

Lerdahl, F., & Jackendoff, R. (1983). An overview of hierarchical structure in music. *Music Perception, 1*(2), 229–252.

Levinson, S.C (1987). Pragmatics and the grammar of anaphora: A partial pragmatic reduction of binding and control phenomena. *Journal of Linguistics, 23*, 379–434.

Levinson, S.C (2000). *Presumptive Meanings: The Theory of Generalised Conversational Implicature.* Cambridge, MA: MIT Press.

Misyak, J., Noguchi, T., & Chater, N. (2016). Instantaneous conventions. *Psychological Science, 27*(12), 1550–1561.

Nicolis, G. and Prigogine, I. (1977). *Self-Organisation in Nonequilibrium Systems: From Dissipative Structures to Order Through Fluctuations.* New York, NY: Wiley.

Ostrom, E. (1990). *Governing the Commons: The Evolution of Institutions for Collective Action.* Cambridge, UK: Cambridge University Press.

Piantadosi, S. T., Tily, H., & Gibson, E. (2012). The communicative function of ambiguity in language. *Cognition, 122*(3), 280–291.

Pinker, S., & Bloom, P. (1990). Natural language and natural selection. *Behavioural and Brain Sciences, 13*(4), 707–727.

Polanyi, M. (1941). The growth of thought in society. *Economica, 8*(32), 428–456.

Polanyi, M. (1951). *The Logic of Liberty.* Chicago: The University of Chicago Press.

Pullum, G. K., & Scholz, B. C. (2002). Empirical assessment of stimulus poverty arguments. *The Linguistic Review, 19*(1–2), 9–50.

Putnam, H. (1967). The 'innateness hypothesis' and explanatory models in linguistics. *Synthese, 17*, 12–22.

Rozenblit, L., & Keil, F. (2002). The misunderstood limits of folk science: An illusion of explanatory depth. *Cognitive science, 26*(5), 521–562.

Russell, B. (1905). On denoting. *Mind, 14*(56), 479–493.

Schmidtz, D. & Boettke, P. (2021). Friedrich Hayek, *The Stanford Encyclopedia of Philosophy* (Summer 2021 Edition), Edward N. Zalta (ed.), URL = ¡https://plato.stanford.edu/archives/sum2021/entries/friedrich-hayek/¿.

Saldana, C., Kirby, S., Truswell, R., & Smith, K. (2019). Compositional hierarchical structure evolves through cultural transmission: An experimental study. *Journal of Language Evolution, 4*(2), 83–107. https://doi.org/10.1093/jole/lzz002

Sugden, R. (1989). Spontaneous order. *Journal of Economic Perspectives, 3*(4), 85–97.

Svarverud, E., Gilson, S., & Glennerster, A. (2012). A demonstration of 'broken' visual space. *PLoS One, 7*(3), e33782.

Stich, S. P. (1975). Logical form and natural language. *Philosophical Studies, 28*(6), 397–418.

Thelen, E., & Smith, L. B. (1996). *A Dynamic Systems Approach to the Development of Cognition and Action.* Cambridge, MA: MIT press.

Tomasello, M. (1992). *First Verbs: A Case Study of Early Grammatical Development.* Cambridge, UK: Cambridge University Press.

Weyl, H. (1952). *Symmetry.* Princeton, NJ: Princeton University Press.

CHAPTER 4

Language is Acquired in Interaction

Eve V. Clark

Stanford University

CONTENTS

> *La parole est moitié à celui qui parle, moitié à celui qui écoute.*
> Michel de Montaigne

ABSTRACT

Conversational interaction supports and enables first language acquisition. From infancy on, children hear language used by more expert speakers, and when they start to use some language themselves, they receive feedback on errors they make and they go in for extensive practice. These three factors – exposure, feedback, and practice – are central to the acquisition of language. Children become increasingly adept at understanding other speakers, at planning what to say next, at timing their turns, and at monitoring their own productions against representations stored in memory for comprehension. They make spontaneous repairs as needed and respond to requests for repairs from others from the earliest stages. In all this, they build up and make use of their current common ground with different interlocutors to take into account what their addressees know and rely on both gestures and words to understand others and to convey what they themselves mean. At the same time, children are learning

DOI: 10.1201/9781003205388-4

to identify and represent patterns of sounds, morphemes, words and phrases in the speech they hear. These patterns are central to children's identification, representation, analysis, and recognition of linguistic elements. They start with sound segments in the first year and continue on to the identification of individual words, short word combinations and word-order patterns as they grasp more of the language they hear every day. These units are what they rely on as they learn how to use language to communicate with others.

4.1   INTERACTION AND LANGUAGE USE

Language has a primary social role in any exchange, and the speakers involved must be able to both understand and produce language. Language is put to use in interaction when speakers convey their intentions to their addressees, and those addressees in turn respond to what they have understood. They need to be able to do this in a timely manner, making use of the conventional forms available in their language. While adult speakers take this for granted, children must master all the ingredients needed, from identifying words, assigning meanings to them, and pronouncing them, to storing knowledge about pronunciations and meanings in memory, to choosing the right words on each occasion to express their intentions, and to planning and producing the relevant utterances fluently and on time. The process of acquiring a language takes time: children have to learn a vocabulary, learn how to combine elements from that vocabulary, how to modify words in various ways, how to construct longer, more complex utterances, and, critically, how to use these elements in order to convey specific goals and information as they coordinate their speech and their activities with others.

Babies get started on this formidable task in their first year. Parents look at their babies, hold them, touch them, and talk to them. When adults talk to young infants in the early months, they rely extensively on frequently used, brief, formulaic utterances as they carry out every day routine activities. Early on, for example, they use numerous routine utterances like *Upsy-daisy* (lifting the baby), *Bath-time, Night-night, Time to eat, Want some more?, Want up?,* and *Do it again,* utterances they have recourse to every time with a specific activity (Tamis-LeMonda et al. 2019). As they talk, adults look at their infants, track their gaze, and pause after speaking in order to give even nonverbal babies "a turn" at contributing, whether with a blink, a kick, a smile, or some kind of vocalisation (Snow 1977).

Infants look at parental faces and follow adult gaze with increasing frequency through their first year (e.g., Del Bianco et al. 2019). They also look at adult hands as they attend to adult activities, again from six to eight months on (Yu & Smith 2013). Their attention to shared activities in this form also appears to play a role in infants' memory for their first words, typically words for objects often handled and played with from around the middle of the first year (Bergelson & Swingley 2012; Chang, de Barbaro, & Deák 2016; Deák et al. 2018).

Adults talk with their children as they run through their daily routines. They use short utterances to very young children, typically relying just on single words or short phrases for talking about the objects and actions relevant to the current activity, again often combined with gaze and gesture directed at the entities being labelled. This helps young children understand what is being said from their knowledge of just a few of the words, together with attention to adult gaze and gesture in context (Rader & Zukow-Goldring 2010; Clark & Estigarribia 2011). Only later do young children begin to make use of combinations of words, as they start to attend to small constructions as well (Müller & Hagoort 2006; You et al. 2021).

The talk accompanying both adult and child actions provides children with words and phrases relevant to many collaborative activities. Adults talk with children as they carry out such daily routines as getting dressed, putting on shoes, putting away clothes, using a spoon, drinking from a cup, helping pull weeds, collecting shells, choosing a book to be read from, and all the other daily activities young children may experience. They also talk to them as they are playing, as they start trying to build towers with two or three blocks, as they put a toy to bed on a cushion, pull a toy dog on wheels around the room, treat a waste-basket as a hat, or construct a garage for toy cars. Talk, in all these cases, accompanies activities.

4.2   INFANT PARTICIPATION

From infancy on, children take an active part in collaborative interaction and play. For example, from around two to three months on, they respond to adult speech with vocalisations, initially overlapping with the adult a lot, and then gradually adjusting to a turn-taking pattern as they come to alternate vocally with adult partners (van Egeren, Barratt, & Roach 2001). They also initiate and persist in peek-a-boo, alternately hiding and looking, and in exchange games, passing an object to-and-fro with the adult, from as early as seven months on (Escalona 1973). As infants get older and start to crawl or navigate on foot while holding on to various pieces of furniture, prior to walking, they also point at and show objects by holding them out towards the adult (Adolph & Tamis-LeMonda 2014). Once they can walk, anywhere from ten to twelve months on, adults talk with them both more and differently, because adult and child can now interact face-to-face (Karasik, Tamis-LeMonda & Adolph 2014).

Also, from around nine to ten months on, infants start to rely on combinations of gestures, vocalisations, and early versions of a few words, as they get to work on constructing a first system for communicating (Clark & Kelly 2021). All these collaborative activities play a central role in children's interactions with adults who look at, touch and talk about objects and ongoing actions as they interact with infants and young children. Furthermore, many of these collaborative activities typically occur in specialised contexts: talk about food in the kitchen, about dressing and undressing in the bedroom, about bathing and cleaning in the bathroom, about going outside in the front hallway, and so on (Roy, Frank, & Roy 2012; Benitez & Smith 2012). In short, particular kinds of activities and the words for those activities are initially associated with particular places.

4.3 EXPOSURE, FEEDBACK, AND PRACTICE

Such interactional settings, where young children can observe both what is going on and hear what adults are saying, provide major contexts for early language acquisition (Clark 2021). Adults typically talk as they interact with their small children, and this provides children with extensive exposure to the language of the community, from more skilled users of that language. When adults talk with their children, they expect them to respond to what has been said. Such exchanges provide children with extensive practise in both understanding what adults are saying and trying to produce language in response, from early on. The more children interact with family members and with other speakers, the more language they hear, and the more language they respond to in the course of their everyday activities (e.g., Clark 2018b; Marcos et al. 2004; Rogoff et al. 1993; Gallaway & Richards 1994; Roy, Frank, & Roy 2012). Adult talk about what is going on, including talk during collaborative book-reading and co-operative play, all contributes to young children's growing understanding of when and how to use language.

At the same time, as they talk with their children, adults frequently check on what the children mean, especially when children's utterances are hard to understand because of errors in pronunciation, in word choice, in the addition of morphological affixes, or in word order. In checking up on what a child has said, adults often ask for clarification and, in doing so, offer a reformulation in a conventional form of the child's utterance apparently intended (e.g., Chouinard & Clark 2003; Clark & de Marneffe 2012; Lustigman & Clark 2019). That is, they produce an adult version of the child's utterance, offering it as an interpretation as they check on what the child is apparently trying to say.

Children generally respond to such feedback (typically offered after errors) and, besides agreeing or disagreeing with the interpretation offered, may repeat the actual repair in their next turn, thus overtly confirming the adult's interpretation. They also make spontaneous repairs to their own speech, from as young as age one, though these are not always successful, when they detect mismatches between what they have stored in memory for comprehension, and what they actually produce on a particular occasion (Clark 2020). Feedback, in the form of clarification requests and reformulations of what the child said, typically targets children's errors, whether errors of pronunciation, of word-choices and word-form, or of constructions, and so complements children's exposure to adult language use, in everyday talk.

Practice represents a third factor in adult-child conversational exchanges that plays an important role in language acquisition. Children practice in exchanges with others, and on their own when as young as one to two years old, in solitary monologues after being put to bed, for example (Weir 1970). They practice using language whenever they listen, whenever they contribute a turn to the current exchange, and whenever they introduce a new topic. When very young, in fact, they appear more likely to pursue topics they themselves have proposed, through several turns, than they are a new topic proposed by their mothers (Veneziano 2014). They also practice when they repeat, in their turns, new information that has just been presented in earlier adult utterances (McTear 1985; Clark & Bernicot 2008; Filipi 2009). In short, children practice using language in everyday exchanges, in pretend-play with parents and with siblings, in talking for toys and dolls, and later also in playing and planning-play interactions with siblings and peers as they assign and take on particular roles and particular things to say (e.g., Garvey & Kramer 1989; Andersen 1990; Hughes & Dunn 1997; Cohen 2009).

4.4   USING LANGUAGE

But that is only part of what is required when using a language. Children must also store more and more word forms heard from others in memory so they can recognise them when they hear those words on subsequent occasions, from different speakers. By storing forms heard from other, more expert speakers, children steadily expand the number of words to which they have assigned some meaning, and can therefore understand more when they hear them on subsequent occasions, from other speakers. This also enables them to acquire more options for expressing their own intentions as well as recognising the intentions of others (Woodward 2009; Henderson & Woodward 2011; Csibra & Gergely 2007).

They also become more flexible in recognising the same words produced with varying pronunciations from a range of speakers. At the same time, they rely on representations in memory based on familiar adults' speech from very early on when they monitor their own productions, as well as when they monitor the speech of others as they try to understand them. These representations for comprehension allow children to produce spontaneous repairs when they detect problems in their own speech, as well as when they respond to requests for clarification from others (Clark & Hecht 1983; Clark 2020a).

Central to practicing their own developing language is understanding what the current speaker is saying, and in planning what to say in the next turn. This requires that children be able to retrieve those words and constructions relevant to what they want to say next, and then to produce, on time, the utterance they are planning as they take the next turn in an exchange, for example in answering a question. The time children take in planning answers to questions depends in large part on how complex the question is and, therefore, how complicated the answer is expected to be. *What* and *where* questions can be understood fairly easily by two-year-olds simply by attending to the noun contained in the question (*Where's your ball?*, *What's that?* + POINT to object); the same holds for simple *Yes/No* questions (*Do you want some apple?*) (see Casillas, Bobb, & Clark 2016; Garvey & Berninger 1981; Moradlou, Zheng & Ginzburg 2021).

Consider also questions like *Do you want an apple or a plum?*, *When did you read that book?* or *Why do you want to go outside?* Very young children find such questions harder to understand, and they only acquire the meanings of these *Wh* question forms considerably later, over the course of the next few years. And they take longer to plan and produce answers to such questions. At the same time, even very young children know that they need to reply as quickly as possible, or else they may lose their turn to another speaker, for example to an older sibling (Dunn & Shatz 1989; Casillas 2014a, 2014b). Where they can answer with a gesture as well as a word, in response to *Where* or *Which* questions, for instance, they generally answer with a gesture first (it is faster) and follow up with a verbal response (Clark & Lindsey 2015). Young children also learn early on, starting from age two, to track who is speaking and to switch their gaze to the speaker when attending to conversations among others, and so learn to anticipate who will be the next speaker (Bakker, Kochukhova, & von Hoftsen 2011; Casillas & Frank 2017).

4.5 COMMON GROUND

In taking turns and so contributing to a conversational exchange, young children must rely to some extent on common ground. They begin to construct common ground from the start with care-giving adults as they attend to the many everyday routines carried out in particular places, at particular times, with specific activities and objects. They keep track of their physical surroundings, where they participate in particular activities – bath-time, dressing, changing, meals, play, walks, book-reading, bedtime, and favourite toys, for instance. They keep track of family vs. non-family members, and of other individuals with whom interactions are common, versus one-off interactions in only a single exchange. By age two, children can take into account what someone does or doesn't know in a particular setting, and make use of gaze and gesture as well as some words to make sure the other person has the requisite knowledge (see O'Neill 1996; Dimitrova, Moro, & Mohr 2015; Abbot-Smith et al. 2016; also Chandler, Fritz, & Hala 1989). Common ground here, of course, also includes the language(s) children are acquiring, as well as any current assumptions about daily routines and activities (Clark 2015a; also Rogoff et al. 1993). Making use of common ground and adding further to common ground during an exchange, by repeating new information from the other speaker, say, is as critical for small children as it is for adults (Clark & Bernicot 2008; see also McTear 1985).

4.6 UNITS OF LANGUAGE

Once children focus in on the sounds of the ambient language and start to distinguish different sounds, they also start attending to recurring sequences of sounds. By eight months, they can identify such sequences (e.g., Saffran et al. 1996; Choi et al. 2020), and can then go on to assign some meaning to them. This in turn leads them to focus on words, generally words for objects and for actions, early on in the second year. They represent sequences of sounds in memory, based on the adult versions they hear, and then use these representations in checking on their own attempts at producing those same sequences (Dodd 1975; Scollon 1976). They may represent unanalysed chunks or short phrases as well as words early on, and take some time to analyse these elements into smaller units such as stems and inflexions (Peters 1983; Arnon, McCauley, & Christiansen 2017) before they actually try to produce any combinations of words themselves.

How do children extract units from the stream of speech? They can track recurring sequences and contexts, physical contexts with recurring objects and actions, picked out by adult gaze and gesture, as well as by adult use of frequent frames like *Look at the –*, or *Give me the –*. Adults also make frequent use of such frames as *That's a – * or *That's called a –* accompanied by pointing or showing gestures (e.g., Clark & Wong 2003; Clark & Estigarribia 2011; Weisleder & Waxman 2010; Bannard & Lieven 2012; Tamis-LeMonda et al. 2019). And, as Mintz (2003) showed, in adult speech, many such frames reliably identify nouns, while others identify verbs. Effectively, children's attention to statistical patterns in the speech they hear allows them to make distributional analyses not only of what to count as words, but also of the kinds of words they have identified, and so ultimately identify different parts of speech. In the second year or so, therefore, children can begin to assign classes of meanings – to words for objects on the one hand, say, and to words for actions on the other.

The first elements children pick out and start assigning some meaning to may be words or chunks consisting of short sequences of words (Arnon 2011; Arnon, Mc-Cauley, & Christiansen 2017). These they then analyse into subparts: words, then stems and grammatical morphemes that can be attached to specific kinds of stems (Lieven 2009; Theakston & Lieven 2017). As children add to their vocabularies, taking up new words as they are offered, they can also start to link related meanings (e.g., *cow, horse, sheep; robin, swallow, hawk*), and so start to build up semantic domains, as well as construct taxonomic hierarchies within those domains (e.g., *animal, dog, collie; tree, oak, ash; bird, thrush*) (Clark 2018a; Clark & Wong 2003; Clark & Estigarribia 2011; Gelman, Wilcox, & Clark 1989; Diesendruck & Shatz 2001; see also Hills et al. 2009; Sagi et al. 2011; Siew 2021).

Added vocabulary in turn enables young children to start combining words to form their first constructions for talking about the events they observe and are interested in. They can begin to link verbs and such roles such as agent, object-affected, and location in talking about events (Goldberg 2006, 2019; Lieven, Pine, & Baldwin 1997). They can also start to construct paradigms, using the morphological affixes that can go on nouns on the one hand, and those that can go on verbs on the other, to extend the range of meanings they can express with a specific word combination in English, such as *Bunny walk*, extended, for instance, to *Bunny is walking, Bunny walked, Bunny (is) going to walk*, and so on, as they discover tense marking, as well as number (singular, plural and dual), gender (masculine, feminine and neuter), and case (nominative, accusative, dative and say), depending on the language being acquired. Identifying which morphemes modulate the meanings of words takes time, but children appear to do this fairly systematically starting as soon as they begin to combine words (Brown 1973).

While grammatical morphemes for tense, modality, possession, and number, for example, allow for variations in the meanings of many basic constructions, free grammatical morphemes in English allow for the expression of spatial and temporal relations, as in *beside* the chair, *on* the table, *in* the cup, *at* the door, or *on* Monday, *in* July, *before* breakfast. And derivational morphemes like those that mark agency with *-er*, as in *rider, jumper, opener*, or with *-ist*, as in *flutist, violinist*, and *pianist*, allow for the coining of words to express new meanings as needed, that is, meanings not already expressed by words already known to the child (Clark & Hecht 1982, Clark & Cohen 1984, Clark 1993). Notice that a number of these coinages would be illegitimate for adult speakers because they are pre-empted by existing words, e.g., *trumpetist* for *trumpeter*.

Another common option here for expressing new meanings is compounding, where children combine two or more existing words with a compound stress pattern in order to express a new meaning, as in *PERSIMMON-tree, DALMATIAN-dog, GARDEN-man* (for a gardener), or *PLATE-egg* vs. *CUP-egg* (for a fried egg vs. a boiled egg). In short, identifying more words and morphemes greatly extends the range of meanings children can express fairly early on. Children take advantage of such options for forming "new" words, beginning with those options that are the most productive in their language and hence heard most often in adult speech. For instance, children learning Germanic languages start to rely on compounding from at least age two onwards, while those learning Romance languages begin to use some derivational morphemes as early as age two to three onwards, and only start to use compounding several years later. Productivity in the adult language plays a major role in these patterns. But as children get older, they typically drop many of their own coinages in favour of the conventional adult terms for the relevant meanings (Clark 1993).

4.7 PARTIAL MEANINGS AND MEANING DOMAINS

When children first assign some meaning to a word, they at first may have only assigned a partial meaning, when compared to the adult's fuller conventional meaning. At the same time, such early partial meanings may often overlap, in particular contexts of use, with the adult meaning. Children, of course, have much less knowledge of the full membership of specific conceptual categories, and much less experience with category instances. It therefore takes time for them to learn the conventional meanings of some words, and many speakers, both adult and child, often rely on a variety of partial meanings for many words in their vocabularies. Take names of trees, e.g., *larch, ash, elm, rowan*, and *beech*. While many adults know that these terms are all names of trees, they are quite unable to identify instances of those trees, and have no idea which leaves belong to each type of tree. In short, they know only that these terms label kinds of trees. Being able to recognise that fact alone involves just enough of the word meaning in each case for most everyday encounters with these words (Clark in press; Lee, Lew-Williams, & Goldberg 2021).

Knowing at least part of the meaning of a word in effect allows for "good enough comprehension" for most purposes, on the one hand, and even good enough production on the other. But as children and adults acquire more knowledge about a domain, they also elaborate their meanings for any words they know that are pertinent to that domain. In doing this, they can add to what were formerly partial meanings, so that their meanings become closer over time to the full conventional meanings. While many adults know a few words for types of dinosaur, for example, it is not until their children get interested in dinosaurs that they too learn the "full" meanings of words for many of the different kinds of dinosaurs as they become more expert along with their children (e.g., Chi & Koeske 1983). The same goes for children learning the names of birds, plants, insects, musical instruments, tools, cars, minerals, and the myriad other domains that children (and adults) learn about as they extend their interests and encounter more and more domains in the natural and man-made worlds around them.

Learning specific words for things, and how those things are related to each other, allows speakers to structure their conceptual knowledge within a domain, and to then maintain it through their reliance on a detailed vocabulary for each domain (e.g., Bross 1973 on teaching anatomy in medicine). As children add more words to each domain, they also structure the domain in terms of superordinate and subordinate terms, and terms that are on the same level within a hierarchy. They also learn adjacent terms relevant to each entity – for parts (*hoof, mane, ears*), for stages in ontogeny (*foal, filly, mare*), for habitats (*stable, field, corral*), for types of motion (*walk, trot, canter, gallop*), for characteristic sounds (*neigh, whinny*), and so on, as each domain is elaborated further (Clark 2018a). As children learn more about a domain, the words they learn for different facets of that domain help them structure and maintain their knowledge (Gelman et al. 1989; Hills et al. 2009). Adults help in all this by supplying links between words that enable children to set up hierarchical relations as well as other connections within a domain (see, e.g., Callanan & Sabbagh 2004; Clark & Wong 2002).

4.8 INFORMATION FLOW

Another dimension in language use concerns information flow. What do the current speakers know, what is their common ground, prior to the current exchange, plus what do they gradually add to that common ground over the course of the exchange? By age two, children can assess what their addressee does and doesn't know, and make use of that knowledge in asking for information and in designing their utterances (O'Neill 1996; Abbot et al. 2016). Also, much as adults do, from at least age two onwards, children start to ratify any new information heard in an adult utterance by repeating it, and thereby adding that information to the current common ground. This is readily apparent, for instance, in conversations between parents and their two-year-olds (Clark & Bernicot 2008). And as children get older, they both ratify what was new in the previous speaker's turn, and also start to add information that is new to the other (the adult in this case) in their own utterances.

Information flow in the adult's utterance, then, provides children early on with a means by which to build up constructions containing both given and new information (Goldberg 2019; Hickmann et al. 1996). But young children may vary in how they order given and new information, sometimes placing new information first, before they settle on the generally preferred adult order of 'given then new' (Narasimhan & Dimroth 2018; Baker & Greenfield 1988). Attention to order also plays a role in children's acquisition of the basic word order needed in transitive utterances as they add subjects and direct objects to their verbs. In both English and French, for example, they add direct objects first as they expand their utterances (e.g., *hit ball*), and only later add subjects (e.g., *Daddy hit ball*). Notice that objects generally present new information, and so will not be known ahead of time to the addressee, while subjects are generally given in context and are therefore already known to both speaker and addressee. Yet both objects and subjects are obligatory in these two languages (Graf et al. 2015; Clark 2022).

4.9   TAKING TURNS

In using language, children learn to attend to turn-taking early on. This also requires planning what one is going to say, as one takes a new turn. And both in taking turns and in planning for a turn, children have to attend to timing. That is, in order to take a turn, speakers need to come in on time, or else miss that turn. The general process of turn-taking, planning, and timing has been studied in how both adults and children answer questions (Holler et al. 2015). In choosing what to say when, speakers need to attend to the current speaker in order to understand what is being said, while simultaneously planning, to some degree in advance, on what to produce in the next turn. If that planning takes longer than expected as the addressee/next speaker tries to retrieve the right words, say, then that next speaker may use a variety of tactics in order to hold the floor until ready to speak, producing a first word followed by *um*, say, or starting with *well*, with drawn out pronunciation and then a pause as they search for the right word(s). Timing is often critical for young children because they take longer to plan and produce their turns than adult speakers do. This may result in the loss of a turn, because an older sibling or an adult jumps in first (see Dunn & Shatz 1989; Rutter & Durkin 1987). But even children as young as two or three know that they need to hold the floor even if they are not quite ready to answer a question or contribute the next turn (Casillas 2014), and they already rely on such forms as *um* as they begin to speak in order to indicate that they are in the process of planning what to say next.

How quickly young children answer questions is initially a function of the complexity of the question and the complexity of the answer actually given. For example, compare the answers to the yes/no question in (1):

(1) Do you want the green crayon?

    a. Yeah.

    b. That one Mommy.

    c. I want a blue too.

The answer in (1a) is minimal, and could be an assent, as here, or a denial with *No*. (1b) is more than minimal, consisting of a non-sentential phrase. And (1c) is also more than minimal, consisting of a full sentential utterance. These answer-types differ in how much planning each requires and how long young children take to produce them after hearing the *yes/no* question (Casillas et al. 2016). As children get older, they become more likely to produce more elaborate answers, and do so more quickly, until they approach the timing found for adult speakers.

In turn taking, more generally, children have to choose what to say when. They therefore need to attend to what the other speaker is saying and then, often simultaneously, start planning what to say in the next turn in the exchange. The processing involved in coordinating comprehension and production is often overlooked, but this coordination is central for a communication system, whether speakers are using speech or sign. Speakers often need to start planning while they are simultaneously processing some of the preceding speaker's utterance(s). In some cases, planning the next turn may be relatively simple, because the follow-up is straightforward, as when one answers a simple *yes/no* question. It becomes a bit more complex, though, when answering various *wh-* questions. *Where is the ball?* requires planning to provide the relevant locative information if the ball itself is not in sight and so can't simply be pointed to, while *When is she arriving?* requires planning to provide relevant information about the time of arrival. In both cases, of course, the next speaker needs to be privy to the pertinent information, in order to take that up further in relation to the question that has just been asked. And contributing a turn may be more complex still when speakers participate in a general discussion of some topic, where some of them know a lot more than others.

4.10   COMMUNICATING INTENTIONS

Even before they start to speak, very young children can display their intention to communicate – asserting or requesting, for example – in their uses of gesture, gaze and prelinguistic vocalisation (e.g., Bates et al. 1975; Golinkoff 1986; Kelly 2001, 2014). In their proto-declaratives, children direct adult attention to some object or action, generally by pointing and looking at the object or event of interest. Such prelinguistic acts precede their uses of one-word labels for objects and actions. These proto-declarations or assertions are later replaced by utterances that continue to command adult attention but also communicate, by providing some propositional content (e.g., *Look doggie, There car*). And in their proto-imperatives or requests, young children may make use of an adult to attain some goal, soliciting help in getting a lid off a jar or reaching a toy that's out of reach. Children also make use of reaching gestures in such cases, with the whole hand extended and fingers "grasping" as they look at the desired object (Bates 1976; Golinkoff 1986; Wu & Gros-Louis 2014). They also distinguish these proto-speech acts prosodically, producing "requests" and "rejections" with a wider pitch range and longer duration than "responses" or "statements", from around seven months on (Esteve-Gibert & Prieto 2013).

As children get older, they become able to produce a greater range of speech acts and so signal their communicative intentions more precisely. While very young children rely primarily on gesture and gaze, and then adding prosody as well, they can later on elaborate their options: they start to produce words, combine them with pointing or reaching, say, along with stance – leaning forward with reaching gestures, but not with points. They continue to rely on pointing as they later produce deictic words like *this* and *there*, or nouns for the objects being indicated. And they rely on iconic gestures as they demonstrate how to move something, how some toy works, or as they show where someone went. They use nods to affirm or agree, and shake their heads to negate or refuse, both from early on, often preverbally. As they get older, they combine such gestures with words, melding them as they learn to elaborate their intentions for their addressees (Kendon 2004).

4.11 CONCLUSION

Multiple processing mechanisms play a role in the acquisition of a language: attention to speech and to the contexts of speech, gaze, and gesture; the statistical analysis of speech signals; representations in memory for segments and sequences of segments in the speech of others; the mapping of words and word-chunks to meanings; the planning and production of utterances; the timing of utterance production; the monitoring of the forms of productions, along with making any spontaneous repairs that are needed, as well as responding to requests for clarification. All these factors play critical roles as infants become immersed in adult language use along with adult reliance on gesture and gaze, in communicative contexts as adults and infants coordinate their activities.

Effectively, what infants need to achieve is some degree of skill in using language as a major ingredient in communication. Adults aid them in this by initially simplifying their own language, for example, at first using only very frequent, very short, utterances, pertinent to the context at hand. But as infants show signs of comprehension and later, of production as well, adults interact with them with utterances that make use of their current lexical knowledge and also extend their experience with language use. They talk about what is happening, what their young children are doing, about their joint activities; they respond to their children's utterances, and ask many questions. They not only expose their children to language, they also offer feedback by checking up on what their children mean when that is unclear, and they offer them all sorts of practice in using language, in a variety of contexts, with an expanding range of addressees, topics, activities, and interests over time. These factors are all integral to learning how to use language.

BIBLIOGRAPHY

Abbot-Smith, K., Nurmsoo, E., Croll, R., Ferguson, H., & Forrester, M. (2016). How children aged 2;6 tailor verbal expressions to interlocutor informational needs. *Journal of Child Language*, **43**, 1277–1291.

Adolph, K. E., & Tamis-LeMonda, C. S. (2014). The costs and benefits of development: The transition from crawling to walking. *Child Development Perspectives*, **8**, 187–192.

Andersen, E. S. (1990). *Speaking with Style*. London: Routledge.

Arnon, I. (2011). Units of learning in language acquisition. In E. V. Clark & B. F. Kelly (Eds), *Experience, Variation and Generalization: Learning a first language* (pp. 167–178). Amsterdam: John Benjamins.

Arnon, I., McCauley, S. M., & Christiansen, M. H. (2017). Digging up the building blocks of language: Age-of-acquisition effects for multiword phrases. *Journal of Memory and Language*, **92**, 265–280.

Baker, N., & Greenfield, P. M. 1988. The development of new and old information in young children's early language. *Language Sciences*, **10**, 3–34.

Bakker, M., Kochukhova, O., & von Hofsten, C. (2011). Development of social perception: A conversation study of 6-, 12-, and 36-month-old children. *Infant Behavior and Development*, 34, 363–370.

Bannard, C., & Lieven, E. (2012). Formulaic language in L1 acquisition. *Annual Review of Applied Linguistics*, **32**, 3–16.

Bates, E., Camaioni, L., & Volterra, V. (1975). The acquisition of performatives prior to speech. *Merrill-Palmer Quarterly*, **21**, 205–226.

Benitez, V. L., & Smith, L. B. (2012). Predictable locations aid early object naming. *Cognition*, **125**, 339–352.

Bergelson, E., & Swingley, D. (2012). At 6–9 months, human infants know the meanings of many common nouns. *Proceedings of the National Academy of Sciences*, **109**, 3253–3258.

Bross, I. D. J. (1973). Languages in cancer research. In G. P. Murphy, D. Pressman, E. A. Mirand (Eds.), *Perspectives in Cancer Research and Treatment* (pp. 213–221). New York: Alan R. Liss.

Casillas, M. (2014). Taking the floor on time: Delay and deferral in children's turn taking. In I. Arnon, M. Casillas, C. Kurumada, & B. Estigarribia (Eds.), *Language in Interaction: Studies in honor of Eve V. Clark* (pp. 101–114). Amsterdam: John Benjamins.

Casillas, M., Bobb, S. B., & Clark, E. V. (2016). Turn taking, timing, and planning in early language acquisition. *Journal of Child Language*, **43**, 1310–1337.

Casillas, M., & Frank, M. C. (2017). The development of children's ability to track and predict turn structure in conversation. *Journal of Memory and Language*, **92**, 234–253.

Chandler, M., Fritz, A. S., & Hala, S. (1989). Small-scale deceit: Deception as a marker of two-, three-, and four-year-olds' early theories of mind. *Child Development*, **59**, 1263–1277.

Chang, L., de Barbaro, K., & Deák, G. (2016). Contingencies between infants' gaze, vocal, and manual actions and mothers' object-naming: Longitudinal changes from 4 to 9 months. *Developmental Neuropsychology*, **41**, 342–361.

Chi, M. T., & Koeske, R. D. (1983). Network representation of a child's dinosaur knowledge. *Developmental Psychology*, **19**, 29–39.

Choi, D., Batterink, L. J., Black, A. K., Paller, K. A., & Werker, J. F. (2020). Preverbal infants discover statistical word patterns at similar rates as adults: Evidence from neural entrainment. *Psychological Science*, **31**, 1161–1173.

Chouinard, M. M., & Clark, E. V. (2003). Adult reformulations of child errors as negative evidence. *Journal of Child Language*, **30**, 637–669.

Clark, E. V. (1993). *The Lexicon in Acquisition*. Cambridge: Cambridge University Press.

Clark, E. V. (2015a). Common ground. In B. MacWhinney & W. O'Grady (Eds.), *The Handbook of Language Emergence* (pp. 328–353). London: Wiley-Blackwell.

Clark, E. V. (2018a). Acquiring meanings and meaning domains. In K. Syrett & S. Arunachalam (Eds.), *Semantics in Language Acquisition* (pp. 21–43). Amsterdam: John Benjamins.

Clark, E. V. (2018b). Conversational partners and common ground: Variation contributes to language acquisition. In M. Hickmann, E. Veneziano, & H. Jisa (Eds.), *Sources of Variation in First Language Acquisition: Languages, contexts, and learners* (pp. 163–182). Amsterdam: John Benjamins.

Clark, Eve V. (2020). Conversational repair and the acquisition of language. *Discourse Processes*, **57**, 441–459.

Clark, E. V. (2021). Language as expertise. Unpublished ms. 110 pp., Stanford University.

Clark, E. V. (2022). Adding subjects on the left. In R. Levie, A. Bar On, O. Ashkenazi, G. Brandes, & E. Dattner (Eds.), *Developing Language and Literacy: In honour of Dorit Ravid*. Berlin: Springerverlag.

Clark, E. V. (in press). A gradualist view of word meaning in language acquisition and language use. *Journal of Linguistics*.

Clark, E. V., & Bernicot, J. (2008). Repetition as ratification: How parents and children place information in common ground. *Journal of Child Language*, **35**, 349–371.

Clark, E. V., & Cohen, S. R. (1984). Productivity and memory for newly formed words. *Journal of Child Language*, **11**, 611–625.

Clark, E. V., & de Marneffe, M. C. (2012). Constructing verb paradigms in French: Adult construals and emerging grammatical contrasts. *Morphology*, **22**, 89–120.

Clark, E. V., & Estigarribia, B. (2011). Using speech and gesture to inform young children about unfamiliar word meanings. *Gesture*, **11**, 1–23.

Clark, E. V., & Hecht, B. F. (1983). Comprehension, production, and language acquisition. *Annual Review of Psychology*, **34**, 325–349.

Clark, E. V., & Kelly, B. F. (2021). Constructing a system of communication: Using gestures and words. In A. Morgenstern & S. Goldin-Meadow (Eds.), *Gesture in Language*: *Development across the Lifespan* (pp. 137–156). Berlin: Walter de Gruyter and Washington, DC: American Psychological Association.

Clark, E. V., & Lindsey, K. L. (2015) Turn-taking: A case study of early gesture and word use in answering *Where* and *Which* questions. *Frontiers in Psychology*, **6**, article 890.

Clark, E. V., & Wong, A. D.-W. (2002). Pragmatic directions about language use: Offers of words and relations. *Language in Society*, **31**, 181–212.

Csibra, G., & Gergely, G. (2007). 'Obsessed with goals': Functions and mechanisms of teleological interpretation of actions in humans. *Acta Psychologica*, **124**, 60–78.

Deák, G., Krasno, A. M., Jasso, H., Triesch, J. (2018). What leads to shared attention? Maternal cues and infant responses during object play. *Infancy*, **23**, 4–28.

Del Bianco, T., Falck-Ytter, T., Thorup, E., & Gredebäck, G. (2019). The developmental origins of gaze-following in human infants. *Infancy*, 24, 433–454.

Diesendruck, G., & Shatz, M. 2001. Two-year-olds' recognition of hierarchies: Evidence from their interpretation of the semantic relation between object labels. *Cognitive Development*, **16**, 577–594.

Dimitrova, N., Moro, C., & Mohr, C. (2015). Caregivers interpret infants' early gestures based on shared knowledge about referents. *Infant Behavior and Development*, **39**, 98–106.

Dodd, B. (1975). Children's understanding of their own phonological forms. *The Quarterly Journal of Experimental Psychology*, **27**, 165–172.

Escalona, S . 1973. Basic modes of social interaction: Their emergence and patterning during the first two years of life. *Merrill-Palmer Quarterly*, **19**, 205–232.

Esteve-Gibert, N., & Prieto, P. (2013). Prosody signals the emergence of intentional communication in the first year of life: evidence from Catalan-babbling infants. *Journal of Child Language*, **40**, 919–944.

Filipi, A. (2009). *Toddler and Parent Interaction: The organization of gaze, pointing, and vocalisation*. Amsterdam: Johns Benjamins.

Gallaway, C., & Richards, B. J. (Eds.), (1994). *Input and Interaction in Language Acquisition*. Cambridge: Cambridge University Press.

Garvey, C., & Berninger, G. (1981). Timing and turn taking in children's conversations. *Discourse Processes*, **4**, 27–57.

Garvey, C., & Kramer, T. (1989). The language of social pretending. *Developmental Review*, **9**, 364–382.

Gelman, S. A., Wilcox, S. A., & Clark, E. V. (1989). Conceptual and lexical hierarchies in young children. *Cognitive Development*, 4, 309–326.

Goldberg, A. E. (2006). *Constructions at Work: The nature of generalization in language*. Oxford: Oxford University Press.

Goldberg, A. E. (2019). *Explain Me This: Creativity, competition, and the partial productivity of constructions*. Princeton, NJ: Princeton University Press.

Golinkoff, R. M. (1986). 'I beg your pardon?': the preverbal negotiation of failed messages. *Journal of Child Language*, **13**, 455–476.

Henderson, A. M. E., & Woodward, A. L. (2011). 'Let's work together': What do infants understand about collaborative goals? *Cognition*, **121**, 12–21.

Hickmann, M., Hendriks, H., Roland, F., & Liang, J. (1996). The marking of new information in children's narratives: a comparison of English, French, German and Mandarin Chinese. *Journal of Child Language*, **23**, 591–619.

Hills, T. T., Maouene, M., Maouene, J., Sheya, A., & Smith, L. (2009). Categorical structure among shared features in networks of early-learned nouns. *Cognition*, **112**, 381–396.

Hughes, C., & Dunn, J. (1997). 'Pretend you didn't know': Preschoolers' talk about mental states in pretend play. *Cognitive Development*, **12,** 477–497.

Karasik, L. B., Tamis-LeMonda, C. S., & Adolph, K. E. (2014). Crawling and walking infants elicit different verbal responses from mothers. *Developmental Science*, **17**, 388–395.

Kelly, B. F. (2001). The development of gesture, speech, and action as communicative strategies. In *Proceedings of the Annual Meeting of the Berkeley Linguistics Society*, 27, 371–380.

Kelly, B. F. (2014). Temporal synchrony in early multi-modal communication. In I. Arnon, M. Casillas, C. Kurumada, & B. Estigarribia (Eds.), *Language in Interaction: Studies in honor of Eve V. Clark* (pp.117–138). Amsterdam: John Benjamin.

Kendon, A. (2004). *Gesture: Visible action as utterance*. Cambridge: Cambridge University Press.

Lieven, E. (2009). Developing constructions. *Cognitive Linguistics*, **20**, 191–199.

Lieven, E. V., Pine, J. M., & Baldwin, G. (1997). Lexically-based learning and early grammatical development. *Journal of Child Language*, *24*(1), 187–219.

Lustigman, L., & Clark, E. V. (2019). Exposure and feedback in language acquisition: adult construals of children's early verb-form use in Hebrew. *Journal of Child Language*, **46**, 241–264.

Marcos, H., Salazar Orvig, A., Bernicot, J., Guidetti, M., Hudelot, C., & Préneron, C. (2004). *Apprendre à Parler: Influence du mode de garde*. Paris: L'Harmattan.

McTear. M. F. (1985). *Children's Conversation*. Oxford: Blackwell.

Mintz, T. H. (2003). Frequent frames as a cue for grammatical categories in child directed speech. *Cognition*, **90**, 91–117.

Moradlou, S., Zheng, X., Ye, T. I. A. N., & Ginzburg, J. (2021). *Wh*-Questions are understood before polar-questions: Evidence from English, German, and Chinese. *Journal of Child Language*, *48*(1), 157–183.

Narasimhan, B., & Dimroth, C. (2018). The influence of discourse context on children's ordering of 'new' and 'old' information. *Linguistics Vanguard*, *4*(s1).

O'Neill, D. K. (1996). Two-year-old children's sensitivity to a parent's knowledge state when making requests. *Child Development*, **67**, 659–677.

Peters, A. M. (1983). *The Units of Language Acquisition*. Cambridge: Cambridge University Press.

Rader, N. de V., & Zukow-Goldring, P. (2010). How the hands control attention during early word learning. *Gesture*, **10**, 202–221.

Rogoff, B., Mistry, J., Göncü, A., & Mosier, C. (1993). *Guided Participation in Cultural Activity by Toddlers and Caregivers. Monographs of the Society for Research in Child Development*, 58 [Serial No. 236].

Roy, B. C., Frank, M. C., & Roy, D. 2012. Relating activity contexts to early word learning in dense longitudinal data. *Proceedings of the Annual Meeting of the Cognitive Science Society*, 34, 935–940.

Saffran, J. R., Aslin, R. N., & Newport, E. L. (1996). Statistical learning by 8-month-old infants. *Science*, **274**, 1926–1928.

Saffran, J. R. (2001). Words in a sea of sounds: The output of infant statistical learning. *Cognition*, **81**, 149–169.

Saji, N., Imai, M., Saalbach, H., Zhang, Y., Shu, H., & Okada, H. (2011). Word learning does not end at fast-mapping: Evolution of verb meanings through reorganization of an entire semantic domain. *Cognition*, **118**, 45–61.

Scollon, R. (1976). *Conversations With a One Year Old: A case study of the developmental foundation of syntax*. Honolulu, HA: University of Hawaii Press.

Siew, C. S. Q. (2021). Global and local feature distinctiveness effects in language acquisition. *Cognitive Science*, **45**, e13008.

Snow, C. E. (1977). The development of conversation between mothers and babies. *Journal of Child Language*, **4**, 1–22.

Tamis-LeMonda, C. S., Custode, S., Kuchirko, Y., Escobar, K., & Lo, T. (2019). Routine language: Speech directed to infants during home activities. *Child Development*, **90**, 2135–2152.

Theakston, A., & Lieven, E. (2017). Multiunit sequences in first language acquisition. *Topics in Cognitive Science*, **9**, 588–603.

van Egeren, L. A., Barratt, M. S., & Roach, M. A. (2001). Mother-infant responsiveness: Timing, mutual regulation, and interactional context. *Developmental Psychology*, 37, 684–697.

Veneziano, E. (2014). Conversation and language acquisition: Unique properties and effects. In I. Arnon, M. Casillas, C. Kurumada, & B. Estigarribia (Eds.), *Language in Interaction* (pp. 83–99). Amsterdam: John Benjamins.

Weir, R. H. (1970). *Language in the Crib*. Amsterdam: Mouton.

Weisleder, A., & Waxman, S. R. (2010). What's in the input? Frequent frames in child-directed speech offer distributional cues to grammatical categories in Spanish and English. *Journal of Child Language*, **37**, 1089–1108.

Woodward, A. L. (2009). Infants' grasp of others' intentions. *Current Directions in Psychological Science*, **18**, 53–57.

Wu, Z., & Gros-Louis, J. (2014). Infants' prelinguistic communicative acts and maternal responses: Relations to linguistic development. *First Language*, **34**, 72–90.

You, G., Bickel, B., Daum, M. M., & Stoll, S. 2021. Child-directed speech is optimized for syntax-free semantic inference. *Nature/Scientific Reports*, **11**, 16527.

Yu, C., & Smith, L. B. (2013). Joint attention without gaze following: Human infants and their parents coordinate visual attention to objects through eye-hand coordination. *PLoS One*, **8**, e79659.

CHAPTER 5

Why Algebraic Systems aren't Sufficient for Syntax: Experimental Evidence from Passives in English, Mandarin, Indonesian, Balinese, and Hebrew

Ben Ambridge

University of Manchester, UK

CONTENTS

ABSTRACT

An intrepid explorer leads us on a global voyage in pursuit of the "affectedness" hypothesis for the passive; the idea that the passive construction (e.g., *Bob got run over by a bus*) has a meaning in and of its own right – here that something happened to Bob; that he was highly affected in some way – and thus that the passive can't be reduced to a formal algebraic rule that generates passives for any verb that you happen to plug in to it. We start in 1980s Minnesota and New York, where two independent research teams found – in support of this hypothesis – that kids struggle with passives that don't have this meaning (e.g., *Superman was remembered by Batman*). We then travel to Michigan and Edinburgh, where evidence is brewing that all passives – regardless of the verb – are equally good at priming other passives; evidence for an abstract, algebraic rule. In Act III, your humble narrator arrives to save the day

DOI: 10.1201/9781003205388-5

with eight – count 'em – studies that provide evidence for the semantic-affectedness constraint across English (adults and children), Indonesian, Balinese, Mandarin, and Hebrew. I conclude that, while you could of course delegate all of this to pragmatics, usage etc., it's more parsimonious to keep it in syntax since the same semantic considerations render certain sentences ungrammatical altogether (e.g., *Three people are slept by this tent*), which is usually considered to be the job of syntax.

5.1 INTRODUCTION

If ever there was a construction that seems particularly well suited to algebraic approaches to language, it is the passive. Even the hackiest programmer could, in a matter of minutes, bash out some code to automatically generate a sentence like *Bob was kicked by Wendy* from the corresponding active *Wendy kicked Bob* (as in the heyday of transformational approaches), or from the VP *kicked Bob*, adding *by Wendy* as an adjunct (as under minimalist approaches). The algorithm is so simple that when I need to generate passive sentences for my experiments, I do so automatically with an Excel spreadsheet. And provided it's furnished with a list of passive participles (e.g., it's *eaten*, not *ate*), this single-line formula *almost never* fails to generate well-formed English passives. The same is true for passives in – to pick just the languages I happen to have worked on – Indonesian, Mandarin, Balinese, and Hebrew.

But appearances can be deceptive. In this chapter I will summarise evidence that, for all of these languages, algebraic rules that operate without reference to the semantics of the construction cannot explain the patterns we see in passive experiments with flesh-and-blood speakers.

Why not? Remember I said that my single-line Excel formula *almost* never fails to generate well-formed passives. Well, those occasional failures hold the key:

> This tent sleeps three people → *Three people are slept by this tent.
>
> Homer resembled Grandpa → *Grandpa was resembled by Homer.
>
> The leak dribbled water → *Water was dribbled by the leak.
>
> The house has four windows → *Four windows are had by the house.

Now, before you try and tell me that some of these passives aren't *that* bad, I asked people to rate them in an acceptability judgement study, and they all scored well below the midpoint of the scale (Ambridge, Bidgood, Pine, Rowland, & Freudenthal, 2016). What went wrong with my trusty spreadsheet? Well unbeknown to Excel, these passives fall foul of a semantic constraint on the passive that was – building on the work of many others of course – neatly summarised by a pre-pop-sci-era Steven Pinker:

> [B] (mapped onto the surface subject [of a passive]) is in a state or circumstance characterised by [A] (mapped onto the *by*-object or an understood argument) having acted upon it. Pinker, Lebeaux and Frost (1987: 249; see also Pinker, 1989)

The passive examples above are bad because they don't satisfy what I will call this "affectedness" constraint. If *Bob was kicked by Wendy*, it's fair to say that he is in a state or circumstance (probably quite a painful one) characterised by *Wendy* having acted upon him. But there is no sense in which *four windows* or *three people* are in a state or circumstance caused by *the house* or *this tent* having acted upon them.

"No problem", you might say, "we can just give the algorithm a list of these very rare exception verbs (there are probably less than 50 in the entire English language, at least based on Pinker, 1989) and go home". The problem is, the same *affectedness* constraint that rules out these rather extreme examples predicts participants' performance with – in a binary sense – "well formed" passives, across production, priming, comprehension and judgement tasks. We certainly *can* say, for example, that *Bob was seen by Wendy*. But, compared to *Bob was hit by Wendy*, we are less likely to say it (production), to be syntactically primed by it (priming), to rapidly select a matching picture or animation (comprehension), or to give it a high acceptability rating (judgement). Unless, that is, the sentence is presented in a context in which Bob *is* highly affected by being seen by Wendy (e.g., Bob was trying very hard to avoid Wendy, because he owed her a huge amount of money he couldn't pay back. Then...).

Before we take a look at this evidence, let's clear up a couple of potential objections. First, am I straw-manning here: Does anyone actually propose "algebraic" rules of passive formation with no role for semantics? Ladies and gentlemen, I give you Noam Chomsky (1993: 4)

> Constructions such as... [the] passive remain only as taxonomic artifacts, collections of phenomena explained through the interaction of the principles of UG, with the values of the parameters fixed.

OK, so Chomsky doesn't explicitly mention semantics here. But he's going even further: He's ruling out *any* special rules or processes that apply to the passive altogether – whether semantics-based or otherwise. Similarly, other Chomskyan approaches to the passive (e.g., Boeckx, 1998; Collins, 2005; Carnie, 2007), while not specifically *ruling out* semantic factors, propose detailed rules and procedures for passive formation that make no mention of them.

At least one (non-Chomskyan) approach goes further, explicitly positing that syntax consists of a single "level of representation [that] includes syntactic category information but not semantic information (e.g., thematic roles) or lexical content" (Branigan & Pickering, 2017: 8). Or, to put it even more starkly, "syntactic representations do not contain semantic information" (Branigan & Pickering, 2017: 8). Are they talking about passives here? Definitely. When they say that "Like adults, 3- and 4-year-olds appear to have abstract syntactic representations that are not specified for lexical or thematic content" (p. 16), two of the four studies they cite as evidence are studies of the passive (Bencini & Valian, 2008; Messenger et al., 2012).

On to the second possible objection: Why does a semantic constraint rule out an algebraic rule? Why can't we have both: an algebraic passive rule with a semantic constraint sitting on top; perhaps somewhere outside of syntax, such as in the discourse-pragmatics system, or as a phenomenon of performance rather than competence? In all fairness, yes, if this is your preferred option, the data I'm about to summarise don't rule it out (though it's difficult to imagine what possible data *could* rule it out). What I *will* argue (in the rather-pretentiously titled "Denouement" section) is that we should prefer an account which explains all of the relevant phenomena in a single mechanism without the need for various add-ons (your mileage – as the Americans say – may vary). What we need, I will argue, is an account under which this probabilistic affectedness constraint emerges in speakers' grammars, as a result of hearing thousands of passives with exactly that type of meaning. I will try to sketch such an account at the end of this chapter. First, here's the evidence that motivates it.

5.2 ACT I: EARLY STUDIES WITH CHILDREN

Our story starts with a pair of studies conducted in the 1980s. Maratsos, Fox, Becker, and Chalkley (1985) presented children with passive sentences (e.g., *Superman was held by Batman*) and asked them verbally "Who did it" or – in separate experiments – to choose the correct picture from a pair (e.g., Batman holding Superman; Superman holding Batman). The manipulation of interest was the type of verb: Four verbs – *find, hold, wash* and *shake* – were "physical action verbs" (p. 170); or, as they later came to be known in the passives literature, AGENT-PATIENT verbs. Eight verbs – *remember, forget, know, like, miss, see, hear,* and *watch* – were "mental state verbs" (p. 170); later called EXPERIENCER-THEME verbs. Although Pinker et al. (1987) was still a couple of years away, Maratsos et al. (1985) clearly had a similar kind of semantic constraint in mind (which they date to Bever, 1970 and Jackendoff, 1972): The actional (AGENT-PATIENT) type verbs all describe events where the PATIENT is clearly affected (i.e., in a state or circumstance characterised by... the *by*-object having acted upon it) in some way (e.g., *Superman was found/held/washed/shaken by Batman*). This is not the case for the mental-state (EXPERIENCER-THEME) verbs (e.g., *Superman was remembered, forgotten, known, liked, missed, seen, heard, watched by Batman*).

So, what happened? Exactly as predicted by a semantic affectedness constraint, children were worse with the mental-state passives than the actional passives. Like, *much* worse: In the "Whodunnit?" study, four to five year-olds scored 40% on mental-state passives and 67% on actional passives. And crucially, the deficit for mental-state verbs was specific to passives. Children were also given active sentences as a control, and scored 89% and 91% for mental-state and actional actives respectively. The contrast in the picture-choice study was even more stark: four-year-olds scored just 34% on mental-state passives, but 85% on actional passives (92% and 97% on actives). Importantly from our perspective, this mental-state-passives deficit was still evident for seven- and even nine-year-olds, at least numerically (the statistical analyses are reported a bit haphazardly, at least by modern standards). Meanwhile in New York, Sudhalter, and Braine (1985) were conducting essentially the same "Whodunnit?" study as Maratsos' Minnesota-based team, with essentially the same results.

In both cases – although, of course, I'm speaking with the benefit of hindsight – these studies' authors don't quite join the dots. On the one hand, both groups are clearly aware that certain passives (e.g., *John was fit by the new suit*) are unacceptable in adult grammar, and that there's "considerable semantic predictability" with regard to which (Maratsos et al., 1985: 168). On the other hand, both can't quite shake off the idea that the semantic constraint they find in their studies is a quirk – a deficit even – of *children's* grammar; one that is long-gone by adulthood. For example, Sudhalter, and Braine (1985) suggest that "*by* is understood as a signaling Actor before it is understood as a signaling experiencer" (p. 469), while Maratsos et al. (1985: 189) discuss how the passive "extends its semantic range after the period of initial restriction.

So let me join the dots for them: The *same* – as near as dammit – semantic constraint on the passive is present in the heads of adults and four-year-olds. The constraint *seems* to go away because adults and older children are very good at "Whodunnit?" and picture-matching tasks, and so show ceiling performance *even if the sentences are slightly weird and unnatural* (e.g., *Superman was missed by Batman*). But, as we will see in a minute, if you use a more sensitive task, even adults show a certain disfluency with – and dislike of – these mental-state/EXPERIENCER-THEME type passives, which are inconsistent with the *affectedness* constraint on the passive construction.

5.3   ACT II: PASSIVE SEMANTICS IN PERIL (EVENTUALLY)

Although they didn't know it yet, Maratsos and his Minnesota colleagues had strong evidence for a semantic constraint on adult passives. But on the other side of Lake Michigan, trouble was brewing for this hypothesis. Bock and Loebell (1990) presented Michigan State University students with Passive "prime" sentences (e.g., *The construction worker was hit by the bulldozer*) along with suitable pictures, and then asked them to describe pictures of their own. They found that participants produced significantly more passives (e.g., *The 747 was alerted by the airport's control tower*) in this condition than in a control condition with active "prime" sentences (e.g., *The construction worker drove the bulldozer*).

OK, but how is this evidence against a semantic constraint on the passive? It isn't – That evidence comes from a third condition, which used locative "prime" sentences (e.g., *The construction worker was digging by the bulldozer*). The key here is that locative sentences are not, by any stretch of the imagination, passive sentences (they're active intransitives [*The construction worker was digging...*] with a prepositional phrase expressing the location [*... by the bulldozer*]). All that they share with passives is a very abstract grammatical structure. Exactly what grammatical structure that is depends on your theory of grammar, but essentially it's along the lines of: [S[NP *The something*] [AUXP[AUX *was*] [VP[V *Verbing*] [PP [P *by*] [NP *The something*]]]]. Now, what Bock and Loebell showed was that these locative primes were *just as effective* at priming participants to produce passive sentences as were genuine bona fide passive primes. This is very bad news for the idea of semantic affectedness constraint on the passive. Why? Well, suppose this constraint takes the form of a semantic prototype construction; something, very roughly speaking, like *[HIGHLY AFFECTED PATIENT] was [ACTIONed] by [HIGHLY AFFECTING AGENT]*). If that were the case, then presumably it wouldn't be possible to prime this structure with something that is semantically *nothing like this at all*. Presumably it wouldn't be possible to prime this structure with a locative, whose first NP slot is filled not by a HIGHLY AFFECTED PATIENT but with the exact opposite: An AFFECTING AGENT or ACTOR (e.g., *The construction worker was digging. . .*).

Now, before we move on, I think it's important to point an often-overlooked fact about Bock and Lobell's findings. My argument doesn't hinge on this, so disregard it if you like, but it seems to me that there's a gaping hole right in the middle of Bock and Lobell (1990) that everyone has somehow missed. Textbook and summary descriptions of these findings (like mine above, and like Bock and Loebell's own summary) focus on the *differences* between conditions. But let's take a moment to look at the actual numbers, or at least the percentages: Following passive and locative primes, participants produced 79% and 80% of passives (21% and 20% of actives) respectively. Following active primes, participants produced 74% passives (26% actives). OK, so 74% is significantly less than both 79% and 80%. But 74% is a *staggeringly* high rate of passive production. Do you know how many passives crop up in spontaneous speech? Neither do I exactly, but I can tell you from some corpus counts that we did for Ambridge, Bidgood, Pine, Rowland, and Freudenthal (2016) that the rate is *well* under 1%. Can you see where I'm going with this? *Participants were consciously aware that the study was about passives, and that they were supposed to produce lots of passives.* So much so, that they produced passives at around *100 times* the usual rate, even when "primed" with actives. Given this context, it is hardly surprising that sentences that share some superficial overlap with the passive – such as the presence of *by* – boost passive production further (and, even then, only by five percentage points).

And here is the smoking gun: Ziegler, Bencini, Goldberg, and Snedeker (2019) replicated Bock and Loebell's main finding, but found that the locative→passive priming disappeared when the locative prime didn't include the word *by* (e.g., *The construction worker has dug near* [c.f. *was digging by*] *the bulldozer*). This is not to say that passive priming always requires *by*; it doesn't. For example, Messenger, Branigan & McLean (2011) found that, for both adults and children, *by*-less short passives (e.g., *The girls are being shocked*) are primed for full *by* passives (e.g., *The king was scratched by the tiger*). But that's passive→passive priming with quite a bit of semantic overlap in terms of SUBJECT-affectedness. Purely structural *locative*→passive priming, with syntactic overlap but no semantic overlap (à la Bock & Loebell, 1990), is a myth; driven by explicit awareness that producing passives is the aim of the game, and/or by the presence of *by*.

Let's set aside, for now, my misgivings about Bock and Loebell (1990), because it's important for the dramatic arc of this chapter that Act II ends with the semantic-affectedness hypothesis for adult passives in peril. But if Bock and Loebell won't provide that peril, then who will?

Not Gordon and Chafetz (1990), that's for sure: Their evidence against the semantic affectedness hypothesis is weak, due to a quite bizarre methodological decision. This is a shame, because Gordon and Chafetz's (1990) passives task is actually rather ingenious. Rather than asking "Whodunnit?" (which is pretty odd for EXPERIENCER-THEME passives, where no one really *does* anything) or using picture pointing (which requires children to keep in mind who is the AGENT/EXPERIENCER and who the PATIENT/THEME), they used non-reversible passives with *yes/no* questions. For example, a child might be told that John hated peas and then asked (a) *Were the peas hated by John?* and (b) *Was John hated by the peas?* This is a clever task, since only children who are truly under-standable passives can answer both *Yes* to (a) and *No* to (b). Using this method, Gordon and Chafetz (1990) again found that children did much better with actional (AGENT-PATIENT) than non-actional (EXPERIENCER-THEME) passives (63% vs 35%) but showed no such difference for actives (85% vs 82%).

Next, in order to see whether this pattern was due to differences in semantic affectedness, Gordon and Chafetz asked six adults to rate the relevant eighteen verbs for affectedness ("How affected is something that is VERBed?") using a seven-point scale. They then ran a correlational analysis to investigate whether these affectedness ratings predicted children's performance with passives on the *yes/no* question task. So far, so good: This is a method I thoroughly approve of – I've done something very similar myself (Ambridge et al., 2016). But here's the bit that's totally bizarre: Because all the non-actional verbs received uniformly low affectedness ratings (a mean of 1.1/7), they were excluded from the correlation analysis. *Wait, what?* So, Gordon and Chafetz (1990) have demonstrated that there is no relationship between affectedness and passivisability, as long as you exclude all the verbs that score very low on both affectedness and passivisability. *Wait, what?!*

No, the real evidence against the semantic-affectedness hypothesis comes from the other side of the Atlantic – Scotland, to be specific – in the form of a series of studies by Messenger, Branigan, McLean, and Sorace (2012). First, Messenger et al. gave children and adults a picture-choice comprehension task, very similar to that used by Maratsos et al. (1985). One difference was that, as well as the familiar AGENT-PATIENT (actional) verbs (*bite, carry, hit, pat, pull, squash*) and EXPERIENCER-THEME (mental-state) verbs (*hear, ignore, like, love, remember, see*), Messenger et al. introduced a third type: THEME-EXPERIENCER verbs (*annoy, frighten, scare, shock, surprise, upset*). Although, in one sense, these verbs are similar to "mental-state" verbs (in that they are "psychological"), in a more important sense – i.e., in terms of semantic affectedness – they are similar to AGENT-PATIENT actional verbs. If anything, they are even more affecting. If *Bob was hit by Wendy* (AGENT-PATIENT), it's possible that he barely even noticed (e.g., if the contact was very light, and he was already being jostled in a crowd, say). But if *Bob was frightened by Wendy* (THEME-EXPERIENCER), he is by-definition affected: If he didn't notice Wendy's Halloween costume, or wasn't bothered by it, we can't even say *Bob was frightened*. Anyway, like the studies before them, Messenger et al. found that children (and even adults, though the age groups weren't analysed separately) did much worse with EXPERIENCER-THEME than AGENT-PATIENT (and also THEME-EXPERIENCER) passives (e.g., *A soldier is being seen < pulled/scared by a horse*). But *unlike* all the studies before them, Messenger et al. found that children and adults did much worse with EXPERIENCER-THEME than AGENT-PATIENT (and also THEME-EXPERIENCER) *actives*. (e.g., *A horse is seeing < scaring/pulling a solider*). But why?

> Not only is it easier to depict action verbs such as *hit* or *kiss* than to depict experiential verbs such as *love* or *hate* or even perception verbs such as *see*, but it is also easier to distinguish the verb's underlying subject – the causer of the event – for pictures involving verbs like *hit* than for verbs like *see* (and therefore easier to distinguish correctly the target picture from the distractor picture containing the same entities but with the roles swapped). (Messenger et al., 2012: 584)

So, after all that, there was never any difficulty with EXPERIENCER-THEME *passives* after all, it was just EXPERIENCER-THEME *verbs*; or maybe just EXPERIENCER-THEME *pictures*. That can't be right, can it?

It certainly looks that way from the other studies in Messenger et al. (2012). Across two priming studies (again with both children and adults, who performed similarly), EXPERIENCER-THEME passives (e.g., *see*) were just as good as AGENT-PATIENT passives (e.g., *pull*) and THEME-EXPERIENCER passives (e.g., *scare*) at priming AGENT-PATIENT passives.

A slight wrinkle is that it's not exactly clear quite what a semantic-affectedness constraint account would predict here. On the one hand, there are quite a few studies (e.g., Bernolet & Hartsuiker, 2010; Jaeger & Snider, 2013) showing that more surprising prime sentences show a bigger priming effect. This means that EXPERIENCER-THEME passives, which don't fit the semantic prototype would show a *bigger* passive priming effect than the other two types (e.g., *pull, scare*). On the other hand, it feels intuitively – to me at least – that more prototypical passives should activate the stored semantic prototype for the passive *more*. This means that EXPERIENCER-THEME passives, which don't fit the semantic prototype would show a *smaller* passive priming effect than the other two types (e.g., *pull, scare*). As I said, it's not clear. What is clear is that – whichever direction it goes in – we'd certainly expect a *different* degree of passive priming from more -versus less-semantically prototypical passive prime sentences. If, that is, the semantic-affectedness account is right. But that's not what Messenger et al. found. Which suggests that it isn't.

Now, if you're up to date with all your methods and stats and the like, you should be feeling a bit queasy at the *argument from absence of evidence* here. Messenger et al. (2012) – and also Branigan and Pickering (2017) – take the *absence of evidence* for any priming differences between EXPERIENCER-THEME versus AGENT-PATIENT/THEME EXPERIENCER passives as *evidence of absence* of any priming differences between the three types. But, hey, we were all doing that way back in 2012, before the replication crisis had really hit: That power-posing study was in 2010, but the you-know-what didn't really hit the fan until that precognition paper in 2011 (Carney, Cuddy & Yap, 2010; Bem, 2011). In fact, the sample size (24 children and 24 adults) was much too small to rule out the possibility of a genuine, but small and hard-to-detect, difference in priming propensity between the three verb types. Again, this isn't to single out Messenger and colleagues, we were all running underpowered studies back in 2011 (yes, even me! e.g., Ambridge, Pine & Rowland, 2011). It just means that we need a suitably powered replication.

So that's what we did (that's me, and a PhD student, Sena Darmasetiyawan). And, in order to ensure fair play, and that the replication was as close as possible, we asked Kate Messenger to come on board as a co-author, which she did. It turns out that the means in the original study were in the direction predicted by the semantic affectedness hypothesis ("intuitive" version): i.e., less priming by EXPERIENCER-THEME passives than the other two types. So, we assumed, for the purposes of a simulation-based power analysis, that an effect of this (very small) size was underlyingly there in Messenger's original data, and worked out how many (adult) participants we'd need to have a 95% chance of detecting it. It turned out to be 240. Undaunted, we (Darmasetiyawan, Messenger & Ambridge, 2022) – well, Sena – recruited the participants and ran an online version of the study (which was just as well when the pandemic came along).

Did we find a passive priming difference between the different semantic verb types? It depends. You could certainly p-hack (or B-hack) your way to one if you were determined to, with the right combination of framework (frequentist/Bayesian), random-effects structure (maximal models or not?) and so on. The (pretty conservative) pre-registered analysis finds a Bayes Factor (with priors based on Messenger's original data) of around 1.5. The presence of an effect is about one and a half times more likely than its absence, but the evidence is "Weak" (Raftery, 1995) or "Anecdotal" (Jeffreys, 1961). So, did we find a semantic effect? Put it this way: If, despite having 240 participants, you are scrabbling around to find an effect that just about meets some criteria for significance, your effect is too small to be worth worrying about; particularly when compared to the absolutely HUGE overall priming effect found in both Messenger et al. (2021) and our replication. Dark days, then, for the semantic-affectedness account of passives.

5.4 ACT III: PASSIVE RESISTANCE

Or so it would seem, until our hero – ahem, your humble narrator – arrives to save the day. Well before I got the idea of trying to replicate Messenger et al. (2012) directly, it seemed to me that this study wasn't quite the final word on the issue, and that things might look rather different with a couple of methodological tweaks.

Thinking about the picture-choice study, it seemed quite right to me that, as noted by Messenger and colleagues, EXPERIENCER-THEME verbs (e.g., *ignore, remember, see, love, hear, like*) are just more difficult to illustrate in pictures. So, I wondered if using animations might make a difference. How exactly do you illustrate – to take one of our sentence stimuli – *Marge was ignored by Homer*? Using still pictures, with great difficulty. But what if Homer approaches Marge, she does a funny dance, and he turns his back and frowns? It's not perfect, but it's pretty clear who is ignoring whom here. And how to address the problem of ceiling effects? Despite the difficulty of illustrating particular actions in still pictures, Messenger et al.'s 24 adults made just sixteen incorrect picture choices between them in the entire study (vs 848 correct choices). This hardly leaves a lot of room for passive-specific by-verb differences. So, what if we asked adults to choose the matching picture *as quickly as possible*, and timed them? And what of trichotomising a continuous variable – verbs' semantic affectedness – into discrete categories (AGENT-PAITENT/THEME-EXPERIENCER/EXPERIENCER-THEME verbs)? Aren't statisticians always telling us that this is "a bad idea" (Royston, Altman & Sauerbrei, 2006)? How about we take a leaf out of Gordon and Chafetz's playbook and use instead a continuous measure of semantic affectedness obtained from adult raters. but – bear with me here– retaining all the verbs, rather than throwing away half of them (Ambridge et al., 2016; Study 1)?

When we did all of this (Ambridge et al., 2016, Study 4; see also Meints, 1999), we found a main effect of semantic affectedness; such that the more "affecting" the verb, the quicker participants chose the matching picture, for active and passive sentences alike: Messenger et al. were quite right that some verbs are just difficult to process, and/or to illustrate in pictures. Crucially, though, we also found a significant interaction: The reaction time "cost" for verbs scoring low on affectedness was greater for passive than active sentences. Verbs scoring low on semantic affectedness really do display "passive resistance". In Bidgood, Pine, Rowland, and Ambridge (2020) we replicated this finding with adults (though using a Messenger et al. style three-way split of verb types, rather than a continuous measure of affectedness) and – using correct/incorrect points rather than reaction time – children.

Wait, what happened to Ambridge et al. (2016) Studies 2 and 3? Thanks for asking! These were grammaticality judgement tasks (or, as some insist I call them, "acceptability judgement" tasks), in which adults simply rated the grammatical acceptability of active and passive sentences with a bunch of verbs. In fact, in Study 2, we went all out and included every verb we could think of from Maratsos et al. (1985), Sudhalter and Braine (1985), Gordon and Chafetz (1990), and Messenger et al. (2012), as well as Pinker et al. (1987: 250–6) and Levin (1993); for a total of 475 (Study 3 was just a replication with a subset of 72 reversible and – in binary sense – passivisable verbs). Again, we found an interaction between semantic affectedness (as rated by a separate group of adults) and sentence type: People don't *love* sentences with low-affectedness verbs, whether those sentences are active or passive. But they dislike them *a lot more* when they're passive, as you can see in Figure 5.1 (the colours are just for convenience – the analysis used a continuous rather than class-based measure of verbs' semantic affectedness).

Personally, I thought these findings were pretty convincing. Branigan and Pickering (2017: 50) did not:

> Ambridge's results suggest that acceptability judgements are affected by semantic factors, a point that reinforces our conclusion that acceptability judgements do not straightforwardly reflect syntactic representation.

This seems to me to be a rather circular – even unfalsifiable – argument: "We know that 'syntactic representations do not contain semantic information' (Branigan & Pickering, 2017: 8). So, any study which suggests that they do *must not actually*

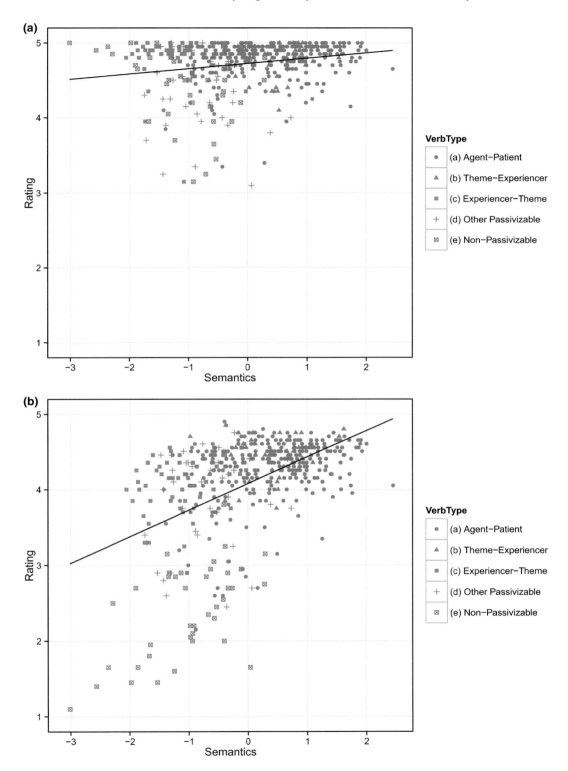

Figure 5.1 Mean grammaticality judgement score for (a) actives and (b) passives as a function of the semantic affectedness predictor (475 verbs; Study 2). Reproduced from Ambridge et al. (2016) under a Creative Commons licence.

be measuring syntactic representations". Presumably following this logic, we should also dismiss the findings from my timed animated-picture-choice studies for the same reason?

No worries: If evidence from syntactic priming studies is what Branigan and Pickering demand, then that's what they shall have. In Bidgood et al. (2020) Study 2, we ran a modified version of Messenger et al.'s priming study, varying the verb type (AGENT-PATIENT, THEME-EXPERIENCER, EXPERIENCER-THEME) of the *target* verb rather than, as in Messenger et al. (2012), the *prime* verb. Why the switch? Well in Messenger et al.'s original study, the target verb was always an AGENT-PATIENT verb. And as we already know from Bock and Loebell (1990) and Ziegler et al. (2019) priming passives with AGENT-PATIENT verbs is almost trivially easy: You can do it using things that *aren't even passives at all* – but that just have a passing resemblance to them (e.g., *The construction worker was digging by the bulldozer*). Particularly when participants can tell fairly easily that the study is about passives, and that they are supposed to produce lots of them (74% remember, in the *active* [!] prime condition of Bock and Loebell). So, it's hardly surprising that – in Messenger et al. (2012) – ever-just-so-slightly awkward EXPERIENCER-THEME passives (e.g., *A soldier is being seen by a horse*) prime passives very effectively; and only – at most – a *shade* less effectively (Darmasetiyawan et al., 2022) than AGENT-PATIENT / THEME-EXPERIENCER passives (e.g., *A soldier is being pulled/scared by a horse*). Flipping around the design of Messenger et al. (2012) – varying the type of the target verb, not the prime verb – makes between-verb differences much easier to see, because it requires participants to *actually say* the slightly awkward EXPERIENCER-THEME passives, which they might be a bit more reluctant to do than the more natural AGENT-PATIENT and THEME-EXPERIENCER passives.

And that's how it turned out: Both adults and children (a) produced fewer passives with EXPERIENCER-THEME verbs than with the other two verb types; and (b) showed a bigger priming effect with EXPERIENCER-THEME verbs than with the other two verb types, exactly as predicted by a semantic-affectedness account of the passive. Game, set, and match.

5.5   DENOUEMENT: A FEW MORE STUDIES AND SOME THEORY

As students of film and theatre will know, the third act doesn't end with the climax, but with the denouement: We go back to our normal everyday life but reflect on how things have changed as a result of the upheaval we've just witnessed: What are the wider implications? What have we learned?

In terms of wider implications, it's worth mentioning just briefly that we have since replicated the production-priming experiment of Bidgood et al. (2020, Study 2) with children with and without autism spectrum conditions (Ambridge, Bidgood & Thomas, 2020; Jones, Dooley & Ambridge, 2021); and the grammaticality judgement experiment of Ambridge et al. (2016, Study 3) in Indonesian (Aryawibawa & Ambridge, 2019), Mandarin (Liu & Ambridge, 2021), Balinese (Darmasetiyawan & Ambridge, submitted), and Hebrew (you'll have to take my word for it on this one: I've got the data but haven't yet got around to writing it up). Interestingly, for

Indonesian, Mandarin, and Balinese, actives show the semantic affectedness effect to pretty much the same extent as passives; or, in the case of the dedicated affectedness ("BA-") construction in Mandarin, even more so. But this doesn't mean that affectedness just predicts something nonspecific like general sentence acceptability. In each case, a semantic affectedness effect is observed for "genuine" passives but not for topicalisation constructions, which mimic passive word order but lack passive morphology. This is not to say that passive affectedness is a semantic universal (e.g., Maratsos et al., 1985 suggest that it may not apply to Gaelic); but it certainly seems to be something that many languages find useful.

This raises the question of just *why* the passive construction in English and many other languages displays a semantic affectedness constraint in the first place. The answer seems to lie with discourse structure. Gordon and Chafetz (1990: 247) – surprisingly, given their overall scepticism regarding a passive affectedness constraint itself – put it best:

> The reason that adults fail to use passives for non-action verbs [i.e., EXPERIENCER-THEME verbs- BA] is that there is usually nothing happening to the logical object of the non-action verb, and hence there is no reason to focus on that argument by passivising the verb. The reason that action verbs [i.e., AGENT-PATIENT and THEME-EXPERIENCER verbs – BA] are good candidates for passivisation... is that PATIENTS of action verbs [including EXPERIENCERs of THEME-EXPERIENCER verbs – BA] are normally affected by the action and hence are things to focus on in discourse.

In order to dig into this idea a bit, I ran just one more study (sorry, I promise I'll stop after this one). If Gordon and Chafetz are right, then it should be possible to increase the rated acceptability of a slightly awkward EXPERIENCER-THEME passive by placing it in a context in which the THEME is quite highly affected. For example:

THEME-affected context: Jack was trying very hard to avoid Emily because he owed her a huge amount of money that he couldn't pay back. Then Jack was seen by Emily.

Neutral context: Jack was looking for his friend in the park. Then Jack was seen by Emily.

My intuition is that the target sentence *Jack was seen by Emily* is slightly more acceptable in the first context than the second, because only here is he really affected by having been seen (e.g., he'll probably feel embarrassed, worried etc.). We've only just started running this study, but the pilot data is broadly supportive. You can see them, and try out the study for yourself, here: `https://osf.io/4cdga/`.

If the final judgement data matches my intuitions, then the implications are really quite radical. These findings, if confirmed, would suggest that grammaticality doesn't depend on the fit between the semantics of the construction (here, affectedness) and the semantics of the verb in some fixed dictionary-definition sense. Rather, grammaticality depends on the fit between the semantics of the construction (here, affectedness) and *the semantics of the whole scene* – i.e., the extent to which the first entity is affected. Even more radically, on this view, grammaticality is no longer a property of particular sentences (remember, the rated sentence is identical in both contexts), but of *pairs* of sentences and real-world meanings+contexts.

Now, let's return to the topic of this volume and to a potential objection I raised back in the Introduction: Why does a sematic constraint rule out an algebraic rule? Why can't we have both: an algebraic passive rule with a semantic constraint sitting on top; perhaps somewhere outside of syntax, such as in the discourse-pragmatics system, or as a phenomenon of performance rather than competence? Well, as I acknowledged in the Introduction, if this is your preferred option, you're welcome to it; the data I've summarised don't rule it out. But it's *clunky* – look at all the components we need to make it work.

To our basic algebraic rule, we first need to add a mechanism that blocks the rule entirely for non-passivisable verbs like *sleep, resemble, dribble,* and *have* (remember the examples from earlier: *Three people are slept by this tent; *Grandpa was resembled by Homer; *Water was dribbled by the leak. *Four windows are had by the house*). Presumably, and standardly, this would be done via the verb's lexical entry (or valance frame etc.). If so, this solution is already starting to look a little clunky, as it treats passivisability – in this binary sense – as an arbitrary lexical property of the verb, rather than as semantically motivated. If, on the other hand, we don't rule out these passives using the verb's lexical entry – postponing everything until a later non-syntactic stage – we would be treating ungrammatical passives as somehow different to ungrammatical transitives, ungrammatical intransitives and all the other ungrammatical utterances that are assumed to result from using a verb in a sentence structure that is not licensed by its lexical entry.

Next, we need to add – in the discourse-pragmatics system, or in performance, a probabilistic constraint that explains the fine-grained semantic differences observed between – broadly speaking – "grammatical" passives in the studies summarised here. We'll also need an explanation of how this constraint interacts with the syntax system to yield the production, judgement and comprehension findings summarised here. But where did this pragmatic constraint come from? Since it varies from language to language, it can only be learned probabilistically from the input. But if children can learn this subtle, fine-grained pragmatic constraint on the passive probabilistically from the input, why can't they learn the (relatively straightforward) *form* of the passive probabilistically from the input too? And if they can, then why do we need an algebraic rule?

Finally, assuming the preliminary findings of my context study hold up, we need to add another mechanism which explains how and why *the same sentence* becomes more or less grammatical in different real-world contexts; that is, how real-world knowledge interacts with the underlying system of pure syntax. And, again, we have to assume that children are skilled and voracious probabilistic input-based learners when it comes to learning which real-world scenarios improve or worsen passives sentences, but hopeless input-based learners when it comes to the apparently much-simpler task of learning the form of the passive construction itself.

You can, of course, build such a system if you want to. But what I don't understand is why anyone *would* want to. Why is it *better* – either for the learner, or for a linguistic analysis – to split the phenomenon of semantic effects on the passive across syntax, the lexicon, discourse-pragmatics and real-world context than to bundle it all into a single probabilistic input-based learning mechanism?

My answer, of course, is that it isn't. So how would this latter possibility work? Let me try to sketch it out. I fully acknowledge, of course, that what follows *is* just a sketch; the proposal would need to be implemented formally – for example as a computational model – before it can be properly tested (as of course is also the case for rival proposals). So, what kind of model of language representation and acquisition could explain all the findings I've set out above (including the very preliminary context findings)? On the one hand, it would need to represent its inputs at a quite *staggering* level of detail: Not just what words were said (e.g., *Jack was seen by Emily*), but the context in which they were said (e.g., that Jack owed Emily a large sum of money and was trying to avoid her). And it would need to store all of this information for every single utterance that it hears. I know this sounds ridiculous, but what's the alternative? How could an affectedness constraint on the passive emerge – on *any* model – if speakers were NOT storing real-world event information that includes (amongst many other linguistically relevant notions) affectedness?

So, on the one hand, the model needs to represent passives at a ludicrously highly-specified level. But on the other hand, the model also needs to represent passives at a ludicrously underspecified level: Remember, utterances that are not passives at all but just have a vague resemblance to a passive (e.g., *The construction worker was digging by the bulldozer*) are sufficient to cause passive priming. They do so, most theorists would agree, by activating some kind of stored abstract representation of the passive construction.

The solution, as I argued in a response to commentators called *Abstractions made of exemplars or 'You're all right, and I've changed my mind'* (Ambridge, 2020), is to assume that (p. 641)

> ... we store all the exemplars that we hear (subject to attention, decay, interference, etc.), but that – in the service of language use – these exemplars are re-represented in such a way as to constitute abstractions ... A useful metaphor for this account is a multiple-level connectionist neural network that stores every exemplar, re-representing it in increasingly abstract ways as we move up the hidden layers... [But] this is not just a metaphor... The brain *really does* contain multiple layers of units (i.e. neurons), each of which aggregates input signals using a nonlinear function and outputs signals to other units.

In a sense, this is nothing more than just a traditional constructivist account (e.g., Goldberg, 1995) which posits that speakers store constructions at every level of generality, from fully lexicalised whole utterances (e.g., *Jack was seen by Emily*) to fully-abstract sentence-level schemas (e.g., [THING] BE/GET [VERB] by [THING]), and everything in between (e.g., partly-lexically specified schemas like *He got VERBed*).

But there is a small difference; at least I think there is. At least on my reading, constructivist accounts assume that the most abstract, top-level constructions are traditional, "human-readable" linguistic constructions like "The English passive" (e.g., [THING] BE/GET [VERB] by [THING]; or even [SUBJECT] BE/GET [VERB] [PP by [NP]]. On my version "it is naïive to expect an explanation couched in terms of 'human-readable' concepts like [NOUN] or [DATIVE CONSTRUCTION] to be anything more than a broad-brush sketch that should not be taken literally" (p. 642):

> To see why, let's use an analogy from a domain that is much closer than language to being 'solved': image classification (McClelland, 2020). Show a multi-level neural network model a picture, and it will tell you whether it's a cat, a dog or a house. How does it work? Well, if you insist on an explanation in terms of 'human-readable' concepts like 'nose', 'tail' and 'window' you can have one. But you know full well that this explanation is just a dumbed-down approximation generated to give humans some vague sense of how the system works. How does it actually work? The point is, nobody really knows; at least, not if you define 'knows' as 'able to give an explanation in terms of human-readable concepts'. The bottom-level, least-abstract layer represents the pixels of the image. As we move up through the layers, the representations become increasingly more abstract. If we plot the activation patterns of these more abstract layers and squint a bit, maybe we can just about make out something that looks sort of like a 'nose detector'. But we know full well that it isn't really one, and that any explanation couched in such simplistic terms is doomed to failure. Sorry, my fellow (psycho-/developmental-)linguists, but language is exactly the same.

And that's where I'll leave it: Far from being a simple algebraic rule, the passive is nothing more than a rough-and-ready human-readable approximation of a certain ever-changing pattern of hidden-unit weightings in a system that maps from real world meaning+contexts to speech sounds, and vice versa. Fade to black. Roll credits:

ACKNOWLEDGEMENTS

The research presented here has received funding from the European Research Council (ERC) under the European Union's Horizon 2020 research and innovation programme (Grant Agreement No. 681296: CLASS). The support of the Economic and Social Research Council [ES/L008955/1] is gratefully acknowledged.

BIBLIOGRAPHY

Ambridge, B, Bidgood, A. & Thomas, K. (2021). Disentangling syntactic, semantic and pragmatic impairments in ASD: Elicited production of passives. Journal of Child Language, 48(1), 184–201 https://doi.org/10.1017/S0305000920000215.

Ambridge, B. (2020). Abstractions made of exemplars or 'You're all right and I've changed my mind' Response to commentators. *First Language, 40*(5-6), 640–659. https://doi.org/10.1177/0142723720949723.

Ambridge, B., Bidgood, A., Pine, J.M., Rowland, C.F. & Freudenthal, D. (2016). Is passive syntax semantically constrained? Evidence from adult grammaticality judgement and comprehension studies. *Cognitive Science, 40*(6), 1435–1459.

Ambridge, B., Pine, J.M. & Rowland, C.F., (2011). Children use verb semantics to retreat from overgeneralization errors: A novel verb grammaticality judgement study. *Cognitive Linguistics, 22*(2), 303–323.

Aryawibawa, I.N & Ambridge, B. (2019). Is syntax semantically constrained? Evidence from a grammaticality judgement study of Indonesian. *Cognitive Science, 42*(8), 3135–3148.

Bem, D. J. (2011). Feeling the future: experimental evidence for anomalous retroactive influences on cognition and affect. *Journal of Personality and Social Psychology, 100*(3), 407–425.

Bencini, G. M. L., & Valian, V. V. (2008). Abstract sentence representations in 3-year-olds: Evidence from language production and comprehension. *Journal of Memory and Language, 59*, 97–113.

Bernolet, S., & Hartsuiker, R. J. (2010). Does verb bias modulate syntactic priming?. *Cognition, 114*(3), 455–461.

Bever, T.G. (1970) The cognitive basis for linguistic structures. In J.R. Hayes (ed.), *Cognitive and the development of language.* New York, Wiley.

Bidgood A., Rowland, C.F., Pine, J.M. & Ambridge, B. (2020). Syntactic representations are both abstract and semantically constrained: Evidence from children's and adults' comprehension and production/priming of the English passive. *Cognitive Science, 44*(9), ee12892. https://doi.org/10.1111/cogs.12892.

Bock, K., & Loebell, H. (1990). Framing sentences. *Cognition, 35*(1), 1–39.

Boeckx, C. (1998). *A Minimalist view on the passive.* Harvard: MIT Press.

Branigan, H. P., & Pickering, M. J. (2017). An experimental approach to linguistic representation. *Behavioral and Brain Sciences, 40*, 1–61.

Carney, D. R., Cuddy, A. J., & Yap, A. J. (2010). Power posing: Brief nonverbal displays affect neuroendocrine levels and risk tolerance. *Psychological Science, 21*(10), 1363–1368.

Carnie, Andrew (2007) *Syntax: A Generative Introduction* (3rd edition) Oxford: Wiley Blackwell.

Chomsky, N. (1993). A minimalist program for linguistic theory. In *The View from Building 20*, by K. Hale & S.J. Keyser (Eds), 1–52. Cambridge, MA: MIT Press.

Collins, C. (2005). A Smuggling approach to the passive in English. *Syntax, 8*(2), 81–120.

Darmasetiyawan, S. & Ambridge, B. (submitted). Syntactic representations contain semantic information: Evidence from Balinese passives. *Collabra: Psychology.*

Darmasetiyawan, S. Messenger, K. & Ambridge, B. (submitted). Is passive priming really impervious to verb semantics? A high-powered replication of Messenger et al. (2012). *Collabra: Psychology.*

Goldberg, A. E. (1995). *Constructions: A construction grammar approach to argument structure.* Chicago: University of Chicago Press.

Gordon, P., & Chafetz, J. (1990). Verb-based versus class-based accounts of actionality effects in children's comprehension of passives. *Cognition, 36*(3), 227–254.

Jackendoff. R. (1972) Semantic Interpretation in Generative Crammer. Cambridge, MA: MIT Press.

Jaeger, T. F., & Snider, N. (2013). Alignment as a consequence of expectation adaptation: Syntactic priming is affected by the prime's prediction error given both prior and recent experience. *Cognition, 127*, 57–83.

Jeffreys, H. (1961). *Theory of probability* (3rd Ed.). Oxford: Oxford University Press.

Liu, L. & Ambridge, B. (2021). Balancing information-structure and semantic constraints on construction choice: building a computational model of passive and passive-like constructions in Mandarin Chinese. *Cognitive Linguistics,* doi.org/10.1515/cog-2019-0100.

Maratsos, M. P., Fox, D. E., Becker, J. A., & Chalkley, M. A. (1985). Semantic restrictions on children's passives. *Cognition, 19*(2), 167–191.

McClelland, J. (2020). Exemplar models are useful and deep neural networks overcome their limitations: A commentary on Ambridge (2020). *First Language, 40*(5-6): 612–615.

Meints, K. (1999) Protoypes and the acquisition of passives. In B. Kokinov (ed.) *Perspectives on Cognitive Science, 4,* 67–77. Sofia: NBU Press.

Messenger, K., Branigan, H. P., & McLean, J. F. (2011). Evidence for (shared) abstract structure underlying children's short and full passives. *Cognition, 121*(2), 268–274.

Messenger, K., Branigan, H.P., McLean, J.F. & Sorace, A. (2012). Is young children's passive syntax semantically constrained? Evidence from syntactic priming. *Journal of Memory and Language, 66*(4), 568–587.

Pinker, S. (1989). *Learnability and cognition: the acquisition of argument structure.* Cambridge, MA; London: MIT.

Pinker, S., Lebeaux, D. S., & Frost, L. A. (1987). Productivity and Constraints in the Acquisition of the Passive. *Cognition, 26*(3), 195–267.

Raftery, A. E. (1995). Bayesian model selection in social re- search. In P. V. Marsden (Ed.), *Sociological methodology 1995* (pp. 111–196). Cambridge, MA: Blackwell.

Royston, P., Altman, D. G., & Sauerbrei, W. (2006). Dichotomizing continuous predictors in multiple regression: a bad idea. *Statistics in Medicine, 25*(1), 127–141.

Sudhalter, V., & Braine, M. D. S. (1985). How does comprehension of passives develop? A Comparison of actional and experiential Verbs. *Journal of Child Language, 12*(2), 455–470.

Ziegler, J., Bencini, G., Goldberg, A., & Snedeker, J. (2019). How abstract is syntax? Evidence from structural priming. *Cognition, 193*, 104045.

CHAPTER 6

Learning Syntactic Structures from String Input

Ethan Gotlieb Wilcox

Harvard University

Jon Gauthier

Massachusetts Institute of Technology

Jennifer Hu

Massachusetts Institute of Technology

Peng Qian

Massachusetts Institute of Technology

Roger Levy

Massachusetts Institute of Technology

CONTENTS

DOI: 10.1201/9781003205388-6

ABSTRACT

This chapter addresses a series of interrelated questions about the origin of syntactic structures: How do language learners generalise from the linguistic stimulus with which they are presented? To what extent does linguistic cognition recruit domain-general (i.e., not language-specific) processes and representations? And to what extent are rules and generalisations about linguistic structure separate from rules and generalisations about linguistic meaning? We address these questions by asking what syntactic generalisations can be acquired by a domain-general learner from string input alone. The learning algorithm we deploy is a neural-network based Language Model (GPT-2; Radford et al., 2019), which has been trained to provide probability distributions over strings of text. We assess its linguistic capabilities by treating it like a human subject in a psycholinguistics experiment, and inspect behaviour in controlled, factorised tests that are designed to reveal the learning outcomes for one particular syntactic generalisation. The tests presented in this chapter focus on a variety of syntactic phenomena in two broad categories: rules about the structure of the sentence and rules about the relationships between smaller lexical units, including scope and binding. Results indicate that our target model has learned many subtle syntactic generalisations, yet it still falls short of humanlike grammatical competence in some areas, notably for cases of parasitic gaps (e.g., "I know what you burned ___ after reading ___ yesterday"). We discuss the implications of these results under three interpretive frameworks, which view the model as (a) a counter-argument against claims of linguistic innateness, (b) a positive example of syntactic emergentism, and (c) a fully articulated model of grammatical competence.

6.1   INTRODUCTION

How do we gain knowledge about the representations that underlie linguistic communication? For the last fifty years, researchers have relied on a combination of introspective judgements and experimental results. This dual approach has been effective, in part because much of the research has focused on adult human subjects, who are capable of both describing internal judgements and producing experimentally controlled behaviour. However, recent advances in computing have produced a new generation of artificial linguistic agents who, for the first time, learn to produce output that could plausibly be called "humanlike" in its sophistication. Their performance has led researchers to ask whether they exhibit the same type of generalisations that underlie human linguistic communication. This chapter addresses both the epistemic question – how can we gain knowledge about what artificial agents have learned? – as well as several possible inferences that can be drawn from these results for linguistic theory. We focus on the learning outcomes of artificial neural networks (ANNs), algorithms that can learn arbitrary relationships between input and output by representing information at one or more intermediary, or hidden, layers of representation. In particular, we investigate application of ANNs, known as language models (LMs): algorithms trained on large amounts of text that assign joint probability distributions over strings, which can be used to produce a probability distribution over a target word given its preceding context. In our case, all of our language models are trained on English. The ANNs we use are domain-general learning algorithms in the sense that they are general-purpose pattern recognisers, and have been used to successfully model data as disparate as photos of flowers and vehicles (Chen et al., 2020; Dosovitskiy et al., 2021) to the structure of proteins (Rives et al., 2021).

We will begin our discussion by presenting one answer to the empirical question – how can we gain knowledge about what artificial agents have learned? We introduce a paradigm for probing these models, dubbed the "psycholinguistics paradigm" because it treats ANNs like human subjects in a psycholinguistics experiment. In Section 6.3 and Section 6.4, we present case studies on specific syntactic phenomena in two different areas. While the ANNs discussed produce surprisingly human-like linguistic behaviour, we argue that they do not in themselves constitute a theory of linguistic cognition – just as a human brain in itself does not constitute a theory of linguistic cognition. In order to make inferences about the knowledge underlying linguistic communication from ANN behaviour, in Section 6.5, we discuss three interpretive frameworks, and discuss their implications for theories and future research.

6.2 METHODS: PSYCHOLINGUISTIC ASSESSMENT OF ANNS

Here we analyse Autoregressive Language Models (henceforth simply LMs) (Elman, 1990, 1991) that are trained to predict the next token x_i given a context of preceding tokens x_{-i}—$P(x_i|x_{-i})$. The theoretical and practical reasons to use LMs to address learnability questions in natural language syntax are compelling. Incremental word prediction plays a major role in human language processing (Hale, 2001; Kuperberg and Jaeger, 2016; Levy, 2008b), demonstrating that the autoregressive LM objective function corresponds to a highly optimised function for language in the human mind. If grammatical abstractions emerge from the application of general-purpose learning models trained on this objective function using human-scale learning data, it places plausible lower bounds on the learnability of those abstractions. From an engineering standpoint, contemporary LMs have achieved impressive apparent fluency in the language they generate (Brown et al., 2020; Jozefowicz et al., 2016; Radford et al., 2019), raising for for the first time the prospect that sophisticated human-like grammatical abstractions could potentially be emergent in models trained without explicit grammatical supervision.

However, these outputs—probability distributions of multi-thousand word vocabularies–are difficult to interpret. How, then, can we evaluate whether a model has "learned" a certain syntactic generalisation? Two classes of approaches to this problem have emerged in recent years. The first is to focus on the internal representations learned by the model, attempting to find homomorphisms between these representations and the representations postulated by linguists (Giulianelli et al., 2018; Hewitt, Hahn, et al., 2020; Hewitt and Manning, 2019 for LMs trained on the closely related Cloze objective function). Here, we take the alternate approach of behavioural testing, elucidating the implications of the models' word-by-word probability distributions for whether they are making human-like grammatical generalisations (building on previous work such as Gulordava et al., 2018; Linzen et al., 2016).

We can reveal what syntactic generalisations have been implicitly learned by an ANN by inspecting their conditional word probabilities values in controlled, factorised tests that are designed to reveal the learning outcomes for one particular syntactic rule, or generalisation. These tests are inspired by the types deployed in psycholinguistic studies (Futrell et al., 2018; Linzen et al., 2016). Because of this, we refer to this methodology as the "Psycholinguistic Assessment Paradigm" for analysis of ANNs. To get an intuition about how these tests can reveal learned generalisations about the structure of a context C and what structures it can co-occur with, consider a comparison between two different contexts, C_1 and C_2, within which a critical word or phrase, w, can only occur with non-negligible probability if a latent structural property X holds of the context. For example, (1-a) is a famous garden-path sentence, where the context C_1 is structurally ambiguous between *man* serving as the head noun of the subject (premodified by the adjective *old*) versus as the main verb of the clause (in which case *The old* is a nounless subject); (1-b) is its unambiguous counterpart.

(1) a. $\overbrace{\text{The old man}}^{C_1}$... the walls. [Ambiguous]

　　b. $\overbrace{\text{The old manned}}^{C_2}$... the walls. [Unambiguous]

In this case, the garden-path disambiguating word *the* requires that the preceding word was the main verb of the clause; this is, the latent property X that must hold of the context. We can rewrite $P(w|C)$ making explicit the marginalisation over whether X holds:

$$P(w|C) = P(w|X, C)P(X|C) + P(w|\neg X, C)P(\neg X|C) \qquad (6.1)$$

and, since $P(w|\neg X, C) \approx 0$,

$$P(w|C) \approx P(w|X, C)P(X|C). \qquad (6.2)$$

Furthermore, we specifically focus on cases where $P(w|X, C_1) \approx P(w|X, C_2)$—that is, if the latent property X holds, there is little difference betweeen the contexts of how likely w is. In Example (1), for example, if *man/manned* is a verb, then the only difference between the variants is whether the verb is in present or past tense; this difference is unlikely to affect whether a direct object comes next or what direct object is likely. In such cases, what pushes around the relative probability of w is $P(X|C_1)$ versus $P(X|C_2)$, namely how strongly the context predicts the latent property X. This means that the $P(w|C_1)$ versus $P(w|C_2)$ comparison, which we can easily compute for any trained LM, can be used to assess whether and how strongly the model's word predictions reflect the latent structural generalisations of interest.

The decomposition of Equation 6.2 offers us something further, too. In practice, we will be testing models using collections of sentence sets, or "items". Across items, the lexical particulars vary but the structural properties of the context are consistent; within an item, the lexical particulars are very tightly controlled. By taking the log of the inverse of the conditional word probability we get its *surprisal* (Hale, 2001; Levy, 2008b), converting a product into sums:

$$S(w|C) \equiv \log \frac{1}{P(w|C)} \approx \log \frac{1}{P(w|X,C)} + \log \frac{1}{P(X|C)}$$

Due to lexical differences, the first term $\log \frac{1}{P(w|X,C)}$ is likely to vary substantially across items, but not within an item. This means that we can use within-items repeated-measures analysis across multiple items to zero in on the presence and robustness of differences across contexts in the second term, $\log \frac{1}{P(X|C)}$, which is what we are really interested in: has the model acquired a generalisation about what latent structures fit in what contexts? We use base-2 logs so that surprisals are measured in *bits*: one bit is associated with observing an event that occurs with probability $1/2$, an event with probability 1 has a surprisal of 0 bits, and an event that is impossible has an infinite number of bits of surprisal. Surprisal also plays a substantial theoretical role in psycholinguistics: a word's surprisal contributes linearly to the amount of time it takes a native speaker to read it in naturalistic text (Goodkind and Bicknell, 2018; Hale, 2001; Smith and Levy, 2013; E. G. Wilcox et al., 2020, though see Brothers and Kuperberg, 2021). Using surprisal as a linking function allows us to make concrete predictions about model outputs based on human behaviour, both in absolute terms (word x_i should be assigned approximate probability p based on human processing times) and in *relative* terms (word x_i should be assigned a lower probability than word y_i).

Connecting with experimental psycholinguistics terminology, we can think of Example (1) as one "item" in two "conditions": UNAMBIGUOUS, in which the sentence up to "the walls", is unambiguously an NP+VP, and AMBIGUOUS, in which the first part is ambiguous between NP and NP+VP interpretations. Each item in the test contains a critical region, which is the underlined NP "the walls." If the model has learned that (1-a) is ambiguous between two interpretations, then it should assign the critical region a lower probability in this condition. Or, in terms of surprisal:

$$S(\text{the walls}|\text{The old manned}) < S(\text{the walls}|\text{The old man}). \tag{6.3}$$

However, the converse is not necessarily true: as this prediction only considers a single sentence pair, a given ANN model could produce output satisfying this criterion without learning the proper generalisation. Thus, in order to abstract away from particular lexical items and sentential contexts, we assess models on *suites* of test items all of which exemplify the syntactic context and continuation of interest, and formulate our predictions over conditions instead of individual items. For example, we would generalise the single-item prediction in Equation (6.3) to

$$S(\text{NP}|\text{UNAMBIGUOUS prefix}) < S(\text{NP}|\text{AMBIGUOUS prefix}), \tag{6.4}$$

and when the word and prefix are sufficiently clear, we will simply write the condition name. Typically, test suites consist of 20–40 items in four conditions, with two predictions that specify an inequality between two conditions. If the model were to assign random probabilities to each word, it should make the correct guess $\sim 50\%$ of the time, for each prediction. All of our test suites come from www.syntaxgym.org, a website for hosting and sharing syntactic test suites (Gauthier et al., 2020). (We encourage readers of this article to explore SyntaxGym and create their own test suites to assess whatever aspect of syntax they wish.)

So far, we have been discussing ANN models only in the abstract. For the rest of this chapter we will look at the learning outcomes of GPT-2 (Radford et al., 2019), a large Transformer-based language model. Transformers (Vaswani et al., 2017) are a type of ANN architecture that has recently become dominant in machine learning research. While previous architectures encoded linear order through a mechanism called recurrence, in which the network sequentially consumed pieces of input (Elman, 1990; Hochreiter and Schmidhuber, 1997), Transformers encode linear order into their input directly and keep track of the relative importance of the relationship between each input piece at each layer of representation. The version of GPT-2 reported here was trained on a corpus of web-text that contained ~8 billion tokens. Under the assumption that children are exposed to about 30,000 words per day ($\approx$11-million words per year) (Hart and Risley, 1995), this model has the linguistic experience comparable to about 8 human lifetimes. Results for other models, including models that implement recurrence, are hosted online at syntaxgym.org.

6.3   GROSS SYNTACTIC STATE: COMPLEMENTISER PHRASES

One of the key features of human language is that groups of adjacent lexical items form larger phrasal units, which are recursively nested within each other. The tests in this section are designed to assess whether the models have learned (1) whether groups of words form larger, cohesive phrases; and (2) whether they have learned to make generalisations about the phrase as a whole. The type of phrase we focus on here are Complementiser Phrases (CPs), which are the theoretical equivalent of sentences. In the base case, chunks of words that form CPs must constitute distinct utterances, which are orthographically distinguished in English with end-of-sentence punctuation. However, there are a variety of strategies that can be used to combine multiple CPs together in a single sentence, including conjunction, subordination and relativisation. The tests deployed here leverage the latter two strategies to assess what models have learned about CPs and how they can be combined.

6.3.1   Subordination

Subordinating conjunctions, such as *when, as,* or *while,* set up temporal relationships between a *matrix* and *subordinate* CP. In order to test whether our model of interest has learned the proper generalisations about these words and the type of phrasal units they conjoin, test suites were created along the lines of (2). (Critical regions are underlined in this and future examples.) Two predictions should hold: First, if models have learned that presence of a subordinator necessitates the presence of two CPs, then end-of-sentence punctuation after the first phrase should be more surprising when a subordinator is present than when it is absent. That is, the period should have higher surprisal in the [+SUBORDINATOR, -MATRIX] condition

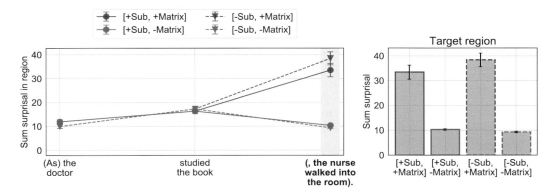

Figure 6.1 **Subordination.** Left: sum GPT-2-derived surprisal in each sentence region, averaged across items in test suite. Target region is highlighted with gray box and shown in boldface. Right: average sum surprisal in target region for each condition. GPT-2 output is consistent with the expectation of a matrix clause when a subordinator is present, and end-of-sentence punctuation when a subordinator is absent.

than the [-SUBORDINATOR, -MATRIX] condition (Prediction 1). Second, if models have learned that two CPs cannot exist in the same sentence without conjunction then the second CP should have higher surprisal when no subordinator is present; i.e., in the [-SUBORDINATOR, +MATRIX] condition compared to the [+SUBORDINATOR, +MATRIX] condition (Prediction 2).

(2) Subordination
   a. As the doctor studied the book, <u>the nurse walked into the office.</u> [+SUB-ORDINATOR, +MATRIX]
   b. *As the doctor studied the book. [+SUBORDINATOR, -MATRIX]
   c. *The doctor studied the book, <u>the nurse walked into the office.</u> [-SUBORDINATOR, +MATRIX]
   d. The doctor studied the book. [-SUBORDINATOR, -MATRIX]

The results for this experiment are shown in Figure 6.1. We first focus on the left panel. Each sentence fed to the model is broken into non-overlapping regions, shown on the x-axis. The region of interest for our two predictions is the main clause, which is highlighted in bold. As a region may contain multiple tokens, the y-axis shows the summed surprisal across tokens for each region, averaged across all the items in a test suite. We now turn to the performance of GPT-2 with respect to the two predictions described above. For Prediction 1, GPT-2 achieves 95.7% accuracy, and for Prediction 2, it achieves 100% accuracy. This is reflected in the relative height of the bars in the right panel (corresponding to surprisal at the target region): Although it is not visually obvious from the scale, the [+SUBORDINATOR, -MATRIX] bar is higher than the [-SUBORDINATOR, -MATRIX] bar, as expected by Prediction 1; more visually evident is the fact that the [-SUBORDINATOR, +MATRIX] bar is higher than the [+SUBORDINATOR, +MATRIX] bar, as expected by Prediction 2. Overall, these results are consistent with the model having learned the relationship between subordiators and CPs.

6.3.2 Relative Clauses

One other way to conjoin CPs in a single sentence is via relativisation, where a CP has been inserted medially into a host clause along the lines of (3), below. In this case, there is a dependency relationship between the top-level subject Noun Phrase and the verb of the embedded CP. Crucially, there are also dependencies that exist between the subject and verb at each CP layer, and because of the rules on relativisation these follow a first-in-first out linear order—the first verb must have as its subject the last noun *(artist/painted)*, and the second verb must have the first noun as its subject *(painting/deteriorated)*.

(3) $[_{CP1}$ The painting$_{N1}$ $[_{CP2}$ that the artist$_{N2}$ with the long dark hair painted$_{V2}$] deteriorated$_{V1}$].

In order to test whether GPT-2 has learned the proper syntactic generalisation about relativisation, we exploit this last-in-first-out rule for subject/verb relationships in test suites following (4), below. Sentences are created with two NPs and two verbs such that one pairing of the two is semantically plausible and the other pairing is implausible. In addition, we use verb transitivity to add an additional element of plausibility; one reason why "deteriorated" is implausible as the first verb in the example above is because it is used intransitively in the vast majority of cases.[1] If the model has learned the last-in-first-out rule for relativised CPs, then it should be less surprised by the condition that forces the plausible pairing than the implausible one. Each sentence also contains a relative clause modifying the second NP, such that a model cannot succeed simply by assigning higher probability to the bigram "artist painted" than "artist deteriorated" without recourse to the rest of the sentence (cf. (3)). In (4), for example, it is implausible that a painting could paint and an artist could deteriorate, at least compared to the more plausible condition where the artist paints and the painting deteriorates. Therefore, we expect a model that has learned the correct relativisation pattern to assign higher surprisal to "deteriorated painted" than "painted deteriorated", given the same prefix "The painting that the artist who lived long ago" (i.e., $S_{\text{IMPLAUSIBLE}} > S_{\text{PLAUSIBLE}}$).

(4)   Relativised Complements (Centre Embedding)

  a.   The painting that the artist who lived long ago <u>painted deteriorated</u>. [PLAUSIBLE]

  b.   The painting that the artist who lived long ago <u>deteriorated painted</u>. [IM-PLAUSIBLE]

The results for this experiment are shown in Figure 6.2, again with regions on the x-axis and summed surprisal for each sentence region on the y-axis. At the critical

---

[1]According to the data from Goldberg and Orwant, 2013, it is used intransitively in over 98% of occurances (see `https://github.com/wilcoxeg/verb_transitivity`).

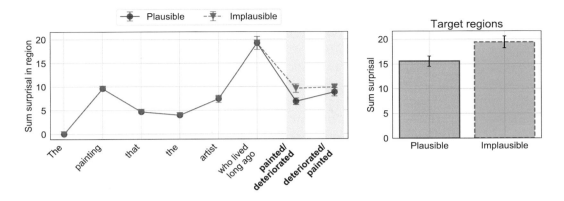

Figure 6.2 **Centre embedding.** Left: sum GPT-2-derived surprisal in each sentence region, averaged across items in test suite. Right: average surprisal summed over target regions for each condition. GPT-2 output is consistent with the last-in-first-out rule for pairing nouns and verbs in relativised CPs.

regions, the blue line, which indicates surprisal in the IMPLAUSIBLE condition is higher than the red line, which indicates surprisal in the PLAUSIBLE condition. Looking at accuracy scores, GPT-2 achieves 85.7% accuracy on this test suite, indicating that it has learned the proper last-in-first-out rule for embedded clause completion.

6.3.3 Main Verb/Reduced Relative Clause Gardenpath Effects

Gardenpath sentences are sentences in which an initial, locally plausible, interpretation becomes globally implausible at a certain point, resulting in a variety of well-studied processing effects, including regressive checking and slowdown in reading times (Ferreira, Christianson, et al., 2001; Ferreira and Henderson, 1991; Pritchett, 1988). At the outset, we introduced our methods using the famous gardenpath sentence "The old man the walls", however here we focus on a different type of gardenpath, called the Main-Verb/Reduced-Relative (MV/RR) gardenpath. For example, the string "The woman brought a sandwich from the kitchen..." is ambiguous between two interpretations: a Main-Verb Interpretation, in which the verb *brought* is a past-tensed verb associated with the matrix clause of the sentence, and the Reduced Relative Interpretation, in which *brought* is a passive participle, associated with a reduced relative clause. The two interpretations are given in (5), below.

(5)   "The woman brought a sandwich..."

     a. $[_{CP} [_{NP}$The woman] $[_{VP}$brought a sandwich]]   (Main-Verb Interpretation)

     b. $[_{NP}$ The woman $[_{CP}$ (who was) brought a sandwich]] (Reduced Relative Interpretation)

Crucially, the two different interpretations should lead to differing expectations for upcoming material. The main-verb interpretation should lead to expectations for end-of-sentence punctuation, adjuncts and other CP-modifiers, or coordinating conjunctions following *sandwich*. The reduced relative interpretation should lead to expectations for a verb, which is still required to complete the sentence. Because the statistics of English heavily favour the main verb interpretation (*brought* is rarely used as a passive particle), most people reading (5) parse the sentence along (5-a) – they are "led down the garden path" – and are surprised if they encounter a subsequent verb. Note that, while the other tests in this chapter discuss model behaviour between sets of items that differ in terms of their grammaticality, gardenpath sentences are not technically ungrammatical. What this test suite does have in common with the others, is that critical regions create a violation of structural expectations. These underlying structural expectations are the object of our interest – grammatical violations and gardenpath sentences are both useful for revealing them.

While garden-path effects have traditionally been used to gain insight into how the human processor manages uncertainty during online interpretation, they rely on assumptions that the processor is forming specific types of representations over which to have uncertainty in the first place. While previous investigation of gardenpath effects in ANNs has demonstrated how they can be used as models of psycholinguistic processing (Futrell et al., 2018; van Schijndel, 2018, 2021), we use them here to build up empirical support for the hypothesis that ANNs have learned abstract phrasal units including complex NPs and CPs. We do so by creating test suites following (6), where items can come in one of four conditions: The main verb can either be AMBIGUOUS or UNAMBIGUOUS between being a main verb and a reduced relative; for example, *brought* is ambiguous but *given* is not. Additionally, sentences can be UNREDUCED in which case they explicitly introduce relative clauses with the relativiser and passiviser *who was*, or else they can be REDUCED, in which case the relative clause is not signaled overtly. Note that the only condition which is a true "gardenpath" is the [REDUCED, AMBIGUOUS] condition; even though *brought* is ambiguous by itself, when it is preceded by a passive verb (as in *was brought*) it can only be analysed as introducing a relative clause. Therefore, if models had correctly learned that both passive participles and overt relativisation and passivisation introduce relative clauses that modify the subject NP, they should find the main verb *tripped* more surprising in this condition than in any of the others. In other terms, we expect an interaction between REDUCTION and AMBIGUITY that results in a superadditive amount of surprisal.

(6) MV/RR Gardenpath Effects:

  a. The woman brought a sandwich from the kitchen <u>tripped</u> on the carpet. [REDUCED, AMBIGUOUS]

  b. The woman who was brought a sandwich from the kitchen <u>tripped</u> on the carpet. [UNREDUCED, AMBIGUOUS]

  c. The woman given a sandwich from the kitchen <u>tripped</u> on the carpet. [REDUCED, UNAMBIGUOUS]

  d. The woman who was given a sandwich from the kitchen <u>tripped</u> on the carpet. [UNREDUCED, UNAMBIGUOUS]

The results for this experiment are shown in Figure 6.3. The top plot shows the region-by-region surprisal for GPT-2, with regions on the x-axis and summed

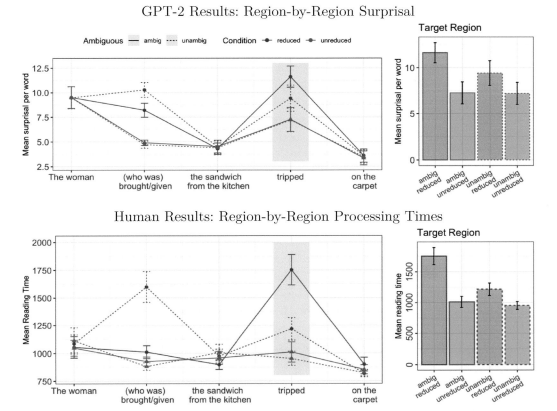

Figure 6.3 **Main Verb/Reduced-Relative Clause Gardenpath Effects.** Top: mean sum surprisal in each sentence region for GPT-2. Bottom: mean reading time (ms) in each sentence region for human subjects. Both GPT-2 and humans show increased processing difficulty when the sentence is ambiguous between two structural interpretations.

surprisal on the y-axis. We can see that, as per our prediction, the [REDUCED, AM-BIGUOUS] condition induces higher surprisal than any of the other conditions in the critical region (the main verb). To compare model-derived surprisal to word-by-word processing times in human subjects, we show reading time data from Vani et al., 2021 on the y-axis of the bottom plot. Processing times are collected using the Maze task (Boyce et al., 2020; Forster et al., 2009), an experimental paradigm in which partici-pants read through a sentence one word at a time. For each word, they must select between a correct and plausible continuation and an implausible distractor word. The time that it takes to make this selection has been shown to be a good measure of incremental processing difficulty, with reduced spillover effects, which are a common feature of other incremental processing measures, such as self-paced-reading (Boyce et al., 2020). By framing the model's incremental predictions as surprisal values, we can see how its behaviour is strikingly similar to that of human subjects in two key ways. First, we find increased RTs and surprisal values for passive participles (i.e., for *given*) in the [REDUCED, UNAMBIGUOUS] condition. And more importantly, we see hugely elevated RTs and surprisal values in the critical region for the [REDUCED, AMBIGUOUS] condition. Overall, these results compatible with the hypothesis that models, like humans, are deriving different structural interpretations of the different conditions, which drive expectation for upcoming material.

One extremely revealing and previously unreported pattern shows up in these data. Even though the verb *given* unambiguously introduces a relative clause, we find that GPT-2 is still slightly "gardenpathed" by it. That is, we find elevated surprisal at *tripped* in the critical region for the [REDUCED, UNAMBIGUOUS] condition (dotted red line). This same 'gardenpath ghost' effect shows up in human reading times, too, where we find elevated RTs for 'tripped' in the same condition. Traces of this effect have been observed in previous studies (F. Ferreira, P.C.), however, the increased sensitivity of the Maze task means Vani et al., 2021 is the first to report the effect as significant. For humans, this effect could be explained by a noisy channel process (Shannon, 1956), which has been hypothesised to be at-play in a number of language processing phenomena (Levy, 2008a). The string "The woman given..." may be so unlikely that participants re-interpret it as the active past-tense "The woman gave...", which leads to a garden-path effect, with similar re-interpretations for other items in the test suite. However, it is unclear whether and how models could implement such reinterpretation. Thus, these data present an interesting and open question that demands further investigation.

6.4 DEPENDENCIES, SCOPE, AND BINDING

In this section, we take a look at the syntactic generalisations learned by GPT-2 that have to do with the co-variation between individual lexical items and phrasal units that are "smaller" than CPs, particularly Noun Phrases.

6.4.1 Filler–Gap Dependencies

Filler–gap dependencies are dependencies between a *filler* (a wh-word such as *who* or *what*) and a gap, which is an empty syntactic position (denoted with underscores in examples below). The relationship is a true bidirectional dependency, in that the presence of a filler necessitates the presence a downstream gap, and gaps are not licensed in the absence of an upstream filler. We assess whether GPT-2 has learned this dependency by creating a test suite with four conditions, outlined in (7). If the model has learned that gaps must be licensed by a filler, then after encountering a transitive verb, the model should expect an NP. Thus, skipping over the NP gap and proceeding directly to an indirect object (*to the patient*) should be less surprising when a filler is present compared to when it is absent. That is, at the indirect object, $S_{[+\text{FILLER}, +\text{GAP}]} < S_{[-\text{FILLER}, +\text{GAP}]}$ (Prediction 1). Conversely, if the model has learned that fillers set up expectations for gaps that must be discharged at likely gap sites, then the direct object of a verb *the new medicine* should be more likely in the absence of a filler than in its presence. That is, at the direct object, $S_{[-\text{FILLER}, -\text{GAP}]} < S_{[+\text{FILLER}, -\text{GAP}]}$ (Prediction 2). For both of these predictions, in order

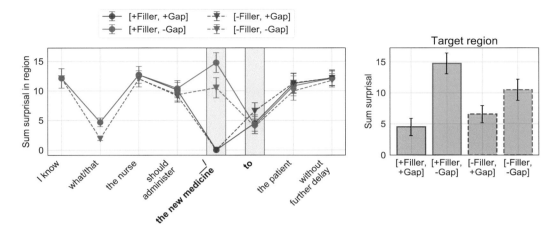

Figure 6.4 Filler–Gap Dependencies (Object Gap). Left: sum GPT-2-derived surprisal in each sentence region, averaged across items in test suite. Surprisal values at the object position in the +GAP conditions are shown as 0 for visualisation purposes. Note that the target region is different for +/−GAP conditions (as indicated by red and blue outlines, respectively). Right: average surprisal summed over target region for each condition. GPT-2 output is consistent with the bidirectional dependency between fillers and gaps in object position.

to appropriately set up expectations for either objects or gaps in object position, we used obligatorily transitive verbs, such as *administer* in our example below.[2]

(7)   Filler–Gap Dependencies

   a.   I remember what the nurse should administer ___ to the patient without further delay. [+FILLER, +GAP]

   b.   *I remember what the nurse should administer <u>the new medicine</u> to the patient without further delay. [+FILLER, -GAP]

   c.   *I remember that the nurse should administer ___ to the patient without further delay. [-FILLER, +GAP]

   d.   I remember that the nurse should administer <u>the new medicine</u> to the patient without further delay. [-FILLER, -GAP]

The results for this experiment are shown in Figure 6.4, with each sentence region on the x-axis and summed surprisal for all the words in that region on the y-axis. As expected from Prediction 1, we find that the post-gap preposition is higher surprisal in the [-FILLER, +GAP] condition than in the [+FILLER, +GAP] condition. The model has an accuracy score of 95.8% for this prediction. Turning towards Prediction 2, GPT-2 exhibits higher surprisal in the filled argument position when a filler is present (i.e., in [+FILLER, -GAP]) compared to when it is absent ([-FILLER, -GAP]), and the model is 100% accurate for this prediction. These high scores suggest that the model has learned the correct bidirectional dependency between fillers and gaps. See

---

[2]These tests are adapted from Wilcox, Levy, Morita, et al., 2018; for a fuller discussion of the paradigm see Wilcox, Futrell, et al., 2021.

`www.syntaxgym.org` for suites that test gaps in subject and indirect object position, for which we find similar, high accuracy performance.

6.4.1.1 Island constraints

Filler–gap dependencies have played an outsised role in generative linguistics, in part because they are one of the few dependencies that are claimed to be truly unbounded. Gaps can be licensed by fillers that are an arbitrary (and possibly infinite!) number of nodes away in a phrase structure. But while the dependency is potentially unbounded in length, it is not entirely unconstrained. For example, gaps are licensed in subject, object, or indirect object position in embedded clauses, but gaps are not licensed when they appear in an adjunct phrase attached to the clause, as demonstrated in (8).

(8)   * I know who the nurse admitted the patient after inspecting ___ yesterday night.

The structural constraints on filler–gap dependency are known as island constraints (Ross, 1967). Island constraints have been one of the core empirical patterns cited as evidence for Nativist approaches to language (Phillips, 2013)—children within the same language community learn island constraints without any direct supervision, and the same types of structural configurations give rise to island constraints in un-related languages. A handful of recent studies (Wilcox, Futrell, et al., 2021; E. Wilcox, Levy, and Futrell, 2019; Wilcox, Levy, Morita, et al., 2018) have assessed whether or not ANN models can learn island constraints using the following methodology: If the model has learned that fillers do not license gaps in islands, then the presence of an upstream filler should not impact the surprisal of a gap inside island structures. That is, in (8), *yesterday* should not be any more or less likely in a minimal-pair counterpart without a filler. Wilcox, Futrell, et al., 2021 find that GPT-2 successfully attenuates its expectations for gaps inside island constructions for eight of the most-studied islands, including adjuncts, suggesting that it has learned the proper grammatical generalisations for the distribution of the filler–gap dependency in English.

Below, we build upon this work and provide one example of the learning limits for GPT-2. While it is true that gaps are not licensed in adjunct clauses in English, there is one exception to this rule: They may be if the adjunct directly follows a clause which hosts a gap, as in (9-d). In this case, the gap inside the adjunct clause is said to be 'parasitic' on the embedded clause gap, and this construction is referred to as the *parasitic gap* construction (Engdahl, 1983; Ross, 1967). To test whether models have learned such adverb phrases as the legitimate loci of gaps, we created sentences following (9), where the HOSTGAP factor indicates variation in the host gap, not the 'parasitic' gap. Two types of sentences were created, one like (9) below where the adverb phrase included a gerund verb, and one in which the verb was tensed. If models have learned the parasitic gap construction, we would expect no difference in surprisal based on the presence of a filler in the -HOSTGAP condition (which is effectively an island). However, we would expect surprisal to be affected by

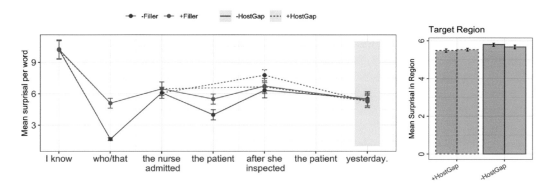

Figure 6.5 **Parasitic Gaps.** If GPT-2 had learned parasitic gaps, we would expect a difference in surprisal between +/-FILLER in the +HOSTGAP condition but not in the -HOSTGAP condition. We see no difference between conditions, indicating that GPT-2 has not learned the proper generalisation.

the presence or absence of a filler in the +HOSTGAP condition, where the presence of a wh-word renders the whole sentence grammatical.[3]

(9)   Parasitic Gaps
    a.   *I know that the nurse admitted the patient after she inspected __ yester-
         day. [-FILLER, -HOSTGAP]
    b.   *I know who the nurse admitted the patient after she inspected __ yester-
         day. [+FILLER, -HOSTGAP]
    c.   *I know that the nurse admitted __ after she inspected __ yesterday. [-
         FILLER, +HOSTGAP]
    d.   I know who the nurse admitted __ after she inspected __ yesterday.
         [+FILLER, +HOSTGAP]

The results of this experiment are shown in Figure 6.5, with mean by-region surprisal on the y-axis. While there is no difference in surprisal based on the presence of an upstream filler in the -HOSTGAP condition, as expected, we also find no effect of *filler* in the +HOSTGAP, which should be the case if the model has learned the proper generalisation.

6.4.2   Reflexive Anaphora

Anaphoric pronouns form dependencies with referring noun phrases (or r-expressions), with which they co-refer. For example, in (10), the anaphoric pronoun *herself* refers to the antecedent *The author with the senators*.

---

[3]We do not include the -GAP conditions, as we predict the expectations for gaps set up by wh-complementisers to be fully discharged at the first gap site. These expectations correspond to the contrast in grammaticality between the filled-gap version of our basic tests (*I know what you read *the paper*.) compared to the filled-gap version of a parasitic gap sentence (*I know what you read ___ before shredding *the paper*.)

(10)   The author with the senators hurt herself.

Unlike fillers and gaps, anaphoric dependencies are not bidirectional: although an anaphoric pronoun requires an r-expression, r-expressions may be used freely without subsequent pronouns. However, like fillers and gaps, the relationship is subject to a number of restrictions, including that the r-expression and pronoun must match in gender and number features and, structurally, that the r-expression must $c-$command the anaphor (Carnie, 2021). To test whether the models have learned the dependency, as well as its structural restrictions, we create test suites following (11). Each sentence contains an anaphoric pronoun, a head-noun that $c-$commands the pronoun, and a modifying prepositional phrase with a secondary noun that does not $c-$command the pronoun. There are four conditions: The head-noun can either be SINGULAR or PLURAL, and it can either MATCH or MISMATCH with the anaphoric pronoun in terms of number. We run two suites of tests, one with feminine anaphoric pronouns like (11), and one with masculine anaphoric pronouns.[4] For these sentences, the non-$c-$commanding NPs always mismatch with the head noun, meaning that they are all "distractors" that could possibly trick the model into expecting the wrong number on the pronoun. If the model has learned the correct generalisations, then it should exhibit lower surprisal in the MATCH condition, both when the head NP is plural (Prediction 1) and singular (Prediction 2).

(11)   Reflexive Anaphora: Number Agreement
    a.   The author with the senators hurt herself. [MATCH, SING]
    b.   The author with the senators hurt themselves. [MISMATCH, SING]
    c.   The authors with the senator hurt themselves. [MATCH, PLURAL]
    d.   The authors with the senator hurt herself. [MISMATCH, PLURAL]

The results for this experiment are shown in Figure 6.6. Beginning with masculine anaphoric pronouns (top), we find that GPT-2 is 89% accurate for both Prediction 1 (plural agreement) and Prediction 2 (singular agreement). Turning to the feminine anaphoric pronoun (bottom), for Prediction 1 GPT-2 is 100% accurate; however, for Prediction 2, where the model must correctly predict a singular pronoun, the model is only 21% accurate. This indicates that the model is distracted by the number mismatching NP in the prepositional clause, but only in cases where the pronoun is feminine.

6.4.3   Negative Polarity Items

Negative Polarity Items (NPIs) are a class of polarity-sensitive items, which must appear in downward-entailing environments, or contexts that license inferences from supersets to subsets (Chierchia, 2013). One way to construct these environments is with negative quantifiers, such as the English determiner *no*. In order for the NPI to be in the scope of the negative quantifier, it must be $c-$commanded by it, thus we can set up suites to determine whether or not GPT-2 has learned the relevant structural

---

[4]Note that while anaphors must agree in gender with the r-expression, we do not test this generalisation.

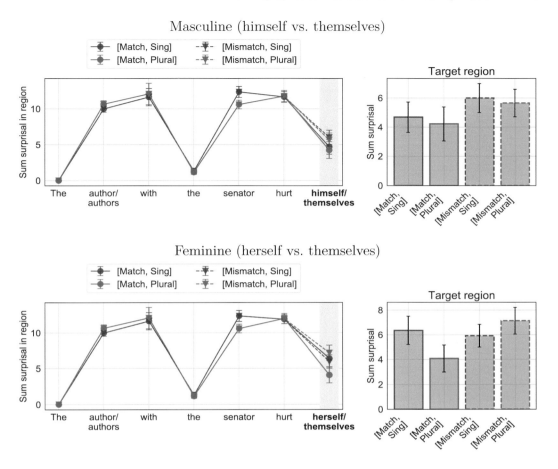

Figure 6.6 **Reflexive Anaphora (Number Agreement).** Top: masculine reflexive pronoun. Bottom: feminine reflexive pronoun. GPT-2 output is broadly consistent with the expected agreement pattern, except in the case where it must correctly predict a singular feminine pronoun ("herself").

relationship that are similar to the tests used for anaphoric pronouns, schematised in (12). Sentences have an NPI, *any*, and a subject NP that contains either a negative determiner or a positive determiner (*the*). Each subject NP is modified with a relative clause whose subject likewise contains either a negative or positive determiner. If models have learned the correct rules for NPI licensing, then surprisal at the NPI should be lower for conditions where the subject NP is headed with *no* than for conditions where it is headed with *the*. We formulate this in terms of three predictions: at the NPI, $S_{[\text{NEG, NEG}]} < S_{[\text{POS, NEG}]}$ (Prediction 1), $S_{[\text{NEG, POS}]} < S_{[\text{POS, NEG}]}$ (Prediction 2), and $S_{[\text{NEG, POS}]} < S_{[\text{POS, POS}]}$ (Prediction 3).

(12)   Negative Polarity Item Licensing

    a.   No author that the senators liked has had any success. [NEG, POS]

    b.   No author that no senators liked has had any success. [NEG, NEG]

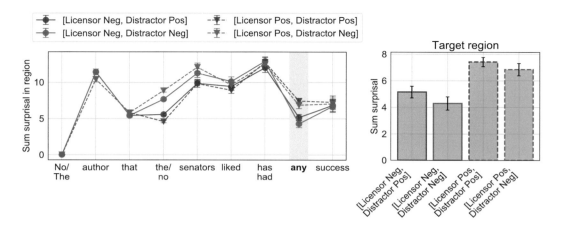

Figure 6.7   Negative Polarity Item Licensing. Left: sum GPT-2-derived surprisal in each sentence region, averaged across items in the test suite. Right: average surprisal summed over the target region for each condition. GPT-2 output is consistent with the structural relationships licensing negative polarity items.

    c. *The author that the senators liked has had any success. [POS, POS]
    d. *The author that no senators liked has had any success. [POS, NEG]

The results for this experiment are shown in Figure 6.7, with sentence regions on the x-axis and surprisal on the y-axis. We find that the model is 100% accurate for Prediction 1, and 97% accurate for Predictions 2 and Prediction 3, suggesting that it has learned the proper generalisations for NPI licensing in English.

6.5 DISCUSSION

The previous sections have introduced several assessments of GPT-2's syntactic capacity. First, we tested the model's ability to represent abstract categories like CPs and NPs, as well as the relationships between them. We next evaluated its ability to learn rules about lexical dependencies, including negative polarity items, anaphoric pronouns, and even empty syntactic positions (gaps). We found that, in the vast majority of cases, GPT-2 successfully learned the relevant grammatical generalisations: the model achieves above 90% accuracy for predictions on suites testing for Subordination, Relative Clause completion, Filler–Gap dependencies, and NPI Licensing. There were two notable cases, however, where the model did not make human-like predictions. These were for predictions about the feminine anaphoric pronoun, *herself*, as well as for cases of *parasitic gaps*, when gaps that appear in typically ungrammatical positions can exist 'parasitically' on the presence of a previous host gap.

What do these results—many positive, some negative—mean for our theoretical understanding of human linguistic cognition? The type of answer that we will explore here is that they can bear on a series of questions about the "origin" of linguistic structures, associated with the generative tradition in linguistics. These questions include: What learning biases do children bring to the task of language acquisition?

How do language learners generalise from the linguistic stimulus with which they are presented? To what extent does linguistic cognition recruit domain general (i.e., not language-specific) processes and representations? And to what extent are rules and generalisations about linguistic structure separate from rules and generalisations about linguistic meaning? Below, we introduce three frameworks for answering these interrelated questions and present the role that the learning outcomes of ANNs can play for each. Finally, we discuss how our results might motivate future development for each approach.

Before moving on to the three interpretive frameworks, we want to return to an issue mentioned during the introduction: the issue of data scale and how it interacts with syntactic generalisation. Because we do not know, precisely, what syntactic structures are present in GPT-2's ~8 billion training tokens, it may be premature to say that our tests capture genuine syntactic generalisation as opposed to, say, mere recapitulation of its training data. In order to interrogate this concern, we want to distinguish between two forms of generalisation—compositional generalisation and what we will call lexico-categorical generalisation. Let's consider the case of Negative Polarity Items, discussed in Section 6.4.3. We argued that what the experiment in this section showed was that GPT-2 had learned that NPIs require negative licensors and also that NPIs must exist in a certain structural relationship *vis a vis* their licensor, using target sentences of the form "*No* + NP + Relative Clause (RC) + *any...*" Now, we can imagine the model learning the structural relationship in two possible ways. First, it could be the case that the model was never exposed to sentences that were structurally similar to our target sentence during training. Rather, the model saw training sentences like (a) "No + NP + *any...*" and (b) "No + NP + RC...". If this were the case, in order to produce the observed behaviour, the model would have to make generalisations about a novel frame by composing (a) and (b) together. This would be an example of compositional generalisation. On the other hand, it may be the case that the model did have experience with sentences of the form "No + NP + RC + *any...*". In this case, in order to produce the correct behaviour, the model had to recognise our target items as similar, and flexibly extend the generalisations it had made during training to sentences that are realised with different items, but share the same structural properties. This would be an example of lexico-categorical generalisation.

Because the experiments we have presented do not control the types of syntactic structures available to the model during training, many of the conclusions we can draw are about lexico-categorical generalisation, rather than compositional generalisation (although our tests certainly don't rule out the latter). But we don't want to downplay the importance of lexico-categorical generalisation. In order to flexibly extend grammatical knowledge, models must learn that words fall into abstract categories and must learn to formulate distributional rules at the level of the category rather than at the level of the word. Both of these behaviours are key features of human linguistic cognition, and they are being learned, here, by a domain-general artificial learning algorithm. Below, we turn back to our main discussion by introducing three interpretive frameworks for understanding the role of GPT-2's learning outcomes.

6.5.1 Syntactic Nativism

This framework posits that language acquisition is powered by innately given and language-specific (rather than domain-general) processes and representations. A primary task of language acquisition is to derive the syntactic generalisations underlying grammatical adult speech using these inbuilt processes and representations. Traditionally, syntactic nativism is motivated by a type of logical argument called The Argument from the Poverty of the Stimulus (APS; Chomsky, 1975; Clark and Lappin, 2010; Legate and Yang, 2002; Pullum and Scholz, 2002). We can present the APS with the following four premises: (i) For a given linguistic generalisation (or rule), it is either learned via a language-specific learning process or via a domain-general learning process. (ii) The linguistic data a child is exposed to are compatible with a large number of possible generalisations $L_0 \ldots L_n$ and yet (iii) the child ends up learning the generalisations associated with their actual language, L_0. (iv) There are no domain-general learning processes that favour L_0 over $L_1 \ldots L_n$. Therefore, the generalisation could not have been learned via a domain-general learning process.

Positive results demonstrating the human-like syntactic behaviour of ANNs complicate premise (iv). If an algorithm that is sufficiently domain general can be found that *does* learn the correct generalisations, given an appropriate approximation of a child's linguistic input, then premise (iv) must be restricted to a smaller set of phenomena. Note, however, that the previous reasoning hinges on three premises: (a) The learning model must be sufficiently domain general; (b) it must have learned the correct generalisation; and (c) its training data must be a "reasonable enough" approximation of the linguistic stimulus of a human child. As for (a), although ANNs – like any learning algorithm – do possess bias, their architecture is designed to handle arbitrary relationships between arbitrary pieces of input, and they have been successfully deployed in a number of domains. Much of the introduction presented an argument that the psycholinguistic assessment paradigm successfully solves (b). This leaves us with (c): Is GPT-2's training data (or the training data of any ANN) a close-enough approximation of the human linguistic stimulus for these models to play a valid role in winnowing down the scope of the APS? There are a number of dimensions along which this question could be asked, including genre, size, and modality, all of which reveal large differences between a human child and GPT-2. In terms of genre, children learn with the assistance of child-directed speech (Rowe, 2008), while GPT-2 was trained on an adult-directed corpus of web text; in terms of size, GPT-2 was trained on about eight lifetimes of human linguistic experience; and in terms of modality, GPT-2 was trained on pre-segmented text, whereas children must induce the relevant representations from the speech stream.

Although these differences are a serious consideration, we believe that they do not rule out the learning outcomes of ANNs as a novel piece of empirical evidence that bears on the APS. As far as genre, if the purpose of child-directed speech is (in part) to assist the child in making the relevant syntactic generalisations, then adult-directed language may pose a more difficult dataset from which to make the necessary syntactic generalisations. Additionally, there is evidence that speech genre does not play an important role in language learning, including a number of cultures that do not practice child-directed speech (Cristia et al., 2019; Weber et al., 2017). Turning towards dataset size, we have focused on GPT-2 because it is one well-studied model that represents the state of the art in machine learning. However, many of the tests presented in this chapter have been conducted on models trained with much smaller datasets (Wilcox, Futrell, et al., 2021), even including a version of GPT-2 trained on the equivalent of the linguistic experience of a four-year old (Hu et al., 2020). In addition, some recurrence-based models, such as the one presented in Gulordava et al., 2018 which was trained on the linguistic experience of an 8-year-old, have shown remarkable success at learning hierarchical-sensitive dependencies. Finally, given the rapid advances in machine learning and recent focus on low-resource and computationally efficient natural language processing, we believe that the amount of data required to learn crucial syntactic generalisations from string input alone will decrease in the future.

6.5.2   Syntactic Emergentism (Non-Syntactic Nativism)

This framework posits that human language learners are endowed with certain (potentially domain-specific) structural biases, but these biases are semantic or logical in nature. Syntactic generalisations such as part of speech, hierarchical relationships and locality constraints are an emergent property, either supervening on patterns in the semantic structures that underlie utterances, or else resulting from fixed constraints in the mapping between these structures and linear-order forms.

Under the syntactic emergentist framework, ANNs provide a positive example of the emergence of syntactic behaviour from a suitably domain-general model, paired with a proxy for the task of human communication. Compare this to the role for ANNs under more nativist approaches, where they are useful only so far as they can provide counter-argument against the APS but not as constructive hypotheses in their own right about how language is learned and implemented. Under this framework, what should be learned from cases where models are not able to learn the relevant facts about syntax? One constructive approach, we suggest, is that these phenomena may point to cases where the relevant structures are acquired either through non-syntactic learning pressures or processing constraints.

6.5.3   Full Emergentism

This framework treats human linguistic knowledge as an emergent phenomenon which arises from the interaction of multiple simple units of an interconnected network (Elman, 1990, 1991; McClelland et al., 1986). The task of language acquisition is to derive syntactic generalisations which accurately replicate the observed distribution of human language. Under this view, ANNs are concrete algorithmic hypotheses — a candidate solution for representing and processing syntactic structures. This position has been summarised recently by Baroni (Chapter 1 of this volume), who suggests that it would be fruitful to take ANNs seriously as "algorithmic linguistic theories making predictions about utterance acceptability." One attractive feature of this approach is that, as far as they are instantiations of a particular theory, ANNs make clear, and explicit predictions about unseen data. Thus, even for researchers who may be averse to emergent approaches to language, ANNs can provide useful baselines against which to clarify and compare algebraic models of linguistic phenomena. Here, however, instead of focusing on unseen data and untested structural phenomena, we have instead focused on providing a sanity check. Does GPT-2 produce reasonable predictions for well-studied syntactic phenomena?

Our results demonstrate that a wide range of syntactic phenomena can emerge from the simple task of predicting the next word, providing strong empirical support for the emergentist perspective. However, model failure to capture some aspects of syntax suggest that in addition to generating novel predictions about untested syntactic structures, researchers may want to continue developing and testing new models on the well-studied grammatical phenomena discussed in this chapter.

BIBLIOGRAPHY

Baroni, Marco (2022). "On the proper role of linguistically-oriented deep net analysis in linguistic theorizing". In: *Algebraic Structures in Natural Language*. Ed. by Shalom Lappin and Jean-Philippe Bernardy. Taylor and Francis.

Boyce, Veronica, Richard Futrell, and Roger P Levy (2020). "Maze Made Easy: Better and easier measurement of incremental processing difficulty". In: *Journal of Memory and Language* 111, p. 104082.

Brothers, Trevor and Gina R Kuperberg (2021). "Word predictability effects are linear, not logarithmic: Implications for probabilistic models of sentence comprehension". In: *Journal of Memory and Language* 116, p. 104174.

Brown, Tom B, Benjamin Mann, Nick Ryder, Melanie Subbiah, Jared Kaplan, Prafulla Dhariwal, Arvind Neelakantan, Pranav Shyam, Girish Sastry, Amanda Askell, et al. (2020). "Language models are few-shot learners". In: *arXiv preprint arXiv:2005.14165*.

Carnie, Andrew (2021). *Syntax: A generative introduction*. John Wiley & Sons.

Chen, Mark, Alec Radford, Rewon Child, Jeffrey Wu, Heewoo Jun, David Luan, and Ilya Sutskever (2020). "Generative pretraining from pixels". In: *International Conference on Machine Learning*. PMLR, pp. 1691–1703.

Chierchia, Gennaro (2013). *Logic in grammar: Polarity, free choice, and intervention*. OUP Oxford.

Chomsky, Noam (1975). "The logical structure of linguistic theory". In:

Clark, Alexander and Shalom Lappin (2010). *Linguistic Nativism and the Poverty of the Stimulus*. John Wiley & Sons.

Cristia, Alejandrina, Emmanuel Dupoux, Michael Gurven, and Jonathan Stieglitz (2019). "Child-Directed speech is infrequent in a forager-farmer population: a time allocation study". In: *Child Development* 90.3, pp. 759–773.

Dosovitskiy, Alexey, Lucas Beyer, Alexander Kolesnikov, Dirk Weissenborn, Xiaohua Zhai, Thomas Unterthiner, Mostafa Dehghani, Matthias Minderer, Georg Heigold, Sylvain Gelly, Jakob Uszkoreit, and Neil Houlsby (2021). "An Image is Worth 16x16 Words: Transformers for Image Recognition at Scale". In: *International Conference on Learning Representations*. URL: https://openreview.net/forum?id=YicbFdNTTy.

Elman, Jeffrey L (1990). "Finding structure in time". In: *Cognitive Science* 14.2, pp. 179–211.

— (1991). "Distributed representations, simple recurrent networks, and grammatical structure". In: *Machine Learning* 7.2-3, pp. 195–225.

Engdahl, Elisabet (1983). "Parasitic gaps". In: *Linguistics and Philosophy*, pp. 5–34.

Ferreira, Fernanda, Kiel Christianson, and Andrew Hollingworth (2001). "Misinterpretations of garden-path sentences: Implications for models of sentence processing and reanalysis". In: *Journal of Psycholinguistic Research* 30.1, pp. 3–20.

Ferreira, Fernanda and John M Henderson (1991). "Recovery from misanalyses of garden-path sentences". In: *Journal of Memory and Language* 30.6, pp. 725–745.

Forster, Kenneth I, Christine Guerrera, and Lisa Elliot (2009). "The maze task: Measuring forced incremental sentence processing time". In: *Behavior Research Methods* 41.1, pp. 163–171.

Futrell, Richard, Ethan Wilcox, Takashi Morita, and Roger Levy (2018). "RNNs as psycholinguistic subjects: Syntactic state and grammatical dependency". In: *arXiv preprint arXiv:1809.01329*.

Gauthier, Jon, Jennifer Hu, Ethan Wilcox, Peng Qian, and Roger Levy (2020). "SyntaxGym: An online platform for targeted evaluation of language models". In: *Proceedings of the 58th Annual Meeting of the Association for Computational Linguistics: System Demonstrations*, pp. 70–76.

Giulianelli, Mario, Jack Harding, Florian Mohnert, Dieuwke Hupkes, and Willem Zuidema (2018). "Under the hood: Using diagnostic classifiers to investigate and improve how language models track agreement information". In: *arXiv preprint arXiv:1808.08079*.

Goldberg, Yoav and Jon Orwant (2013). "A dataset of syntactic-ngrams over time from a very large corpus of english books". In:

Goodkind, Adam and Klinton Bicknell (2018). "Predictive power of word surprisal for reading times is a linear function of language model quality". In: *Proceedings of the 8th Workshop on Cognitive Modeling and Computational Linguistics (CMCL 2018)*, pp. 10–18.

Gulordava, Kristina, Piotr Bojanowski, Edouard Grave, Tal Linzen, and Marco Baroni (2018). "Colorless green recurrent networks dream hierarchically". In: *arXiv preprint arXiv:1803.11138*.

Hale, John (2001). "A probabilistic Earley parser as a psycholinguistic model". In: *Proceedings of the Second Meeting of the North American Chapter of the Association for Computational Linguistics on Language Technologies*. Association for Computational Linguistics, pp. 1–8.

Hart, Betty and Todd R Risley (1995). *Meaningful differences in the everyday experience of young American children*. Paul H Brookes Publishing.

Hewitt, John, Michael Hahn, Surya Ganguli, Percy Liang, and Christopher D Manning (2020). "RNNs can generate bounded hierarchical languages with optimal memory". In: *arXiv preprint arXiv:2010.07515*.

Hewitt, John and Christopher D Manning (2019). "A structural probe for finding syntax in word representations". In: *Proceedings of the 2019 Conference of the*

North American Chapter of the Association for Computational Linguistics: Human Language Technologies, Volume 1 (Long and Short Papers), pp. 4129–4138.

Hochreiter, Sepp and Jürgen Schmidhuber (1997). "Long short-term memory". In: *Neural computation* 9.8, pp. 1735–1780.

Hu, Jennifer, Jon Gauthier, Peng Qian, Ethan Wilcox, and Roger Levy (July 2020). "A Systematic Assessment of Syntactic Generalization in Neural Language Models". In: *Proceedings of the 58th Annual Meeting of the Association for Computational Linguistics*. Online: Association for Computational Linguistics, pp. 1725–1744. DOI: 10.18653/v1/2020.acl-main.158. URL: https://aclanthology.org/2020.acl-main.158.

Jozefowicz, Rafal, Oriol Vinyals, Mike Schuster, Noam Shazeer, and Yonghui Wu (2016). "Exploring the limits of language modeling". In: *arXiv preprint arXiv:1602.02410*.

Kuperberg, Gina R and T Florian Jaeger (2016). "What do we mean by prediction in language comprehension?" In: *Language, Cognition and Neuroscience* 31.1, pp. 32–59.

Legate, Julie Anne and Charles D Yang (2002). "Empirical re-assessment of stimulus poverty arguments". In: *The Linguistic Review* 18.1-2, pp. 151–162.

Levy, Roger (2008a). "A noisy-channel model of human sentence comprehension under uncertain input". In: *Proceedings of the 2008 conference on empirical methods in natural language processing*, pp. 234–243.

— (2008b). "Expectation-based syntactic comprehension". In: *Cognition* 106.3, pp. 1126–1177.

Linzen, Tal, Emmanuel Dupoux, and Yoav Goldberg (2016). "Assessing the ability of LSTMs to learn syntax-sensitive dependencies". In: *Transactions of the Association for Computational Linguistics* 4, pp. 521–535.

McClelland, James L, David E Rumelhart, PDP Research Group, et al. (1986). *Parallel distributed processing*. Vol. 2. MIT Press Cambridge, MA.

Phillips, Colin (2013). "On the nature of island constraints II: Language learning and innateness". In: *Experimental syntax and island effects*, pp. 132–157.

Pritchett, Bradley L (1988). "Garden path phenomena and the grammatical basis of language processing". In: *Language*, pp. 539–576.

Pullum, Geoffrey K and Barbara C Scholz (2002). "Empirical assessment of stimulus poverty arguments". In: *The Linguistic Review* 18.1-2, pp. 9–50.

Radford, Alec, Jeffrey Wu, Rewon Child, David Luan, Dario Amodei, and Ilya Sutskever (2019). "Language models are unsupervised multitask learners". In: *OpenAI Blog* 1.8.

Rives, Alexander, Joshua Meier, Tom Sercu, Siddharth Goyal, Zeming Lin, Jason Liu, Demi Guo, Myle Ott, C Lawrence Zitnick, Jerry Ma, et al. (2021). "Biological structure and function emerge from scaling unsupervised learning to 250 million protein sequences". In: *Proceedings of the National Academy of Sciences* 118.15.

Ross, John Robert (1967). "Constraints on variables in syntax." In:

Rowe, Meredith L (2008). "Child-directed speech: Relation to socioeconomic status, knowledge of child development and child vocabulary skill". In: *Journal of Child Language* 35.1, pp. 185–205.

Shannon, Claude (1956). "The zero error capacity of a noisy channel". In: *IRE Transactions on Information Theory* 2.3, pp. 8–19.

Smith, Nathaniel J and Roger Levy (2013). "The effect of word predictability on reading time is logarithmic". In: *Cognition* 128.3, pp. 302–319.

van Schijndel, M., & Linzen T. (2018). "Modeling garden path effects without explicit hierarchical syntax. In *Proceedings of the 40th annual meeting of the Cognitive Science Society (CogSci)* (pp. 2603–2608). Austin, TX: Cognitive Science Society." In: *CogSci*.

— (2021). "Single-Stage Prediction Models Do Not Explain the Magnitude of Syntactic Disambiguation Difficulty". In: *Cognitive Science* 45.6, e12988.

Vani, Pranali, Ethan Wilcox, and Roger Levy (2021). "I(nterpolated) Maze: High-sensitivity measurement of ungrammatical input processing". In: URL: `https://www.cuny2021.io/wp-content/uploads/2021/02/CUNY_2021_abstract_339.pdf`.

Vaswani, Ashish, Noam Shazeer, Niki Parmar, Jakob Uszkoreit, Llion Jones, Aidan N Gomez, Łukasz Kaiser, and Illia Polosukhin (2017). "Attention is all you need". In: *Advances in neural information processing systems*, pp. 5998–6008.

Weber, Ann, Anne Fernald, and Yatma Diop (2017). "When cultural norms discourage talking to babies: Effectiveness of a parenting program in rural Senegal". In: *Child Development* 88.5, pp. 1513–1526.

Wilcox, Ethan Gotlieb, Jon Gauthier, Jennifer Hu, Peng Qian, and Roger Levy (2020). "On the Predictive Power of Neural Language Models for Human Real-Time Comprehension Behavior". In: *arXiv preprint arXiv:2006.01912*.

Wilcox, Ethan, Richard Futrell, and Roger Levy (2021). "Using Computational Models to Test Syntactic Learnability". In: *Lingbuzz Preprint: lingbuzz/006327*.

Wilcox, Ethan, Roger Levy, and Richard Futrell (2019). "Hierarchical Representation in Neural Language Models: Suppression and Recovery of Expectations". In: *arXiv preprint arXiv:1906.04068*.

Wilcox, Ethan, Roger Levy, Takashi Morita, and Richard Futrell (2018). "What do RNN Language Models Learn about Filler-Gap Dependencies?" In: *arXiv preprint arXiv:1809.00042*.

CHAPTER 7

Analysing Discourse Knowledge in Pre-Trained Language Models: From Constructed Data to Deep Neural Networks

Sharid Loáiciga

University of Gothenburg

CONTENTS

ABSTRACT

Two case studies, discourse deixis and discourse entity representations, are presented in this chapter as examples of central themes in theories of discourse representation that can also be explored by means of deep neural network (DNN) models.

DOI: 10.1201/9781003205388-7

We argue in favour of a methodology combining the controlled settings of psycholinguistic experimentation with the large coverage of current computational linguistics approaches using DNN models.

In the case of discourse deixis, we first show experiments using standard psycholinguistic constructed examples and contrast them with experiments using corpus data. In both of these sets of experiments, the verbs participating in the causative-inchoative alternation have an effect on the choice between an event or entity antecedent for the pronouns *it/this*. Then, we propose a method to identify verbs presenting this property in an unsupervised way using pre-trained language models. In the case of discourse entity representations, we test the sensitivity of pre-trained language models to different referring expressions re-mentioning the same entity.

The results of the experiments relying on DNNs turned out to be inconclusive, but they illustrate some of the challenges and advantages in scaling up the methods from psycholinguistics in order to test linguistic generalisations from theories of discourse representation.

7.1 INTRODUCTION

Formal models of discourse structure and interpretation build meaning representations by describing how events and entities are introduced and how they evolve throughout the discourse. They describe them using true or false conditions about their temporal and aspectual features, the participants involved, and the logical relations between them. In contrast, the linguistic representations that deep learning models build are targeted towards solving highly specific tasks and are less intelligible, thus motivating a surge in probing approaches. In this chapter, we look at two study cases, discourse deixis and entity representations. We look into what discourse theories have contributed to the analysis of these phenomena and what we can learn using deep learning models.

Discourse theories describe context as a series of segments joined by a complex system of constraint verification. The validation or not of the verification constraints permits the construction of coherence, the resolution of anaphoric phenomena and the disambiguation of tense and aspect. Since they are not only focused on written discourse but also on dialog, they take into account speaker phenomena such as presupposition and intentions.

Two well known such theories are Discourse Representation Theory (DRT) (Kamp and Reyle, 1993) and Centering Theory (CT) (Grosz and Sidner, 1986). These are theories that model the interpretation of discourse. As such, they are complex and intricate, modelling many levels of linguistic phenomena. It follows that algebraic systems developed specifically for these theories will be equally complex and intertwined, presumably part of the reasons why they are not the prevalent paradigm. DRT and CT are frequently cited in the discourse literature, but systems built on top of these type of theories have not developed as successfully as those we have seen with deep neural network (DNN) approaches.

DNNs, on the other hand, are not theories but task solving machines. One key aspect of the success of machine learning for discourse modelling is the division of this daunting interpretation task into subtasks. As a result, discourse segmentation, discourse relation parsing, temporal parsing, coreference resolution, and event coreference are conceived as different tasks, and many of them are subdivided into even more specific tasks such as bridging anaphora resolution. This subdivision of the large discourse interpretation task has paved the way for incredible results on the individual tasks, but at the same time discouraged the development of the theoretical exploration of discourse phenomena.

Here we argue in favour of using DNN approaches not only for pushing the baselines of the tasks we have and the tasks yet to come, but also for studying their limits and learning capabilities in order to inform theoretical linguistic knowledge of discourse. DNNs have proved more than adequate for a number of tasks and research geared towards understanding the extent of their potential might give us new theoretical insights regarding discourse.

Taking a cue from the syntax-level studies interested in the properties of DNNs (Baroni, 2022; Kulmizev and Nivre, 2021), and given the current renewed interest in discourse problems such as discourse parsing, coherence models, discourse related representation learning, among others, the conditions are right to encourage learning about discourse theory using neural networks alongside system development for specific tasks and baselines. We propose an approach that combines the methodologies of psycholinguistics with DNNs in order to reconcile the rigor of the first with the breadth and robustness of the second. This idea is not new and has been applied in very specific topics such as script knowledge (**modi-etal-2017-modelling**). We believe that it is a suitable approach to extract knowledge from DNNs.

We examine two examples of this approach in the areas of discourse deixis and entity representation. Discourse deixis, i.e., reference to chunks of context with the demonstratives *this/that*, is a less studied phenomenon within the discourse community. It has long been considered a difficult phenomenon to tackle too, as the antecedents to these pronouns do not have clear boundaries as opposed to standard nominal antecedents. Antecedents can be an event or situation or idea, without a clear correspondent syntactic constituent. We present multilingual experiments in relation to the questions of when and to what degree event instances serve as antecedents when a competing entity referent is also available. These experiments have followed a psycholinguistic methodology in order to control for the features of interest and have led to deep learning experiments about the properties of verbs.

Our second case study is about entity representations. A key idea of theoretical models like DRT and CT is that entities and events change dynamically as the discourse structure evolves. We explore if and how pre-trained language models keep track of the notion of entity. We discuss recent papers that have delved into this subject and offer some ideas for future research.

Our experiments with DNNs show some of the challenges in scaling up the methods from pyscholinguistics. Unfortunately, they also fail to point towards firm conclusions, unlike the case for syntax. In our experiments, pre-trained models like GPT2 do not implicitly encode the kind of discourse knowledge tested. With the expectation that they serve as an example of the kind of considerations and experimental design that could lead to new theoretical insights, we reflect on the reasons behind our results.

7.2 CASE STUDY 1: DISCOURSE DEIXIS

Discourse deixis is defined in the context of written discourse by Webber (1988) as the reference of pronouns *this/that* to previous segments of discourse. Demonstrative pronouns are different from personal pronouns in that they are intrinsically ambiguous, they are often compatible with several possible antecedents or segments, while personal pronouns often refer to a specific noun[1]. She defines their interpretation process in terms of the hierarchical structural segmentation typical of DRT or CT, meaning that possible antecedents are found in the right frontier, i.e., the right outer branches of a discourse tree.

Discourse deixis is a type of abstract anaphora: anaphora that involve reference to abstract entities such as events or states (Asher, 1993). It is a less studied type of anaphora within computational linguistics, as evidenced by the little amount of annotated data available (Dipper and Zinsmeister, 2010; Poesio, 2015).

The study of reference to non-nominal antecedents has largely been a niche area in computational linguistics research (see review by Kolhatkar, Roussel, et al. (2018)). From corpus-based studies of pronouns done in relationship to the texts on which co-reference resolution systems will be trained and tested, we know that about 5% of referential pronouns and 71% of demonstratives in dialog data refer to events (Müller, 2007; Poesio, 2015), whereas about 3% of referential *it* pronouns in written text of various genres refer to events (Evans, 2001).

The most extensive annotation efforts in the field of coreference resolution have focused on English nominal coreference. OntoNotes (Pradhan et al., 2013), the largest and most frequently used corpus for training coreference resolution systems, for instance, only includes verbs if "they can be coreferenced with an existing noun phrase" according to its guidelines. Corpora with a richer annotation of event pronouns exist, but are much smaller. One such resource is the ARRAU corpus (Uryupina et al., 2020), whose size amounts to about 20% of version 5 of OntoNotes. ParCorFull (Lapshinova-Koltunski et al., 2018) also contains annotations of event pronouns in English, German, and French.

The scarcity of manually annotated resources has led to the use of artificial training data for coreference resolution systems of English non-nominal anaphora. Kolhatkar, Zinsmeister, et al. (2013) study the resolution of anaphoric shell nouns such as "this issue" or "this fact" by exploiting instances such as "the fact that...". Marasović et al. (2017) construct training examples based on specific patterns of verbs governing embedded sentences.

In psycholinguistic research, on the other hand, the focus has been on using theoretical constructs of complexity, salience, and focus to capture co-reference patterns. The demonstratives *this* and *that* have been grouped together, assuming that they behave in the same manner, but potentially differently from *it*. Brown-Schmidt et al.

---

[1]This discussion does not include first and second person pronouns.

(2005) analyse *it* vs *that* and report a preference for *that* if what is referred to is a composite (e.g., *Put the cup on the saucer. Now put that [the cup and the saucer]* ...), independent of other metrics of the salience of the referent. Building on the Centering co-reference model (Grosz, Joshi, et al., 1995), Passonneau (1989) analyses intra-sentential instances of *it* vs *that* with an explicit NP antecedent. She reports that *it* is used to refer to the centre (most often the subject), whereas *that* favours non-centres.

7.2.1 An English Psycholinguistic Study

The methodology from psycholinguistic studies offers systematic control over the possible variables behind a phenomenon. This methodology has actually been used to different degrees in many of the studies about syntax-based knowledge and DNNs. We therefore turn to psycholinguistics to try to understand the patterns of coreference of *it/this* found in naturally occurring data.

Loáiciga, Bevacqua, Rohde, et al. (2018) present a study using the setting of story-continuation, which requires participants to enter a free text continuation to a given prompt. The study asks when and to what degree event instances serve as antecedents when a competing entity referent is also available. This study targeted only the demonstrative pronoun *this* and compared it with the personal pronoun *it*.

Two experiments were completed. Experiment 1 uses standard hand-crafted, constructed examples (1)–(2), while Experiment 2 breaks with convention and uses corpus examples (3). The corpus passages are minimally edited sentences extracted from the ParCorFull corpus (Lapshinova-Koltunski et al., 2018). This is a English-German-French parallel corpus annotated with full co-reference. It includes annotations of two types of antecedents: entities and events. Entities can be either pronouns or NPs, whereas events can be VPs, clauses or a set of clauses.

With the constructed examples experiment, we establish a baseline rate at which participants assign *it/this* pronouns to entity vs event antecedents. By varying a property of the context sentence, we test how malleable the two pronouns' respective co-reference preferences are. Participants are then presented with the context sentence and either pronoun prompt *it* or *this*, as in (1)–(2).

(1)   The train from the Highlands arrived promptly. It/This ____

(2)   The balloon with the red hearts popped noiselessly. It/This ____

(3)   You carry a phone. It/This ____
        (original co-reference: entity~*it*: *You carry a phone. It knows where you are.*)

One factor that was controlled for was the availability of entities for anaphoric resolution in the context, which is dependent on the argument structure of the previous predicates. Different verbs have different frames and hence entities involved. Alternating verbs, the focus of this study, can have an intransitive as well as a transitive use: the first usually describes a change of state (4-a), and the latter specifies, in subject position, which entity brought on the change (4-b). Conversely, non-alternating verbs only have an intransitive use (5-a)–(5-b). Attention should be paid to the fact that the alternating property involves the semantic roles of the verb arguments, as both (4-a) and (5-a) are intransitive sentences. Without adscribing to any specific theory on semantic roles, a verb like *melt* differs from a verb like *die* in that *melt* can have either an agent (transitive use) or a theme/patient subject (intransitive) whereas *die* only has a theme/patient subject.

(4)   a.   The snow melted.
       b.   The heat melted the snow.

(5)   a.   The battery died.
       b.   * The heat died the battery.

Manipulating the verb in the context sentence affects the argument realisation options associated with the predicate: Non-alternating verbs like *arrive* permit only a single realisation with the entity that arrives always in subject position; alternating verbs like *pop* are compatible with realisations where the entity that pops appears in subject position or object position. For alternating verbs, an explicit agent entity can be introduced (*I popped the balloon*) or left implicit, as in (2).

The continuations provided by the participants were collected via Amazon Mechanical Turk and annotated by the authors. The analysis used mixed-effects logistic regression: we modeled the binary outcome of entity or event co-reference with fixed effects for prompt type, verb class, and their interaction, with maximal random effects structure when supported by the data (Barr et al., 2013).

The results of these experiments paint a different picture depending on the type of examples used. While both experiments show a bias to use *it* to refer to entities and *this* to refer to events, the pattern is stronger with the constructed examples and much more nuanced with the corpus examples (compare Figures 7.1 and 7.2).

Moreover, the first experiment shows that alternation impacts co-reference, whereby verbs that permit alternations yield more event co-reference than non-alternating verbs. This confirms our hypothesis that the salience of the single argument of non-alternating verbs may have attracted more entity co-reference. This effect, however, could not be confirmed with the second experiment since the corpus examples did not include annotations for the type of verb of the antecedents.

7.2.2   Do the Effects of Referring Expression and Type of Verb Observed in English Extend to Other Languages?

In previous work (Bevacqua et al., 2021), we extend the study presented above (§7.2.1) to four additional languages (English, French, German, Italian, and Spanish) to investigate the similarities and differences that arise due to structural differences in the languages. The languages are related typologically but differ in their use of grammatical gender and case and their pronominal systems, most notably the availability of a null pronoun.

As in the previous study, the story continuation setting was used, targeting the following pronominal forms: *It* vs *This* in English[2], *Il* vs *Cela* vs *C'est* in French, *Es*

---

[2]This English experiment serves thus as a replication study.

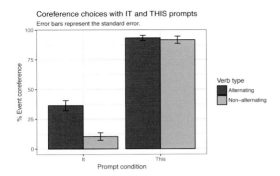

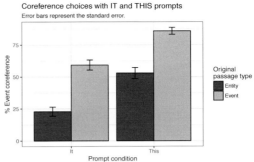

Figure 7.1 Experiment 1 (constructed examples) results by prompt and verb type.

Figure 7.2 Experiment 2 (corpus examples) results by prompt and original coreference (collapsing over original *it/this* pronoun type).

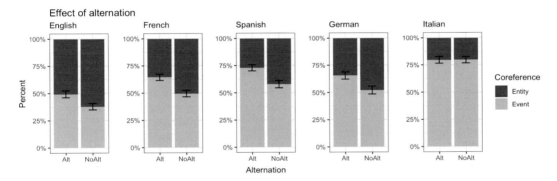

Figure 7.3 Event and entity coreference by verb type in the five languages.

vs *Das* vs *Dies* in German, *Ciò* vs *Questo* vs zero pronoun in Italian, and *Esto* vs *Este* vs zero pronoun in Spanish.

The multilingual aspect of the study made it harder to work with corpus examples in a controlled way, which is why this study was limited to constructed examples. In addition to alternation, this study also targeted the verbal feature of aspect, but we will limit ourselves to the results of alternation here.

Regarding antecedent complexity, in this study we also targeted the impact of the availability of an additional explicit argument to the verb, namely the complexity created via the alternation pattern of verbs like *to pop*. We refer to Bevacqua et al. (2021) for the design details of the experiment.

The results yielded similarities between the languages. As in the English-only study, in all languages, demonstrative pronouns had a bias towards event continuations, confirming expectations from the linguistic literature. Concerning alternation, however, there was some variation between the languages. Alternating verbs yielded more event continuations in all languages except Italian, with different levels of strength for the effect.

Since we only worked with constructed examples, we also looked to compare the patterns from the psycholinguistic experiments with an annotated coreference corpus. Specifically, we sought to confirm the alternation status of the verbs in the coreferential chains of the corpus. To achieve this, once again, we worked with the ParCorFull corpus, which includes annotations for the English, German, and French languages.

We first extracted all coreference chains headed by lexical entity or event antecedents, thus excluding cataphora. We then retained all mentions of the pronouns of interest (EN: *this, it*; DE: *es, das, dies*; FR: *c', il, cela*) in a subject position and ordered them according to their appearance in the text. For entity antecedents, we extracted the verb to which the head of the noun phrase is attached. For event antecedents, we extracted the verb from the antecedent itself. With a list of verbs of interest, we then looked for resources annotated with the alternation status of verbs but unfortunately found only a few with limited coverage. The most well-known one is Levin's 1993 English list consisting of 354 verbs. Hoewever, even using this list, we only found a handful of the verbs.

7.2.3 Automatic Detection of the Alternating Verbs

In work described by Loáiciga, Bevacqua, and Hardmeier (2021), we exploited DNNs to fill this gap. We present a method to detect alternating verbs automatically.

From the several types of verb frame alternation in the literature, the one we discussed in the previous experiments concerns the ability of the entity with the semantic role of patient to be promoted from object to subject, and most theoretical accounts focus on this transitive to intransitive frame change (Samardžić, 2014, among others). This particular alternation frame is also found in the literature as the causative-inchoative alternation.

One key aspect of this alternation is that if a particular verb is in its intransitive form, it is syntactically indistinguishable from any other intransitive verb construction. Besides, the meaning of both the transitive and intransitive versions remains virtually the same, with equal grammatical acceptability regardless of their frequency. With these conditions, a disambiguation by context is highly unlikely and attention must be paid to the semantic roles of the arguments involved.

7.2.3.1 *Probing Sentences*

To generate probing sentences, we start by extracting transitive verb frames from a parsed corpus (Europarl (Koehn, 2005) with dependency annotations automatically generated with the Stanza parser (Qi et al., 2020) trained on Universal Dependencies v2.5). We extracted examples consisting of a triplet of *(subject, verb, object)* lemmas, if both the subject and the object are nouns. We assumed that the *subjects* of transitive verbs are typically in an *agent*-like relation with the predicate, so we treated them as agent candidates, whereas the *objects* are more likely to be in a *patient*-like relation and are used as patient candidates.

In a next step, we expanded the set of agent and patient nouns by using it to seed the lookup of semantically related words using GloVe (Pennington et al., 2014).

We started with the pretrained 300-dimensional *glove-wiki-gigaword-300* model from the *gensim* library (Řehůřek and Sojka, 2010). After filtering the vocabulary of the GloVe model so that it only contains nouns, we expanded the word sets according to the following procedure (reproduced here from Loáiciga, Bevacqua, and Hardmeier (2021)):

1. Let V be the original vocabulary of the embedding space, and S and O be the sets of words observed in subject and object position of transitive verb frames, respectively.

2. Disjoint sets of seed words are created as $S' = V \cap S \setminus O$ and $O' = V \cap O \setminus S$.

3. We proceed as follows to create expanded sets S^+ and O^+ from S' and O', respectively:

   (a) We draw 20 samples of 10 items from the seed word list, S' or O'.

   (b) For each sample, we find the 50 nearest neighbours in the embedding space using the 3CosMul similarity metric of Levy and Goldberg (2014). The union of these 20 sets of nearest neighbours forms the expansion candidates.

   (c) Disjoint sets S^+ and O^+ are created by taking the 30 highest-scoring expansion candidates generated from S' and O' respectively, but ignoring items that occur in the subject and object expansion candidates of the same verb.

Probing sentences, fixed sentences where only one word of interest varies, are generated by inserting the items of the agent-like and patient-like expanded sets into templates of the form

        \<s\> The NOUN VERBS . \</s\>

These sentences are then scored with the pre-trained language model GPT-2 (Radford et al., 2019), resulting in a probability for each NOUN-VERB pair. Finally, we sum up the probability of the agent-like and patient-like nouns separately. We classify a verb as alternating if the total probability of the sentences with patient-like fillers exceeds that of the sentence with agent-like fillers, and as non-alternating otherwise.

7.2.3.2 Results

We tested our method on three data sets. The first is a small set with manually constructed examples containing 10 verbs of each category. The second is the subset of causative-inchoative alternating verbs from the FAVA data set (Kann et al., 2019). This means that it only contains verbs that are positive examples. The FAVA data set includes both the transitive and intransitive variants of each verb. The third evaluation data set is composed of the subset of FrameNet verbs annotated as alternating or non-alternating. We randomly sampled 50% of the verbs each time we

TABLE 7.1   Precision, recall, and F-scores using a constructed data set with 20 verbs. We present results using the present tense.

GPT-2	Alternating			Non-alternating		
	P	R	F1	P	R	F1
	0.62	0.80	0.70	0.71	0.50	0.59

queried the language model. For the first two data sets, we present results both with the manually curated sentences and with generated sentences (according to Section 7.2.3.1); for the FrameNet data set, we only provide results with generated sentences.

The language model has a maximal precision of 0.69 in the constructed set and a precision of 0.60 in the FrameNet set. The results of the evaluation on the Constructed set using simple sentences (Table 7.1) and those with the expanded sentences (Table 7.2) are comparable, with an improvement of 0.07 in precision and of 0.1 in recall using the expansion. This suggests that the language model does catch the underlying thematic role relationships to some extent, but the expansion method does not add as much extra identification capacity as we had expected. However, it is worth noting that the method predicts labels for a large number of verbs unattested in the existing gold standards, i.e., we cannot know whether the predicted labels are correct.

We produced expanded sets of potential agents and patients using different corpus sources for the probing sentences. In Table 7.2, we report results using any word tagged as NOUN by Stanza in English Europarl (vocabulary size of 22,923 words), and also probing sentences generated with all nouns listed in the English dictionary Lefff (Sagot, 2010) (vocabulary size of 49,932 words). We observe similar precision results, with the Europarl expansion yielding better recall, in reversed correlation with the vocabulary sizes. We also report results computed two probability normalisations according to Lau et al. (2015). Although lower than the unnormalised scores, these results presumably provide a more realistic scenario as they account for sentence length and lexical frequency.

Comparisons with similar methods are difficult. We have a set up close to Seyffarth (2019), however, while they query their neural model with argument sequences, we probe ours with inflected sentences. In addition, while Kann et al. (2019) report results between 66% and 85% accuracy for the causative-inchoative (alternating) verbs, their task is supervised and only considers verbs known to alternate.

We saw in the psycholinguistics experiments that the alternating property influences coreference patterns in humans. However, it seems that this property is not easily caught by relying on the frequency of nominal patterns as tested here. When tested on its own, the GPT-2 model, on the other hand, has some moderate success. While this is just one pre-trained model, we do not have reason to believe that other pre-trained models will behave differently.

TABLE 7.2 Precision, recall, and F-scores for the GPT-2 model on the different evaluation sets. We present results using the present tense. Notation: Expanded_EP refers to probing sentences generated with any word tagged as NOUN in English Europarl; Expanded_Lefff refers to probing sentences generated with all nouns listed in the English dictionary Lefff. We normalised the sentence log probabilities produced by GPT-2 by sentence length and lexical frequency following Lau et al. (2015). The normalisation LP-div is defined as $-\frac{\log P_m(\xi)}{\log P_u(\xi)}$, while the SLOR (syntactic log-odds ratio) is defined as $\frac{\log P_m(\xi) - \log P_u(\xi)}{|\xi|}$, where $P_m(\xi)$ is the probability of the sentence given by the model and $P_u(\xi)$ is the unigram probability of the sentence.

| | Verbs | GPT-2 unnormalised | | | | | |
| | | Alternating | | | Non-alternating | | |
		P	R	F1	P	R	F1
Constructed	20						
Expanded_EP		0.69	0.90	0.78	0.86	0.60	0.71
Expanded_Lefff		0.69	0.90	0.78	0.86	0.60	0.71
FAVA	120						
Expanded_EP		0.69	0.34	0.45	0.56	0.69	0.62
Expanded_Lefff		0.70	0.30	0.42	0.66	0.65	0.65
FrameNet	329						
Expanded_EP		0.60	0.15	0.24	0.40	0.15	0.22
Expanded_Lefff		0.62	0.09	0.16	0.43	0.13	0.20

| | Verbs | GPT-2 norm-LP-div | | | | | |
| | | Alternating | | | Non-alternating | | |
		P	R	F1	P	R	F1
Constructed	20						
Expanded_EP		0.62	0.80	0.70	0.71	0.50	0.59
Expanded_Lefff		0.54	0.70	0.61	0.57	0.40	0.47
FAVA	120						
Expanded_EP		0.50	0.32	0.39	0.45	0.45	0.45
Expanded_Lefff		0.63	0.31	0.42	0.64	0.57	0.60
FrameNet	329						
Expanded_EP		0.59	0.15	0.24	0.38	0.14	0.20
Expanded_Lefff		0.61	0.13	0.22	0.43	0.10	0.16

| | Verbs | GPT-2 norm-SLOR | | | | | |
| | | Alternating | | | Non-alternating | | |
		P	R	F1	P	R	F1
Constructed	20						
Expanded_EP		0.62	0.80	0.70	0.71	0.50	0.59
Expanded_Lefff		0.54	0.70	0.61	0.57	0.40	0.47
FAVA	120						
Expanded_EP		0.49	0.32	0.39	0.44	0.43	0.43
Expanded_Lefff		0.67	0.31	0.42	0.66	0.61	0.63
FrameNet	329						
Expanded_EP		0.59	0.15	0.24	0.38	0.14	0.20
Expanded_Lefff		0.67	0.14	0.23	0.49	0.12	0.19

7.3 FROM PSYCHOLINGUISTICS TO PROBING TASKS

The diverse properties of the verbs, like the alternation property of verbs like *pop* studied here, are left to specifications in the lexicon in discourse theories such as DRT or CT. In contrast, lexical semantic properties, encoded in the form of distributed word representations, are tightly connected to higher level tasks in DNNs.

The alternating vs non-alternating study (Section 7.2.3) was motivated by our psycholinguistic investigation into the coreference patterns of *this* vs *it*. However, it did not need to be. Studies where DNNs are the subject of study are worthwhile in their own right. As DNNs become the standard tools in the domain, understanding their capabilities is essential, in particular, if they can help us confirm or even capture the cognitive processes behind naturally occurring phenomena.

Psycholinguistic studies offer suitable methods for measuring linguistic processing in humans through controlled experimentation, where each variable is isolated and accounted for. While this facilitates the investigation of specific effects, it has limitations on how many effects can be traced simultaneously. It also does not allow for natural non-constructed data such as those found in corpora.

Through psycholinguistic experimentation, we tested the hypothesis that verbs with multiple participants trigger more event readings than verbs with a single participant. This finding echoes the idea within discourse theory that coreference patterns are influenced by different elements in the context, such as verbs and discourse relations, and not merely by the mentions within the coreference chain. This would suggest that large DNN models should also be able to identify the pattern, as they are the best machines yet to capture the context in a single representation, and seem extremely good at semantic modelling. However, at least in our experiments, the GPT-2 model is only moderately successful on this task. More investigation is needed in order to verify whether DNNs can pick up subtle distinctions such as that of alternating and non-alternating verb frames.

As part of what Baroni (Chapter 1 of this volume) has called Linguistically Oriented Deep Net Analysis (LODNA), there is an increasing number of papers on probing pre-trained language models for some linguistic phenomenon. This research area started with the influential paper by Linzen et al. (2016) on verb-subject agreement which was quickly followed by many others and by diverse linguistic phenomena such as bridging (Pandit and Hou, 2021) and numerical quantification (Lin et al., 2020). The probing approach has its own problems, as pointed in the literature. Probing consist of a simple auxiliary task trained on the encoded representations of another system. If the probe succeeds in the task for which it is trained, we conclude that the input (and hence the original system) had the necessary knowledge to solve the task. The main issue with this approach is that depending on the setup, it can become difficult to differentiate between the capacity of the input representations and the capacity of the probe system itself to solve the task. Nevertheless, it has the advantage of being able to deal with naturalistic data from corpora in large amounts.

Using a probing approach, our next case study focuses on probing discourse entities in pre-trained language models. While these experiments do not use constructed examples, they have been inspired by the same type of psycholinguistic methodology to hypothesis testing.

7.4 CASE STUDY 2: DISCOURSE ENTITY REPRESENTATIONS

Discourse entities are central to discourse theories in general and to coreference resolution in particular. The idea that a discourse entity is first introduced and that it subsequently undergoes updates or changes as the context evolves is present in both. In this work we understand discourse entities to be as defined by Karttunen (1969) and Webber (1988), i.e., referents in the text which are introduced and referred to by pronouns and noun phrases; they exist in the current discourse and they may or may not refer to real world entities.

7.4.1 Form of Referring Expression

In Beyer et al. (2021), several criteria contributing to coherence from the linguistic literature are selected to probe large pre-trained language models using surprisal measures. Although we will concentrate on the re-mention of entities in this section, we also looked at sentence ordering, cloze story, pronoun resolution, and connectives in the cited paper. While the notion of sentence acceptability is well studied from a linguistic point of view and in terms of neural language model representations (Hu et al., 2020; Lau et al., 2017; Marvin and Linzen, 2018; Warstadt, Parrish, et al., 2020; Warstadt, Singh, et al., 2019, among others), it remains less clear what neural models are capable of capturing when modelling language across sentence boundaries.

In line with theories proposing an accessibility hierarchy that position pronouns requiring the highest level of accessibility and lexical noun phrases (indefinites and definites) the lowest level (Ariel, 2004; Givón, 1983), we tested whether pre-trained language models were sensitive to a violation in the use of referring expressions according to their accessibility status. While an adequate referring expression ensures cohesion, strictly speaking, for keeping in topic from one sentence to the other, entities need only to be re-mentioned, regardless of their form.

For this experiment, we constructed a test suite based on the ARRAU corpus (Uryupina et al., 2020). We extracted coreferential chains with mentions spanning consecutive sentences and with at least one pronominal mention. The probing sentences consisted of minimal pairs (6) where a same-context sentence containing the antecedent is followed by a sentence with the original pronoun re-mentioning the antecedent (6-a) or by a manipulated sentence in which the pronoun is replaced by a repetition of the antecedent (6-b).

(6)   And there's a ladder coming out of the tree and there's a man at the top of the ladder
    a.   you can't see *him* yet.
    b.   you can't see *the man at the top of the ladder* yet.

In this experiment, in addition to the language model GPT-2 (Radford et al., 2019), the dialogue model DIALOGPT (Zhang et al., 2020) was tested. Both models were presented with the probing sentences and surprisal scores $s(t_i) = -\log_2(p(t_i|t_0...t_{i-1}))$ were collected from the language model's conditional token probabilities p. The token scores were normalised over the number of tokens in the portion of the sentence of interest.

Table 7.3 reports the prediction accuracy of whether the model found the manipulated version more surprising than the coherent counterpart. We found that when presented with a new lexical entity, neither model has a clear preference for a pronominal re-mention of the entity. The very nature of the language model will drive it to topic continuity, as it is designed to generate tokens based on a previous history. However, both pronominalisation and repetition represent cohesive ties to the previous context recoverable from surface cues. The difference is that the first involves a stronger link with the context, licensing the use of the pronoun, which the models evaluated in the study fail to pick up.

TABLE 7.3 Accuracy results on entity re-mention test suite. WSJ and VPC refer to the News portion of the ARRAU corpus.

	WSJ	VPC	Dialogue	Fiction
GPT-2	0.53	0.56	0.47	0.42
DIALOGPT	0.44	0.51	0.47	0.36
#items	512	75	68	98

7.4.2 Discourse New vs Discourse Old

The experiments in the previous section assumed that pre-trained language models had some knowledge of discourse entities and asked whether they would be sensitive to encoding changes in their form. In this section, we address the more primitive question of whether the model recognises a discourse entity at all.

The intuition that language models implicitly capture and, in turn also benefit from entity knowledge has been explored for some time now (Ji et al., 2017; Yang et al., 2017), with recent papers focusing on how to inject some explicit entity representation into the system (Aina et al., 2019; Gupta and Durrett, 2019, among others). Concerning discourse entity knowledge specifically, there are two works that stand out. We refer to the papers by Sorodoc et al. (2020) and Li et al. (2021).

Both of these works are interested in probing entity knowledge in pre-trained language models and they both take a semantic approach in that they are interested in a global discourse entity representation as understood in this Chapter (Section 7.4). Sorodoc et al. (2020) assess whether the word vectors of a pronoun and its antecedent are similar enough so that we can consider them to be the same entity. They evaluate their morpho-syntactic information and their content similarity. Li et al. (2021), on their side, evaluate the True/False values of logical propositions about entities in simplified, synthetic data (Alchemy, derived from SCONE (Long et al., 2016) and Textworld (Côté et al., 2018)). Probing the dynamic nature of the discourse entities, the propositions are designed to verify the status of the entities at different points in the discourse (e.g., From the text *You see an open chest. The only thing in the chest is an old key*, the proposition *contains(chest, apple) = False*).

In both of these pieces of research, the authors used a simple classifier for their probing task and report positive results indicating some degree of discourse entity knowledge on the pre-trained models (Transformer XL (Dai et al., 2019) by Sorodoc et al. (2020); BART (Lewis et al., 2020); and T5 (Raffel et al., 2020a) by Li et al. (2021)). We believe that these initial reports are worth investigating further. Their analyses are limited to pronouns-antecedent pairs in the first case and very simple data in the second. Pronoun-antecedent pairs are only a part of a discourse entity which is represented by all mentions within a same coreferential chain. Synthetic data on the other hand, might not capture the much more nuanced picture found in naturally occurring data as exemplified in our psycholinguistic experiments (Section 7.2.1).

The next step, in our opinion, would be to investigate whereas the pre-trained models keep track of the discourse entities. One way to approach such a question would be through a task that relies on the distinction between discourse new and discourse old (Kamp and Reyle, 1993; Prince, 1992). This task would help in assessing whether the model is able to discriminate between the introduction of a new entity and the re-mention of an old one. We are currently working on this question.

7.5 WHAT WENT WRONG?

The pre-trained models used in the experiments presented here do not seem to encode the kind of discourse knowledge relevant for the identification of alternating verbs and discourse entities. Given the nature and size of the models, one can only speculate about the possible reasons.

It is possible that there is a corpus domain effect. In our first case study, the alternating verbs, the expansion procedure relied on the Europarl corpus, while the GPT-2 model is trained on web-crawled data. Therefore, there might be only a small overlap between the two. That being said, the training data for the GPT-2 model was in principle selected to be diverse enough to ensure generalisation over various domains and potential down-stream applications (Radford et al., 2019). Concerning the discourse entities, one could imagine such a corpus domain effect with GPT-2, but less so with DialoGPT, since the probing sentences were extracted from a dialog corpus. A corpus-domain effect would be an argument in favour of testing even bigger models such as T5 (Raffel et al., 2020b) or some other model trained on gigantic amounts of data. Yet, this does not guarantee positive results (Marton and Sayeed, 2022).

Another possible reason is that the pre-training procedure and learning objective are not of the right kind to capture these linguistic properties. It is not currently clear how much information across sentence boundaries is captured by these language models. Although the training sentences are delimited by start and end tokens, current DNN models are not fed strictly one sentence at a time, so they should be able to encode at least *some* discourse knowledge.

A third reason may be that these linguistic distinctions are artificial and thus not as clear-cut as currently stated by discourse linguistic theory, at least in the case of alternating verb distinctions and the use of referring expressions for discourse entities. As shown with the experiment using constructed vs corpus examples (Section 7.2.1), linguistic generalisations become much more nuanced when confronted with naturalistic corpus data. Although more experiments are needed in order to draw any firm conclusions, it might very well be the case that the theories need expanding or even updating. That is precisely why large-scale studies of the type DNNs make possible are valuable for linguistic knowledge.

7.6 THE WORK AHEAD

The computational linguistics community has been busy with discourse processing in the last few years. This is evidenced by the ever raising baselines in tasks such as coreference resolution (Lee et al., 2017), discourse parsing (Noord et al., 2018), and implicit relation classification (Kim et al., 2020). This progress is outstanding and well beyond what algebraic implementations of discourse theories have accomplished.

Nevertheless, in contrast to the classic discourse theories, more can be said about the cognitive processes behind the diverse discourse phenomena that these tasks tackle. As the DNNs have become the new standard, the time is right to assume this challenge. Following the example from syntax-level studies with DNNs, the fact that a DNN is capable of learning some particular feature from context alone tells us something about the interactions of this feature with other aspects of the context, and about the easiness of access to this feature for humans.

To continue the parallel with syntax, attention should be drawn to the fact that syntax has the advantage of being just simple enough to be captured in the task of parsing. However, discourse is more complex with several phenomena not necessarily combinable under a single task. The closest to a single discourse task is probably the coherence classification and prediction task (Moon et al., 2019, among others). We should also remember that discourse-level resources and studies for other languages are scarce, even in comparison to the standards of computational linguistics at large, a community heavily biased towards English.

This situation makes us argue in favour of an empirical theorising so to speak, by which building systems is accompanied by the investigation of the limits and capabilities of the DNNs behind the systems. What is there to gain? Potentially a better understanding of the cognitive processes yielding the patterns observed in naturally occurring data and their interpretation by humans, a true multilingual perspective on discourse/linguistic processing, insights as to how to best design DNNs going forward, and robust contributions to linguistic theory.

7.7 CONCLUSION

In this chapter, we have presented a line of research that combines the rigor of psycholinguistic studies with the robustness of DNNs. In psycholinguistics we have a methodology that facilitates targeting specific linguistic phenomena, while in DNNs we have the possibility to explore what are the limits in terms of how much generalisation can be extracted from data alone. By combining these frameworks, we can exploit unrestricted corpus data to either verify hypotheses or build linguistic knowledge in a bottom up fashion, supporting new research and bridging linguistics and computational linguistics.

BIBLIOGRAPHY

Aina, Laura, Carina Silberer, Ionut-Teodor Sorodoc, Matthijs Westera, and Gemma Boleda (June 2019). "What do Entity-Centric Models Learn? Insights from Entity Linking in Multi-Party Dialogue". In: *Proceedings of the 2019 Conference of the North American Chapter of the Association for Computational Linguistics: Human Language Technologies, Volume 1 (Long and Short Papers)*. Minneapolis, Minnesota: Association for Computational Linguistics, pp. 3772–3783. DOI: 10.18653/v1/N19-1378. URL: https://aclanthology.org/N19-1378.

Ariel, Mira (2004). "Accessibility Marking: Discourse Functions, Discourse Profiles, and Processing Cues". In: *Discourse Processes* 37.2, pp. 91–116.

Asher, Nicholas (1993). *Reference to Abstract Objects in Discourse*. Netherlands: Springer.

Baroni, Marco (2022). "On the proper role of linguistically-oriented deep net analysis in linguistic theorizing". In: *Algebraic Structures in Natural Language*. Ed. by Shalom Lappin and Jean-Philippe Bernardy. Taylor and Francis.

Barr, Dale J., Roger Levy, Christoph Scheepers, and Harry J. Tily (2013). "Random effects structure for confirmatory hypothesis testing: Keep it maximal". In: *Journal of memory and language* 68.3, pp. 255–278.

Bevacqua, Luca, Sharid Loáiciga, Hannah Rohde, and Christian Hardmeier (2021). "Event and entity coreference across five languages: Effects of context and referring expression". In: *Dialogue and Discourse* 12.2, pp. 192–226. DOI: https://doi.org/10.5210/dad.2021.207.

Beyer, Anne, Sharid Loáiciga, and David Schlangen (June 2021). "Is Incoherence Surprising? Targeted Evaluation of Coherence Prediction from Language Models". In: *Proceedings of the 2021 Conference of the North American Chapter of the Association for Computational Linguistics: Human Language Technologies*. Online: Association for Computational Linguistics, pp. 4164–4173. DOI: 10.18653/v1/2021.naacl-main.328. URL: https://aclanthology.org/2021.naacl-main.328.

Brown-Schmidt, Sarah, Donna K. Byron, and Michael K. Tanenhaus (2005). "Beyond salience: Interpretation of personal and demonstrative pronouns". In: *Journal of Memory and Language* 53.2, pp. 292–313.

Côté, Marc-Alexandre, Ákos Kádár, Xingdi Yuan, Ben Kybartas, Tavian Barnes, Emery Fine, James Moore, Ruo Yu Tao, Matthew Hausknecht, Layla El Asri, Mahmoud Adada, Wendy Tay, and Adam Trischler (2018). "TextWorld: A Learning Environment for Text-based Games". In: *CoRR* abs/1806.11532.

Dai, Zihang, Zhilin Yang, Yiming Yang, Jaime Carbonell, Quoc Le, and Ruslan Salakhutdinov (July 2019). "Transformer-XL: Attentive Language Models beyond a Fixed-Length Context". In: *Proceedings of the 57th Annual Meeting of the Association for Computational Linguistics*. Florence, Italy: Association for Computational Linguistics, pp. 2978–2988. DOI: 10.18653/v1/P19-1285. URL: https://aclanthology.org/P19-1285.

Dipper, Stefanie and Heike Zinsmeister (2010). "Towards a Standard for Annotating Abstract Anaphora". In: *Proceedings of the LREC Workshop on Language Resource and Language Technology Standards – state of the art, emerging needs, and future developments*. LREC10-W4. Valletta, Malta: European Language Resources Association (ELRA), pp. 54–59.

Evans, Richard (2001). "Applying Machine Learning Toward an Automatic Classification of IT". In: *Literary and Linguistic Computing* 16.1, pp. 45–57.

Givón, Thomas (1983). *Topic Continuity in Discourse: A Quantitative Cross-Language Study*. Amsterdam: John Benjamin.

Grosz, Barbara J., Aravind K. Joshi, and Scott Weinstein (1995). "Centering: A Framework for Modelling the Local Coherence of Discourse". In: *Computational Linguistics* 21.2, pp. 203–225.

Grosz, Barbara J. and Candace L. Sidner (1986). "Attention, Intentions, and the Structure of Discourse". In: *Computational Linguistics* 12.3, pp. 175–204. URL: https://aclanthology.org/J86-3001.

Gupta, Aditya and Greg Durrett (Nov. 2019). "Effective Use of Transformer Networks for Entity Tracking". In: *Proceedings of the 2019 Conference on Empirical Methods in Natural Language Processing and the 9th International Joint Conference on Natural Language Processing (EMNLP-IJCNLP)*. Hong Kong, China: Association for Computational Linguistics, pp. 759–769. DOI: 10.18653/v1/D19-1070. URL: https://aclanthology.org/D19-1070.

Hu, Jennifer, Jon Gauthier, Peng Qian, Ethan Wilcox, and Roger Levy (July 2020). "A Systematic Assessment of Syntactic Generalization in Neural Language Models". In: *Proceedings of the 58th Annual Meeting of the Association for Computational Linguistics*. Online: Association for Computational Linguistics, pp. 1725–1744. DOI: 10.18653/v1/2020.acl-main.158. URL: https://aclanthology.org/2020.acl-main.158.

Ji, Yangfeng, Chenhao Tan, Sebastian Martschat, Yejin Choi, and Noah A. Smith (Sept. 2017). "Dynamic Entity Representations in Neural Language Models". In: *Proceedings of the 2017 Conference on Empirical Methods in Natural Language Processing*. Copenhagen, Denmark: Association for Computational Linguistics, pp. 1830–1839. DOI: 10.18653/v1/D17-1195. URL: https://aclanthology.org/D17-1195.

Kamp, Hans and Uwe Reyle (1993). *From Discourse to Logic. Introduction to Modeltheorectic Semantics of Natural Language, Formal Logic and Discourse Representation Theory*. Dordrecht: Kluwer Academic Publishers.

Kann, Katharina, Alex Warstadt, Adina Williams, and Samuel R. Bowman (2019). "Verb Argument Structure Alternations in Word and Sentence Embeddings". In: *Proceedings of the Society for Computation in Linguistics (SCiL) 2019*, pp. 287–297. DOI: 10.7275/q5js-4y86. URL: https://aclanthology.org/W19-0129.

Karttunen, Lauri (Sept. 1969). "Discourse Referents". In: *International Conference on Computational Linguistics COLING 1969: Preprint No. 70*. Sånga Säby, Sweden. URL: `https://www.aclweb.org/anthology/C69-7001`.

Kim, Najoung, Song Feng, Chulaka Gunasekara, and Luis Lastras (July 2020). "Implicit Discourse Relation Classification: We Need to Talk about Evaluation". In: *Proceedings of the 58th Annual Meeting of the Association for Computational Linguistics*. Online: Association for Computational Linguistics, pp. 5404–5414. DOI: `10.18653/v1/2020.acl-main.480`. URL: `https://aclanthology.org/2020.acl-main.480`.

Koehn, Philipp (2005). "Europarl: A Parallel Corpus for Statistical Machine Translation". In: *Conference Proceedings: the tenth Machine Translation Summit*. AAMT. Phuket, Thailand: AAMT, pp. 79–86. URL: `http://mt-archive.info/MTS-2005-Koehn.pdf`.

Kolhatkar, Varada, Adam Roussel, Stefanie Dipper, and Heike Zinsmeister (Sept. 2018). "Survey: Anaphora With Non-nominal Antecedents in Computational Linguistics: a Survey". In: *Computational Linguistics* 44.3, pp. 547–612. DOI: `10.1162/coli\_a\_00327`. URL: `https://aclanthology.org/J18-3007`.

Kolhatkar, Varada, Heike Zinsmeister, and Graeme Hirst (Oct. 2013). "Interpreting Anaphoric Shell Nouns using Antecedents of Cataphoric Shell Nouns as Training Data". In: *Proceedings of the 2013 Conference on Empirical Methods in Natural Language Processing*. Seattle, Washington, USA: Association for Computational Linguistics, pp. 300–310. URL: `https://aclanthology.org/D13-1030`.

Kulmizev, Artur and Joakim Nivre (2021). *Schrödinger's Tree – On Syntax and Neural Language Models*. arXiv: `2110.08887 [cs.CL]`.

Lapshinova-Koltunski, Ekaterina, Christian Hardmeier, and Pauline Krielke (2018). "ParCorFull: a Parallel Corpus Annotated with Full Coreference". In: *Proceedings of 11th Language Resources and Evaluation Conference*. to appear. Miyazaki, Japan: European Language Resources Association (ELRA), pp. 00–00.

Lau, Jey Han, Alexander Clark, and Shalom Lappin (July 2015). "Unsupervised Prediction of Acceptability Judgements". In: *Proceedings of the 53rd Annual Meeting of the Association for Computational Linguistics and the 7th International Joint Conference on Natural Language Processing (Volume 1: Long Papers)*. Beijing, China: Association for Computational Linguistics, pp. 1618–1628. DOI: `10.3115/v1/P15-1156`. URL: `https://aclanthology.org/P15-1156`.

— (2017). "Grammaticality, Acceptability and Probability: A probabilistic view of linguistic knowledge". In: *Cognitive Science* 41.5, pp. 1202–1241.

Lee, Kenton, Luheng He, Mike Lewis, and Luke Zettlemoyer (Sept. 2017). "End-to-end Neural Coreference Resolution". In: *Proceedings of the 2017 Conference on Empirical Methods in Natural Language Processing*. Copenhagen, Denmark: Association for Computational Linguistics, pp. 188–197. DOI: `10.18653/v1/D17-1018`. URL: `https://aclanthology.org/D17-1018`.

Levin, Beth (1993). *English verb classes and alternations: a preliminary investigation*. Chicago: The University of Chicago Press.

Levy, Omer and Yoav Goldberg (June 2014). "Linguistic Regularities in Sparse and Explicit Word Representations". In: *Proceedings of the Eighteenth Conference on*

Computational Natural Language Learning. Ann Arbor, Michigan: Association for Computational Linguistics, pp. 171–180. DOI: `10.3115/v1/W14-1618`. URL: `https://aclanthology.org/W14-1618`.

Lewis, Mike, Yinhan Liu, Naman Goyal, Marjan Ghazvininejad, Abdelrahman Mohamed, Omer Levy, Veselin Stoyanov, and Luke Zettlemoyer (July 2020). "BART: Denoising Sequence-to-Sequence Pre-training for Natural Language Generation, Translation, and Comprehension". In: *Proceedings of the 58th Annual Meeting of the Association for Computational Linguistics*. Online: Association for Computational Linguistics, pp. 7871–7880. DOI: `10.18653/v1/2020.acl-main.703`. URL: `https://aclanthology.org/2020.acl-main.703`.

Li, Belinda Z., Maxwell Nye, and Jacob Andreas (Aug. 2021). "Implicit Representations of Meaning in Neural Language Models". In: *Proceedings of the 59th Annual Meeting of the Association for Computational Linguistics and the 11th International Joint Conference on Natural Language Processing (Volume 1: Long Papers)*. Online: Association for Computational Linguistics, pp. 1813–1827. DOI: `10.18653/v1/2021.acl-long.143`. URL: `https://aclanthology.org/2021.acl-long.143`.

Lin, Bill Yuchen, Seyeon Lee, Rahul Khanna, and Xiang Ren (Nov. 2020). "Birds have four legs?! NumerSense: Probing Numerical Commonsense Knowledge of Pre-Trained Language Models". In: *Proceedings of the 2020 Conference on Empirical Methods in Natural Language Processing (EMNLP)*. Online: Association for Computational Linguistics, pp. 6862–6868. DOI: `10.18653/v1/2020.emnlp-main.557`. URL: `https://aclanthology.org/2020.emnlp-main.557`.

Linzen, Tal, Emmanuel Dupoux, and Yoav Goldberg (2016). "Assessing the ability of LSTMs to learn syntax-sensitive dependencies". In: *Transactions of the Association for Computational Linguistics* 4, pp. 521–535.

Loáiciga, Sharid, Luca Bevacqua, and Christian Hardmeier (2021). "Unsupervised Discovery of Unaccusative and Unergative Verbs". In: *CoRR* abs/2111.00808. arXiv: `2111.00808`. URL: `https://arxiv.org/abs/2111.00808`.

Loáiciga, Sharid, Luca Bevacqua, Hannah Rohde, and Christian Hardmeier (June 2018). "Event versus entity co-reference: Effects of context and form of referring expression". In: *Proceedings of the First Workshop on Computational Models of Reference, Anaphora and Coreference*. New Orleans, Louisiana: Association for Computational Linguistics, pp. 97–103. DOI: `10.18653/v1/W18-0711`. URL: `https://aclanthology.org/W18-0711`.

Long, Reginald, Panupong Pasupat, and Percy Liang (Aug. 2016). "Simpler Context-Dependent Logical Forms via Model Projections". In: *Proceedings of the 54th Annual Meeting of the Association for Computational Linguistics (Volume 1: Long Papers)*. Berlin, Germany: Association for Computational Linguistics, pp. 1456–1465. DOI: `10.18653/v1/P16-1138`. URL: `https://aclanthology.org/P16-1138`.

Marasović, Ana, Leo Born, Juri Opitz, and Anette Frank (Sept. 2017). "A Mention-Ranking Model for Abstract Anaphora Resolution". In: *Proceedings of the 2017 Conference on Empirical Methods in Natural Language Processing*. Copenhagen,

Denmark: Association for Computational Linguistics, pp. 221–232. DOI: 10 . 18653/v1/D17-1021. URL: https://aclanthology.org/D17-1021.

Marton, Yuval and Asad Sayeed (2022). "Thematic fit bits: Annotation quality and quantity for event participant representation". In: *Proceedings of the Language Resources and Evaluation Conference 2022*. To appear. Marseilles, France.

Marvin, Rebecca and Tal Linzen (Oct. 2018). "Targeted Syntactic Evaluation of Language Models". In: *Proceedings of the 2018 Conference on Empirical Methods in Natural Language Processing*. Brussels, Belgium: Association for Computational Linguistics, pp. 1192–1202. DOI: 10.18653/v1/D18-1151. URL: https://aclanthology.org/D18-1151.

Modi, Ashutosh, Ivan Titov, Vera Demberg, Asad Sayeed, and Manfred Pinkal (2017). "Modeling Semantic Expectation: Using Script Knowledge for Referent Prediction". In: *Transactions of the Association for Computational Linguistics* 5, pp. 31–44. DOI: 10.1162/tacl_a_00044. URL: https://aclanthology.org/Q17-1003.

Moon, Han Cheol, Tasnim Mohiuddin, Shafiq Joty, and Chi Xu (Nov. 2019). "A Unified Neural Coherence Model". In: *Proceedings of the 2019 Conference on Empirical Methods in Natural Language Processing and the 9th International Joint Conference on Natural Language Processing (EMNLP-IJCNLP)*. Hong Kong, China: Association for Computational Linguistics, pp. 2262–2272. DOI: 10.18653/v1/D19-1231. URL: https://aclanthology.org/D19-1231.

Müller, Christoph (2007). "Resolving *It*, *This*, and *That* in Unrestricted Multi-Party Dialog". In: *Proceedings of the 45th Annual Meeting of the Association for Computational Linguistics*. ACL07. Prague, Czech Republic: Association for Computational Linguistics (ACL), pp. 816–823.

Noord, Rik van, Lasha Abzianidze, Antonio Toral, and Johan Bos (2018). "Exploring Neural Methods for Parsing Discourse Representation Structures". In: *Transactions of the Association for Computational Linguistics* 6, pp. 619–633. DOI: 10.1162/tacl_a_00241. URL: https://aclanthology.org/Q18-1043.

Pandit, Onkar and Yufang Hou (June 2021). "Probing for Bridging Inference in Transformer Language Models". In: *Proceedings of the 2021 Conference of the North American Chapter of the Association for Computational Linguistics: Human Language Technologies*. Online: Association for Computational Linguistics, pp. 4153–4163. DOI: 10.18653/v1/2021.naacl-main.327. URL: https://aclanthology.org/2021.naacl-main.327.

Passonneau, Rebecca J. (1989). "Getting at Discourse Referents". In: *Proceedings of the 27th Annual Meeting of the Association for Computational Linguistics*. Vancouver, British Columbia, Canada: Association for Computational Linguistics, pp. 51–59.

Pennington, Jeffrey, Richard Socher, and Christopher D. Manning (2014). "GloVe: Global Vectors for Word Representation". In: *Empirical Methods in Natural Language Processing (EMNLP)*, pp. 1532–1543. URL: http://www.aclweb.org/anthology/D14-1162.

Poesio, Massimo (2015). "Linguistic and Cognitive Evidence About Anaphora". In: *Anaphora Resolution: Algorithms, Resources and Application*. Ed. by Massimo

Poesio, Roland Stuckardt, and Yannick Versley. Berlin Heidelberg: Springer-Verlag, pp. 23–54.

Pradhan, Sameer, Alessandro Moschitti, Nianwen Xue, Hwee Tou Ng, Anders Björkelund, Olga Uryupina, Yuchen Zhang, and Zhi Zhong (Aug. 2013). "Towards Robust Linguistic Analysis using OntoNotes". In: *Proceedings of the Seventeenth Conference on Computational Natural Language Learning.* Sofia, Bulgaria: Association for Computational Linguistics, pp. 143–152. URL: `http://www.aclweb.org/anthology/W13-3516`.

Prince, Ellen F. (1992). "The ZPG letter: Subjects, definiteness, and information status". In: *Discourse description: Diverse linguistic analysis of a fund-raising text.* Ed. by W. Mann and S. Thompson. Amsterdam: John Benjamins, pp. 223–255.

Qi, Peng, Yuhao Zhang, Yuhui Zhang, Jason Bolton, and Christopher D. Manning (2020). "Stanza: A Python Natural Language Processing Toolkit for Many Human Languages". In: *Proceedings of the 58th Annual Meeting of the Association for Computational Linguistics: System Demonstrations.* URL: `https://nlp.stanford.edu/pubs/qi2020stanza.pdf`.

Radford, Alec, Jeff Wu, Rewon Child, David Luan, Dario Amodei, and Ilya Sutskever (2019). "Language Models are Unsupervised Multitask Learners". In: *Technical report, OpenAI.* URL: `https://github.com/openai/gpt-2`.

Raffel, Colin, Noam Shazeer, Adam Roberts, Katherine Lee, Sharan Narang, Michael Matena, Yanqi Zhou, Wei Li, and Peter J. Liu (2020a). "Exploring the Limits of Transfer Learning with a Unified Text-to-Text Transformer". In: *Journal of Machine Learning Research* 21.140, pp. 1–67. URL: `http://jmlr.org/papers/v21/20-074.html`.

— (2020b). "Exploring the Limits of Transfer Learning with a Unified Text-to-Text Transformer". In: *Journal of Machine Learning Research* 21.140, pp. 1–67. URL: `http://jmlr.org/papers/v21/20-074.html`.

Řehůřek, Radim and Petr Sojka (May 2010). "Software Framework for Topic Modelling with Large Corpora". English. In: *Proceedings of the LREC 2010 Workshop on New Challenges for NLP Frameworks.* Valletta, Malta: ELRA, pp. 45–50. URL: `http://is.muni.cz/publication/884893/en`.

Sagot, BenoıFIXME: combining circumflex accent!t (May 2010). "The Lefff, a Freely Available and Large-coverage Morphological and Syntactic Lexicon for French". In: *Proceedings of the Seventh International Conference on Language Resources and Evaluation (LREC'10).* Valletta, Malta: European Language Resources Association (ELRA). URL: `http://www.lrec-conf.org/proceedings/lrec2010/pdf/701%5C_Paper.pdf`.

Samardžić, Tanja (2014). "Dynamics, causation, duration in the predicate-argument structure of verbs: A computational approach based on parallel corpora". PhD thesis. Geneva, Switzerland: University of Geneva.

Seyffarth, Esther (2019). "Identifying Participation of Individual Verbs or VerbNet Classes in the Causative Alternation". In: *Proceedings of the Society for Computation in Linguistics (SCiL) 2019*, pp. 146–155. DOI: `10.7275/efvz-jy59`. URL: `https://aclanthology.org/W19-0115`.

Sorodoc, Ionut-Teodor, Kristina Gulordava, and Gemma Boleda (July 2020). "Probing for Referential Information in Language Models". In: *Proceedings of the 58th Annual Meeting of the Association for Computational Linguistics*. Online: Association for Computational Linguistics, pp. 4177–4189. DOI: 10.18653/v1/2020.acl-main.384. URL: https://aclanthology.org/2020.acl-main.384.

Uryupina, Olga, Ron Artstein, Antonella Bristot, Federica Cavicchio, Francesca Delogu, Kepa Rodriguez, and Massimo Poesio (2020). "Annotating a broad range of anaphoric phenomena, in multiple genres: the ARRAU Corpus". In: *Natural Language Engineering* 26, pp. 95–128.

Warstadt, Alex, Alicia Parrish, Haokun Liu, Anhad Mohananey, Wei Peng, Sheng-Fu Wang, and Samuel R. Bowman (2020). "BLiMP: The Benchmark of Linguistic Minimal Pairs for English". In: *Transactions of the Association for Computational Linguistics* 8, pp. 377–392. DOI: 10.1162/tacl_a_00321. URL: https://aclanthology.org/2020.tacl-1.25.

Warstadt, Alex, Amanpreet Singh, and Samuel R. Bowman (Mar. 2019). "Neural Network Acceptability Judgments". In: *Transactions of the Association for Computational Linguistics* 7, pp. 625–641. DOI: 10.1162/tacl_a_00290. URL: https://aclanthology.org/Q19-1040.

Webber, Bonnie Lynn (June 1988). "Discourse Deixis: Reference to Discourse Segments". In: *26th Annual Meeting of the Association for Computational Linguistics*. Buffalo, New York, USA: Association for Computational Linguistics, pp. 113–122. DOI: 10.3115/982023.982037. URL: https://aclanthology.org/P88-1014.

Yang, Zichao, Phil Blunsom, Chris Dyer, and Wang Ling (Sept. 2017). "Reference-Aware Language Models". In: *Proceedings of the 2017 Conference on Empirical Methods in Natural Language Processing*. Copenhagen, Denmark: Association for Computational Linguistics, pp. 1850–1859. DOI: 10.18653/v1/D17-1197. URL: https://aclanthology.org/D17-1197.

Zhang, Yizhe, Siqi Sun, Michel Galley, Yen-Chun Chen, Chris Brockett, Xiang Gao, Jianfeng Gao, Jingjing Liu, and Bill Dolan (July 2020). "DIALOGPT : Large-Scale Generative Pre-training for Conversational Response Generation". In: *Proceedings of the 58th Annual Meeting of the Association for Computational Linguistics: System Demonstrations*. Online: Association for Computational Linguistics, pp. 270–278. DOI: 10.18653/v1/2020.acl-demos.30. URL: https://aclanthology.org/2020.acl-demos.30.

CHAPTER 8

Linguistically Guided Multilingual NLP: Current Approaches, Challenges, and Future Perspectives

Olga Majewska

Language Technology Lab, University of Cambridge

Ivan Vulić

Language Technology Lab, University of Cambridge

Anna Korhonen

Language Technology Lab, University of Cambridge

CONTENTS

ABSTRACT

The neural revolution has redefined – and many would argue, undermined – the place of traditional linguistics in natural language processing. The pace at which large unsupervised deep learning models conquer new territories of language understanding raises doubts as to the utility of rule-driven approaches and formalised linguistic knowledge in solving the challenges facing future language technology. Strikingly, the potential of leading neural architectures goes beyond solving well-defined problems and learning shortcuts to specific datasets: A growing body of evidence has revealed that they are capable of implicitly acquiring deeper linguistic knowledge directly from text. And yet, their success is only as certain as the availability of ever growing

DOI: 10.1201/9781003205388-8

volumes of language data and resources, inevitable for the small elite of languages dominating the Web but far from guaranteed for thousands of others. It is clear that, to overcome data scarcity, neural models need to become smarter and more sample-efficient as language learners, strategically leveraging information available in one language to help perform a task in another. Could explicit, structured linguistic information help achieve this goal after all? From another perspective, could such human-tailored expert linguistic and symbolic knowledge provide adequate inductive biases to data-hungry neural NLP architectures, where such biases would be invaluable, especially in low-resource scenarios? In this chapter, we consider the empirical evidence for the ability of neural networks to autonomously acquire deeper linguistic understanding from data and discuss what they are still missing. To fill those gaps, we weigh the potential of typological information, intermediate dependency parsing training, linguistic knowledge transfer, and native speaker introspection to provide guidance for multilingual NLP in resource-lean scenarios.

8.1 INTRODUCTION

The virtually unlimited access to vast amounts of language data together with the development of efficient text representation learners have created a situation in NLP research where breakthroughs are conditioned on a combination of modelling work and data scale rather than linguistic guidance and grammar formalisms. While the success of large language models in tackling downstream tasks is the ultimate measure of their utility in real-world applications (Devlin et al., 2019; Peters, Neumann, Iyyer, et al., 2018; Yang et al., 2019), a plethora of targeted probes have since revealed their capacity to develop remarkably rich representations of linguistic structure at different levels of analysis (Hewitt and Manning, 2019; Jawahar et al., 2019; Liu et al., 2019; Tenney, Das, et al., 2019). If exposure to large volumes of raw text is enough to acquire an understanding of hierarchical dependencies in text or fine-grained distinctions between several senses of an ambiguous word, can the new generation of text encoders still benefit from discrete, structured information and algebraic representations of linguistic knowledge? Or are they sophisticated enough linguistic learners to autonomously acquire all they need to know from the implicit cues extracted directly from examples of language in use?

In this contribution, we approach these questions through the lens of an important goal and challenge in natural language processing: *its multilingual expansion*. The availability of large annotated datasets and even unlabelled corpora cannot be taken for granted in the vast majority of languages spoken worldwide, and the data-dependence of current approaches to representation learning makes them prone to fall short in low-resource scenarios. What is more, sophisticated natural language tasks often rely on a nuanced grasp of linguistic properties specific to the language in question, and massively multilingual models prove incapable of capturing all dimensions of cross-lingual variation in an already large set of parameters, resulting in degraded task performance. A better computational understanding of typological distance and closeness between languages should help guide the transfer of information from resource-rich to resource-poor languages, thus mitigating the consequences of the digital language divide. Further, infusing the model with linguistic knowledge relevant to the task at hand could help it become a more robust, sample-efficient learner, capable of maintaining the same level performance even when faced with training data shortages.

In what follows, we weigh the potential of automatic bottom-up linguistic knowledge acquisition on the one hand, and explicit knowledge injection on the other, to support and improve multilingual NLP. In Section 8.2, we discuss the ways in which linguistic typology could give contemporary NLP the predictive power to deal with the challenge of data scarcity, considering how and to what effect recent works have integrated typological knowledge into NLP systems. Next, in Section 8.3 we review the empirical evidence generated in recent years for the existence of deeper linguistic structure in automatically learned text representations and deliberate on whether this makes linguistic annotation superfluous. Then, in Section 8.4, we discuss the results of our empirical study of the usefulness of supervised parsing for semantic language understanding, evaluating the monolingual, and cross-lingual zero-shot performance of the state-of-the-art Transformer-based networks with and without intermediary dependency parsing training. Finally, in Section 8.5, we assess the relevance of structured semantic(-syntactic) knowledge about verbs for large pretrained models' success in downstream tasks, focusing on the challenging problem of reasoning about events. While our analyses undermine the hitherto assumed importance of explicit syntactic training for a range of natural language understanding tasks, the performance boosts offered by injected knowledge about verbs' commonalities with respect to semantic properties and predicate-argument structures reaffirm the continuing relevance of linguistic expertise – and native-speaker introspection – for filling the models' knowledge gaps.

8.2 CAN TYPOLOGISTS HELP MODELS TACKLE CROSS-LINGUAL VARIATION?

Despite the evident commonalities in how humans acquire and then use language to interact with the outside world, true linguistic universals are few and far between and notoriously hard to pin down (Evans and Levinson, 2009; Perfors et al., 2011). The richly varied ways in which similar concepts are expressed and combined to produce more complex meanings across the world's languages constitute one of the major obstacles to the generalisability of modern language technology. Striving for language independence, a prerequisite of scalable, cross-lingually applicable natural language processing methods, researchers inadvertently let biases from few well-resourced languages used for model development percolate into algorithm design (Bender, 2011), resulting in sometimes drastically degraded performance when faced with languages from outside the digitally prominent elite (Blasi et al., 2021; Joshi et al., 2020).

Although the discrepancies found in the structures and lexica of the world's languages are profound, the inter connectedness of humans' language faculty with other cognitive mechanisms imposes constraints on cross-lingual variation, giving rise to certain universal tendencies (Comrie, 1989; Corbett, 2010; Greenberg, 1966). The search for such recurrent patterns and the classification and description of linguistic properties which distinguish languages and language clusters from each other, carried out by linguistic typologists, have given rise to rich inventories of linguistic data systematically organised into attributes and their language-specific values (Dryer and Haspelmath, 2013; Littell et al., 2017; Michaelis et al., 2013). More recently, in order to overcome the bottleneck of slow manual construction and extension of typological databases, and their resultant incompleteness, automatic approaches to acquiring typological information directly from multilingual corpora have been increasingly advocated (Asgari and Schütze, 2017; Bjerva and Augenstein, 2018; Bjerva, Salesky, et al., 2020; Malaviya et al., 2017; Östling and Tiedemann, 2017, *inter alia*).

Given the practical infeasibility of manually constructing linguistic resources and expert-annotated data to support supervised learning in all of the over seven thousand languages spoken worldwide, large typological databases hold promise to help NLP systems intelligently navigate linguistic diversity, providing tools for estimating language closeness, and allowing for leveraging and sharing the limited data available in some languages to make more accurate predictions in others that are similar with respect to certain properties of interest.

In algebraic approaches, typological databases can come in handy as sources of rules. For example, Bender's (Bender and Goss-Grubbs, 2008) Grammar Matrix framework enables generation of rule-based grammars for diverse languages from typological features, bidirectionally mapping surface strings to Minimal Recursion Semantics (Copestake et al., 2005) representations, allowing parsing and generation. Non-algebraic learning methods, on the other hand, have mostly resorted to typological information to guide feature engineering and the design of constraints for machine learning algorithms. To make the discrete linguistic information encoded in attribute-value pairs in typological databases compatible with machine learning techniques, it is typically represented in the form of feature vectors, where each dimension corresponds to a feature value.

One task which has widely benefited from typological guidance is syntactic parsing: the subset of entries in WALS (Dryer and Haspelmath, 2013) providing information on word order has been used with success in a number of studies (Naseem et al., 2012; Täckström et al., 2013; Y. Zhang and Barzilay, 2015). Here, typological information is leveraged within the framework of selective sharing in a language transfer setting, where dependency relations between sentence elements are learned from the whole set of source (resource-rich) languages, but their ordering, which is language-specific, is only learned from languages typologically close to the target.

Another type of approaches has drawn on typological knowledge in order to bias the shared parameters of a joint multilingual model towards some linguistic properties characteristic of a given language. For instance, in the joint multilingual parser of (Ammar et al., 2016), language embeddings consisting of an averaged one-hot vector of WALS typological properties are used to make the parser aware of the input language it is currently dealing with. Typological guidance is further exploited by Daiber et al. (2016), who demonstrate the usefulness of typological word order features in a universal reordering model, trained to predict the word order in the target language based on the syntactic structure of the source language and all WALS parameter settings available for each of the 22 target languages involved in the study.

Used for preordering in a machine translation pipeline, the typologically savvy algorithm was shown to yield strong downstream performance across many pairs of diverse languages.

More recently, there have also been attempts to condition various multilingual neural architectures on dense language vectors, where such vectors are created from the initial discrete, sparse WALS language vectors. The mapping from sparse to dense language vectors can also be optimised as part of the neural model. In this line of work Ustun et al. (2020) and Ansell et al. (2021) demonstrated that such language vectors are useful in adapting large pretrained multilingual language models to specific low-resource languages, even in the absence of any data in the particular target language. In this extremely resource-poor scenario, the model is able to leverage typological similarities between the target language and its related language(s) which are better represented in the model: e.g., adapting to Faroese is possible because the model can utilise its knowledge acquired for Icelandic and other related Germanic languages. Using such vectors with some *a priori* knowledge properties typically outperfomed model variants with randomly initialised language vectors. A similar observation was made by Ponti, Vulić, Cotterell, et al. (2019), where it was shown that conditioning character-level modelling on typological information stored in such dense WALS-based language vectors also yields performance gains.

In addition to their usefulness when integrated into machine learning algorithms, typological databases have been mined to inform the process of data selection. This has been particularly important in language transfer approaches, where the choice of source language data has a large bearing on the success of a method in the target. Deri and Knight (2016) demonstrated this by leveraging the information about genealogical, geographic, syntactic, and phonetic properties available in the URIEL language typology database (Littell et al., 2017) to map high-resource languages to related low-resource counterparts, align phoneme inventories and thus support language transfer of grapheme-to-phoneme models. Beyond its utility in guiding the choice of typologically akin source data for a particular target language, typological information can benefit language transfer at the stage of data pre-processing. For example, Ponti, Reichart, et al. (2018) employ typological features to pre-process treebanks and thus reduce their cross-lingual variation: source-language syntactic trees are adapted in a rule-based fashion to the typological properties of a target language with respect to certain syntactic constructions. Using such pre-processed, structurally compatible trees as input into lexicalised syntax-based neural models is then shown to yield state-of-the-art results in downstream tasks such as Neural Machine Translation and cross-lingual sentence similarity.

These studies, among many others, point towards a greater potential of typological knowledge to provide systematic guidance for the development of cross-lingually robust NLP systems, informing algorithm design and evaluation. In practice, however, its incorporation has so far led to modest improvements rather than significant breakthroughs (Lhoneux et al., 2018; Ponti, O'horan, et al., 2019). While typology-savvy methods achieve stronger results than the linguistically unaware baselines, the margins of improvement are mostly slim. There are a number of potential reasons behind their limited success, including the focus of these methods on only narrow subsets of features, as well as the still restricted, incomplete coverage of the existing databases (e.g., on average, WALS provides values for only around 14% of features for each of its over 2600 included languages (Oncevay et al., 2020)) and the coarse, approximate nature of the features stored in them. Automatic acquisition of typological knowledge from raw text corpora could remedy these limitations, allowing for more complete inclusion of linguistic patterns across various contexts and frequencies of occurrence and capturing language phenomena as gradients rather than discrete by means of continuous representations, immediately usable in deep neural models. Nonetheless, the richness and scope of the information encoded in data-driven representations relies on the language diversity of the corpora used in the process, which is still limited. A promising avenue of research involves combining the signals learned from data with existing discrete knowledge, achieving a synergistic effect. For instance, Oncevay et al. (2020) demonstrated that merging language embeddings learned via multilingual machine translation with syntactic typological features from WALS in a single shared feature space preserves both types of knowledge and can benefit downstream neural machine translation.

However, another, more elusive factor dampening performance gains of linguistically informed systems may be the redundancy of the external information provided to the system. The new generation of neural models have been shown to implicitly develop substantial awareness of linguistic phenomena based on exposure to unannotated text alone, and expert-curated external information nudges them only slightly beyond their baseline performance. In order to truly leverage the evident potential of linguistic information in the current language technology, it is vital to understand what the state-of-the-art models already know. In the next section, we discuss some of the insights provided by the growing body of research focused on dissecting the knowledge stored in the parameters of large language models.

8.3 IN SEARCH OF LINGUISTIC STRUCTURE: HOW DEEP IS THE NEURAL MODELS' UNDERSTANDING OF LANGUAGE?

The excitement sparked within the NLP community at the impressive achievements of recent large self-supervised sentence encoders (Devlin et al., 2019; Peters, Neumann, Iyyer, et al., 2018) has been matched by cautious reluctance to hail these purely data-driven architectures as a panacea for all challenges posed by natural language problems. Their data requirements alone make them available to a small minority of digitally dominant languages, while their size imposes prohibitive demands on computational resources, thus hindering experimentation with different pre-training hyperparameters and objectives. Understandably, much recent work has aimed to pry open the lid of the omnipresent Transformer-based models to help answer the question whether their impressive task-solving capabilities are grounded in a deeper, more nuanced appreciation of the complexity of linguistic expressions than their predecessors. Impressively, there is a growing body of evidence suggesting that these new architectures are indeed far from oblivious to the linguistic structure underlying the observed natural language text.

Some of the first works probing the new generation of token-level deep contextual representations revealed they encode hierarchical relations along with linear word order information (Lin et al., 2019), and at least partial information about parts of speech, syntactic chunks, and thematic roles (Liu et al., 2019; Tenney, Xia, et al., 2019). The impressive extent to which many of the key linguistic notions that have been hitherto manually labelled by experts in syntactic treebanks are learned by large encoders without explicit supervision was demonstrated in a series of syntactic probes designed by Hewitt and Manning (2019) and Manning et al. (2020). Probing BERT vectors (Devlin et al., 2019) for traces of the Stanford Dependencies formalism, they showed that entire dependency trees are recoverable from linear transformations of the network's word representation space. Despite only observing linear word token sequences in text corpora, BERT has demonstrated awareness of the latent syntactic structure and relationships between non-adjacent sentence elements, instead of simply relying on sequential co-occurrence statistics, by successfully predicting subject-verb agreement in English sentences regardless of intervening nouns being present (e.g., *The girl with ponytails was there*), achieving human-like accuracy (Goldberg, 2019). The model's appreciation of long-distance relationships in text has also been demonstrated in the task of coreference resolution, where it outperformed rule-based systems (Manning et al., 2020). The implications of these findings are far-reaching, putting into question the utility of collecting large volumes of syntactically hand-annotated training data to aid downstream tasks.

The search for linguistic structure in pretrained models has not been limited to English alone. Given the discrepancy in the availability of state-of-the-art language technology between English (and few other dominant languages) and the thousand other varieties spoken worldwide, multilingual extension of the existing models has been vigorously pursued, giving rise to large multilingual encoders such as multilingual BERT (Devlin et al., 2019) and XLM-R (Conneau, Khandelwal, et al., 2020). Jointly pretrained on a hundred of languages, these architectures encode text sequences into a shared multilingual representation space, which endows them with powerful cross-lingual transfer capabilities, proven in a variety of morphological, syntactic and semantic downstream tasks (Artetxe, Labaka, et al., 2020; Hu et al., 2020; Kondratyuk and Straka, 2019; Mueller et al., 2020; Pires et al., 2019; Qiu et al., 2020; Y. Wang et al., 2019; Wu and Dredze, 2019). Their success in zero-shot model transfer scenarios implies that they capture some higher-order, language-agnostic information in their parameters. Which parts of their representations are cross-lingually shared, how much language-specific information they preserve and to what extent the shared embedding space encodes patterns of typological variation, are some of the main questions guiding recent probing analyses of massively multilingual models.

Whether the source of effectiveness of the multilingual BERT (mBERT) in cross-lingual dependency parsing, among others, lies in its capacity to learn a cross-lingual representation of syntactic structure was investigated by Chi et al. (2020), in an extension of their earlier English-centric syntactic probes. Notably, their analysis showed that linear transformations of the word embeddings output from the multilingual model recover syntactic tree distances across ten languages, and that the probes trained on one language can recover syntactic structure in other languages in a zero-shot setting, suggesting the presence of cross-lingual syntactic features embedded in a cross-lingual syntactic subspace in mBERT. Indeed, transfer performance between languages was shown to correlate strongly with the degree of overlap between their syntactic subspaces. Intriguingly, the study revealed that the topology of the model's shared syntactic subspace exhibits fine-grained distinctions between dependency relations which align considerably with those captured by the Universal Dependencies (UD) taxonomy, despite no prior exposure to UD dependency labels. Although mBERT is not immune to biases from word order (e.g., separating pre- and post-nominal adjectival modifiers, grouped together under one UD label `amod`), some of the fine-grained distinctions, although in disagreement with the UD formalism, are linguistically valid (e.g., determiners (`det`) are split into definite articles, indefinite articles, possessives, and demonstratives). This finding reveals that massively multilingual models pick up on cross-lingual patterns and universal tendencies without any explicit guidance, and therefore may constitute a powerful tool for unsupervised large-scale linguistic discovery and expansion of existing databases, thus circumventing the bottleneck of manual annotation.

The ability of large multilingual models to capture cross-lingual commonalities within a joint representation space has been shown to extend to other levels of linguistic analysis. The work of Cao et al. (2020) revealed that mBERT embeddings of similar words in similar sentential contexts in different languages demonstrate approximate alignment. This suggests that despite not being trained on parallel corpora, mBERT aligns semantic information across languages within the shared embedding space. Language neutrality of multilingual representations was directly studied by Libovický et al. (2020). They discovered that the contextualised representations are more language-agnostic than the previous generation of static word embeddings, even those explicitly trained to represent words constituting translation pairs similarly using bilingual dictionaries. However, they are not free from language-specific signals, allowing easy recovery of language identity; moreover, clustering of language centroids of the mean-pooled representations largely reflects membership of language families. Interestingly, Beinborn, and Choenni (2020) study of variation in the semantic organisation of concepts across languages using word-level (Conneau, Lample, et al., 2018) and sentence-level multilingual representations (Artetxe and Schwenk, 2019) revealed that they indeed encode subtle cross-lingual differences (i.e. *multilingual semantic drift*), and enable reconstruction of phylogenetic language trees that align with those proposed by etymologists, which points towards the potential of data-driven multilingual models to support theoretical comparative linguistics.

What is note-worthy, cross-lingual commonalities in the organisation of the inferred lexical-semantic information in the contextualised models are found even when the representation space is not shared. Vulić, Ponti, et al. (2020) demonstrated that the representations from language-specific monolingual language models, trained independently on monolingual corpora, sill exhibit latent cross-lingual commonalities, as reflected in the similarities between the embeddings learned for translational equivalents, even if the degree of similarity depends on the typological distance between the two languages (a case of approximate isomorphism (Søgaard et al., 2018)).

Given the structural and semantic cross-lingual commonalities encoded in multilingual representations and the demonstrated ability of the large prertained models to pick up on linguistic cues which had so far been out of reach of distributional methods, the question to what extent they recover typological patterns naturally arises. Choenni and Shutova (2020) probed sentence-level representations from a range of multilingual encoders (LASER (Artetxe and Schwenk, 2019), M-BERT, XLM (Conneau and Lample, 2019), and XLM-R) for lexical, morphological, and syntactic typological features from the WALS database, focusing on 14 typologically diverse languages. Their experiments revealed that all the studied architectures encode information about word order, negation, and pronouns, however, M-BERT and XLM-R generally outperform the other two on lexical and morphological features, and the models differ in terms of where and how the information is stored.

As hinted in the previous section, the richness of linguistic information captured by self-supervised encoders, and the awareness that they develop of cross-lingual patterns of variation, suggest that supplying them with external, discrete typological information, similarly to the approaches discussed in the previous section, may have little bearing on downstream performance due to information redundancy. Bjerva and Augenstein (2021) investigated this problem directly, testing the hypothesis of whether cross-lingual training induces the model to implicitly learn relevant typological information directly from input text, thus diminishing the utility of providing expert typological knowledge explicitly. To do so, they used adversarial techniques to blind the model to typological signals, and subsequently evaluated the impact of this strategy on cross-lingual performance and sharing, governed by latent weights learnt during training. The experiments revealed that impeding access to typological cues indeed damages performance (with the largest effects in POS tagging) and hinders sharing between typologically similar languages, while enabling access to such information has the opposite effect.

These analyses corroborate the hypothesis about the redundancy of information in high-resource settings, where the model picks up on the salient typological patterns independently based on training data and external guidance is superfluous, as reflected in meagre improvements in downstream performance. However, access to typological features stored in a database such as WALS can be critical in low-resource scenarios, where even unannotated data is scarce. In such cases, even a limited number of language-specific properties recorded in an external database can provide guidance useful for cross-lingual sharing and positively impact cross-lingual performance.

8.4 DO LARGE LANGUAGE MODELS NEED TO KNOW GRAMMAR?

As discussed in Section 8.2, integrating typological knowledge into data-driven models has found some success mostly for syntactically oriented NLP tasks such as part-of-speech tagging and syntactic parsing with 'pre-Transformer' model architectures. On the other hand, as discussed in Section 8.3, large Transformer-based language models do seem to capture and encode plenty of implicit syntactic knowledge (Kulmizev et al., 2020). This raises the question: Is external, explicit syntactic knowledge, that is, human-generated syntactic annotations, useful at all when combined with knowledge implicitly encoded within the neural architectures, especially in light of their down-the-line employment in language understanding tasks and applications? While the necessity of supervised syntactic parsing for successful higher-level semantic language understanding has been long advocated in traditional NLP (Chen and Manning, 2014; Klein and Manning, 2003; Kondratyuk and Straka, 2019), recent empirical studies on the interplay between syntax and semantic understanding tasks (Glavaš and Vulić, 2021; Kuncoro et al., 2020) directly challenge this belief. However, this dispute is not a new one by any means: Back in 2007, Bod questioned the superiority of supervised parsing over inducing syntactic structures directly (or implicitly) from the data, but in the context of statistical machine translation.

In particular, a recent empirical study of Glavaš and Vulić (2021) brings the usefulness of syntactic annotations for high-level natural language understanding under renewed scrutiny. Do such syntactic annotations help at all or do large language models already contain all the syntactic knowledge they need to tackle language understanding tasks such as natural language inference, commonsense reasoning, and paraphrase identification? Their main *modus operandi* is to inject syntactic knowledge into the parameters of the language models via intermediate (dependency) parsing training based on a state-of-the-art dependency parser, and then tune such a syntactically enriched model in a series of aforementioned language understanding tasks. Results from both monolingual English and zero-shot language transfer experiments suggest that linguistic knowledge in the form of syntactic annotations, when injected into language models with intermediate source-language and target-language parsing training, has very limited or non-existent effect on downstream semantic understanding performance. A potential explanation of these empirical findings emerges from a deeper examination of the representation spaces: The structural knowledge obtained through simple language modelling pretraining typically overlaps with the structural knowledge injected through intermediate parsing training, especially for languages which do contain sufficient amounts of raw pretraining data. In effect, this might render the external syntactic information redundant. Even if some positive empirical evidence (i.e., performance gains for some tasks) is observed, it appears to be mostly due to the model's exposure to more text data, as in the case of lower-resource languages, not well represented in the massively multilingual language model such as mBERT, and not due to leveraging the information on the syntactic structure in that particular language. This has been demonstrated through experiments that conduct simple masked language modelling instead of parsing training as the chosen 'post-pretraining' task.

While the study of Glavaš and Vulić (2021), which analysed monolingual and multilingual setups, along with similar studies focused on monolingual settings only (Kuncoro et al., 2020; Swayamdipta et al., 2019), renders supervised parsing and syntactic annotations largely inconsequential to semantic understanding tasks, much more work in this area is needed before reaching solid long-standing conclusions, especially in light of (massive) multilinguality and cross-lingual variation. First, one hypothesis that has not been disproved by the observed results is that syntactic supervision might seem superficially redundant simply because current benchmarks do not really test true language understanding (Bender and Koller, 2020). Second, the reported results come with an important caveat: The study drew conclusions from experiments conducted on languages which are considered 'resource-rich' from the NLP perspective (English, German, French, Chinese, and Turkish). One can safely assume that these languages are well represented within the shared multilingual space of a multilingual language model, and also boast large-enough repositories of syntactic annotations. In other words, this redundancy between the knowledge captured in the model's parameters and syntactic annotations might be present and apparent only for such resource-rich languages. Future research should aim to understand whether the more formal knowledge on grammar and structure for other, under-represented languages could indeed bring in useful language-learning-oriented inductive biases in situations where large amounts of raw text data are more difficult to procure. In order to reach a deeper understanding of the (im)balance between the size of available text data for large model pretraining on the one side, versus language-specific and language-universal syntactic and semantic properties on the other side, a wider set of probes and evaluation protocols with a wider set of representative languages is crucially required.

Another potential hypothesis – originating from these recent analytical studies on the connections between syntax and semantic applications – is that the use of linguistic and symbolic knowledge with neural NLP architectures must be tuned and adapted to the task at hand. For instance, while there might be a large mismatch between UD-style general structural knowledge and the knowledge needed to tackle commonsense reasoning with pretrained language models, this does not preclude that some other type of linguistic knowledge might be beneficial for the same task, or that this very type of linguistic knowledge might be proven useful for some other task. Going forward, we advocate more research in this area of understanding knowledge–language–task alignments, with further and finer-grained analyses of such (mis)matches: What do large language models need to know to solve a particular task in a particular language, and can they acquire some of that knowledge from particular linguistic resources? We delve deeper into this question in what follows.

8.5 WHAT CAN MODELS STILL LEARN FROM LINGUISTS (AND NATIVE SPEAKERS)?

The momentum with which progressively more challenging baselines are being surpassed by self-supervised text encoders seems to leave little scope for explicit linguistic guidance. However, despite impressive results in probing experiments targeting specific aspects of linguistic structure, tasks requiring nuanced linguistic reasoning capabilities still pose a considerable challenge for state-of-the-art architectures. Indeed, the fact that some type of information is encoded in a model's parameters does not guarantee that it is being used to solve the downstream task at hand. There is a body of evidence that suggests current models are still prone to fall back on spurious correlations and superficial clues when tackling a natural language problem (Niven and Kao, 2019), rather than relying on their encodings of linguistic information (Rogers et al., 2020).

Within the textual domain, two central problem areas for current approaches are (i) natural language tasks requiring heterogeneous knowledge and making inferences about implicit events and their consequences, left out from text or expressed figuratively (e.g., causal commonsense reasoning (Ponti, Glavaš, et al., 2020; Roemmele et al., 2011), metaphor detection (Song et al., 2021)) and (ii) low-resource scenarios, where the target language training data are scarce or non-existent. Even massively multilingual encoders only cover a fraction of the linguistic territory, and their scores drop to random performance levels when faced with languages not seen in pretraining. Although there are promising post-hoc strategies to boost their capacity to tackle out-of-sample languages (Ponti, Glavaš, et al., 2020), there is still a long way to go until they attain a human-like ability to deal with pragmatic aspects of language (e.g., humour, irony) and derive a full representation of a situation, with its real-world context and constraints, its participating entities and the relations between them, from just a few lines of text.

While the ultimate goal is endowing machines with the capacity to derive the knowledge necessary to fill in gaps and missing connections autonomously, in the meantime, developing methods for explicitly injecting external information to remedy their shortcomings and thus reduce the human-machine performance gap is a worthwhile pursuit. The important prerequisites for the success of such endeavours are (i) identifying what information may benefit the task in question and is lacking in the distributed representations, and (ii) packaging this information effectively, without harming the knowledge already encoded by the model through pretraining on raw text corpora. Recently, a rich body of work has emerged that explores the possibility to boost large pretrained language models with external knowledge, for example, by injecting explicit syntactic biases into BERT pretraining (Kuncoro et al., 2020), adding additional pretraining objectives based on external knowledge sources (Calixto et al., 2021; Lauscher et al., 2020), or using such objectives to fine-tune the parameters of the pretained model post hoc (Liu et al., 2019; Peters, Neumann, Logan, et al., 2019; Zhang et al., 2019).

A lot of reasoning that humans engage in an everyday basis involves making sense of chains of events, their causes and implications, and the roles played by the actors involved. As we read, we implicitly fill in a schematic representation of an event with information based on mentions of agents, objects, and the settings within which they interact, and naturally make inferences about their mutual relations, motivations and goals. Mastering this skill is vital for machine reading systems and has many practical applications, including information retrieval, question answering or text summarisation. Correctly identifying tokens and text spans which refer to events and their participants, and classifying the temporal and causal links between them, are necessary prerequisites for understanding the structure of a story or dialogue (Carlson et al., 2002; Eisenberg and Finlayson, 2017; Miltsakaki et al., 2004). Current event processing evaluation benchmarks test the ability of NLP systems to detect what type of occurrence took place, identifying, and classifying the token(s) corresponding to the event trigger (i.e., the word(s) which evoke the event), when, with respect to other events (based on temporal expressions), and what entities were involved (by identifying entity mentions and assigning them one of the pre-defined roles).

Across languages, the function of evoking an event and acting as its organisational core is predominantly fulfilled by verbs. Acting as pivots within sentence structure, verbs bear important information about the event taking place and its unfolding through time, as well as the relations between and roles of the participating entities. Expressive representations of verbs need to capture the inter-connectedness between verbs' semantics and syntactic behaviour, however, their complex properties are difficult to automatically derive from unlabelled text. Indeed, partitioning the verb lexicon into coherent semantic classes and making nuanced, fine-grained distinctions between degrees of similarity between related verbs still eludes state-of-the-art models (Majewska, McCarthy, et al., 2021), and this deficiency is even more pronounced in languages other than English (Majewska, Vulić, McCarthy, and Korhonen, 2020). In theoretical and computational linguistics, there is an extensive body of work providing rich descriptions and classifications of verb semantics (Croft, 2012; Fillmore, 1976; Levin, 1993; Levin and Hovav, 2005) and corresponding structured databases (Baker et al., 1998; Kipper et al., 2006). The latter, which organise fine-grained semantic-syntactic information about verbs in computer-readable form, have the potential to help refine distributional models' grasp of verbs' properties. The challenge lies in incorporating and combining this discrete knowledge with the continuous, contextualised representations learned by large text encoders from patterns in corpora, which in itself may be one of the milestones towards achieving a general form of intelligence (Cartuyvels et al., 2021).

Given the central role of verbs in expressions of events, and the close link between the cognitive representations of events and verb semantics (Jackendoff and Jackendoff, 2002; Warglien et al., 2012), the quality of verb representations computed by a model should have a bearing on its success in an event processing task. Starting from this assumption, we investigated the extent to which the rich verb-related information stored in structured language resources can be utilised to help large language models tackle the tasks of event extraction and classification (Majewska, Vulić, Glavaš, et al., 2021). To this end, we developed a modular, efficient approach to infuse discrete verb knowledge into a contextualised self-supervised encoder by means of an intermediate pre-training step that avoids the computationally expensive retraining of the entire architecture from scratch, while enabling easy integration with other, diverse types of information.

As a source of expert-curated information about English verbs, we selected two large online lexicons, VerbNet (Kipper Schuler, 2005) and FrameNet (Baker et al., 1998). The former, entirely dedicated to verbs, classifies them into 329 classes (and 272 subclasses) based on the overlap in their semantic and syntactic properties. Central to it is the underlying assumption of predictability between a verb's lexical semantic representation and the syntactic realisation of its arguments (Levin and Hovav, 2005), a principle which is thought to apply cross-lingually (Jackendoff, 1992; Levin, 1993), as illustrated by verb class translatability (Majewska, Vulić, McCarthy, Huang, et al., 2018; Vulić, Mrkšić, et al., 2017). FrameNet has a more semantic focus and organises concepts into 1,224 semantic frames (Fillmore, 1976, 1977, 1982) (i.e., schematic representations of situations and events) which they evoke, characterised by a set of typical roles assumed by its participants. Each frame is thus associated with a set of word senses, which share semantic content and typical argument structures. Given the semantic criteria defining each frame, analogous frames are attested in languages other than English, regardless of different syntactic properties (Bick, 2011; Ohara, 2012; Subirats and Sato, 2004).

To efficiently package the information drawn from each source, we designed an intermediary training task, framed as a binary classification problem: Given a pair of verbs, the goal is to predict if they share the same Verbnet class or FrameNet frame. To disentangle the contribution of each resource, we extracted training examples from each database separately. In order to avoid the trap of catastrophic forgetting, we only trained a small dedicated set of adapter parameters (Houlsby et al., 2019; Pfeiffer et al., 2020) on this auxiliary task, without affecting the knowledge derived in pretraining. Subsequently, we combined the linguistic knowledge encoded in the original model parameters and the additional verb knowledge contained within the verb adapters and evaluated the impact of the latter on event processing tasks. We compared the strengths of three approaches, a) fine-tuning both sets of parameters, (b) freezing both sets of parameters and inserting an additional set of task-specific adapter parameters, and (c) sequentially fine-tuning the full model first on the auxiliary verb-focused task, and then on the downstream task.

We evaluated the success of our proposed verb knowledge injection on two datasets, the TimeML-annotated corpus from TempEval tasks (UzZaman et al., 2013; Verhagen et al., 2010), and the ACE dataset (Doddington et al., 2004), and two corresponding tasks, (i) token-level event trigger identification and classification and (ii) span extraction for event triggers and arguments. Encouragingly, the results on English showed that indeed, complementing the distributional signals in the parameters of the pretrained model boosts its event reasoning capabilities, translating to improvements in downstream task performance. While these results suggest that language resources maintain their relevance for self-supervised text encoders and can provide useful guidance in tasks where accurate verb processing is key, there is a follow-up question that immediately arises: What to do if no such resources are available? Although there have been a number of successful attempts to create VerbNets and FrameNet in languages other than English, such endeavours are costly and time-consuming, and therefore very few languages boast databases of the same quality and scope. Given the cross-lingual applicability of the rationale underlying each resource, in the second phase of this study, we tested the transferability of discrete verb knowledge across languages, without any target-language adjustments.

To this end, we evaluated two cross-lingual transfer approaches: direct model transfer and annotation transfer. In the former, we leveraged the widely used multilingual BERT model (Devlin et al., 2019) and fine-tuned it first on the English verb knowledge (via the word pair classification task), then on the English task data, and finally, we made predictions on the test data in the target language. In the second approach, we took inspiration from previous work on cross-lingual transfer of semantic specialisation for static word embeddings (Glavaš, Ponti, et al., 2019; Ponti, Vulić, Glavaš, et al., 2019; S. Wang et al., 2020). The method starts from the positive training instances used for auxiliary verb-oriented training (e.g., verb pairs sharing a class or frame) and involves (1) automatic translation of verbs in each pair into the target language by retrieving their nearest neighbour in the target language in a shared cross-lingual embedding space, (2) cleaning of the noisy target language verb pairs (due to polysemy and out-of-context translation) by means of a transferred relation prediction model (Glavaš and Vulić, 2018), trained on the English examples to distinguish verb pairs that share an English class or frame from those that do not, and (3) training target-language verb adapters injected into the pretrained model on the translated and filtered target-language verb pairs.

The evaluation of our transfer approaches on Chinese, Spanish, and Arabic revealed that both approaches succeed in supporting the underlying model in solving the problem at hand. Relative typological closeness of Spanish to English, compared to the other two languages, renders direct transfer of semantic-syntactic information more viable, as reflected in significant improvements over the baselines yielded by the translation-based transfer method. Even though automatic verb pair transfer inevitably introduces some noise into the training data, there is a non-negligible amount of information about commonalities in verbs' semantic-syntactic patterns of behaviour that is relevant beyond the source language and can aid event processing in the target language. Nevertheless, while this is encouraging news for cross-lingual transfer scenarios where no in-target lexicons are available, the direct automatic transfer of source linguistic knowledge has obvious limitations. First, there is the anticipated problem of noisy translation, which is only partly addressed by the constraint filtering step (2). Given that automatic translation of verb pairs is based on cross-lingual semantic similarity alone, the closest translation equivalents in the target language may no longer display the shared syntactic behaviour of the source verb pair that makes them fellow VerbNet class members in the source language (i.e., words close in meaning may belong to different VerbNet classes due to differences in syntactic behaviour). Hence, such target language verb pairs may be erroneously labelled as positive training instances. Further, there is the issue of cross-lingual variation with respect to the semantic-syntactic properties of individual verb classes or frame members. Despite the stipulated universal nature of the interplay between verbs' semantics and syntax and the semantically syntactically defined verb class as a lexical organisational unit, verb class membership is language-specific, and therefore they cannot be transplanted from one language to another without adjustments taking into account the properties of the language in question. This contrasts with the wide cross-lingual portability of synonyms and antonyms demonstrated in prior work on semantic specialisation transfer (Mrkšić et al., 2017; Ponti, Vulić, Glavaš, et al., 2019), where cross-lingual semantic similarity is a reliable criterion for generating target language training examples.

As a way of verifying if noisy automatic translation is indeed to blame for limiting the positive impact of injected verb knowledge on event processing performance, we additionally experimented with leveraging clean target language verb knowledge derived from a small lexical database available in one of the target languages – Spanish FrameNet (Subirats and Sato, 2004), using the same procedure as in English. Notably, despite the much smaller scale of the resource (12 times fewer positive instances for training the verb adapter compared to the English FrameNet), the evaluation results revealed that the language-specific Spanish verb adapter outperforms its translation-based counterpart, compensating the limited coverage with gold standard quality. This finding indicates that existing expert-curated databases can still support distributional models in tackling tasks benefiting from a nuanced grasp of verb meaning and syntactic behaviour. However, the inequality in terms of access to such resources across the world's languages remains a fundamental obstacle, together with the slow and expensive construction process involved in their creation.

Given that current models benefit from human linguistic guidance, one potential solution lies in optimising the resource creation methodology. In scenarios where access to target language experts is limited and their work costly, can we turn to untrained native speakers instead? We conclude our investigation by examining the potential of harnessing non-expert linguistic intuitions of native speakers as an alternative source of supplementary knowledge on verb behaviour. To this end, we leverage the verb classes and verb similarity data generated in our precursor work (Majewska, McCarthy, et al., 2021; Majewska, Vulić, McCarthy, and Korhonen, 2020) based on a two-phase data collection approach. First, broad semantic verb classes are produced in a manual clustering task, and are subsequently fed as input into the second phase, where fine-grained semantic similarity judgements are expressed (through drag-and-drop operations) by means of iterative spatial arrangements of verb labels in a two-dimensional space. The multi-arrangement method (Kriegeskorte and Mur, 2012) used to derive symmetric representational dissimilarity matrices for each verb sample was first proposed in the field of cognitive neuroscience for capturing multi-way similarity judgements of visual stimuli. In our adaptation to the textual domain, the technique elicits relative, multi-way, continuous similarity judgements, leveraging the intuitive metaphor of distance in a geometric space as a measure of closeness in meaning and tapping into the spatial nature of the representation of concept similarity in the mental lexicon (Casasanto, 2008; Gärdenfors, 2004; Lakoff and Johnson, 1999).

To inject the information encoded in our multilingual resource, we derived positive instances for adapter training based on the criterion of shared verb class membership, analogously to the experiments with VerbNet and FrameNet data. The evaluation on English and Chinese showed that the classes based on non-expert judgements about verb meaning can indeed be mined for valuable, supplementary information that can augment the knowledge automatically acquired by models from large text corpora. Crucially, experimental results revealed that the impact of non-expert knowledge on downstream performance compares favourably to direct cross-lingual transfer of information from English expert-curated lexicons to the target language. This suggests that native-speaker intuitions about verb semantics can provide important language-specific guidance missing from the automatically translated and refined lexical constraints.

Overall, the results of this inquiry point towards the continuing relevance of linguistic annotations and their underlying formalisms for current deep learning NLP solutions. The experiments using the data generated by non-expert native speakers, as well as the small expert-built dataset in Spanish, reaffirm the value of dedicating efforts to the optimisation and acceleration of annotation methodologies, and the potential of language-specific resources to enrich state-of-the-art NLP models.

While automatic cross-lingual transfer methods offer ways to reuse the structured databases we already have in well-resourced languages, discrete information generated by linguists (or even native speakers) still has a role to play in remedying the models' linguistic knowledge deficiencies. As discussed in the preceding sections, this expertise becomes invaluable in scenarios where not even unannotated text corpora are easily available. Combining the two sources of information – automatic bottom-up acquisition and algebraic representations rooted in linguistic theory – in a joint knowledge augmentation method may offer the key to extending the success of large pretrained models to tasks and languages where these are still under-performing.

8.6 CONCLUSION

The new possibilities brought about by the advent of large pretrained language models are vast, and their utility as engines behind natural language processing solutions unquestionable. And yet, we argued, there is still room in the NLP toolbox for methods that utilise discrete, symbolic linguistic knowledge; in fact, the two paradigms can be successfully combined for an amplified effect. Crucially, much potential of linguistic information remains untapped, given the overwhelming focus of current work on a few resource-rich languages. Future research in multilingual NLP could greatly benefit from using typological information to guide all critical stages of model development, from data selection and pre-processing, to algorithm design, hyperparameter choice, and evaluation. The depth and richness of linguistic knowledge automatically acquired by text encoders is invariably dependant on the scale and diversity of the data, which, in turn, are tightly linked to the language's status. Methods that draw on linguistic insights may therefore play an essential role in helping extend the reach of state-of-the-art language technology to the multitude of under-represented varieties spoken around the world. The key, however, is to use them wisely and purposefully, tuning the weight and extent of the relative contributions of continuous distributional and discrete symbolic information based on the specific requirements of the language and task at hand. Complex natural language understanding tasks still pose a challenge for neural NLP models, and this is further exacerbated in the absence of training data. Correctly identifying and then remedying their shortcomings through targeted linguistic knowledge injection or incorporation of linguistically informed inductive biases can help them become less data-dependent and more robust to cross-lingual variation, the key qualities of truly multilingual, generalisable NLP technology.

BIBLIOGRAPHY

Ammar, Waleed, George Mulcaire, Miguel Ballesteros, Chris Dyer, and Noah A Smith (2016). "Many languages, one parser". In: *Transactions of the Association for Computational Linguistics* 4, pp. 431–444.

Ansell, Alan, Edoardo Maria Ponti, Jonas Pfeiffer, Sebastian Ruder, Goran Glavaš, Ivan Vulić, and Anna Korhonen (2021). "MAD-G: Multilingual adapter generation for efficient cross-lingual transfer". In: *Findings of EMNLP*, pp. 4762–4781. URL: https://aclanthology.org/2021.findings-emnlp.410.

Artetxe, Mikel, Gorka Labaka, and Eneko Agirre (2020). "Translation artifacts in cross-lingual transfer learning". In: *Proceedings of EMNLP*, pp. 7674–7684. URL: `https://aclanthology.org/2020.emnlp-main.618`.

Artetxe, Mikel and Holger Schwenk (2019). "Massively multilingual sentence embeddings for zero-shot cross-lingual transfer and beyond". In: *Transactions of the Association for Computational Linguistics* 7, pp. 597–610.

Asgari, Ehsaneddin and Hinrich Schütze (2017). "Past, Present, future: A computational investigation of the typology of tense in 1000 languages". In: *Proceedings of EMNLP*, pp. 113–124. DOI: `10.18653/v1/D17-1011`. URL: `https://aclanthology.org/D17-1011`.

Baker, Collin F., Charles J. Fillmore, and John B. Lowe (1998). "The Berkeley FrameNet Project". In: *Proceedings of COLING*, pp. 86–90. URL: `http://aclweb.org/anthology/C98-1013`.

Beinborn, Lisa and Rochelle Choenni (2020). "Semantic drift in multilingual representations". In: *Computational Linguistics* 46.3, pp. 571–603.

Bender, Emily M. (2011). "On achieving and evaluating language-independence in NLP". In: *Linguistic Issues in Language Technology* 6.3, pp. 1–26.

Bender, Emily M. and David Goss-Grubbs (2008). "Semantic representations of syntactically marked discourse status in crosslinguistic perspective". In: *Semantics in Text Processing. STEP 2008 Conference Proceedings*, pp. 17–29.

Bender, Emily M. and Alexander Koller (2020). "Climbing towards NLU: On meaning, form, and understanding in the age of data". In: *Proceedings of ACL*, pp. 5185–5198. URL: `https://aclanthology.org/2020.acl-main.463`.

Bick, Eckhard (2011). "A FrameNet for Danish". In: *Proceedings of the 18th Nordic Conference of Computational Linguistics*, pp. 34–41. URL: `https://www.aclweb.org/anthology/W11-4606`.

Bjerva, Johannes and Isabelle Augenstein (June 2018). "From Phonology to Syntax: Unsupervised linguistic typology at different levels with language embeddings". In: *Proceedings of NAACL–HLT*, pp. 907–916. DOI: `10.18653/v1/N18-1083`. URL: `https://aclanthology.org/N18-1083`.

— (Apr. 2021). "Does typological blinding impede cross-lingual sharing?" In: *Proceedings of EACL*, pp. 480–486. DOI: `10.18653/v1/2021.eacl-main.38`. URL: `https://aclanthology.org/2021.eacl-main.38`.

Bjerva, Johannes, Elizabeth Salesky, Sabrina J. Mielke, Aditi Chaudhary, Giuseppe G. A. Celano, Edoardo Maria Ponti, Ekaterina Vylomova, Ryan Cotterell, and Isabelle Augenstein (2020). "SIGTYP 2020 shared task: Prediction of typological features". In: *Proceedings of the Second Workshop on Computational Research in Linguistic Typology*, pp. 1–11. DOI: `10.18653/v1/2020.sigtyp-1.1`. URL: `https://aclanthology.org/2020.sigtyp-1.1`.

Blasi, Damián, Antonios Anastasopoulos, and Graham Neubig (2021). "Systematic inequalities in language technology performance across the world's languages". In: *arXiv preprint arXiv:2110.06733*. URL: `https://arxiv.org/pdf/2110.06733.pdf`.

Bod, Rens (2007). "Is the End of supervised parsing in sight?" In: *Proceedings of ACL*, pp. 400–407.

Calixto, Iacer, Alessandro Raganato, and Tommaso Pasini (June 2021). "Wikipedia entities as rendezvous across languages: Grounding multilingual language models by predicting Wikipedia Hyperlinks". In: *Proceedings of NAACL–HLT*, pp. 3651–3661. URL: `https://aclanthology.org/2021.naacl-main.286`.

Cao, Steven, Nikita Kitaev, and Dan Klein (2020). "Multilingual alignment of contextual word representations". In: *Proceedings of ICLR*.

Carlson, Lynn, Daniel Marcu, and Mary Ellen Okurowski (2002). *RST Discourse Treebank LDC2002T07*. Tech. rep. Web Download. Philadelphia: Linguistic Data Consortium.

Cartuyvels, Ruben, Graham Spinks, and Marie-Francine Moens (2021). "Discrete and continuous representations and processing in deep learning: Looking forward". In: *AI Open* 2, pp. 143–159.

Casasanto, Daniel (2008). "Similarity and proximity: When Does close in space mean close in mind?" In: *Memory & Cognition* 36.6, pp. 1047–1056. URL: `https://doi.org/10.3758/MC.36.6.1047`.

Chen, Danqi and Christopher D Manning (2014). "A fast and accurate dependency parser using neural networks". In: *Proceedings of EMNLP 2014*, pp. 740–750.

Chi, Ethan A., John Hewitt, and Christopher D. Manning (July 2020). "Finding universal grammatical relations in multilingual BERT". In: *Proceedings of the 58th Annual Meeting of the Association for Computational Linguistics*, pp. 5564–5577. DOI: `10.18653/v1/2020.acl-main.493`. URL: `https://aclanthology.org/2020.acl-main.493`.

Choenni, Rochelle and Ekaterina Shutova (2020). "What does it mean to be language-agnostic? Probing multilingual sentence encoders for typological properties". In: *arXiv preprint arXiv:2009.12862*.

Comrie, Bernard (1989). *Language Universals and Linguistic Typology: Syntax and Morphology*. University of Chicago Press.

Conneau, Alexis, Kartikay Khandelwal, Naman Goyal, Vishrav Chaudhary, Guillaume Wenzek, Francisco Guzmán, Edouard Grave, Myle Ott, Luke Zettlemoyer, and Veselin Stoyanov (July 2020). "Unsupervised cross-lingual representation learning at scale". In: *Proceedings of ACL*, pp. 8440–8451. DOI: `10.18653/v1/2020.acl-main.747`. URL: `https://aclanthology.org/2020.acl-main.747`.

Conneau, Alexis and Guillaume Lample (2019). "Cross-lingual language model pre-training". In: *Advances in Neural Information Processing Systems* 32.

Conneau, Alexis, Guillaume Lample, Marc'Aurelio Ranzato, Ludovic Denoyer, and Hervé Jégou (2018). "Word translation without parallel data". In: *Proceedings of ICLR*.

Copestake, Ann, Dan Flickinger, Carl Pollard, and Ivan A Sag (2005). "Minimal recursion semantics: An introduction". In: *Research on Language and Computation* 3.2, pp. 281–332.

Corbett, Greville G. (2010). "Implicational hierarchies". In: *The Oxford Handbook of Language Typology*. Ed. by Jae Jung Song. OUP Oxford, pp. 190–205.

Croft, William (2012). *Verbs: Aspect and Causal Structure*. OUP Oxford.

Daiber, Joachim, Miloš Stanojević, and Khalil Sima'an (2016). "Universal reordering via linguistic typology". In: *Proceedings of COLING*, pp. 3167–3176.

Deri, Aliya and Kevin Knight (2016). "Grapheme-to-phoneme models for (almost) any language". In: *Proceedings of ACL*, pp. 399–408.

Devlin, Jacob, Ming-Wei Chang, Kenton Lee, and Kristina Toutanova (2019). "BERT: Pre-training of deep bidirectional transformers for language understanding". In: *Proceedings of NAACL–HLT*, pp. 4171–4186.

Doddington, George R., Alexis Mitchell, Mark A. Przybocki, Lance A. Ramshaw, Stephanie M. Strassel, and Ralph M. Weischedel (2004). "The automatic content extraction (ACE) program – tasks, data, and evaluation." In: *Proceedings of LREC*. Vol. 2. 1, pp. 837–840.

Dryer, Matthew S. and Martin Haspelmath (2013). "The World Atlas of Language Structures Online". In:

Eisenberg, Joshua and Mark Finlayson (2017). "A simpler and more generalizable story detector using verb and character features". In: *Proceedings of EMNLP*, pp. 2708–2715.

Evans, Nicholas and Stephen C Levinson (2009). "The myth of language universals: Language diversity and its importance for cognitive science". In: *Behavioral and brain sciences* 32.5, pp. 429–448.

Fillmore, Charles J. (1976). "Frame semantics and the nature of language". In: *Annals of the New York Academy of Sciences: Conference on the Origin and Development of Language and Speech*. Vol. 280. New York, New York, pp. 20–32. URL: http://www.icsi.berkeley.edu/pubs/ai/framesemantics76.pdf.

— (1977). "The need for a frame semantics in linguistics". In: *Statistical Methods in Linguistics*. Ed. Hans Karlgren. Scriptor, pp. 5–29.

— (1982). "Frame Semantics". In: *Linguistics in the Morning Calm*. Ed. The Linguistic Society of Korea. Hanshin Publishing Co., pp. 111–137.

Gärdenfors, Peter (2004). *Conceptual Spaces: The Geometry of Thought*. MIT Press.

Glavaš, Goran, Edoardo Maria Ponti, and Ivan Vulić (2019). "Semantic Specialization of Distributional Word Vectors". In: *Proceedings of EMNLP: Tutorial Abstracts*. URL: https://www.aclweb.org/anthology/D19-2007.

Glavaš, Goran and Ivan Vulić (June 2018). "Discriminating between Lexico-semantic relations with the specialization tensor model". In: *Proceedings of NAACL–HLT*, pp. 181–187. DOI: 10.18653/v1/N18-2029. URL: https://www.aclweb.org/anthology/N18-2029.

— (2021). "Is supervised syntactic parsing beneficial for language understanding tasks? An empirical investigation". In: *Proceedings of EACL*, pp. 3090–3104. URL: https://aclanthology.org/2021.eacl-main.270.

Goldberg, Yoav (2019). "Assessing BERT's syntactic abilities". In: *arXiv preprint arXiv:1901.05287*.

Greenberg, Joseph H (1966). "Synchronic and diachronic universals in phonology". In: *Language* 42.2, pp. 508–517.

Hewitt, John and Christopher D. Manning (2019). "A structural probe for finding syntax in word representations". In: *Proceedings of NAACL–HLT*, pp. 4129–4138.

Houlsby, Neil, Andrei Giurgiu, Stanislaw Jastrzebski, Bruna Morrone, Quentin De Laroussilhe, Andrea Gesmundo, Mona Attariyan, and Sylvain Gelly (2019). "Parameter-efficient transfer learning for NLP". In:

Hu, Junjie, Sebastian Ruder, Aditya Siddhant, Graham Neubig, Orhan Firat, and Melvin Johnson (2020). "Xtreme: A massively multilingual multi-task benchmark for evaluating cross-lingual generalisation". In: *International Conference on Machine Learning*. PMLR, pp. 4411–4421.

Jackendoff, Ray (1992). *Semantic Structures*. Vol. 18. MIT Press.

Jackendoff, Ray and Ray S Jackendoff (2002). *Foundations of Language: Brain, Meaning, Grammar, Evolution*. Oxford University Press, USA.

Jawahar, Ganesh, Benoît Sagot, and Djamé Seddah (July 2019). "What does BERT learn about the structure of language?" In: *Proceedings of ACL*, pp. 3651–3657. DOI: 10.18653/v1/P19-1356. URL: https://aclanthology.org/P19-1356.

Joshi, Pratik, Sebastin Santy, Amar Budhiraja, Kalika Bali, and Monojit Choudhury (2020). "The state and fate of linguistic diversity and inclusion in the NLP world". In: *Proceedings of ACL*, pp. 6282–6293. URL: https://www.aclweb.org/anthology/2020.acl-main.560.

Kipper Schuler, Karin (2005). "VerbNet: A Broad-Coverage, Comprehensive Verb Lexicon". PhD thesis. University of Pennsylvania. URL: https://repository.upenn.edu/dissertations/AAI3179808.

Kipper, Karin, Anna Korhonen, Neville Ryant, and Martha Palmer (2006). "Extending VerbNet with Novel Verb Classes". In: *Proceedings of LREC*, pp. 1027–1032. URL: http://www.lrec-conf.org/proceedings/lrec2006/pdf/468_pdf.pdf.

Klein, Dan and Christopher D. Manning (2003). "Accurate unlexicalized parsing". In: *Proceedings of ACL 2003*, pp. 423–430.

Kondratyuk, Dan and Milan Straka (2019). "75 Languages, 1 Model: Parsing Universal Dependencies Universally". In: *Proceedings of EMNLP 2019*, pp. 2779–2795.

Kriegeskorte, Nikolaus and Marieke Mur (2012). "Inverse MDS: Inferring dissimilarity structure from multiple item arrangements". In: *Frontiers in Psychology* 3, p. 245. URL: https://doi.org/10.3389/fpsyg.2012.00245.

Kulmizev, Artur, Vinit Ravishankar, Mostafa Abdou, and Joakim Nivre (2020). "Do neural language models show preferences for syntactic formalisms?" In: *Proceedings of ACL*, pp. 4077–4091.

Kuncoro, Adhiguna, Lingpeng Kong, Daniel Fried, Dani Yogatama, Laura Rimell, Chris Dyer, and Phil Blunsom (2020). "Syntactic structure distillation pretraining for bidirectional encoders". In: *Transactions of the Association for Computational Linguistics* 8, pp. 776–794. DOI: 10.1162/tacl_a_00345. URL: https://aclanthology.org/2020.tacl-1.50.

Lakoff, George and Mark Johnson (1999). *Philosophy in the Flesh: The Embodied Mind and Its Challenge to Western Thought*. Vol. 4. University of Chicago Press.

Lauscher, Anne, Ivan Vulić, Edoardo Maria Ponti, Anna Korhonen, and Goran Glavaš (Dec. 2020). "Specializing Unsupervised Pretraining Models for Word-Level Semantic Similarity". In: *Proceedings of COLING*, pp. 1371–1383. DOI: 10.18653/v1/2020.coling-main.118. URL: https://www.aclweb.org/anthology/2020.coling-main.118.

Levin, Beth (1993). *English Verb Classes and Alternations: A Preliminary Investigation*. University of Chicago Press.

Levin, Beth and Malka Rappaport Hovav (2005). *Argument Realization*. Cambridge: Cambridge University Press.

Lhoneux, Miryam de, Johannes Bjerva, Isabelle Augenstein, and Anders Søgaard (Oct. 2018). "Parameter sharing between dependency parsers for related languages". In: *Proceedings of EMNLP*, pp. 4992–4997. DOI: 10.18653/v1/D18-1543. URL: https://aclanthology.org/D18-1543.

Libovický, Jindřich, Rudolf Rosa, and Alexander Fraser (Nov. 2020). "On the language neutrality of pre-trained multilingual representations". In: *Findings of the Association for Computational Linguistics: EMNLP 2020*, pp. 1663–1674. DOI: 10.18653/v1/2020.findings-emnlp.150. URL: https://aclanthology.org/2020.findings-emnlp.150.

Lin, Yongjie, Yi Chern Tan, and Robert Frank (Aug. 2019). "Open sesame: Getting inside BERT's linguistic knowledge". In: *Proceedings of the 2019 ACL Workshop BlackboxNLP: Analyzing and Interpreting Neural Networks for NLP*, pp. 241–253. DOI: 10.18653/v1/W19-4825. URL: https://aclanthology.org/W19-4825.

Littell, Patrick, David R. Mortensen, Ke Lin, Katherine Kairis, Carlisle Turner, and Lori Levin (2017). "Uriel and lang2vec: Representing languages as typological, geographical, and phylogenetic vectors". In: *Proceedings of EACL*, pp. 8–14.

Liu, Nelson F., Matt Gardner, Yonatan Belinkov, Matthew E. Peters, and Noah A. Smith (June 2019). "Linguistic knowledge and transferability of contextual representations". In: *Proceedings of NAACL–HLT*, pp. 1073–1094. DOI: 10.18653/v1/N19-1112. URL: https://aclanthology.org/N19-1112.

Liu, Qianchu, Diana McCarthy, Ivan Vulić, and Anna Korhonen (2019). "Investigating cross-lingual alignment methods for contextualized embeddings with token-level evaluation". In: *Proceedings of CoNLL*, pp. 33–43. URL: https://www.aclweb.org/anthology/K19-1004.

Majewska, Olga, Diana McCarthy, Jasper van den Bosch, Nikolaus Kriegeskorte, Ivan Vulić, and Anna Korhonen (2021). "Semantic Data set construction from human clustering and spatial arrangement". In: *Computational Linguistics* 47.1, pp. 69–116.

Majewska, Olga, Ivan Vulić, Goran Glavaš, Edoardo Maria Ponti, and Anna Korhonen (Aug. 2021). "Verb Knowledge injection for multilingual event processing". In: *Proceedings of ACL*, pp. 6952–6969. DOI: 10.18653/v1/2021.acl-long.541. URL: https://aclanthology.org/2021.acl-long.541.

Majewska, Olga, Ivan Vulić, Diana McCarthy, Yan Huang, Akira Murakami, Veronika Laippala, and Anna Korhonen (2018). "Investigating the cross-lingual translatability of VerbNet-style classification". In: *Language Resources and Evaluation* 52.3, pp. 771–799.

Majewska, Olga, Ivan Vulić, Diana McCarthy, and Anna Korhonen (2020). "Manual clustering and spatial arrangement of verbs for multilingual evaluation and typology analysis". In: *Proceedings of COLING*, pp. 4810–4824.

Malaviya, Chaitanya, Graham Neubig, and Patrick Littell (Sept. 2017). "Learning language representations for typology prediction". In: *Proceedings of EMNLP*, pp. 2529–2535. DOI: 10.18653/v1/D17-1268. URL: https://aclanthology.org/D17-1268.

Manning, Christopher D., Kevin Clark, John Hewitt, Urvashi Khandelwal, and Omer Levy (2020). "Emergent linguistic structure in artificial neural networks trained by self-supervision". In: *Proceedings of the National Academy of Sciences* 117.48, pp. 30046–30054.

Michaelis, Susanne Maria, Philippe Maurer, Martin Haspelmath, and Magnus Huber (2013). *The Atlas of Pidgin and Creole Language Structures.* Oxford University Press.

Miltsakaki, Eleni, Rashmi Prasad, Aravind K. Joshi, and Bonnie L. Webber (2004). "The Penn Discourse Treebank". In: *Proceedings of LREC.*

Mrkšić, Nikola, Ivan Vulić, Diarmuid Ó Séaghdha, Ira Leviant, Roi Reichart, Milica Gašić, Anna Korhonen, and Steve Young (2017). "Semantic specialization of distributional word vector spaces using monolingual and cross-lingual constraints". In: *Transactions of the Association for Computational Linguistics* 5, pp. 309–324.

Mueller, David, Nicholas Andrews, and Mark Dredze (July 2020). "Sources of transfer in multilingual named entity recognition". In: *Proceedings of ACL*, pp. 8093–8104. DOI: 10.18653/v1/2020.acl-main.720. URL: https://aclanthology.org/2020.acl-main.720.

Naseem, Tahira, Regina Barzilay, and Amir Globerson (July 2012). "Selective sharing for multilingual dependency parsing". In: *Proceedings of ACL*, pp. 629–637. URL: https://aclanthology.org/P12-1066.

Niven, Timothy and Hung-Yu Kao (July 2019). "Probing neural network comprehension of natural language arguments". In: *Proceedings of ACL*, pp. 4658–4664. DOI: 10.18653/v1/P19-1459. URL: https://aclanthology.org/P19-1459.

Ohara, Kyoko (2012). "Semantic Annotations in Japanese FrameNet: Comparing Frames in Japanese and English." In: *Proceedings of LREC.* Citeseer, pp. 1559–1562.

Oncevay, Arturo, Barry Haddow, and Alexandra Birch (Nov. 2020). "Bridging linguistic typology and multilingual machine translation with multi-view language representations". In: *Proceedings of EMNLP*, pp. 2391–2406. DOI: 10.18653/v1/2020.emnlp-main.187. URL: https://aclanthology.org/2020.emnlp-main.187.

Östling, Robert and Jörg Tiedemann (Apr. 2017). "Continuous multilinguality with language vectors". In: *Proceedings of EACL*, pp. 644–649. URL: https://aclanthology.org/E17-2102.

Perfors, Amy, Joshua B. Tenenbaum, and Terry Regier (2011). "The learnability of abstract syntactic principles". In: *Cognition* 118.3, pp. 306–338.

Peters, Matthew E., Mark Neumann, Mohit Iyyer, Matt Gardner, Christopher Clark, Kenton Lee, and Luke Zettlemoyer (2018). "Deep contextualized word representations". In: *Proceedings of NAACL–HLT*, pp. 2227–2237.

Peters, Matthew E., Mark Neumann, Robert Logan, Roy Schwartz, Vidur Joshi, Sameer Singh, and Noah A. Smith (2019). "Knowledge enhanced contextual word representations". In: *Proceedings of EMNLP–IJCNLP*, pp. 43–54.

Pfeiffer, Jonas, Andreas Rücklé, Clifton Poth, Aishwarya Kamath, Ivan Vulić, Sebastian Ruder, Kyunghyun Cho, and Iryna Gurevych (Oct. 2020). "AdapterHub: A framework for adapting transformers". In: *Proceedings of EMNLP*, pp. 46–54.

DOI: 10.18653/v1/2020.emnlp-demos.7. URL: https://aclanthology.org/2020.emnlp-demos.7.

Pires, Telmo, Eva Schlinger, and Dan Garrette (July 2019). "How multilingual is multilingual BERT?" In: *Proceedings of ACL*, pp. 4996–5001. DOI: 10.18653/v1/P19-1493. URL: https://aclanthology.org/P19-1493.

Ponti, Edoardo Maria, Goran Glavaš, Olga Majewska, Qianchu Liu, Ivan Vulić, and Anna Korhonen (Nov. 2020). "XCOPA: A multilingual dataset for causal commonsense reasoning". In: *Proceedings of EMNLP*, pp. 2362–2376. DOI: 10.18653/v1/2020.emnlp-main.185. URL: https://aclanthology.org/2020.emnlp-main.185.

Ponti, Edoardo Maria, Helen O'horan, Yevgeni Berzak, Ivan Vulić, Roi Reichart, Thierry Poibeau, Ekaterina Shutova, and Anna Korhonen (2019). "Modeling language variation and universals: A survey on typological linguistics for natural language processing". In: *Computational Linguistics* 45.3, pp. 559–601.

Ponti, Edoardo Maria, Roi Reichart, Anna Korhonen, and Ivan Vulić (2018). "Isomorphic transfer of syntactic structures in cross-lingual NLP". In: *Proceedings of ACL*, pp. 1531–1542.

Ponti, Edoardo Maria, Ivan Vulić, Ryan Cotterell, Roi Reichart, and Anna Korhonen (2019). "Towards zero-shot language modeling". In: *Proceedings of EMNLP-IJCNLP*, pp. 2900–2910. URL: https://aclanthology.org/D19-1288.

Ponti, Edoardo Maria, Ivan Vulić, Goran Glavaš, Roi Reichart, and Anna Korhonen (Nov. 2019). "Cross-lingual semantic specialization via lexical relation induction". In: *Proceedings of EMNLP–IJCNLP*, pp. 2206–2217. DOI: 10.18653/v1/D19-1226. URL: https://www.aclweb.org/anthology/D19-1226.

Qiu, Xipeng, Tianxiang Sun, Yige Xu, Yunfan Shao, Ning Dai, and Xuanjing Huang (2020). "Pre-trained models for natural language processing: A survey". In: *Science China Technological Sciences*, pp. 1–26.

Roemmele, Melissa, Cosmin Adrian Bejan, and Andrew S Gordon (2011). "Choice of plausible alternatives: An evaluation of commonsense causal reasoning". In: *2011 AAAI Spring Symposium Series*. URL: https://people.ict.usc.edu/~gordon/publications/AAAI-SPRING11A.PDF.

Rogers, Anna, Olga Kovaleva, and Anna Rumshisky (2020). "A Primer in BERTology: What we know about how BERT works". In: *Transactions of the ACL*. URL: https://arxiv.org/abs/2002.12327.

Søgaard, Anders, Sebastian Ruder, and Ivan Vulić (July 2018). "On the Limitations of Unsupervised Bilingual Dictionary Induction". In: *Proceedings of ACL*, pp. 778–788. DOI: 10.18653/v1/P18-1072. URL: https://aclanthology.org/P18-1072.

Song, Wei, Shuhui Zhou, Ruiji Fu, Ting Liu, and Lizhen Liu (Aug. 2021). "Verb metaphor detection via contextual relation learning". In: *Proceedings of ACL–IJCNLP*, pp. 4240–4251. DOI: 10.18653/v1/2021.acl-long.327. URL: https://aclanthology.org/2021.acl-long.327.

Subirats, Carlos and Hiroaki Sato (2004). "Spanish framenet and framesql". In: *Proceedings of LREC Workshop on Building Lexical Resources from Semantically Annotated Corpora*. Citeseer. Lisbon, Portugal.

Swayamdipta, Swabha, Matthew Peters, Brendan Roof, Chris Dyer, and Noah A. Smith (2019). "Shallow syntax in deep water". In: *arXiv preprint arXiv:1908.11047*.

Täckström, Oscar, Ryan McDonald, and Joakim Nivre (2013). "Target language adaptation of discriminative transfer parsers". In: *Proceedings of NAACL–HLT*, pp. 1061–1071.

Tenney, Ian, Dipanjan Das, and Ellie Pavlick (July 2019). "BERT Rediscovers the Classical NLP Pipeline". In: *Proceedings of ACL*, pp. 4593–4601. DOI: 10.18653/v1/P19-1452. URL: https://aclanthology.org/P19-1452.

Tenney, Ian, Patrick Xia, Berlin Chen, Alex Wang, Adam Poliak, R. Thomas Mc-Coy, Najoung Kim, Benjamin Van Durme, Samuel R. Bowman, Dipanjan Das, et al. (2019). "What do you learn from context? Probing for sentence structure in contextualized word representations". In: *Proceedings of ICLR*.

Ustun, Ahmet, Arianna Bisazza, Gosse Bouma, and Gertjan van Noord (2020). "UDapter: Language adaptation for truly universal dependency parsing". In: *Proceedings of EMNLP*, pp. 2302–2315. URL: https://aclanthology.org/2020.emnlp-main.180.

UzZaman, Naushad, Hector Llorens, Leon Derczynski, James Allen, Marc Verhagen, and James Pustejovsky (2013). "Semeval-2013 task 1: Tempeval-3: Evaluating time expressions, events, and temporal relations". In: *Proceedings of the Second Joint Conference on Lexical and Computational Semantics (* SEM), Volume 2: Proceedings of SemEval*, pp. 1–9.

Verhagen, Marc, Roser Sauri, Tommaso Caselli, and James Pustejovsky (2010). "SemEval-2010 Task 13: TempEval-2". In: *Proceedings of SemEval*, pp. 57–62.

Vulić, Ivan, Nikola Mrkšić, and Anna Korhonen (Sept. 2017). "Cross-lingual induction and transfer of verb classes based on word vector space specialisation". In: *Proceedings of EMNLP*, pp. 2546–2558. DOI: 10.18653/v1/D17-1270. URL: https://aclanthology.org/D17-1270.

Vulić, Ivan, Edoardo Maria Ponti, Robert Litschko, Goran Glavaš, and Anna Korhonen (Nov. 2020). "Probing pretrained language models for lexical semantics". In: *Proceedings of EMNLP*, pp. 7222–7240. DOI: 10.18653/v1/2020.emnlp-main.586. URL: https://aclanthology.org/2020.emnlp-main.586.

Wang, Shike, Yuchen Fan, Xiangying Luo, and Dong Yu (Dec. 2020). "SHIKEBLCU at SemEval-2020 Task 2: An external knowledge-enhanced matrix for multilingual and cross-lingual lexical entailment". In: *Proceedings of SemEval*, pp. 255–262. URL: https://www.aclweb.org/anthology/2020.semeval-1.31.

Wang, Yuxuan, Wanxiang Che, Jiang Guo, Yijia Liu, and Ting Liu (Nov. 2019). "Cross-Lingual BERT Transformation for Zero-Shot Dependency Parsing". In: *Proceedings of EMNLP-IJCNLP*, pp. 5721–5727. DOI: 10.18653/v1/D19-1575. URL: https://aclanthology.org/D19-1575.

Warglien, Massimo, Peter Gärdenfors, and Matthijs Westera (2012). "Event structure, conceptual spaces and the semantics of verbs". In: *Theoretical Linguistics* 38.3-4, pp. 159–193.

Wu, Shijie and Mark Dredze (Nov. 2019). "Beto, Bentz, Becas: The Surprising Cross-Lingual Effectiveness of BERT". In: *Proceedings of EMNLP-IJCNLP*, pp. 833–844. DOI: 10.18653/v1/D19-1077. URL: https://aclanthology.org/D19-1077.

Yang, Zhilin, Zihang Dai, Yiming Yang, Jaime Carbonell, Russ R. Salakhutdinov, and Quoc V. Le (2019). "Xlnet: Generalized autoregressive pretraining for language understanding". In: *Advances in Neural Information Processing systems* 32.

Zhang, Yuan and Regina Barzilay (Sept. 2015). "Hierarchical low-rank tensors for multilingual transfer parsing". In: *Proceedings of EMNLP*, pp. 1857–1867. DOI: 10.18653/v1/D15-1213. URL: https://aclanthology.org/D15-1213.

Zhang, Zhengyan, Xu Han, Zhiyuan Liu, Xin Jiang, Maosong Sun, and Qun Liu (July 2019). "ERNIE: Enhanced language representation with informative entities". In: *Proceedings of ACL*, pp. 1441–1451. DOI: 10.18653/v1/P19-1139. URL: https://www.aclweb.org/anthology/P19-1139.

CHAPTER 9

Word Embeddings are Word Story Embeddings (and That's Fine)

Katrin Erk

The University of Texas at Austin

Gabriella Chronis

The University of Texas at Austin

CONTENTS

ABSTRACT

Many words are polysemous, and most of them in a manner that is entirely idiosyncratic, not regular. Word embeddings give us a window into idiosyncratic polysemy: They are computed as an aggregate of many observed word uses, from different speakers. Interestingly, they also pick up what could be called traces of stories: text topics, judgements and sentiment, and cultural trends. This holds for all types of

DOI: 10.1201/9781003205388-9

word embeddings, from count-based vectors to word type embeddings and word token embeddings. In this chapter, we trace the many ways in which stories show up in word vectors, and we argue that this is actually an interesting signal and not a bug. We also perform an in-depth analysis of clusters of contextualised word embeddings, again finding traces of stories, along with an interesting pattern of clustering that could be described equally well as driven by lexico-syntactic patterns and story traces.

9.1 INTRODUCTION: WORD EMBEDDINGS AND STORIES

Deep learning models in machine learning are universal function approximators. Given enough pairs of inputs and outputs of some function, they can learn to approximate it. They project the inputs to latent representations, combine and re-combine them through multiple layers, and thereby learn internal features to best match the data they have seen. This is interesting from a linguistic point of view, not just for the performance of these models on natural language processing tasks but for the latent features that the models learn. Baroni (Chapter 1 of this volume) contends that language models should be treated as linguistic theories in their own right. What linguistic representations, if any, do these models build when they solve natural language tasks? Deep learning models that are language models are particularly intriguing because they are trained on very general and basic tasks such as predicting a held-out word in context, so that we can observe what the models learn when they are simply pushed to observe statistical regularities in texts.

There is a lively ongoing discussion about the syntactic information that deep learning models encode, for example, Gulordava et al. (2018), Lake and Baroni (2018), Lappin (2021), and Linzen et al. (2016), about what syntactic knowledge these models notice, how systematic they are in observing syntactic regularities, and whether they encode syntactic knowledge in a way that is different from standard linguistic formalisms. In the same way, we can ask what machine learning models learn about lexical semantics – and this is what we want to do in this chapter. The questions that we want to look at are analogous to those that are being asked about syntax: What differences in word meaning do machine learning models observe, and encode in word embeddings? And do their observations of lexical regularities differ from how we usually describe word senses?

Word embeddings to some extent reflect categories of things and events in the world, in that words that belong to the same categories tend to be more distributionally similar than words that do not share a category (Burgess and Lund, 1997). Padó and Lapata (2003) and Sahlgren (2008) remark that distributional similarity encompasses a wide array of semantic relations, including (but not limited to) taxonomic relations such as synonymy, hyponymy, and co-hyponymy. There is even work which sets inferring taxonomic structure as an objective for distributional modelling. For example, Kruszewski et al. (2015) and Nickel and Kiela (2017) construct hierarchical taxonomic spaces, Mrkšić et al. (2017) aim to separate antonyms, and Roller et al. (2014) tackle lexical entailment and hypernymy. Webson et al. (2020) remove connotative associations. When one does so, one is selecting meanings related to categorisation as the particular kind of meaning to represent faithfully in the model.

Sahlgren notes that these relations are neither axiomatic nor all-encompassing, and cautions against a prescriptive perspective that would construe any particular kind of meaning as the *a priori* goal of distributional modelling. It is certainly useful to have a lexical model with taxonomic knowledge, but it is a mistake to think that distributional similarity is merely a noisy measure of taxonomic relatedness. That "noise" can contain information about other kinds of meaning, which we are calling stories.

Word embeddings do not just learn about categories of things and events in the world, they also pick up on stories connected to words. This is not an entirely new insight, it has been mentioned over and over again, in bits and pieces, and not just with recent word embeddings but also with old-fashioned count-based vector spaces. For example, word sense induction models seem to pick up not only on what we would call dictionary senses but also more fine-grained usage context (Reisinger and Mooney, 2010). Such usage context can be used to study changes in word connotations (Kozlowski et al., 2019; Kutuzov et al., 2017), but it has also been found to be shot through with harmful social biases that reflect stereotypes. We believe it is useful to view all these observations as facets of the same larger phenomenon: that word embeddings record how humans view the world, what they find important, useful, and useless, what judgements they make, and what stories they like to tell using the words.

What we mean by *stories that people tell with words* is an amalgam of several things, including but not limited to affordances (ways that humans typically use an object), judgements and emotions, and the topical contexts in which words frequently appear. In this chapter, we will explore how these aspects of meaning are reflected in the organisation of contextual distributional space.

When putting a deep learning model into production, there are very real concerns about unforeseen negative impacts lurking inside the black box: cultural bias, prejudice, and misinformation potential. NLP research oriented towards applications often asks how models trained on text can be shaped to more accurately reflect the shape of the world, for example through de-biasing. The same characteristics that pose an obstacle for NLP practitioners present an opportunity to linguists and social scientists: a chance to study the interaction between many different factors which contribute to the meaning and interpretation of language. The traditional distinction between semantics and pragmatics leads to the desire for a transparent model in which we think of the factors which contribute to meaning as separate or separable; there are extensional ('actual world') factors and social factors. On the other hand, Potts (2019) suggests that if we follow the cue that word embeddings give us, we are likely to view these categories as connected and influenced by one another.

In addition to providing a framework for studying distributional semantic similarity, the holistic idea of story meanings is useful for discussions about the mental lexicon. McRae and Matsuki (2009) show that during sentence processing, listeners make use of story knowledge in forming expectations about upcoming words. This could mean that story knowledge is part of the lexicon, or that it is used in sentence processing in addition to the lexicon, or even, as Elman (2009) points out, it could mean that there is no mental lexicon, just mental story knowledge. We think that if there is a mental lexicon, it must contain some story knowledge, for prominent affordances, emotions, and topical contexts. Listeners can draw on this knowledge in sentence understanding and in metaphorical uses of a word that may foreground its social and emotional facets. It may not be possible to draw a clear, principled line between story knowledge in the lexicon and story knowledge that is used in addition to the lexicon, and we do not see it as necessary to draw such a line. Our aim in this paper is to point to work in lexical semantics that is compatible with story knowledge in the lexicon and to the many ways in which embeddings exhibit traces of such knowledge.

The debate about the nature of the lexicon is an old one. In Section 9.2, we look at some theories in linguistics and psychology that consider scenes, events, and background knowledge to be important to word meaning, both out of context and in context. We want to see to what extent the information that we find in word embeddings matches what these theories say about the human mental lexicon and human sentence processing, and whether therefore word embeddings can be used in linguistic analyses informed by those theories. In Section 9.3 we take a tour through research about word embeddings, from count-based word vectors to very recent models, to point out all the different observations that are glimpses of a general "story bias."

The most recent addition to word embedding frameworks are contextualised word embeddings (CWEs), embeddings for individual word tokens instead of word types. These embeddings constitute a fascinating new opportunity for studying lexical meaning in context. It was possible to some extent to do this with word type embeddings that were modified based on their sentence context (Erk and Padó, 2008; Schütze, 1998; Thater et al., 2011) but recent contextualised embeddings have the potential to observe higher-order co-occurrence regularities and therefore much more subtle meaning differences. Do we indeed observe more subtle meaning differences, and can we actually interpret them? This is not a question that we can settle in this chapter, but to get some insight into contextualised word embeddings as lexical representations, we perform an in-depth qualitative analysis of contextualised word embeddings for a small sample of nouns and verbs in Section 9.4. We close the text by speculating on how word embeddings can help us understand how humans understand sentences: how the stories connected to individual words combine to form a story for the overall sentence, and how the sentence story in turn modulates the meanings of the words from which it is constructed.

9.2 FRAMES, AFFORDANCES, EVENTS, AND CONTEXTUAL MODULATION IN WORD MEANING

When you know the meaning of a word, what do you know? When you know the word *cat*, you certainly know properties of cats, such as: that they are furry, whiskered, and carnivorous. You may also know what things in the world you can label as cats. But that is not all. Words are also connected to connotations, emotional affects, larger scenes, pieces of background knowledge, typical events, circumstances, even perspectives. When a speaker (or signer, or reader) encounters a word in context, the word might evoke for them a particular referent. It might also evoke for them any and all of these other dimensions of meaning. To refer to these facets in a theory-neutral way, we use the term *stories*. Story meaning is related to referential meaning, but it is not the same. The idea of story meaning is not new. It had been translated into theoretical frameworks and motivated by psycholinguistic evidence. In this section, we trace these different notions through the literature in linguistics and psychology. What arises, in spite of all differences, is a clear picture of story-like knowledge as an important part of word meaning, both lexicalised and in context.

Fillmore (1982) describes words as connected to *frames*. A frame is a "categorisation of experience" (p. 112), a piece of background knowledge connected to a word. Fillmore's frames are prototypes in the sense of Rosch (1973). They are part of a word's memorised meaning; when the word is used, it evokes its frame. A frame can be a scene with typical participants. For example, the scene for the word *criticise* involves a Judge and a Defendant. In an utterance, these scene participants are verbalised as semantic roles of the verb *criticise*. Frames also include cultural knowledge. Fillmore uses the example of *breakfast*, writing (p. 118): "to understand this word is to understand the practice in our culture of having three meals a day, at more or less conventionally established times of the day, and for one of those meals to be the one which is eaten early in the day, after a period of sleep."

The frame that forms the background of a word can be highly specific. Fillmore's example is the word *decedent*. A decedent is a dead person, but the word is only used in the context of inheritance. The frame concept is later developed into a "semantics of understanding", or U-semantics which contrasts with T-semantics, a semantics of truth (Fillmore, 1985). Fillmore argues that truth values are not enough to describe what it means to understand a sentence, that it is important to consider the frames evoked by the words. Multiple words can connect to the same prototypical scene but take different perspectives on it. This is the case with *buy* and *sell*, which both describe a commerce scene, but differ in who is the profiled agent, and which other participants are typically named. Emotions and judgements, too, are important parts of frames. Fillmore (1985) uses the example *My dad wasted most of the morning on the bus* (p. 230), where the choice of the word *dad* instead of *father* lets us draw conclusions about the speaker's relationship with his father, and the word *wasted* "brings into play a judgement that the time was not used profitably [...] and this depends on a framing of time as a limited resource (Lakoff and Johnson, 1980)."

Prototypical scenes can have participants that are heroes and villains, so evoking a frame can mean passing a judgement. This connects frames to the notion of *framing* in the social sciences (Kuypers, 2009), where a framing is a schema of interpretation. Linguistically, framing can take the form of a frame in the sense of Fillmore, or a conceptual metaphor (Lakoff and Johnson, 1980). Lakoff (2004, p. 56) uses the example of *tax relief*. The word *relief* evokes a frame with clear heroes and villains. The term *tax relief* casts taxes as a scourge, taxpayers as suffering victims, and politicians who lower taxes are the rescuers. So the notion of *framing*, like Fillmore's frames, involves stored, prototypical scenes but focuses on the judgements, in some cases the biases, imparted by the use of a particular frame.

In contextualism, the focus is on the contextual *modulation* of word meaning: the influence of context on word meaning, including what could be called story context. In a classical example by Travis (1997, p. 89), Pia has a red-leaf shrub but does not like the red, so she paints the leaves green. If, upon completion of her task, she says: "This is better. The leaves of my tree are now green," she has spoken the truth. But imagine that now a botanist asks around for some green leaves for a study on photosynthesis, and Pia says, "The leaves of my tree are green, you can use them." This time, so the argument goes, she has not spoken the truth – the point being that context can interfere with word meanings to an extent that the truth conditions of a sentence are changed. The context influence in the *green leaves* example is a story influence, but one that comes from the discourse context, imposed on the word *green* from the outside, if you will, rather than evoked lexically.[1] Recanati (2017) connects these dynamic context influences back to the lexicon, building on the theory of Meaning Eliminativism from Recanati (2003, ch. 9). In that earlier work, Recanati offers several accounts of word meaning that allow for context influences. One of them is Meaning Eliminativism, where the idea is that listeners do not generalise over observed word uses to form abstract word senses, they just remember observed occurrences in all their story context. In a new situation, the speaker chooses to use the word if the situation is sufficiently (contextually) similar to a previous use of the word. Recanati (2017) sketches how polysemy can arise in a Meaning Eliminativism setting: The listener remembers the observed usages, so if a usage context is sufficiently frequent, it will be remembered strongly enough to function as a separate sense.

In psychology, a number of studies have shown the influence of event knowledge on human sentence processing, measured through priming effects, and effects on reading times (McRae and Matsuki, 2009). Event verbs cue typical arguments, but conversely, nouns cue event verbs for which they are typical agents, patients, or instruments (McRae, Hare, et al., 2005): *Chef* cues *cooking*, *tax* cues *paid*, and *chainsaw* cues *cutting*. This could be interpreted, at least in part, as objects cueing their affordances (Gibson, 1966), that is, the actions that humans typically do with them. The event knowledge that affects human sentence processing can be very fine-grained, such that different patients are cued depending on different agents of the action. *Journalists* are expected to *check the spelling*, while *mechanics* are expected to *check the brakes* (Bicknell et al., 2010). Bicknell et al. (2010) use words where this expectation cannot be explained by a direct association between the agent and patient, for example, *journalist* does not cue *spelling*. The effect is only found in the presence of the verb – which means that it is hard to describe this effect in any way as lexical. In fact, Elman (2009) speculates about "lexical knowledge without a lexicon:" Given that event knowledge affects sentence processing strongly and early on, and given that this knowledge does not seem to be lexical, is it possible that there is no lexicon at all? Intriguingly, the computational mechanism that Elman uses to demonstrate lexical knowledge without a lexicon is a language model (an RNN). We

---

[1]Del Pinal (2018) affirms the effect of context on word meaning but seeks to rein in context effects on a lexical basis: Context can only modify specific lexically given dimensions, which coincide with the qualia used in Pustejovsky (1991).

TABLE 9.1   Some annotator choices for lexical substitutes for the noun *charge* in the sense of a person in one's care, from Kremer et al. (2014).

Now, how can I help the elegantly mannered friend of my Nepthys and his surprising young <u>charge</u>?	dependent, companion, person, lass, protégé
The distinctive whuffle of pleasure rippled through the betas on the bridge, and Rakal let loose a small growl, as if to caution his <u>charges</u> against false hope.	dependent, companion, private, underling, prisoner, troop

will return to the question of "lexical knowledge without a lexicon" below, when we look at recent contextualised language models.

Summing up, there are many different notions of story-like influences connection with word meaning. There are affordances, prototypical scenes and events, and pieces of background knowledge, sometimes with a focus on the facts of the situation, sometimes with explicit inclusion of cultural contexts as well as emotions and judgements connected to a scene. (Fillmore's frames encompass all of these notions of stories when they are prototypical; we use the term *story* to encompass both frames and dynamic, non-prototypical story contexts.)[2] In the next section, we check which of these different types of lexicalised story influences we can observe in word embeddings.

Words lexically evoke stories, but they also jointly cue stories that they do not evoke lexically. And their meanings are dynamically modulated by the story told by the sentence, and the discourse, as a whole. This interaction between frequent, lexicalised meanings and the story at hand can be clearly seen in the lexical substitution data we collected in Kremer et al. (2014), where annotators provided lexical substitutes for words in context. Many substitutes are not WordNet-synonyms, -hypernyms or -hyponyms of the original target but context-specific, story-specific. Table 9.1 shows two example sentences, both with the target noun *charge* in the sense of someone that you take care of or that you oversee. The substitutes reflect this commonality: we get *dependent* and *companion* in both sentences. But the first sentence seems to be from some kind of ballroom story, and the *charge* in question is likely a young girl. The second sentence seems to be part of a war story, where the *charges* are more likely to be prisoners or subordinates. With respect to word embeddings, this raises the question of whether contextualised word embeddings are fine-grained enough to capture not only frequent usage contexts but also these subtle effects that the context at hand exerts on word meaning.

---

[2]Trott et al. (2020) argue for the importance of *construal* in language, and in natural language processing. Construal is about how "linguistic choices subtly colour meaning." The notion of construal overlaps with what we call story influences, for example Trott et al. include metaphor in their list of dimensions of construed meaning, but they explicitly exclude background knowledge evoked by words and other effects that Fillmore includes in U-semantics. So construal has some overlap with story-like influences, but it is not the same.

9.3 STORIES, FROM COUNT-BASED WORD VECTORS TO CONTEXTUALISED EMBEDDINGS

Word embeddings computed from text corpora record statistical regularities about how the words are used. Patterns of language use encode many different kinds of information, about word senses, human concept representation and the mental lexicon, sizeable amounts of world knowledge, and social and cultural contexts of use. This is all well known. But we think it is instructive to look at story-like influences in word embeddings comprehensively, across all the tasks in which they have shown up, to see that they come together to paint a single picture: Word embeddings capture how humans engage with words and with the world, the typical stories they tell and kinds of value judgements they make.

To start, there is the distinction of *similarity* and *relatedness* in lexical items. *Similar* words have properties in common and are close to one another in a taxonomy. *Related* words pertain to the same topics. (We italicise the terms *similar* and *related* to distinguish this specific meaning of the terms from their general-language use.) A jug is *similar* to a bucket. A hammer is *related* to a nail. Distributional models reflect both kinds of relations. In fact, they can be tuned to focus on one or the other by changing the size of the context window. Count-based co-occurrence models which use smaller context windows are better at predicting similarity relations, while those with larger windows are better at predicting semantic relatedness judgements. Sahlgren (2006) noted this phenomenon anecdotally, and subsequent empirical testing has confirmed the context window effect both in Dutch (Peirsman, 2008) and English (Baroni and Lenci, 2011). Felix Hill and colleagues exploit the fact that distributional models can be tuned to focus on either similarity or relatedness to study lexical concreteness (Hill et al., 2013) and to tune distributional spaces towards particular tasks (Kiela et al., 2015). This difference between *similarity* prediction and *relatedness* prediction has been shown for contextualised language models as well. Chronis and Erk (2020) show that the final layers of BERT (Devlin et al., 2019), which contain more propagation of contextual information, are better at relatedness, but earlier layers best predict similarity. We will make use of this fact in our qualitative analysis in Section 9.4. Linking the notions of *relatedness* and *similarity* to the theories from the previous section, Fillmore's (1982) notion of frames is very general, so that both groups of *related* words and groups of *similar* words should be frames, though the frames in the FrameNet resource (Fillmore et al., 2003) are groups of *similar* words. The words that fill roles in a frame could be characterised as being *related* to the lexical units in the frame. *Relatedness* links words that tend to appear in the same stories, or in the same generalised events in the sense of McRae and colleagues.

As a second piece of the puzzle, when distributional models are used to extract context items that are interpretable in themselves, as in Baroni, Murphy, et al. (2010) and Baroni and Lenci (2010), they do not tend to extract typical attributes. Baroni, Murphy, et al. (2010) write about the extracted context items for *motorcycle*: "we clearly see here the tendency of [the model] [...] to prefer actional and situational properties (riding, parking, colliding, being on the road) over parts (such as wheels and engines)" (p. 233). These actional properties are similar to affordances and to the event verbs that McRae, Hare, et al. (2005) found to be primed from the mention of nouns that are typical agents, patients, or instruments.

Again and again, story effects show up as noise in natural language processing tasks. Reisinger and Mooney (2010), doing word sense induction, notice that their clustering algorithm sometimes picked up on what they call "thematic polysemy" (p. 1174). For instance, it discovered two very distinct "senses" for the word *wizard*, one of them the "King Arthur wizard", the other "Hogwarts wizard". Is there an analytic difference between this thematic polysemy and the distinct related word senses like *running a computer program* and *running a marathon*? Intriguingly, humans feel that these usages clearly constitute the same sense of *wizard* but in different contexts. We will see similar story effects in clusters made from contextualised embeddings below in Section 9.4.

Story effects are also visible in diachronic studies. A similar issue appears as with word sense induction, in that if you try to detect changes in sense, you also observe changes in the social context of a word while the sense stays the same. This leads to spurious detected sense changes, as reported in Rosenfeld (2019) and Del Tredici (2020). Strikingly, Kutuzov et al. (2017) employ the same methods that are being used to find diachronic changes in word sense but use them to detect changes in cultural context, in particular outbreaks of armed conflict. The analysis of word embeddings for the cultural context of words is still in its beginnings, but is growing. In the social sciences, Kozlowski et al. (2019) analyse word embeddings over time for dimensions representative of social class.

There is much recent research on mitigating and detecting social bias in word embeddings, starting with Bolukbasi et al. (2016). Webson et al. (2020) characterised the de-biasing task as a task of distinguishing denotation from connotation. When we view the task in this way, bias can be viewed as just another type of story effect– where the stories that people tell often involve judgements, or are dependent on particular cultural associations. One problem with existing work on de-biasing is that it needs to define a bias in order to remove it, so it always focuses on some particular, well-defined type of bias, often gender bias, or left-versus-right political bias in the case of Webson et al. (2020). Maybe seeing bias as a story effect can help us find more general techniques to (at least partly) separate the categories of items, and their properties, from the stories that people tell about them.

9.4 ET TU, BERT?

As a language model, BERT (Devlin et al., 2019) is emblematic of the current transformer architecture paradigm. In contrast to type-level distributional models, BERT leverages representations of individual word occurrences, or tokens, which take into account the surrounding sentential context. For word token embeddings, as for word type embeddings, we can ask to what extent they reflect stories. We first again check the existing literature, before moving on to a qualitative analysis of BERT embeddings for a small sample of lemmas.

In the NLP literature, the natural first place to look is the task of sense disambiguation and sense induction. Contextualised language models achieve state of the art accuracy on several word sense disambiguation benchmarks, achieving F1 scores 10 or 20 percent higher than the baseline of selecting the most frequent sense (Wiedemann et al., 2019). Contextualised language models also lead to massive leaps in the harder task of word sense induction, though the best models still perform well below human levels (Amrami and Goldberg, 2019). This gap in performance between language models and humans is intriguing; the error analysis in Amrami and Goldberg (2019) hints that the model sometimes creates clusters specific to particular topics.

In the realm of lexical semantics, contextual word embeddings have been employed most commonly to study semantic change. Giulianelli et al. (2020) coin the phrase "usage types" to describe the kinds of clusters formed by BERT tokens. In some cases, they found them to make distinctions based on metaphoricity, syntactic roles and argument structure, as well as phrasal collocations (conventional multi-word expressions) and named entities. Finally, looking at de-biasing, most research on this topic has been done on type embeddings, but biases have also been found, and de-biasing efforts undertaken, for contextualised language models (Bommasani and Cardie, 2020; Kaneko and Bollegala, 2021). This research indicates that many words "list" to one side of a cultural axis of meaning.

9.4.1 A Qualitative Analysis of BERT Tokens

To get a clearer sense of the kinds of story effects we find in contextualised embeddings, we perform a qualitative analysis of word token embeddings in BERT for a small number of noun and verb lemmas. As our main basis of the analysis, we use clusters of BERT token embeddings.[3] Following our previous work (Chronis and Erk, 2020), where we found that multi-prototype embeddings derived from the middle layers of BERT best approximate word *similarity* (as opposed to *relatedness*), we look at clusters for the 8th layer of the 12 layer BERT. If any layer were to distinguish senses while not being overly sensitive to story effects, we would expect it to be layer 8, based on its ability to predict word similarity. As in 2020, we sample a number of tokens for each lemma, drawn from the British National Corpus (BNC; here, we use a maximum of 100 tokens per lemma), and use a fixed number of five clusters per lemma, obtained using k-means clustering. In order to counteract distortions introduced by the fixed number of clusters, we additionally visualise token vectors in the Context Atlas visualisation tool, which shows T-SNE plots of BERT tokens from Wikipedia (Coenen et al., 2019).[4]

---

[3]For this study, we use the 12 layer `bert-base-uncased` model available from the HuggingFace Python API (Wolf et al., 2020). The model is pre-trained with standard training objectives on English Wikipedia and the BookCorpus (Zhu et al., 2015). We interpret the hidden representations above a token as the contextual embeddings for that token. Since there are twelve layers, this yields 12 vector representations of each token. For words consisting of more than one sub-word token, like 'in #depend ##ence', we follow the precedent of averaging the embeddings of each of its tokens.

[4]Interactive demo available at `https://storage.googleapis.com/bert-wsd-vis/demo/index.html`. The clusters apparent from observing the Context Atlas are neither more comprehensive, nor identical to the clusters we generate. The kinds of organisation we see according to genre/topic/framing are not as prevalent in Context Atlas, which is limited to usages from Wikipedia. This goes to show that when conducting statistical research into lexical semantics, one must be very mindful of the distribution one draws from and whose language it represents.

Our main analysis comprises 45 nouns, sampled from nouns that appear at least 25 times in the BNC. We sampled 5 nouns each from three polysemy bands (1 sense, 2-5 senses, 6 and more senses) in WordNet 3.0 crossed with three bands of concreteness according to the concreteness norms of Brysbaert et al. (2014) (average concreteness ratings 0-2.3, 2.3-4.5, 4.5-5.0). In addition, we inspected some verbs from the stimulus list of Bicknell et al. (2010). This study, which we discussed in Section 9.2, studies effects of generalised event knowledge on expectations in sentence processing, with stimuli pairing, for example *the mechanic checked the brakes* with *the journalist checked the spelling*. Here we want to know whether BERT will separate the Bicknell agent/verb/patient combinations. We again focus on BERT layer 8.

In the following, we discuss particularly interesting lemmas as well as general trends we observe across all the lemmas. This study has all the advantages and disadvantages of a qualitative study: Because we look at the data 'by hand', we may notice subtleties that a quantitative analysis may miss, and patterns we had not anticipated. The downside is that the analysis is subjective. We even observed differences in our interpretation of the clusters between the two authors. It is also small in scale, and we may simply not be able to perceive some higher-order statistical regularities underlying the data because they are too different from surface co-occurrences. However, in most cases, the rough groupings have natural interpretations and/or particular features, both syntactic and semantic, which distinguish them from one another. In our analysis, we see some story effects, especially in verbs and high-polysemy nouns. In addition to distinguishing senses, BERT notices subtle distinctions which look a lot like affordances, narrative and topic effects, and is also sensitive to syntactic and collocation effects.

9.4.2 Sense Separation

Among mildly polysemous nouns (2-5 senses), there is great variation on the extent to which the clusters reflect WordNet senses. For some concrete words, senses are clearly separated into different clusters: a smoking *pipe* is distinguished from a plumbing *pipe*, programming *libraries* are distinguished from lending *libraries*. For *bottle*, one cluster focuses on the physical object while others focus on the contents. *Shoe* behaves similarly. Most of its WordNet senses are very rare. Here the clusters organise according to topic/genre as well as to grammatical cues. There is one cluster dedicated to actions done by or to a shoe, such as kicking in a door or getting-some-sticky-substance-stuck-to-the-bottom-of. This cluster could be described as "shoe in a narrative." Another cluster focuses topically on the shoe industry. This cluster could alternatively be described as involving compound nouns with shoe, such as *shoe store, shoe repairer, shoe factory*. Interestingly, a separate compound noun cluster isolates the topic of shoe-related items like *shoe laces* and *shoe polish*. Syntactic patterns and topic jointly yield clusters with definite perspectives on shoes: as a commodity, as an

---

Some kinds of story effects are more prevalent in scientific literature, others in fiction. The topics we can discern are not necessarily definitive or most significant to the meaning of the English word, but they are the most significant in our corpus.

TABLE 9.2   WordNet senses for *load*.

Sense	Example
(a) fill or place a load on	*load the truck with hay*
(b) put (something) on a structure or conveyance	*load hay onto the truck*
(c) supply (a device) with something necessary to function	*load the gun*
(d) transfer from storage to a computer's memory	*load the software*
(e) corrupt, debase, or make impure	*load the servers* (as in overload)

object functionally consisting of several components, or as a participant in a narrative event.

Abstract nouns with a mild degree of polysemy tend to have closely related senses. WordNet lists four senses for *admission,* where the first is a confession, and the other three are to do with entry to an event or location. Admission can refer to the cost of entry, the permission to enter, or the act of entering. BERT distinguishes the confession sense quite clearly. However, it mixes the other three senses between different clusters.

Verbs tend to display a greater degree of polysemy than nouns, and on average are more abstract. We find that for verbs, grammatical cues are a stronger organising principle than topics. In Layers 7 and 8, clusters can typically be recognised as distinguishing different grammatical constructions in which the verb is used. In many cases this corresponds to sense separation—for instance, in a given construction that is only used for one or two of a verb's many senses. We observe that more topical separation is sometimes reached in the final layer.

Take for example the word *load,* whose five WordNet senses are shown in Table 9.2. At layer 8, there are two distinct clusters which capture the computer loading sense (d) and one cluster which captures the "put" sense (b). The clusters seem to group both by syntactic and topical similarity. Examples of *load* in the "put" cluster (Table 9.3, cluster 3) all have an overt direct object corresponding to the Patient argument, as well as a locative phrase denoting the Location or Goal of movement. Sentences in the computer cluster of *load* all have topical words related to computers, and the direct object position is always overt. Cluster 1 contains most of the "fill" senses (in which the Location or Goal occupy direct object position) as well as sentences which do not contain enough context to disambiguate between uses. In the final layer of the network, we see separations that more closely correspond with the topic and less with grammatical cues. Sometimes this results in the separation of a sense, and sometimes it results in the collapse of several senses. The "fill" and "put" senses are merged in a cluster to do with loading vehicles. The "corrupt/overload" sense is separate.

In attempting to relate the degree to which BERT distinguishes dictionary senses, we were forced to countenance the many ways in which BERT organises meaning; it is difficult to talk about BERT's separation of senses without talking about other kinds of stories. Story effects crop up at all levels of polysemy and concreteness. In *library,* there are clusters corresponding to different metonymic senses of library, as

TABLE 9.3   Tokens of *load* from the BNC clustered according to their representations at layer 7 of BERT base.

Cluster	Description	Examples
0	adjectival nominal	... that 's not even a half **load**. straps at top of shoulder slings for fine adjustment to **load** carrying.
1	ambiguous "fill" "charge"	Others will **load** at Mareham in Norfolk. to **load** our jeep up from the magazine Although slow to **load** and fire, hand guns can penetrate armour more easily than arrows. The alternative, when plutonium is seen as a fuel, is to **load** it into existing Russian reactors ...
2	computer infinitival/modal	It only took six seconds to **load** each room but some puzzles require you to operate buttons in several rooms, so you would obviously be running between rooms for a while. If it does, they will be overwritten when you **load** the line editor.
3	"put"	Standing up, she began to **load** the tea-things on to a tray. The defendant helped to **load** the goods into Ballay's van. Some way away a couple of humans were using some sort of machines to **load** boxes into a hole in the side of the plane.
4	computer imperative first position	**Load** it from starting Window. Bulk **load** a wrong formulation or a not a wrong formulation. **Load** it up, arrange your features into a smirk and invite the nearest Mac user to come and have a butcher's.

an organisation or as a building. We also see a cluster that focuses on the books and people in the library. This latter distinction corresponds to different attitudes or perspectives surrounding a single sense of the word. There are two separate clusters for the "hollow tube" sense of *pipe*: one in which a pipe is seen as a medium through which a substance moves (such as water, waste, in one case sea otters!), and the other in which pipes are seen as raw material for constructing or engineering a system. It is hard to tease apart different kinds of story effects, because they tend to interact. Story effects also often coincide with syntactic cues. In some cases, when BERT manages to isolate a sense (as with admission to a hospital), it is a consequence of isolating a topic which only makes use of one of those senses. To see how the different types of story effects interact, we take a detailed look at one word: *independence*.

9.4.3 Interaction between Topic, Sense, and Narrative Type: *Independence*

The noun *independence* has one main WordNet sense: freedom from control over others. This encompasses both individual freedoms and state sovereignty, though the line between encyclopedic and lexical meanings is drawn differently in different lexical resources.[5] Of the five clusters generated for *independence* (Table 9.4), three pertain exclusively to political independence. Of the other two, one small cluster pertains to collective independence of non-political bodies and abstract bodies ("the press," "phonemes," "interpreters.") The final, large cluster, pertains to independence of individuals ("one's manhood and independence," "her independence and organising ability.")

With the separation between state and individual independence, the clusters for *independence* demonstrate something like sense distinctions (even if WordNet does not list state sovereignty and the personality trait as separate senses—perhaps it should!) The three clusters relating to political independence exhibit differences in the type of narrative. We mentioned that *independence* has two clusters of state independence. Of these, one seems to be anticipatory ("432 votes in favour of party independence," "vague promises about independence," "The vote for independence") and the other seems to reflect on an accomplished event ("The DEMOS...had led Slovenia to independence," "smaller than anticipated flows of aid after independence," "Qatar gained full independence"). In both clusters is the same sense of independence, but the perspective on the event of independence is different. This does not correspond with any single grammatical cue. This close look at *independence* demonstrates how senses, selectional preferences, and topical information all interact to organise meanings.

9.4.4 Affordances, Narratives, Events

Affordances, in the sense of Gibson (1966), are the properties of an object which allow it to function in different capacities. Embeddings organised according to affordances encode manners in which the word is experienced by a subject. Embeddings are subjective not just in the sense that they encode emotional and affective meaning (which they do), but also in the sense that they encode different phenomenological perspectives on a word. This phenomenon is clearly observed for the word *desk*. Only one sense for desk is recorded in WordNet, but The New Oxford American Dictionary distinguishes a subsense for the counter where one checks in or receives information (the front desk) (in addition to two more uncommon senses). The BERT clusters for *desk* (Table 9.5) mirror these sub-senses, and make further distinctions seemingly related to topic. Two of the five clusters (1, 3) contain the information desk subsense. Two clusters (0, 2) seem to refer to desks as a surface holding objects, where cluster

---

[5]WordNet also lists a second sense with a highly limited meaning, for references specific to the successful conclusion of the American war for independence from Britain.

TABLE 9.4   Tokens of *independence* from the BNC clustered according to their representations at layer 8 of BERT base.

Cluster	Description	Examples
0	sovereignty	At the Estonian CP congress there were 432 votes in favour of party **independence**, three votes against and six abstentions. They were then on the verge of **independence**. The politicians made vague promises about **independence**. By 1814 [...] the prospects for **independence** were gloomy; Bolívar had been driven out of Venezuela and New Granada was about to be recaptured.
1	political entity (other than state)	The **independence** of the cities was effectively strangled. The test by this time was no longer '**independence** of Moscow' but 'Human Rights'. The older though continuing tensions between cultural authority and cultural **independence** have been transformed by the increasingly dominant social relations of the new means of production and reproduction. In his resignation speech, Gorbachev asserted that although he had been in favour of "the **independence** and self-determination of peoples and the sovereignty of republics," he had also believed in "preserving the union state and the country's integrity"
2	organisation	The existence of these characteristics required the **independence** of the profession from interference by government. Other systems have used different strategies [...], for example, the HMM 's erroneous assumption about **independence** between adjacent phonemes means that the acoustic evidence is underestimated. That is that practices in theoretical, moral-practical, and aesthetic spheres become 'contingent' in their **independence** from externally imposed order. The concept of the 'freedom of the press' must, therefore, be appraised with reference to the structural and organisational **independence** of the press from the state.
3	personality	His films reflect his background, a masculine world where one's manhood and **independence** can only survive through violence. Joshua's physical **independence** was achieved because he was young and motivated. Departments [...] have received instructions that–whatever the precise degree of **independence**–the minister is answerable to Parliament for whether the body is working efficiently and economically. Her **independence** and organising ability had been displayed early when she joined the Girl Scouts in 1909 and formed the first Bournemouth troop of guides.
4	colonialism	The Islamic Republic of Mauritania, formerly part of French West Africa, gained full **independence** in 1960. Launch of the Burma **Independence** Army (1942) **Independence** of Lithuania, Estonia and Latvia Qatar gained full **independence** from the United Kingdom in 1971.

TABLE 9.5 Tokens of *desk* from the BNC clustered according to their representations at layer 8 of BERT base.

Cluster	Description	Examples
0	surface for papers	Small machines like the Olivetti PCS 33 and the Packard Bell Elite 1000 don't take up much **desk** space, but they don't leave you with much room for future expansion either. In New Scotland Yard John McLeish was trying, increasingly irritably, to clear his **desk** so he could go home. Would you really, and think carefully about this, trust all your personal information; diary, telephone list and so on to the memory of that recalcitrant computer on your office **desk**? Nigel himself vacillated between belief in and total rejection of death, and busied himself with sorting out his **desk** and jettisoning surplus papers.
1	reception; location; direct object/ prepositional phrase	In the hotel lobby, Bodie came away from the **desk** and spoke briefly to Cowley . When she turned again she saw Mahoney approaching the **desk**. Madame Gauthier was perched on a stool at the reception **desk**, making up her accounts. She ushered them into a small cluttered room where a middle-aged woman in a navy dress sat behind a littered **desk**.
2	movement across surface; definite article	Edward 's fingers drummed on the edge of the **desk**. There was the thin voice beating at him across the **desk**. He showed her into another bare cubicle where two hatchet-faced men were scribbling, and pointed to a phone that lay scratched and bruised on the **desk**. The draft position paper goes sliding over the edge of the **desk** into the waste-paper basket as I snatch up the receiver.
3	reception; function	Rather, the offer is made by the customer when he takes the goods to the cash **desk** [...] The information **desk** was manned throughout the weekend, the timetable was strictly adhered to and everyone benefited from the efficiency. We do need a **desk** in both places–a desk to welcome people is important.
4	somebody's desk; workstation source/destination of movement	If you have to leave your **desk** [...] When he got to Kafka's **desk**, he spoke. Dyson took off his overcoat and went to his **desk**, frowning heavily. My mother was working at her **desk**. He arrived at his **desk**, squinted at the offering tucked into his blotter and sat down to read it properly: [...]

0 focuses more on clutter ("clear his desk so he could go home", "busied himself with sorting out his desk" but also "desk lamp") and cluster 2 more on movement across the surface ("the draft position paper goes sliding over the edge of the desk", "flipped the five ten-pound notes across the desk .", "fingers drummed on the edge of the desk", "reached over the desk for a bottle of pills", "the receiver was dangling under the desk"). While the clusters are only partly distinguishable topically, they differ grammatically, where cluster 2 but not 0 uses past tense and the definite determiner 'the' on *desk*. Comparing clusters 2 and 3, we see that tokens exemplifying the same sense of desk (a furniture with a flat surface at which one can work) cluster together according to their affordances: as a surface, or as a location at which a person is working. The same participants might be present in the situations described by these sentences—a person, the furniture, papers strewn about—but the aspect of the desk afforded to the reader shifts. And BERT picks up on these shifts.

Box, a concrete word with high polysemy, also pays attention to affordances. One cluster specifies boxes full of stuff—that is, boxes seen as containers ("box of matches", "box of dolls", "box of bullets". Another cluster specifies boxes that *do* things—boxes which contain or comprise some kind of mechanism ("phone box", "connection box", "junction box").

Context clues to affordances blend into context clues for associated events, which seem the organising principle for the word *letter*. The alphabet sense of the word is not attested enough in the BNC.[6] We almost exclusively see the epistle sense of the word. Letters in this sense participate in different kinds of events—sending, reading, producing. These events afford or emphasise different prototypical participants. The clusters for *letter* are given in Table 9.6. Cluster 0 contains uses that overtly refer to the act of sending or receiving. This event information interacts with topic information: cluster 0 is also largely limited to letters sent in an official capacity. Cluster 1 contains usages in which personal letters are exchanged between individuals. Here we find letters as texts that are being read, or else as physical objects with which people interact. Cluster 2 usages focus on the speech act of communicating information by way of a letter. Grammatically, they contain overt reference to both author and recipient/audience, as well as a subordinate clause detailing the thematic content of the letter.

We see a similar sort of topic/event interaction in the word *admission*. Recall that BERT recognises very distinct senses (admission of guilt vs. admission to an event/location), but does not distinguish between the metonymic senses listed in WordNet (cost of access, right to access, or the act of giving access). Rather, BERT distinguishes topic clusters (admission to an event, admission to a hospital, admission to an institution or school). What's interesting about these clusters is that in some of them, you see all three metonymic senses, but in some of them, only one or two senses apply: the hospital cluster contains only the act of entering/giving access, because in the hospital frame, admission does not prototypically incur a fee or require an application.

---

[6]The alphabet sense of *letter* however forms a distinct cluster at layer 8 in Context Atlas.

TABLE 9.6 Tokens of *letter* from the BNC clustered according to their representations at layer 8 of BERT base.

Cluster	Description	Examples
0	official letter;	They had received yet another **letter** from the school ...
	recipient named;	It is probably a surprise to you to receive a **letter** from me. The next morning a letter came for Matthew.
	sending event	**Letter** to the Editor: Tie is staying in place well
1	personal letter;	Please, old friend, come to my house at once with this **letter** in your hand.
	movement events; reading events	It was a good **letter**, if a little pompous.
		He pulled a crumpled **letter** out of his shirt pocket, opened it and handed it to her to read.
2	sender named;	But, as Olga said in her **letter** to me, one weeps more often because one is not free.
	recipient named;	One **letter** from 12 senators, including Edward Kennedy, spoke of the 'continuing human rights abuses of British security forces'.
	speech act	Thank you for your **letter** of 2 November 1992 regarding the problems associated with the above property.
		In that connection, I should like to quote from a **letter** that the Secretary of State wrote to the right hon. Member for Selby (Mr. Alison)...
3	noun complement	The contract required the yard to open a **letter** of credit . . .
		POST OF CONFIRMATION OF **LETTER** OF OFFER
		A proper **letter** of instruction is vital.
		This month's **letter** of the month prize is a luxurious Cotman Watercolour Box from Winsor & Newton.
4	alphabet letter; unclear	These consist of a capital **letter** followed by numbers.
		Points referred to in accompanying **letter**.
		This is a standard record update **letter** to be sent to a client
		In seperate [sic] incidents, two farmers were injured by **letter** bombs thought to be from animal rights extremists.
		Activity in the target **letter**'s detector will therefore be inhibited (switched off).

9.4.5 Framing

The lemmas in this study are too broadly chosen to show clear instances of the kind of bias targeted in the de-biasing literature. We do, however, see cases where BERT distinguishes separate framings of a noun, as when different contexts invite different value judgements. In the clusters for fire (Table 9.7), there is a distinction between dangerous, destructive fire (cluster 1), small domesticated fires (cluster 3), and fire which is characterised in terms of how it is physically experienced, both physically and metaphorically (cluster 0). The latter cluster contains both literal and figurative references to the experience of fire, but in each case, the fire is framed as an intense or transformative experience rather than a destructive one. Note that different fire-related experiences are allocated to different clusters: "He was tired, and the heat of the fire was making him sleepy," is assigned to the hearth cluster, and "I was as much arsonist as alchemist now, swinging the axe gleefully, impervious to everything but the fire's appetite," is assigned to the destructive event cluster. What we are seeing here is an organisation of the human emotions towards fire into several attitudes. Different kinds of fire are categorised into stories that come pre-packaged with judgements.

9.4.6 Syntactic cues and their interaction with senses, topics, and affordances

As noted in several above cases, BERT consistently groups common syntactic constructions together. Sometimes these syntactic differences seem to be the only distinguishing trait of clusters, but in many cases the differences in syntax coincide with differences in sense, or other kinds of story outlined above. In short, *subtly different uses of a word tend to have their own syntactic fingerprint.*

The noun *train* offers a good illustration of this phenomenon. One cluster groups together tokens of *train* which serve as the argument to a preposition ("on the train", "in the train", "straight off the London train"), as well as those which serve as an argument to the verb *board* ("She boarded the train in advance of him.") Semantically, these usages all convey the meaning of a train as a container, with people inside it. Movement of the train is not typically entailed in these usages. There is another cluster which groups together tokens of *train* which are syntactic subjects. This group clusters together sentences in which the movement of the train is foregrounded ("This train would take her there," "And the train is getting nearer," "The train stops at Greenwich"). This cluster also contains tokens which contain words related to movement, without the syntactic cues ("The sheep gazed through the bars at the departing train," "He was left behind by the rest of the wagon train"). So in the usages where the train is more likely to be the subject, it is also more likely to be in motion. In contrast with this story, which foregrounds the train, another cluster of *train* tokens entails motion from a different perspective: as a connection between two locations or a journey as a whole. These instances of *train* are often syntactically objects, with animate subjects ("get a train from Glasgow down to Girran," "Needs to catch uncrowded train," "they took the train to London.")

The close ties between syntactic behaviour and variations in meaning has been well studied. In her now standard book on verb classes and alternations, Levin (1993) hypothesised that differences in meaning influence syntactic behaviour. BERT, in

TABLE 9.7   Tokens of *fire* from the BNC clustered according to their representations at layer 8 of BERT base.

Cluster	Description	Examples
0	transformative fire;	An occasional shaft of sunlight penetrated the foliage and lit up the bronze trunks of the pines, touching them with **fire**.
	intense feeling;	Adam swiftly read the titles, most of which contained romantic words like 'love', 'heart', 'arrow', 'passionate', '**fire**', 'dream', 'kiss', and 'enchanted'.
	emotion	Changez said nothing, but shuffled backwards, away from the **fire** of Anwar's blazing contempt, which was fuelled by bottomless disappointment.
		Never again, except in the nostalgic hopefulness of a few—would the ceremonies be performed; gone were the offerings, the blood-shedding, the **fire** and incense, the gorgeous (and the plain) robes . . .
1	destructive fire; arson	There was a **fire** at Mr's store and they called it arson.
		An electrical short circuit started the **fire**, they think.
		Mr Green hopes the **fire** will provoke further pledges of aid to People In Need at 1113 Maryhill Road, Glasgow.
		A woman and seven children left a house in nearby Gudmunsen Avenue after a **fire** was discovered in a bedroom at around 7.30am on Saturday.
2	artillery;	Small-arms **fire** scorched a web of gaps through the foam.
	metaphorical artillery	Almost immediately, there was a brief burst of machine-gun **fire**, which destroyed the three remaining wheels.
		'The hierarchy are now under **fire** because of the team's performance and are seeking to deflect criticism by blaming me.
		Following an exchange of **fire** the Ju88 flew back to Sicily in a damaged condition and with one crewman wounded, but one Beaufighter—T3239 'B' crewed by Flt.Lt.
3	hearth	or reading in the shadow of a **fire**;
		They all went over to the **fire** for plates of meat and bread.
		The light from the **fire** bathed her in a warm flickering glow as he lay down beside her.
		The bar is warm and cosy, with an open **fire** and oak beams.
4	compound nouns;	Now add the top of the fireback, bedding it on top of the lower half with a layer of **fire** cement
	control over fire	That's when the **fire** brigade arrived.
		Mr Small said **fire** alarms were installed and special voice tapes would tell people to leave the premises.
		A **FIRE** station is to be put up for sale, a council report has revealed.

picking up on rather complex syntactic patterns, may be finding semantic groups of usages to which these patterns correspond.

We do not want to be overly optimistic. Sometimes, *all* you can see are syntactic patterns, without any specific meanings (story-related or otherwise) separated out. Sometimes not even that, for example in the clusters for the verb *fix* and the noun *analysis*.

9.4.7 Fine-grained Story Effects on Individual Occurrences?

In Section 9.2 we discussed how some theories focus on memorised, lexicalised story contexts, while others primarily look at dynamic, ad-hoc context effects on individual tokens. In our qualitative analysis in this section, we have seen plenty of evidence for something like memorisation of frequent senses: Frequent usage contexts form coherent clusters. But it remains unclear to what extent contextualised embeddings are sensitive to the fine-grained context effects like those that contextualism discusses and those that we observe in lexical substitutes (Table 9.1). Manual inspection of token clusters is a tool that is much too blunt to answer this question, but it remains an important question to be probed with quantitative measures in the future.

Looking specifically at the verbs in our study, which as mentioned above were pulled from the stimuli of Bicknell et al. (2010), we can ask whether we see the fine-grained event knowledge effects that Bicknell and colleagues found in their participants: does BERT make a difference between *journalist checks spelling* and *mechanic checks brakes*? Here we find that when the different usages each are sufficiently frequent (as with *worker operates machinery* versus *druglord operates cartel*), we see the stimuli falling in different usage groups,[7] but when a usage is not very frequent, or when many uses are blurred without clear clusters (which is the case with *check*), we cannot see a distinction. Again, this could be because some patterns influencing embedding locations may not be discernible in manual inspection.

9.4.8 Discussion

In this section we examined a number of nouns, both concrete and abstract, both polysemous and 'monosemous' (at least according to WordNet), along with some verbs, and explored how BERT organises tokens of these word in relation to each other. Our aim has been to get a clearer sense of the semantic generalisations (and their syntactic reflections) that contextualised language models are able to see. We found that tokens are often grouped by shared syntactic constructions or prototypical topics, where sometimes differences in syntax can be a cue to differences in topics. What is interesting for the study of word meaning is that division along these lines often leads to organisation according to particular stories, which are sometimes at odds with traditional sense distinctions. There are distinctions along the lines of prototypical affordances, events, and evaluative framing—the meaning of *train* (Section 9.4.6)

---

[7]Again, sometimes we see this in our BNC-based clusters, sometimes only in the Wikipedia tokens of the Context Atlas. These are genre effects, which we get even with such a general corpus as the BNC.

emerges from the situated perspectives from which trains are encountered—as containers, as conveyances, as moving objects.

This understanding invites new strategies for building applied machine learning systems in which it is important to control the types of meaning used. Work on the discovery and mitigation of biases in word embeddings is often framed in terms of untangling the 'truth' of the matter from spurious correlations in the data or separating out denotation from connotation. We hope that our analysis complicates the idea that there *is* some truth of the matter which can be abstracted from the perspectives according to which it is perceived.

Work on bias focuses on instances where the model exhibits discriminatory behaviour towards oppressed and minority groups. Ideally, debiasing language models constitutes a separation of fact from stereotype, denotation from connotation, events from their emotional framings. It is important to recognise that, given the close-knit relation between sense and story in word embeddings, denotation from connotation, debiasing efforts are likely to yield tools which allow for greater *control* over the narrative or story before they enable the elimination of story effects entirely. Further analyses should examine the kinds of stories by which contextualised language models organise culturally loaded terms, and experiment with tuning the model in or out to different kinds of story.

Through qualitative evaluation of what information BERT collapses and what distinctions are represented, we can approximate whether the representations accord with any extant theory of the lexicon. This is a question not of which theory is 'correct', but which one(s) the model has found suitable to its task of language modelling.

Some of the usage groups found by BERT match word senses that we find in dictionaries; others match distinct stories told around words in what might be called the same dictionary sense. But to what extent can we distinguish between word senses and stories? Story meanings are already inherent in the way many words are analysed into senses, for example in the senses of *admission*, which reflect admission as a price, as a permission, and as an action, and which are arguably distinguished by prototypical events. On the other hand, word embeddings miss generalisations like in the case of *wizard* discussed in Section 9.3, maybe because they miss information on real-world attributes that Hogwarts wizards and King Arthur wizards have in common.

In Section 9.2 we mentioned Elman's proposal of "lexical knowledge without a lexicon" (Elman, 2009). Is that what modern language models such as BERT are? The architecture of transformer encoders makes it possible to fulfill Elman's vision: tokens are never represented independently of their left and right neighbours, and representations can vary continuously across tokens of the same word.[8] It is certainly the case that BERT contextual embeddings encode lexical knowledge at the level

---

[8]This might also have been said of the RNN developed by Elman himself, but in an RNN the lexical knowledge is all mixed into a single vector which represents "the text so far". Transformer models such as BERT build representations which can be interpreted as corresponding to individual words in the text. Thus, the model produces on the fly representations of each token of a word on the basis of the surrounding context, without selecting a specific sense of the word.

of the lemma. BERT token vectors of a lemma vary, but they do tend to cluster together (apart from tokens of other lemmas). Mickus et al. (2020) measure how well BERT-space is divided by lemmas by calculating the silhouette score of token vectors with respect to other vectors of the same lemma.[9] In the last layer of `bert-large-uncased`, the authors determine, one quarter of BERT tokens would be better assigned to a word-type other than their own. Put another way, three quarters of tokens cluster together well with their own type. In the large majority of cases, the lemma would appear to be a significant level of organisation, much as with a lexicon. In our qualitative analysis, we observe some token groups that correspond to clear senses, another representation level important to the construction of a lexicon. But is it a lexicon, a collection of identifiable representations of senses that we can point to? This requires more analysis, with better tools than we currently have, but given how strongly some usage patterns stand out as token groups, it would be reasonable to assume that the language model has memorised frequent co-occurrence patterns as 'senses'.

9.5 CONCLUSION

Word embeddings that are computed from text capture statistical regularities about how words are used. It has often been noted, in the context of many different tasks, that this usage context includes what may be called stories connected to the words. When these pieces of evidence are put together, as we did in Section 9.3, they form a strong picture of a "story bias" that includes typical events, typical stories that people tell when they use a word, affordances (ways in which people interact with objects), as well as judgements and biases.

We think that it is useful to see all the different instances of "story bias" as part of a whole. With an eye on natural language processing applications, we see individual instances of bias and prejudice as types of stories that people tell around words, which may give us new ways of addressing bias. For linguistics and social science, word embeddings are also a resource, a distilled corpus, which we may be able to use to get additional insights about people's relation to words and objects from the way they talk about them; we have seen some glimpses of this in the qualitative analysis in Section 9.4.

There are some approaches in formal semantics that propose integrating word embeddings as fine-grained representations of word and phrase meaning, including Asher et al. (2016), Baroni, Bernardi, et al. (2014), Bernardy et al. (2018), Clark et al. (2008), Emerson (2018), McNally (2017), Muskens and Sadrzadeh (2018), and Zeevat et al. (2017). In these approaches, there is a tendency to interpret embeddings as denotational, or to create explicitly denotational embeddings (in Bernardy et al. (2018),

---

[9]The silhouette score is used to determine whether an observation $\mathbf{v}$ assigned to cluster $C_i \in C$ is well-assigned to that cluster, or whether it would be better off assigned to another cluster in C. It is calculated as a function of the 'cohesion' of the vector to other vectors in the assigned cluster and the 'separation' between the vector and other observations outside the cluster; a vector with a high silhouette score is maximally close to other observations in the cluster and maximally distant from observations in other clusters.

Herbelot (2020), and Herbelot and Copestake (2021) and Lappin (2021, ch. 6)). We think it will be interesting to integrate such frameworks with fine-grained representations of stories, and of story-modulated word meanings. As noted in Baroni, Murphy, et al. (2010), text-based word vectors seem not to notice object properties as strongly as human participants do, and denotational embeddings tend to foreground particularly those object properties. So it will be interesting to explore mechanisms for how object properties and "story context" interact in determining meaning in context – mechanisms that might underlie Fillmore's U-semantics: How is a "sentence story" constructed from the individual components of the sentence, and how can we both construct the whole from its parts and have the parts be modulated by the whole? Two formal/distributional approaches, Chersoni et al. (2019) and our own Erk and Herbelot (2020), explicitly model story effects at the sentence level, and could serve as a basis for studying these questions. In such a framework, word embeddings could serve either as representations of lexicalised, stored meanings, or as representations of meaning in a particular sentence context.

BIBLIOGRAPHY

Amrami, Asaf and Yoav Goldberg (May 2019). "Towards Better Substitution-Based Word Sense Induction". In: *arXiv:1905.12598 [cs]*. arXiv: 1905.12598 [cs].

Asher, Nicholas, Tim Van de Cruys, and Márta Abrusán (2016). "Integrating type theory and distributional semantics: a case study on adjective-noun compositions. Computational Linguistics". In: *Computational Linguistics* 42.4, pp. 703–725.

Baroni, Marco (2022). "On the proper role of linguistically-oriented deep net analysis in linguistic theorizing". In: *Algebraic Structures in Natural Language*. Ed. by Shalom Lappin and Jean-Philippe Bernardy. Taylor and Francis.

Baroni, Marco, Raffaella Bernardi, and Roberto Zamparelli (2014). "Frege in Space: A program for compositional distributional semantics". In: *Linguistic Issues in Language Technology* 9.6, pp. 5–110. URL: http://elanguage.net/journals/lilt/article/view/3746.

Baroni, Marco and Alessandro Lenci (2010). "Distributional Memory: A general framework for corpus-based semantics". In: *Computational Linguistics* 36.4, pp. 673–721.

— (2011). "How we BLESSed distributional semantic evaluation". In: *Workshop on GEometrical Models of Natural Language Semantics (GEMS)*. Edinburgh, Great Britain. URL: www.aclweb.org/anthology/W11-2501.

Baroni, Marco, Brian Murphy, Eduard Barbu, and Massimo Poesio (2010). "Strudel: A corpus-based semantic model based on properties and types". In: *Cognitive Science* 34.2, pp. 222–254. ISSN: 03640213. DOI: 10.1111/j.1551-6709.2009.01068.x.

Bernardy, Jean-Philippe, Rasmus Blanck, Stergios Chatzikyriakidis, and Shalom Lappin (2018). "A compositional Bayesian semantics for natural language". In: *First International Workshop on Language Cognition and Computational Models*. Santa Fe, NM, United States, pp. 1–10.

Bicknell, Klinton, Jeffrey L. Elman, Mary Hare, Ken McRae, and Marta Kutas (2010). "Effects of event knowledge in processing verbal arguments". In: *Journal of Memory and Language* 63.4, pp. 489–505. ISSN: 0749596X. DOI: 10.1016/j.jml.2010.08.004.

Bolukbasi, Tolga, Kai-Wei Chang, James Y Zou, Venkatesh Saligrama, and Adam T Kalai (2016). "Man is to computer programmer as woman is to homemaker? Debiasing word embeddings". In: *Advances in Neural Information Processing Systems.* Ed. by D. Lee, M. Sugiyama, U. Luxburg, I. Guyon, and R. Garnett. Vol. 29.

Bommasani, Rishi and Claire Cardie (Nov. 2020). "Intrinsic evaluation of summarization datasets". In: *Proceedings of the 2020 Conference on Empirical Methods in Natural Language Processing (EMNLP).* Online: Association for Computational Linguistics, pp. 8075–8096. DOI: 10.18653/v1/2020.emnlp-main.649.

Brysbaert, Marc, AB Warriner, and V Kuperman (2014). "Concreteness ratings for 40 thousand generally known English word lemmas". In: *BEHAVIOR RESEARCH METHODS* 46.3, pp. 904–911. ISSN: 1554-351X.

Burgess, Curt and Kevin Lund (Mar. 1997). "Modelling parsing constraints with high-dimensional context space". en. In: *Language and Cognitive Processes* 12.2-3, pp. 177–210. ISSN: 0169-0965, 1464-0732. DOI: 10.1080/016909697386844. URL: https://www.tandfonline.com/doi/full/10.1080/016909697386844 (visited on 04/23/2022).

Chersoni, E., E. Santus, L. Pannitto, A. Lenci, P. Blache, and C.-R. Huang (2019). "A structured distributional model of sentence meaning and processing". In: *Natural Language Engineering* 25.4, pp. 483–502. DOI: 10.1017/S1351324919000214.

Chronis, Gabriella and Katrin Erk (2020). "When is a bishop not like a rook? When it's like a rabbi! Multi-prototype BERT embeddings for estimating semantic relationships". In: *Proceedings of CoNLL.*

Clark, S., B. Coecke, and M. Sadrzadeh (2008). "A compositional distributional model of meaning". In: *Proceedings of QI.* Oxford, UK, pp. 133–140.

Coenen, Andy, Emily Reif, Ann Yuan, Been Kim, Adam Pearce, F. Viégas, and M. Wattenberg (2019). "Visualizing and measuring the geometry of BERT". In: *NeurIPS.*

Del Pinal, Guillermo (Apr. 2018). "Meaning, modulation, and context: A multidimensional semantics for truth-conditional pragmatics". en. In: *Linguistics and Philosophy* 41.2, pp. 165–207. ISSN: 0165-0157, 1573-0549. DOI: 10.1007/s10988-017-9221-z.

Del Tredici, Marco (2020). "Linguistic Variation in Online Communities: A Computational Perspective". PhD thesis. Universiteit van Amsterdam.

Devlin, Jacob, Ming-Wei Chang, Kenton Lee, and Kristina Toutanova (2019). "BERT: Pre-training of deep bidirectional transformers for language understanding". In: *Proceedings of NAACL.*

Elman, Jeffrey L. (2009). "On the meaning of words and dinosaur bones: Lexical knowledge without a lexicon". In: *Cognitive Science* 33, pp. 547–582. ISSN: 03640213. DOI: 10.1111/j.1551-6709.2009.01023.x.

Emerson, Guy (2018). "Functional Distributional Semantics: Learning Linguistically Informed Representations from a Precisely Annotated Corpus". PhD thesis. University of Cambridge.

Erk, Katrin and Aurélie Herbelot (2020). How to marry a star: probabilistic constraints for meaning in context. arXiv 2009.07936. arXiv: 2009.07936 [cs.CL].

Erk, Katrin and Sebastian Padó (Oct. 2008). "A structured vector space model for word meaning in context". In: *Proceedings of the 2008 Conference on Empirical Methods in Natural Language Processing*. Honolulu, Hawaii: Association for Computational Linguistics, pp. 897–906. URL: https://aclanthology.org/D08-1094.

Fillmore, Charles J. (1982). "Frame semantics". In: *Linguistics in the morning calm*. Ed. by The linguistic society of Korea. Seoul: Hanshin Publishing Co., pp. 111–137.

— (1985). "Frames and the semantics of understanding". In: *Quaderni di Semantica* 6, pp. 222–254.

Fillmore, Charles J., Christopher R. Johnson, and Miriam R.L. Petruck (2003). "Background to FrameNet". In: *International Journal of Lexicography* 16.3, pp. 235–250. ISSN: 09503846. DOI: 10.1093/ijl/16.3.235.

Gibson, J. J. (1966). *The Senses Considered as Perceptual Systems*. London: Allen and Unwin.

Giulianelli, Mario, Marco Del Tredici, and Raquel Fernández (July 2020). "Analysing lexical semantic change with contextualised word representations". In: *Proceedings of the 58th Annual Meeting of the Association for Computational Linguistics*. Online: Association for Computational Linguistics, pp. 3960–3973.

Gulordava, Kristina, Piotr Bojanowski, Edouard Grave, Tal Linzen, and Marco Baroni (2018). "Colorless green recurrent networks dream hierarchically". In: *Proceedings of the 2018 Conference of the North American Chapter of the Association for Computational Linguistics: Human Language Technologies, Volume 1 (Long Papers)*. New Orleans, Louisiana: Association for Computational Linguistics, pp. 1195–1205. URL: http://aclweb.org/anthology/N18-1108.

Herbelot, Aurélie (2020). "Re-solve it: simulating the acquisition of core semantic competences from small data". In: *Proceedings of CoNLL*.

Herbelot, Aurélie and Ann Copestake (2021). "Ideal words: A vector-based formalisation of semantic competence". In: *Künstliche Intelligenz*.

Hill, Felix, Douwe Kiela, and Anna Korhonen (Aug. 2013). "Concreteness and Corpora: A Theoretical and Practical Study". In: *Proceedings of the Fourth Annual Workshop on Cognitive Modeling and Computational Linguistics (CMCL)*. Sofia, Bulgaria: Association for Computational Linguistics, pp. 75–83.

Kaneko, Masahiro and Danushka Bollegala (2021). "Debiasing pre-trained contextualised embeddings". In: *Proceedings of EACL*.

Kiela, Douwe, Felix Hill, and Stephen Clark (Sept. 2015). "Specializing word embeddings for similarity or relatedness". In: *Proceedings of the 2015 Conference on Empirical Methods in Natural Language Processing*. Lisbon, Portugal: Association for Computational Linguistics, pp. 2044–2048. DOI: 10.18653/v1/D15-1242. URL: https://aclanthology.org/D15-1242.

Kozlowski, Austin C., Matt Taddy, and James A. Evans (Oct. 2019). "The geometry of culture: Analyzing the meanings of class through word embeddings". en. In: *American Sociological Review* 84.5, pp. 905–949. ISSN: 0003-1224. DOI: 10.1177/0003122419877135.

Kremer, Gerhard, Katrin Erk, Sebastian Padó, and Stefan Thater (2014). "What substitutes tell us - Analysis of an "All-Words" Lexical Substitution Corpus". In: *Proceedings of EACL*.

Kruszewski, Germán, Denis Paperno, and Marco Baroni (July 2015). "Deriving Boolean structures from distributional vectors". en. In: *Transactions of the Association for Computational Linguistics* 3, pp. 375–388. ISSN: 2307-387X. URL: https://transacl.org/ojs/index.php/tacl/article/view/616 (visited on 04/24/2022).

Kutuzov, Andrey, Erik Velldal, and Lilja Øvrelid (2017). "Tracing armed conflicts with diachronic word embedding models". In: *Proceedings of the Events and Stories in the News Workshop*. Vancouver, Canada.

Kuypers, Jim A. (2009). "Framing analysis". In: *Rhetorical Criticism: Perspectives in Action*. Ed. by Jim A. Kuypers. Lanham: Lexiongton Press, pp. 181–204.

Lake, Brenden and Marco Baroni (2018). "Generalization without systematicity: On the compositional skills of sequence-to-sequence recurrent networks". In: *35th International Conference on Machine Learning*. Vol. 7, pp. 4487–4499. ISBN: 978-1-5108-6796-3.

Lakoff, George (2004). *Don't Think of an Elephant!: Know Your Values and Frame the Debate*. Chelsea Green Publishing.

Lakoff, George and Mark Johnson (1980). *Metaphors we Live By*. Chicago: University of Chicago Press.

Lappin, Shalom (2021). *Deep Learning and Linguistic Representation*. London: Chapman and Hall.

Levin, Beth (1993). *English Verb Classes and Alternations: A Preliminary Investigation*. Chicago: University of Chicago Press. ISBN: 978-0-226-47532-5 978-0-226-47533-2.

Linzen, T., E. Dupoux, and Y. Goldberg (2016). "Assessing the ability of LSTMs to learn syntax-sensitive dependencies". In: *Transactions of the Association for Computational Linguistics* 4, pp. 521–535.

McNally, Louise (2017). "Kinds, descriptions of kinds, concepts, and distributions". In: *Bridging Formal and Conceptual Semantics. Selected Papers of BRIDGE-14*. Ed. by K Balogh and W Petersen, pp. 39–61.

McRae, Ken, Mary Hare, Jeffrey L. Elman, and Todd Ferretti (2005). "A basis for generating expectancies for verbs from nouns". In: *Memory and Cognition* 33.7, pp. 1174–1184. ISSN: 0090502X. DOI: 10.3758/BF03193221.

McRae, Ken and Kazunaga Matsuki (2009). "People use their knowledge of common events to understand language, and do so as quickly as possible". In: *Linguistics and Language Compass* 3.6, pp. 1417–1429. ISSN: 1749818X. DOI: 10.1111/j.1749-818X.2009.00174.x.

Mickus, Timothee, Denis Paperno, Mathieu Constant, and Kees van Deemter (Jan. 2020). "What do you mean, BERT?" In: *Proceedings of the Society for Compu-*

tation in Linguistics 2020. New York, New York: Association for Computational Linguistics, pp. 279–290. URL: https://aclanthology.org/2020.scil-1.35.

Mrkšić, Nikola, Ivan Vulić, Diarmuid Ó Séaghdha, Ira Leviant, Roi Reichart, Milica Gašić, Anna Korhonen, and Steve Young (June 2017). "Semantic Specialisation of Distributional Word Vector Spaces using Monolingual and Cross-Lingual Constraints". In: *arXiv:1706.00374 [cs]*. arXiv: 1706.00374. URL: http://arxiv.org/abs/1706.00374 (visited on 04/24/2022).

Muskens, Reinhard and Mehrnoosh Sadrzadeh (2018). "Static and dynamic vector semantics for lambda calculus models of natural language". In: *Journal of Language Modelling* 6.2, pp. 319–351.

Nickel, Maximilian and Douwe Kiela (May 2017). "Poincaré Embeddings for Learning Hierarchical Representations". In: *arXiv:1705.08039 [cs, stat]*. arXiv: 1705.08039. URL: http://arxiv.org/abs/1705.08039 (visited on 04/21/2022).

Padó, Sebastian and Mirella Lapata (July 2003). "Constructing semantic space models from parsed Corpora". In: *Proceedings of the 41st Annual Meeting of the Association for Computational Linguistics*. Sapporo, Japan: Association for Computational Linguistics, pp. 128–135. DOI: 10.3115/1075096.1075113. URL: https://aclanthology.org/P03-1017 (visited on 04/24/2022).

Peirsman, Yves (2008). "Word Space Models of Semantic Similarity and Relatedness". In: *European Summer School in Logic, Language and Information (ESSLLI) Student Session*. Hamburg, Germany.

Potts, Christopher (2019). "A case for deep learning in semantics: Response to Pater". In: *Language*. DOI: 10.1353/lan.2019.0003.

Pustejovsky, James (Dec. 1991). "The Generative Lexicon". In: *Comput. Linguist.* 17.4, pp. 409–441. ISSN: 0891-2017.

Recanati, François (2003). *Literal Meaning*. Cambridge University Press.

— (2017). "Contextualism and Polysemy". In: *dialectica* 71.3, pp. 379–397. DOI: 10.1111/1746-8361.12179.

Reisinger, Joseph and Raymond Mooney (Oct. 2010). "A mixture model with sharing for lexical semantics". In: *Proceedings of the 2010 Conference on Empirical Methods in Natural Language Processing*. Cambridge, MA: Association for Computational Linguistics, pp. 1173–1182.

Roller, Stephen, Katrin Erk, and Gemma Boleda (Aug. 2014). "Inclusive yet selective: Supervised distributional Hypernymy detection". In: *Proceedings of COLING 2014, the 25th International Conference on Computational Linguistics: Technical Papers*. Dublin, Ireland: Dublin City University and Association for Computational Linguistics, pp. 1025–1036. URL: https://aclanthology.org/C14-1097 (visited on 04/24/2022).

Rosch, Eleanor (1973). "On the internal structure of perceptual and semantic categories". In: *Cognitive Development and the Acquisition of Language*. Ed. by T. E. Moore. New York: Academic Press, pp. 111–144.

Rosenfeld, Alex (2019). "Computational Models of Lexical Change". PhD thesis. University of Texas at Austin.

Sahlgren, Magnus (2006). "The Word-Space Model. Using Distributional Analysis to Represent Syntagmatic and Paradigmatic Relations Between Words in High-dimensional Vector Spaces". PhD thesis. Stockholm University. URL: https://www.sics.se/~mange/TheWordSpaceModel.pdf.

— (2008). "The distributional hypothesis". en. In: *Rivista di Linguistica* 2.1, pp. 33–53.

Schütze, Hinrich (1998). "Automatic word sense discrimination". In: *Computational Linguistics* 24.1, pp. 97–123.

Thater, Stefan, Hagen Fürstenau, and Manfred Pinkal (Nov. 2011). "Word meaning in context: A simple and effective vector model". In: *Proceedings of 5th International Joint Conference on Natural Language Processing*. Chiang Mai, Thailand: Asian Federation of Natural Language Processing, pp. 1134–1143. URL: https://aclanthology.org/I11-1127.

Travis, Charles (1997). "Pragmatics". In: *A Companion to the Philosophy of Language*. Ed. by Bob Hale and Crispin Wright. Blackwell, pp. 87–107.

Trott, Sean, Tiago Timponi Torrent, Nancy Chang, and Nathan Schneider (2020). "(Re)construing Meaning in NLP". en. In: *Proceedings of the 58th Annual Meeting of the Association for Computational Linguistics*. Online: Association for Computational Linguistics, pp. 5170–5184. DOI: 10.18653/v1/2020.acl-main.462. URL: https://www.aclweb.org/anthology/2020.acl-main.462 (visited on 10/21/2020).

Webson, Albert, Zhizhong Chen, Carsten Eickhoff, and Ellie Pavlick (2020). "Are "Undocumented Workers" the Same as "Illegal Aliens"? Disentangling denotation and connotation in vector spaces". In: *Proceedings of EMNLP*.

Wiedemann, Gregor, Steffen Remus, Avi Chawla, and Chris Biemann (2019). "Does BERT Make Any Sense? Interpretable word sense disambiguation with contextualized embeddings". In: *Konferenz zur Verarbeitung natürlicher Sprache / Conference on Natural Language Processing (KONVENS)*. Erlangen, Germany, p. 10.

Wolf, Thomas, Lysandre Debut, Victor Sanh, Julien Chaumond, Clement Delangue, Anthony Moi, Pierric Cistac, Tim Rault, Rémi Louf, Morgan Funtowicz, Joe Davison, Sam Shleifer, Patrick von Platen, Clara Ma, Yacine Jernite, Julien Plu, Canwen Xu, Teven Le Scao, Sylvain Gugger, Mariama Drame, Quentin Lhoest, and Alexander M. Rush (Oct. 2020). "Transformers: State-of-the-Art Natural Language Processing". In: *Proceedings of the 2020 Conference on Empirical Methods in Natural Language Processing: System Demonstrations*. Online: Association for Computational Linguistics, pp. 38–45. URL: https://www.aclweb.org/anthology/2020.emnlp-demos.6.

Zeevat, Henk, Scott Grimm, Lotte Hogeweg, Sander Lestrade, and E. Smith (2017). "Representing the Lexicon". In: *Bridging Formal and Conceptual Semantics. Selected Papers of BRIDGE-14*. Ed. by K Balogh and W Petersen. Düsseldorf: düsseldorf university press, pp. 153–186.

Zhu, Yukun, Ryan Kiros, Rich Zemel, Ruslan Salakhutdinov, Raquel Urtasun, Antonio Torralba, and Sanja Fidler (Dec. 2015). "Aligning books and movies: Towards story-like visual explanations by watching movies and reading books". In: *The IEEE International Conference on Computer Vision (ICCV)*.

CHAPTER 10

Algebra and Language: Reasons for (Dis)content

Lawrence S. Moss

Indiana University

CONTENTS

ABSTRACT

This chapter offers reasons to be contented with algebraic methods in the study of language, and also reasons to be discontented. The reasons for discontent include the failure of algebraic methods to predict and understand deep learning models, and the fact that algebraic methods do not typically take learning into account. The reasons to be content include the fact that algebraic methods lead us to facts about linguistic structure that seem to be otherwise unavailable. In addition, algebraic methods generalise in elegant ways. We hold that the generalisations of algebraic methods offered by category theory and coalgebra might eventually be as important for the study of language as they are in contemporary theoretical computer science. We illustrate this by looking at coalgebraic formulations of Markov decision processes, bringing out their relation to automata. We discuss at length the interplay of algebraic and deep learning methods in natural language inference, showing that both sides make strong contributions.

DOI: 10.1201/9781003205388-10

10.1 INTRODUCTION

This article discusses several points related to the overall theme of the volume. I explore "algebraic methods" in the study of language, especially in the wake of the success of deep learning models. I start with the recognition that deep learning models outperform approaches to language based on formal grammars, model theory, and proof theory – the "algebraic" tools under discussion. This should give pause to those of us who have spent many years developing those tools. The main vehicle for this discussion will be work on natural language inference (NLI), where one sees neural learners outperform systems that use symbolic methods. Having worked on one symbolic approach, I have to wonder why it is that neural learners do better, and whether representational methods are of permanent interest in understanding human language.

My overall question is in the title of the paper. Do we now view algebraic methods with Content or Discontent? Like all good questions, there is no easy answer. I will be presenting both sides, partly to clarify the debate and also because my own views are nuanced. There are reasons for both Content and Discontent, and the NLI field will show this. In addition to the reason for Discontent coming from deep learning models, there always had been reasons to be sceptical of formal work in the study of language, and so this paper will review some of that discussion.

In addition to discussing the volume's question through the lens of NLI, I will discuss it from a mathematical angle as well. The "algebraic systems" found in our volume's title are something of a "straw person." I say this based on looking at progress in areas of theoretical computer science, yielding work that is just as "algebraic" as anything and yet is suitable for discussing probabilistic models, for example. I will present a taste of this large body of work, one particular point coming from one of my projects in that direction. And when one looks at all of this (generalised) algebraic work, I will make the case that algebraic tools do have a place in the study of language after all. It might be a place shared with other tools, but it will be a place nevertheless.

I didn't originally intend to write a paper that is as "personal" as this one turned out to be. But I think it will help in presenting my points.

Long ago, I became involved in teaching a course called Mathematics and Logic for Cognitive Science to graduate students in Cognitive Science, AI, Computational Linguistics, and related fields. This started at a time when work on neural networks was seen as something unlikely to succeed, so while I taught a little about perceptrons, the main work of the class was in probabilistic models like Bayesian networks, hidden Markov models, and the basics of information theory; in addition, there was some of the linear algebra that one would need to understand latent semantic analysis. Finally, there was a tiny bit about logic. I threw in logic to make the case for some kind of representation, and the main vehicle that I used was dynamic epistemic logic. But over time I realised that many of the assumptions that we make when we do logic are questionable when used in connection with the problems of cognitive science. The "algebraic tools" of formal grammars and model theory could seem quaint from a very applied point of view. On the other hand, everything I was teaching was mathematics.

How different is linear algebra from logic, especially to end users for whom both are a second language? In time, I became much less attached to my own staring discipline, logic, and more committed to mathematical modelling of all sorts.

I think this progression explains some of the way that I approach the question that underlies this volume. The overall question in the volume seems to contrast or oppose tools from algebra with those from probability. I don't think that this is a particularly good way to think about mathematical tools, and in particular I want to start with a look at *coalgebraic generalisations of automata* as providing "algebraic" tools that go beyond the narrow confines of algebra that we are thinking of in this discussion. This is the content of Section 10.2. The main message is that when suitably generalised, the algebraic tools that lead to discontent might be more attractive. After that, I turn in Section 10.3 to a longer discussion of work in natural language inference where one can see both algebraic and deep learning methods used. So this leads to a very long meditation on the themes of the volume and of the paper itself. Those themes are laid out in Section 10.1.1 just below.

10.1.1   What are the Reasons to be (Dis)contented?

I find it useful to put down some of the reasons to be both discontented and contented with algebraic methods in the study of language.

On the discontented side:

(D1) Algebraic methods did not predict that deep learning models would do as well as they did do. In fact, people used to algebraic methods found deep learning to be surprising. A corollary is that the success of deep learning models points us away from methods that were not used in constructing them.

(D2) Algebraic methods are "sharp", permitting no shades of gray. They are based on assumptions that have taken us far but which increasingly lead us astray: languages are well-defined sets of strings. Competence is more important than practice. Real-life data pertaining to language always is "fuzzy", graded and imprecise.

(D3) The overwhelming proportion of work using algebraic methods ignores the matter of learning. Learning is a crucial aspect of language at every level, and so methods which ignore it are bound to fail.

On the contented side:

(C1) Algebraic methods get at something important. The show pattens in language that are not obvious from the data. In retrospect, a deep learning model might be able to grasp such a pattern, but it is not clear how one would find the pattern without a hint that it is there. Algebraic methods hint at important structure.

(C2) The way to blend symbolic and statistical methods in NLP is bound to use algebraic ideas in some form. To some extent, this is already happening.

(C3) "Algebraic methods" is not a closed class of mathematical ideas. When faced with challenges like (D2) and (D3), they will rise to the occasion. In areas of theoretical computer science, this has already happened. Even for neural network models, there is a reason to be optimistic about the future.

As contradictory as it sounds, I think all of these points are valid. My discussions in the rest of this paper are mainly going to support them, and sometimes to refine or challenge them. At the time of this writing, I do not know what the other papers in this volume are going to say. My guess is that they will fall on the D side more than the C side, mainly because this is a newer point and it is easier to make. Read against them, this paper is likely to be an apology for algebraic methods based on the C points that I make. But I can see both sides, and so this paper will not come to an easy conclusion.

10.2 ALGEBRAS AND COALGEBRAS: CATEGORY-THEORETIC MODELS OF STRUCTURE

The types of mathematics pertinent to the overall discussion in this book incorporate *structure* to some extent. This is part of why they work, and this structural emphasis is what is challenged by deep learning systems that learn (D3), apparently without structure. My goal in this section is to show that the generalisations of the "algebraic systems" that come from branches of category theory are a better tools for many problems in language.

The notion of structurality in mathematics is not exhausted by grammars, automata, logics, and proof theory. These topics are just one corner of the mathematical universe. People who specialise in branches of abstract algebra, for example, might never have even heard of a formal grammar. Such specialists are often interested doing algebra as a technical tool in areas of mathematics such as number theory. In this discussion, we are interested in structurality as it applies to *state-based systems* of various types. To see what mean, it will be useful to bring in concepts and examples from category theory, especially from the parts of the subject developed in the area called *coalgebra*.

To carry out this discussion, I will need to assume some familiarity with the notions of a *category* and *functor*. If you do not know what these are, you still could read on and catch the overall ideological points related to this chapter and this book, but obviously you won't understand much of the technical details.

Let us begin with the general definition of algebras and coalgebras. For both definitions, one begins with a category C and an endofunctor $F: C \to C$. (An endofunctor is a functor from some category to itself.)

An *F-algebra* is a pair (A, α), where $\alpha: FA \to A$ is a morphism in the underlying category C. Given algebras (A, α) and (B, β), an *algebra morphism* is a morphism

$h\colon A \to B$ so that $h \cdot \alpha = \beta \cdot Fh$. See the square on the left just below:

$$
\begin{array}{ccc}
FA \xrightarrow{\ \alpha\ } A & \qquad & A \xrightarrow{\ \alpha\ } FA \\
\scriptstyle{Fh}\downarrow \quad \downarrow\scriptstyle{h} & & \scriptstyle{h}\downarrow \quad \downarrow\scriptstyle{Fh} \\
FB \xrightarrow[\ \beta\ ]{} B & & B \xrightarrow[\ \beta\ ]{} FB
\end{array}
\qquad (10.1)
$$

Frequently, one elides the name of the functor and the underlying category, and just speaks of *algebras*. For example: an algebra is *initial* if it has a unique algebra morphism to every algebra.

Dually, an *F-coalgebra* is a pair (A, α), where $\alpha\colon A \to FA$ is a morphism in C. Given coalgebras (A, α) and (B, β), a *coalgebra morphism* is a morphism $h\colon A \to B$ so that $\beta \cdot h = Fh \cdot \alpha$. See the square on the right above. A coalgebra is *final* if every coalgebra has a unique coalgebra morphism into it.

Here is a motivating example relevant to our volume. *Deterministic automata.* Let A be a set of inputs (also called an input alphabet). A deterministic automaton on a set S of states is given by a state transition function $\delta_s\colon S \to S$ for every $a \in A$ and a set $Acc \subseteq S$ of *accepting states*. We can "re-package" the state transition functions δ_a in the curried form by

$$
\delta\colon S \to S^A.
$$

Thus $\delta(s)$ is a function which, to each $a \in A$, gives $\delta_a(s)$. We also re-package the set Acc of accepting states as its characteristic function

$$
\gamma\colon S \to \{0, 1\}.
$$

Here $\gamma(s) = 1$ iff $s \in Acc$. The two re-packagings, δ and γ together give us $\langle \gamma, \delta \rangle\colon S \to \{0, 1 \times S^A\}$. Thus, deterministic automata are coalgebras for the functor

$$
FX = \{0, 1\} \times X^A
$$

To summarise: a deterministic automaton with input alphabet may be re-packaged as a function $\alpha\colon S \to FS$, where S is its state set, and F is the functor $FX = \{0, 1\} \times X^A$.

Even more, the notion of *formal languages* and their relation to automata comes up in a natural way as the final coalgebra of this functor. Here is what this means. A formal language L over the alphabet A is a set of words on A; this means that $L \subseteq A^*$. Let us write $\mathcal{L}$ for the set of formal languages L over A. L now may be endowed with a coalgebra structure for the same functor F; this means that there is a natural function

$$
\ell\colon \mathcal{L} \to \{0, 1\} \times \mathcal{L}^A = F(\mathcal{L}). \qquad (10.2)
$$

This function is called a *coalgebra structure*. Here is how ℓ works: Given a formal language L, the first component of $\ell(L)$ is 1 iff the empty word ε belongs to L. Let us write f for the second component of $\ell(L)$. Given an alphabet symbol a, $f(L)(a) = \{w \in A^*\colon aw \in L\}$. This is sometimes called the *Brzozowski derivative* of L. All of this gives us ℓ in (10.2). We have turned the set of languages into an automaton(!). It is not finite-state, but it lives under the same conceptual roof as an automaton, since both are coalgebras of the same functor.

For every automaton (S, α) and every state $s \in S$ we form the language $L(s)$ of words accepted in the state s in (S, α). Observe that

1. s is accepting iff $L(s)$ contains ε, i.e. iff $\ell(L(a)) = 1$.

2. for every $a \in A$, the language of words accepted in the state $\delta_a(s)$ is exactly the Brzozowski derivative that we saw above: $f(L(s))(a)$.

From these points one can check that $L \colon A \to \mathcal{L}$ is a coalgebra morphism, i.e., the square below commutes:

$$
\begin{array}{ccc}
S & \xrightarrow{\ \alpha\ } & F(S) \\
{\scriptstyle L}\downarrow & & \downarrow{\scriptstyle FL} \\
\mathcal{L} & \xrightarrow[\ \ell\ ]{} & F(\mathcal{L})
\end{array}
$$

In fact, L is the unique function that makes this square commute. This means that the coalgebra of languages on the bottom is a *final coalgebra* for the functor related to automata. (Recall the left diagram in (10.1).) For our purposes in this paper, we only need a very high-level look at this topic. If everything in the last paragraph is unfamiliar, fear not: an impressionistic treatment will make the point that I want. (And if you do wish to read more on this topic, a place to start for many readers with a background in theoretical computer science would be Rutten, 2000.)

The next point to be made is that all of this coalgebra generalises in a pretty straightforward way to many other flavors of structure. To do this, one sometimes has to vary the underlying category, moving from sets to (say) vector spaces or some other category. Even more, one has to vary the functor. Among the flavors of structure that one can find in this way are non-deterministic automata, automata with output (transducers), weighted automata, probabilistic automata, Markov chains, graphs, labelled transition systems, context-free grammars, and Kripke models. Furthermore, many of the natural "semantic spaces" for these kinds of objects fall out as final coalgebras, just as the formal languages were the semantic space of deterministic automata. The natural notions of equivalence of structure also turn out to be related to coalgebra morphisms of the type which we saw above in connection with languages. And other aspects of the particular theory of all of these kinds of objects turns out to be special cases of the general theory of coalgebra. (This is not to say that absolutely everything related to, probabilistic automata, for example, is just an application of coalgebra. That would be completely misleading. The point is that *some key first results* could be seen as applications, and this conceptual unification is frequently useful.)

10.2.1 Case Study: Markov Decision Processes

Many of the claims in this paper, both in their Content and Discontent thrusts, may be illustrated by some recent work on *Markov decision processes* (MDPs). These are mathematical objects which are used in *reinforcement learning* (RL), and so they would seem to be good candidates to someday be used in the overall area of language learning. Indeed, MDPs have been used in connection with language, but my sense is that most of the showcase applications of RLs are in motion planning (think self-driving cars), gaming (TD-Gammon, AlphaGo), and other areas. On the other hand, MDPs and reinforcement learning are probably not part of the algebraic toolkit. So as an opener, we have a reason for discontent.

My goal in this section is to show that some of the mathematics concerning MDPs can be understood as a "cousin" of the mathematics of automata. What I mean by a "cousin" is that one can take the math of automata, generalise it to the level of categories, algebras, and coalgebras, and then specialise that more general view to arrive at something which illuminates something about MDPs. My aim is to connect with the issues of *discounted infinite sums* and with the justification of *policy improvement* (Howard, 1960). This section is based on Feys et al. (2018), and what we do here is really a hint to the fuller treatment there.

To see what the subject is about, consider the MDP shown below, taken from course lecture slides (Moore, 2002).[1] As with an automaton, there are four *states*. These are abbreviated PU, PF, RU, and RF, and we let S be the set of these states. A startup company makes receives an *immediate reward* (also called *utility*) which we write as $u(s)$ at the beginning of each time period, and as typical with Markov-type processes, this immediate reward depends (only) on the state. The startup chooses to either *advertise* or *save*; these are the two elements of the set Act of actions in this example. The effect of an action in a state is in general probabilistic (D2): in PU, the effect of *advertise* is to go to PF with probability $\frac{1}{2}$ and to remain in PU with the same probability. A *policy* σ is a function from states to actions: $\sigma : S \to Act$. It tells the agent which action to perform in the different states. A policy is a one-player version of a *strategy* from game theory. (Incidentally, there are also probabilistic policies, but we will not need them. To be sure, the matter of whether having probabilistic policies is necessary for the theory is interesting, and the math that we present has something to say about it. But like everything in this discussion, we are going to work mainly at a suggestive level.)

Naturally, the main problem in the area is to ask whether there is always a *best policy*, and if so, to find one. Further, one would like to *learn* the best policy from experience (D3). This leads to the more fundamental question of how we evaluate policies. The easiest way is to use *discounted infinite sums of expected rewards*. Given a policy σ, a state s, and a time step $n \geq 0$, we can calculate the probability of being in each state t at the start of step n. Let $r_\sigma^n(s)$ be the expected reward earned at the beginning of the nth step, if the starting state is s and if σ is

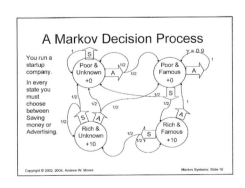

---

[1]My thanks to Andrew Moore for permission to use this figure.

followed. Then we take a *discount factor* $\gamma \in (0,1)$. In our example, $\gamma = .9$. And we define the *long-term value* function for σ as follows:

$$LTV_\sigma(s) = r_\sigma^0(s) + \gamma r_\sigma^1(s) + \cdots + \gamma^n r_\sigma^n(s) + \cdots \qquad (10.3)$$

The idea is that we value today's reward over tomorrow's by a factor of γ, we value the reward today over the reward in n days by a factor of γ^n. The specific value of γ is a pale reflection of the agent's ability to delay their instant gratification and thus make choices which are good in the long run but not necessarily in the short run. In any case, assuming that we have only finitely many states, $\max_s r_\sigma^0(s)$ is a real number, not ∞. This implies that $LTV_\sigma(s)$ in (10.3) is a well-defined number, again not ∞. This leads to an ordering on policies: $\sigma \leq \tau$ iff $LTV_\sigma(s) \leq LTV_\tau(s)$ for all states s. The main question in the area can now be stated: prove that there is a policy which is maximal in $\leq$, and give an algorithm to find such a policy. I am not sure whether work on this question counts as algebra in the sense of this volume: the methods are not those that one first thinks of as "algebra". But my goal is to point out the commonalities so that we start thinking of algebraic methods in a more general way.

We have already mentioned coalgebra as a useful generalisation of automata. Let us look at the coalgebraic formulation of MDPs and also at a concrete calculation of the LTV of an example policy. We recast MDPs as functions $m : S \to \mathbb{R} \times (\Delta S)^{Act}$. So again, we have coalgebras, but for a functor different from what we saw on automata. Here and below, ΔS is the set of discrete probability measures on S, that is, the set of functions on the set S with values in $[0,1]$ and with the property that they sum to 1. This functor Δ evidently a key component of the MDP functor. If you are seeing this for the first time, you might try to see how, given a function $f : S \to T$, we can obtain a map of measures $\Delta f : \Delta S \to \Delta T$. And for that matter, you might think about the *expectation* operation as an algebra $\Delta \mathbb{R} \to \mathbb{R}$.

In every state of an MDP, we get an immediate reward $u(s) = \pi_1(m(s)) \in \mathbb{R}$ and a function from actions to probability distributions $t = \pi_2(m(s)) \in (\Delta S)^{Act}$. (The t stands for *transition*; π_1 and π_2 are *projections*.) Given a fixed policy σ, we get

$$m_\sigma : S \to \mathbb{R} \times \Delta S.$$

For example, let us take the "miserly" policy σ to be $\sigma(s) = save$ for all states s. We would have the equations on the left below.

$m_\sigma(PU)$	$=$	$\langle 0, 1 \cdot PU \rangle$	$LTV_\sigma(PU)$	$=$	$0 + \gamma LTV_\sigma(PU)$
$m_\sigma(PF)$	$=$	$\langle 0, \frac{1}{2} \cdot PU + \frac{1}{2} \cdot RF \rangle$	$LTV_\sigma(PF)$	$=$	$0 + \gamma(\frac{1}{2} LTV_\sigma(PU) + \frac{1}{2} LTV_\sigma(RF))$
$m_\sigma(RU)$	$=$	$\langle 10, \frac{1}{2} \cdot PU + \frac{1}{2} \cdot RU \rangle$	$LTV_\sigma(RU)$	$=$	$10 + \gamma(\frac{1}{2} LTV_\sigma(PU) + \frac{1}{2} LTV_\sigma(RU))$
$m_\sigma(RF)$	$=$	$\langle 10, \frac{1}{2} \cdot RU + \frac{1}{2} \cdot RF \rangle$	$LTV_\sigma(RF)$	$=$	$10 + \gamma(\frac{1}{2} LTV_\sigma(RU) + \frac{1}{2} LTV_\sigma(RF))$

$$(10.4)$$

We next come to the first "algebraic" connection. It is possible to re-express (10.3) as a kind of *fixed-point equation*, leading us to a more algebraic mindset. For each state s, the long-term discounted expected earnings from s is the sum of the immediate earnings and the discounted weighted average of the values $LTV_\sigma(t)$, where t ranges over S and the the weighting factor is the probability that σ takes us from s to t in one step. Seen this way, (10.3) may be re-written to the equations on the right in (10.4) above. This is a linear system and we thus can solve it to get $LTV_\sigma(s)$ for each s. We get $LTV_\sigma(PU) = 0$, $LTV_\sigma(PF) = 14.876$, $LTV_\sigma(RU) = 18.182$, and $LTV_\sigma(RF) = 33.058$.

Thinking more categorically, we regard $LTV_\sigma \colon S \to \mathbb{R}$ as a function which makes the diagram below commute:

The reason we say that this is more categorical is that the vertical arrow on the right makes use of $\Delta(LTV_\sigma)$; that is, we are using the fact that Δ is a functor here – it works on functions and not just on sets. We have seen m_σ in (10.4). $E \colon \Delta\mathbb{R} \to \mathbb{R}$ computes expected value, and α_γ is the function given by $\alpha_\gamma(x, y) = x + (\gamma \cdot y)$. Notice that m_σ on the top of the diagram is a coalgebra of the functor $FX = \mathbb{R} \times \Delta X$, since it is a function from S to $F(S) = \mathbb{R} \times \Delta S$. And the composite on the bottom, $\alpha_\gamma \cdot (\mathbb{R} \times E)$, is an algebra for this same functor F, and LTV_σ is a coalgebra-to-algebra map. In fact, this algebra is what is called a *corecursive algebra* (Capretta et al., 2009): for every coalgebra $f \colon S \to FS$ there is a unique coalgebra-to-algebra map $f^\dagger \colon S \to \mathbb{R}$ making the diagram commute. (There is an issue about infinite state spaces that we are ignoring.) A corecursive algebra is another very useful type of structure in the same general family as final coalgebras and initial algebras, and so the fact that we find the long-term value function LTV_σ for a fixed policy showing up in this way suggests that we are on the right track.

Policy improvement I especially want to mention *policy improvement* and to connnect it to the matter of *coinduction*. Policy improvement was introduced by Howard in his book Howard, 1960. Fix a policy σ, and define a new policy τ in terms of σ by

$$\tau(s) \;=\; \operatorname{argmax}_a \left[\sum_{t \in S} (\text{the probability that } a \text{ takes } s \text{ to } t) \cdot LTV_\sigma(t) \right].$$

Here is an example, with our policy σ from above. Let us determine $\tau(PF)$, the action that new policy τ recommends when one is Poor & Famous. The actions available in the PF state are *advertise* and *save*. If one advertises on the first step, then one for sure remains in PF. Following the the old policy σ gives an LTV of 14.876. If one saves on the first step, there's a 50/50 chance of going to PU and of going to RF. We take the expected LTV of following the old policy σ from those states, getting $(\frac{1}{2} \cdot 0) + (\frac{1}{2} \cdot 33.058)$. Since this number is larger than 14.876, we would have $\tau(PF) = save$. Now we call τ an *an improvement of* σ, but it is not prima facie clear that τ is an improvement in the sense of the order $\leq$ on policies which we mentioned above. Does following τ "forever" (not just for one step) really do better than σ in every state? The way we defined τ is like saying, "take the action which looks the long term best, and then continue just like *this*." In fact, when I first saw policy improvement, I very quickly smelled *circularity*. From the point of view of this paper, work on circularity in semantics would probably count as one of the algebraic areas that we would want to set aside. Think about the Liar Paradox and its elegant treatment in work such as Barwise and Etchemendy, 1987. That work calls on an unusual form of set theory, of all things. It brings in *coinduction* as a kind of circular form of induction. In any case, the main result on policy improvement is that indeed the new policy really does improve the old one. While the proofs in the literature do not make the connection to coinduction, the connection can indeed be made. Making this connection takes a fair amount of work, none of which is highly relevant to the programmatic points in this paper. So I won't present any of it.

But what is the overall point? Does it really help us to know that policy improvement may be put under the same general roof as circularity in semantics? Is the fairly involved algebraic work worth the effort? Just as with the other points in this paper, the results are mixed. I am aware of just one paper that made use of Feys et al. (2018), a paper that does one of the things algebraic treatments are good for: mechanising proofs about algorithms and that exist. That paper is Vajjha et al. (2021). It "closely follows the work of" (Feys et al., 2018). It is perhaps useful to quote from its abstract: "Reinforcement learning algorithms solve sequential decision-making problems in probabilistic environments by optimizing for long-term reward. ... The CertRL development [presented in the paper] exemplifies how the Giry monad and mechanised metric coinduction streamline optimality proofs for reinforcement learning algorithms." So we have a reason for Contentment.

On the other hand, the algebraic treatment of policy iteration is not the same thing as the algebraic treatment of learning in general. It is open to extend the work of Feys et al. (2018) by accounting for Q-learning in an algebraic way. This would be an interesting next step, of course.

The conclusion which we draw from this discussion is that work on MDPs was not part of automata theory, or the algebraic tradition which is examined in this volume. But when one generalises *automata* to the level of *coalgebra* and MDP to the level of *corecursive algebra*, it is possible to make a useful contribution. This is especially the case when one brings in concepts like monads, coinduction, and category-theoretic generalisations of automata theory. Of course, one has to think probabilistically also, and that was missing from the earlier incarnation of algebraic work. One also has to think about flavors of MDPs that might be more useful in practice and farther from the kind of modelling that we have discussed. Finally, it is possible that the best applications of reinforcement learning are driven by practice rather than theory, or that they use theoretical frameworks that are distant from what we mentioned here. If that were the case, it would be hard to make the case for the kind of work we are discussing and advocating in this section.

10.2.2 Addendum: Category Theory and Neural Networks

I wanted to mention a line of work that brings together category theory and neural networks. There are a number of reasons why one might like to do this: one might like a theoretical clarification of what learning is in the first place (D3), and for this the algebraic tools of category theory are a good place to start. (But one should expect categories with additional structure; I have not discussed that.) With a better understanding of learning, one might hope for better algorithms and architectures, or for proofs that various of these meet some given specifications. One of the first papers in this area is Fong et al. (2019) using symmetric monoidal categories and also notions that come up in generalisations of game theory. Another paper in this line is Jacobs and Sprunger (2019), where the aim is to provide a categorical treatment of backpropagation paired with stochastic gradient descent. Much closer to linguistics is the work on categorical distributional semantics pioneered in Coecke et al. (2010) and developed in its own line of work and leading to *quantum NLP* (Kartsaklis et al., 2021). Overall, the papers mentioned here and the topics that I am only hinting at make the case that the strongly algebraic work coming from category theory might be relevant to contemporary NLP.

10.3 INFERENCE

The remainder of this paper is a discussion of the matter of *inference* in language, especially as it connects to the D and C points mentioned in Section 10.1.1. As we shall see, all of our very general points about algebraic methods become extremely salient in connection with this topic.

Textbooks on natural language semantics often start by saying that their end goal is to characterise *inference*: what follows from what? This would parallel syntax, where the main goal is to characterise the sentences that a speaker finds grammatical. But in the case of semantics, one rarely, if ever gets to the matter of inference. Instead, one finds *fragments* and *truth conditions*, and to be sure the problems in natural language semantics are notoriously difficult. But somehow one never gets to thinking about inference as such. In the past year I had the opportunity to raise this point with a prominent pioneer in semantics. They basically conceded that their subject was not about inference at all. The points in the beginning of textbooks were just there as a motivation, but the subject of semantics is not really about inference in the sense that I was asking about. On the other hand, the matter of inference is prominent in NLP from tasks like Recognising Textual Entailment and (now) Natural Language Inference (NLI).

Natural language semantics is not alone in this respect. I think of this matter of inference as of some interest to several other disciplines besides linguistic semantics. To make progress on inference, each gives up something. Mathematical logic gives up on people and natural language. It does a perfect job of accounting for inference, but the account doesn't apply to natural language in any meaningful sense. Good-old-fashioned-AI seems close to mathematical logic on this score. It is closer in the sense of wanting to actually do inference, but the tools used would seem to be those from standard logic. As we have seen, linguistic semantics gives up on inference, preferring to focus on truth conditions and related matters. Psychological studies of syllogistic inference give up on complex inferences of all types; mainly they focus on syllogistic reasoning. And the NLI field gives up on a precise definition of logicality – that is, it is not studying something closely connected to formal semantics – and to some extent it also gives up on explainability. This last field is the one that I am mainly addressing in this section; of all the ones mentioned in this paragraph it is undoubtably the one closest to other papers in this volume.

I would like to pause here to mention the very important work on *proof-theoretic semantics*, since it is an active area that in some ways addresses inference. I think of books such as Chatzikyriakidis and Luo, 2020; Francez, 2015; and many articles by the same authors and a number of others. Proof theoretic semantics is concerned with "meaning as use" rather than "meaning in terms of models," and so some of the criticism that I leveled against the mainstream areas of natural language semantics do not apply to this area. In addition, it is highly "algebraic". On the other hand, I have yet to myself see insights from proof-theoretic semantics contributing to work on computational semantics in a big way, especially to areas where deep learning models are used. So while proof-theoretic semantics is relevant to this chapter, I won't have more to say on it.

10.3.1 Natural logic

I became interested in inference some time ago, and so I constructed fragments of language with fairly standard semantics and with complete characterisations of the inference relations. Some of these may be found in Moss, 2015. I will mention one other. First a small fragment from Moss and Kruckman, 2017. This fragment is an extended syllogistic logic. We start with a set N of *nouns* and a set V of (transitive) *verbs*, and we make *terms* in the following way: nouns are terms, and if t is a term and v is a verb, then v *only* t is a term. Finally, we have sentences of the form *all t u*, where t and u are terms. So we get sentences like *All (eat only vegetables) vegetarians*, with the understanding that this should mean *All who eat only vegetables are vegetarians*. And we even allow nesting in the terms, giving us sentences like *All (see only (chase only cats)) dogs*. This tiny language has a very natural semantics, where one interprets terms t as subsets of a given model, and then *All t u* is true in a given model iff the interpretation of t is a subset of the interpretation of u.

To continue the story on inference, we say that a set of sentences Γ *semantically entails* a sentence φ if every model which makes all sentences in Γ true also makes φ true. Then to give the "full story" on inference means to characterise this relation of semantic entailment in terms of something else, for example, a proof system. The proof system here means that we have logical rules like those shown below:

$$\frac{}{All\ t\ t} \qquad \frac{All\ s\ t \quad All\ t\ v}{All\ s\ u} \qquad \frac{All\ s\ (v\ only\ t) \quad All\ t\ u}{All\ s\ (v\ only\ u)}$$

It is not so hard to show that this proof system is *sound and complete*: given a set Γ of sentences and another sentence φ, Γ semantically entails φ if and only if there is a formal proof of φ using the three rules above. Moreover, it is algorithmically feasible to tell whether a given (finite) set Γ entails a given sentence φ or not. This all means that we have understood the semantic entailment relation so well that it can be dealt with by computational systems with no understanding whatsoever. A possibly related point: once we have a sound and complete logic, we might ask if we can forget about the semantics entirely and just use the proof system. Perhaps the proof system *is* a kind of semantics.

By now, there are dozens of small fragments in the natural logic literature. Some, like the logic above, are subsystems of first-order logic. But others are not. For example, one can formulate logics that use determiners like *most*, or NPs like *at least as many x as y*. One needs to settle on a semantics, and in the case of *most*, this is controversial. But once one does this, it is then possible to investigate proof systems.

How does the natural logic program related to the (dis)contents in Section 10.1.1? The motivation to pursue the program came from a discontent with the move of *explaining inference by means of translating into first-order logic*, for several reasons. First of all, the translation is "expensive". In retrospect, to the extent that it could be done at all, translation seems as hard as inference. Based on a lot of interaction with linguistics, cognitive science, computer science, I advocate the use of "lighter" methods, ones which are algorithmically decidable and hopefully of low computational complexity. The validity problem in first-order logic (the *Entscheidungsproblem*) is famously undecidable, a fact shown independently by Alonzo Church and Alan Turing in papers published in 1936. This is not a knock-down argument agains using first-order logic, but to me it is suggestive. It parallels the development in linguistics a generation later where an approach in syntax using *transformations* was abandoned, due to the Peters-Ritchie Theorem that shows (informally) that when transformations are added to context-free grammars, the resulting formalism is weakly equivalent to unrestricted grammars. The lesson from that was that transformations are too powerful to be cognitively plausible. So we should be discontented with any formalism which is so strong. On the other hand, with syntax we quickly formulate restrictions to transformations and other formalisms as well, which respond to the Peters-Ritchie Theorem. In a sense, work on natural logic is the same kind of response. It seeks low-complexity approaches to inference in language.

The natural logic program is very "algebraic". It aims for an encoding of "linguistic knowledge ... in formal grammars, model theories, proof theories, as well as other rule driven devices." Recalling the performance/competence distinction, one could take it to be a competence characterisation of inference in small fragments. So this is a reason for both Content and Discontent. The reason for Content is (C1): it does get something right. And because it characterises the semantic entailment relation in proof-theoretic terms, one can also investigate whether machine learning systems could acquire the complete logical systems for the tiny fragments in the natural logic family. At the same time, there are reasons for discontent. Perhaps the overly simple syntax makes these systems uninteresting for the understanding of inference. And perhaps what is captured by these logical systems bears only a slight resemblance to actual human inference. To make this point more forcefully, many of the natural logic proof systems include rules that do not strike us as self-evident. They would seem to be more like mathematical theorems than rules of inference. In some cases,

I have to wonder whether anyone "in the real world" ever used them. For example,

$$\frac{\text{There are at least as many } x \text{ as non-}x}{\text{There are at least as many non-}y \text{ as } y}$$
$$\overline{\text{There are at least as many } x \text{ as } y}$$

This is not the only "strange" rule. Would a neural learner possibly learn this? If humans don't use this rule, should a machine somehow infer this from the data?

Having said all of this, the program still is subject to all the discontents: it does not have a connection to deep learning models it usually is not gradient (but some related work such as Geurts and Slik, 2005 really is gradient in an interesting way). Learning is absent.

10.3.2 Arrow tagging

Eventually, I could see that even with 100 small fragments of language and their completeness theorems and algorithms, I would simply never get very far with inference in the sense that people in NLI want to see it. In a way, this is a discontent with the strict logic tradition, but it is not as thoroughgoing a discontent as (D1)–(D3). In a sense parallel to our opening of this section, I had to give up on something to make progress. I decided to give up on the kind of totally naive syntax like in the example above. But I still wanted to use the algebraic tools of the kind I am happiest with, and so I became involved in advancing the integration of *monotonicity reasoning* with *categorial grammar*. The idea for doing this goes back to Johan van Benthem Benthem, 1986, 1991, 2008 and his PhD student Victor Sánchez Valencia Valencia, 1991. The basic idea is that we have parsers for grammatical frameworks that have something approximating a clear mathematical semantics, and so one could marry some "algebraic" work on monotonicity with a parer that runs on text as it comes, and thereby get a very "lightweight" approach to inference. To be sure, the kind of grammar used in van Benthem's work was Ajdukiewicz/Bar-Hillel CG, probably the simplest kind of grammar, and one has to work a bit to extend it to a framework like CCG. That is, one has to "do the math"; see Moss and Hu, 2022.

The goal is to do automatic "arrow tagging." We would like to add inferential information to a parse from CCG, say the one below for the sentence *Every cat that Fido chased ran*:

$$
\frac{\text{every} : \text{NP/N} \quad \dfrac{\text{cat} : \text{N} \quad \dfrac{\text{that} : (\text{N}\backslash\text{N})/(\text{S/NP}) \quad \dfrac{\dfrac{\dfrac{\text{F} : \text{NP}}{\text{F} : \text{S}/(\text{S}\backslash\text{NP})}\,{}^{\mathsf{T}} \quad \text{ch} : (\text{S}\backslash\text{NP})/\text{NP}}{\text{Fido chased} : \text{S/NP}}\,{}^{B}}{\text{that Fido chased} : \text{N}\backslash\text{N}}\,{}^{>}}{\text{cat that Fido chased} : \text{N}}\,{}^{<}}{\text{every cat that Fido chased} : \text{NP}}\,{}^{>} \qquad \text{ran} : \text{S}\backslash\text{NP}}{\text{every cat that Fido chased ran} : \text{S}}\,{}^{<}
$$

The details of this parse should not matter much to this discussion. What matters is that (1) a parser can reliably construct a parse like this; (2) there is a formal semantics for this kind of representation, a clear instance of algebraic thinking related to language; Then we would like to automatically come up with a slightly different tree, with extra arrows and extra $+/-$ notations on some of the types:

$$
\cfrac{
  \text{every}^\uparrow : pr \xrightarrow{-} np^+ \qquad
  \cfrac{
    \cfrac{
      \text{cat}^\downarrow : pr \qquad
      \cfrac{
        \text{that}^\downarrow : (e \to t) \xrightarrow{+} (pr \xrightarrow{+} pr) \qquad
        \cfrac{
          F^\downarrow : e \qquad \text{ch}^\downarrow : e \to (e \to t)
        }{\text{Fido chased}^\downarrow : e \to t}\ {\scriptstyle >}
      }{\text{that Fido chased}^\downarrow : pr \xrightarrow{+} pr}\ {\scriptstyle <}
    }{\text{cat that Fido chased}^\downarrow : pr}\ {\scriptstyle >}
  }{\text{every cat that Fido chased}^\uparrow : np^+}
}{\text{every cat that Fido chased ran}^\uparrow : t}
$$

(with on the right)

$$
\cfrac{
  \cfrac{\text{ran}^\uparrow : e \xrightarrow{+} t}{\text{ran}^\uparrow : \text{NP}^+ \xrightarrow{+} t}\ \text{K}
}{}\ {\scriptstyle <}
$$

We are not going to discuss this in detail, but a few points about this are in order. The types have changed. This is analogous to what we find in semantics, where we move from syntactic categories like nouns, transitive and intransitive verbs, etc., and translate them to Montagovian e, t types. The arrows are like sites for inference: words that are marked $\uparrow$ can be replaced by words which are "greater" in some relevant sense (see below), and we should get an entailment. Words that are marked $\downarrow$ can be replaced by words which are "lesser" in the same relevant sense, and again we should get an entailment. For example, we should have on-hand a *knowledge base* containing entries like

dog $\leq$ animal	run $\leq$ move	every $\leq$ most
cat $\leq$ animal	hit $\leq$ touch	most $\leq$ some
poodle $\leq$ dog	thrash $\leq$ hit	one $\leq$ two
Ragdoll $\leq$ cat	hit vigorously $\leq$ hit	two $\leq$ three
bird $\leq$ scooter	hit lightly $\leq$ hit	three $\leq$ four

We could take our sentence *Every cat that Fido chased ran* and replace *every* by *most*, *cat* with *Ragdoll*, and *move* with *run* and get *Every Ragdoll that Fido chased moved.*

In order to do the polarity tagging, one doesn't need the knowledge base. One needs the additional information provided on the leaves of the second tree. That is, in addition to the syntactic types that we find in the first tree, we need lexical information pertaining to inference. For example, here is a small part of the syntactic and semantic entries in the lexicon in our work.

item	category	type
every	DET = NP/N	$pr \xrightarrow{-} np^+$
some	NP/N	$pr \xrightarrow{+} np^+$
no	NP/N	$pr \xrightarrow{-} np^-$
most	NP/N	$pr \xrightarrow{\cdot} np^+$

Here, pr is an abbreviation of the semantic type $e \to t$. The somewhat complex entries in the right column point us to what happens when we bring the order structure into the semantics directly, so this points in the direction of an algebraic direction within work on the syntax-semantics interface. We aren't going to discuss any of this, except to say that it is an algebraic development that comes about mainly when one puts the matter of inference on centre stage. So this is a reason to be content. On the other side, there is the matter of learning. In our work, we didn't learn the new lexicon as shown above (D3), we simply gave it to our system. But we know that others would like to learn this inferential semantic information.

What is the difference between a marking and a polarity? The way we are thinking about things, a marking goes over an arrow. It is typically given in a lexicon, and for the most part one would not want to change it. That is, the markings reflect important semantic features of words. On the other hand, the polarities are attached to constituents in parse trees. They will not appear on arrows. The polarities of individual lexical items are not given in a lexicon; they typically vary from parse tree to parse tree.

Now given these differences, it is not surprising that some authors use the same symbols for what we are calling markings and polarities. The similarity in the tables which we have seen for the two operations all suggests that one could do with the markings (or polarities) alone. We prefer to separate the two, mostly for conceptual clarity.

But what does it all mean? The explanation of what is going on in this subject would seem to be a prime example of algebraic reasoning in the sense of our book. It involves *higher-order functions* as we find in standard work on the syntax-semantics interface Jacobson, 2014; Moot and Retoré, 2012; Steedman, 2012. In fact, work on this topic extends the usual treatments. That is, to give an account of what is going on has led to new mathematics of a strongly "algebraic" character. In a little more detail, recall that with any two sets A and B, we have a *function set* $A \to B$; this is the set of all functions from A to B. In the ordered setting, this idea of function set gives us three ordered versions: we have $A \xrightarrow{+} B$, the set of all monotone (order-preserving) functions from A to B. These are the ones where $x \leq y$ in A implies $f(x) \leq f(y)$ in B. We also have the set $A \xrightarrow{-} B$ of antitone (order-reversing) functions. And we have the set $A \to B$ of absolutely all functions. It turns out that all of this is relevant to natural language semantics (see Dowty, 1994), and the mathematics behind Dowty's work is developed by Moss (2012).

How does all of this relate to our overall question? As we mentioned, work on arrow-tagging would mainly be on the algebraic side. The theory is thoroughly algebraic. It calls on higher-order functions, indeed it extends this connection from the world of sets to the world of preorders. (A preorder is a relation $\leq$ which is reflexive and transitive; its better-known cousin the partial order also adds anti-symmetry.) A preorder is sometimes called a "poor person's category": in a general category, there may be many morphisms from one object to another (this is typical), while in a preorder either there is exactly one such morphism, or none.

But the "practice" is not completely on the algebraic side. A running system depends on a parser. It can only perform as well as the input from the parser, actually. Using different parsers gives different results sometimes. There certainly were times when we needed to *systematically correct* the parser in various ways. With sentences from newspaper text, for example, we are not able to do much. And what went into the parser? With a massively ambiguous framework like CCG, we only want the very best input from the parser. So this means that we are using a parser that itself was statistically trained; so at the root of our running system are tools derived from Discontent with algebraic work.

10.3.3 Using Arrow Tagging in NLI

At this point, we return to the main thread of the paper. Arrow-tagging gives us a very "cheap" theory of inference: build a good database of background facts, do the tagging, and make replacements. This will not cover for hard-core logical entailment, but perhaps it will do for everyday "unconscious" inference. There is something right (C1) about this view, I think.

Arrow-tagging by itself is not competitive as an approach to NLI. The main reason is that in the existing datasets for NLI, one rarely comes across a premise/hypothesis pair that where the hypothesis comes from the premise by making *exact replacements*. One typically needs more; replacement on polarity arrows is not enough for the test sets, let alone day-to-day inference. For example, consider the sentence

SICK 1627
Premise: A man is mixing a few ingredients in a bowl
Hypothesis: Some ingredients are being mixed in a bowl by a person

Intuitively this should be an entailment. But what could the formal account look like? A computational system could put the arrow on $man^\uparrow$. It's background knowledge should include $man \leq person$. So by replacement, the premise implies *A man is mixing a few ingredients in a bowl*. Going further, the system might well tag the constituent *a few* as $\uparrow$, and it also "know" that *a few* $\leq$ *some*. Thus it would be able to conclude *A person is mixing some ingredients in a bowl*. But our Hypothesis is the passive of this, and this is not obtainable by replacement alone. One needs a tool to compute passives, clearly. But this is not sufficient: in addition to passives, we find paraphrases coming from *there*-insertion, fronting, movement of prepositional phrases, and many other things. Of special interest here are times when one wants to do a logical inference as in the extended syllogistic reasoning which we mentioned in Section 10.3.1. Overall, what we find is that monotonicity is a good strong first tool (C1), perhaps unexpectedly so. Other algebraic tools like logic rules are good as well (C1). At the same time, BERT base does better, as we see in Table 10.1.

10.3.4 Using Arrow Tagging in Inference, and Related Work

The work on polarity annotation of CCG trees typifies the overall theme of this paper. On the one hand, we'll see that it is a qualified success. On the other hand, there are still areas to explore that seem to call into question the overall framework.

There are two downstream end-to-end NLI systems that make heavy use of the arrow-tagging work. The first is based on my PhD student Hai Hu's implementation

TABLE 10.1   Performance on the SICK test set. [†] = corrected SICK. [‡] = P/R for MonaLog averaged across three labels. Results involving BERT are averaged across six runs; same for later experiments.

system	P	R	acc.
majority baseline	–	–	56.36
ML/DL-based systems			
BERT (base, uncased)	86.81	85.37	86.74
Yin and Schütze, 2017	–	–	87.1
Beltagy et al., 2016	–	–	85.1
Logic-based systems			
Bjerva et al., 2014	93.6	60.6	81.6
Abzianidze, 2017	97.95	58.11	81.35
Martínez-Gómez et al., 2016	97.04	63.64	83.13
Yanaka et al., 2018	84.2	77.3	84.3
MonaLog + transformations	89.91	74.23	81.66[†]
Hybrid systems			
Hybrid: MonaLog + BERT	85.65	87.33	85.95[†]
Kalouli et al. (2020)	–	–	86.5
NeuralLog (full system)	88.0	**87.6**	**90.3**
– syntactic variation	68.9	79.3	71.4
– monotonicity	74.5	75.1	74.7

of the calculus: see Hu, Chen, et al., 2019; Hu and Moss, 2018, 2020. Here is what these accomplish. One can indeed take an off-the-shelf parse, follow an algorithm to tag the arrows, and use this as the basis of an NLI system. The architecture of the system is shown in Figure 10.1, and the performance of the system may be found in Figure 10.1. As mentioned, a simple use of monotonicity/polarity tagging alone cannot go very far. It is fairly easy to supplement it with natural logic rules of various kinds, or with transformations like active to passive. Once this is done, the system is not as good as BERT (base, uncased), but it is close.

At this point, we also want to mention the other "algebraic" or "logic-based" work in this area, especially the papers mentioned in Table 10.1. While MonaLog makes use of monotonicity arrow tagging and natural logic rules (hence the name), other systems use tableau methods or other tools from logic. These would all qualify as "algebraic" in the sense of this volume. These systems all perform at roughly the same level, and somewhat below what ML/DL systems can do. The entries in Table 10.1 are, in a sense, out of date since transformer models such as DeBERTa were not around when the entries were found. All of these systems are very good in the Precision column. This is not surprising, since when a logic-based system will report an entailment, it typically has a proof in some formal system. And the requirements on such a system are stringent, so the proof that is found is very likely to correspond to human reasoning in some sense. This is a good reason to be content with this entire line of work (C1).

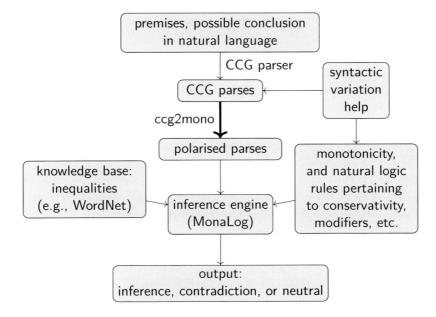

Figure 10.1 Architecture the NLI system MonaLog, using monotonicity tagging, and other "algebraic" components.

Readers familiar with NLI are likely to complain that the SICK dataset is not of current interest: it is much smaller than datasets like MNLI and SNLI, and SICK itself is limited in the kinds of inferences that are found. Is there any hope of using methods like arrow tagging in connection with the larger datasets? While I do not have a full set of statistics, I do have second-hand reports that it will be difficult to extend the qualified success that we mentioned above to the larger datasets. These datasets typically have more syntactic variation, and inference in them often requires much more real-world knowledge. So the performance of systems like MonoLog are not going to do well. But in a sense, they were not intended as general-purpose tools for NLI. They were intended to do well on one small facet of NLI, namely monotonicity inference. What would be more in the spirit of this paper would be to take some other interesting feature of NLI, say temporal/spatial inference, or causal inference, or something else which is somehow limited and amenable to an "algebraic" treatment, and to craft a computational system which does well on that particular feature. In some ways, work on *probabilistic inference in language* is doing something similar to what I advocate; see, for example Bernardy et al. (2019); and Goodman and Frank (2016).

We conclude with the matter of hybridising logic-based and deep learning systems in the area of NLI. This directly relates to point (C2) from the beginning of the paper. Work on hybridisation in MonoLog was primarily a matter of calling on BERT when the logic-based method failed; so this was a weak form of hybridisation. More serious was the work of Kalouli et al. (2020). And the most successful work to date is the NeuralLog system of Chen, Gao, and Moss (2021). Because this work is currently the state of the art and because aspects of it pertain to the theme of the paper, we discuss it in more detail.

Our algebraic discussion of arrow tagging seemed to suggest that one would need CCG to do arrow tagging in the first place. As it turns out, it isn't really neccessary in practice. This was shown in Chen and Gao (2021) One can use dependency parses instead. Doing this means that there is less of a connection to formal semantics, since dependency grammars are not as connected to formal semantics as categorial grammars. Put another way, one can *prove* a soundness result about arrow-tagging for CCG trees, and I do not see how to do this for dependency trees. Nevertheless, the system in Chen and Gao (2021) works somewhat better than the original one system Hu and Moss (2018), even for tagging. Here is one reason for this: the dependency parses themselves are somewhat more accurate than the CCG parses. The later system had the benefit of seeing phenomena that were hard for the earlier system to handle. Retuning to the topic of this paper, it was very useful to work out the details of arrow-tagging in a highly algebraic setting. So even if turns out that one would prefer to use semantic parses of some kind rather than CCG for "in practice" work, it still seems to me that the algebraic approach is better in order to understand what is going on "in theory."

But the more serious reason that NeuralLog does so well is that it found a way to use neural net learners in connection with syntactic variation, a topic which we mentioned earlier as a bottleneck for MonaLog and all of the logic-based systems. The result of this hybridisation is shown in the ablation studies indicated at the bottom of Table 10.1. The row marked -*syntactic variation* shows what happened when the syntactic variation module was turned off, and the final row shows what happened without the monotonicity module. The cheerful conclusion is that both were needed: algebra and deep learning.

10.4 CONCLUSION

We have tried to show reasons for both content and discontent with algebraic methods in the study and modelling of natural language. It is a fairly balanced case, and much of our conclusions can already be read off of the way we stated the reasons for both sides back in Section 10.1.1. Section 10.2 suggested that a more general understanding of algebraic methods will be important for NLP and for language, and the work on monotonicity arrow tagging in Section 10.3 also shows that it has something to say for the core semantic area of inference. At the same time, I also feel the underlying discontent that comes from watching deep learning models outperform the logic-based systems in NLI. For those interested in the overall issue of this volume, I hope that the nuanced presentation here offers some clarification and some new points to consider.

This work is supported by grant #586136 from the Simons Foundation. My thanks to an anonymous reviewer for comments and helpful criticisms of a draft of this paper.

BIBLIOGRAPHY

Abzianidze, Lasha (2017). "LangPro: Natural Language Theorem Prover". In: *CoRR* abs/1708.09417.

Barwise, Jon and John Etchemendy (1987). *The Liar.* An essay on truth and circularity. The Clarendon Press, Oxford University Press, New York, pp. xii+185. ISBN: 0-19-505072-X.

Beltagy, Islam, Stephen Roller, Pengxiang Cheng, Katrin Erk, and Raymond J Mooney (2016). "Representing meaning with a combination of logical and distributional models". In: *Computational Linguistics* 42.4, pp. 763–808.

Benthem, Johan van (1986). *Essays in Logical Semantics.* Vol. 29. Studies in Linguistics and Philosophy. Dordrecht: D. Reidel Publishing Co., pp. xii+225.

— (1991). *Language in Action: Categories, Lambdas, and Dynamic Logic.* Vol. 130. Studies in Logic. Elsevier, Amsterdam.

— (2008). "A Brief History of Natural Logic". In: *Logic, Navya-Nyaya and Applications, Homage to Bimal Krishna Matilal.* Ed. by M. Chakraborty, B. Löwe, M. Nath Mitra, and S. Sarukkai. London: College Publications.

Bernardy, Jean-Philippe, Rasmus Blanck, Stergios Chatzikyriakidis, Shalom Lappin, and Aleksandre Maskharashvili (2019). "Bayesian Inference Semantics: A Modelling System and A Test Suite". In: *Proceedings of the Eighth Joint Conference on Lexical and Computational Semantics, *SEM@NAACL-HLT 2019, Minneapolis, MN, USA, June 6-7, 2019.* Ed. by Rada Mihalcea, Ekaterina Shutova, Lun-Wei Ku, Kilian Evang, and Soujanya Poria. Association for Computational Linguistics, pp. 263–272.

Bjerva, Johannes, Johan Bos, Rob Van der Goot, and Malvina Nissim (2014). "The meaning factory: Formal semantics for recognizing textual entailment and determining semantic similarity". In: *Proceedings of the 8th International Workshop on Semantic Evaluation (SemEval 2014)*, pp. 642–646.

Capretta, Venanzio, Tarmo Uustalu, and Varmo Vene (2009). "Corecursive Algebras: A Study of General Structured Corecursion". English. In: *Formal Methods: Foundations and Applications.* Ed. by M. Oliveira and J. Woodcock. Vol. 5902. Lecture Notes in Computer Science. Springer Berlin Heidelberg, pp. 84–100. ISBN: 978-3-642-10451-0. DOI: 10.1007/978-3-642-10452-7_7. URL: http://dx.doi.org/10.1007/978-3-642-10452-7_7.

Chatzikyriakidis, Stergios and Zhaohui Luo (2020). *Formal Semantics in Modern Type Theories.* Wiley.

Chen, Zeming and Qiyue Gao (2021). "Monotonicity Marking from Universal Dependency Trees". In: *CoRR* abs/2104.08659. arXiv: 2104.08659. URL: https://arxiv.org/abs/2104.08659.

Chen, Zeming, Qiyue Gao, and Lawrence S. Moss (2021). "NeuralLog: Natural Language Inference with Joint Neural and Logical Reasoning". In: *Proceedings of *SEM 2021: The Tenth Joint Conference on Lexical and Computational Semantics, *SEM 2021, Online, August 5-6, 2021.* Ed. by Vivi Nastase and Ivan Vulic. Association for Computational Linguistics, pp. 78–88.

Coecke, Bob, Mehrnoosh Sadrzadeh, and Stephen Clark (2010). "Mathematical Foundations for a Compositional Distributional Model of Meaning". In: *CoRR* abs/1003.4394.

Dowty, David (1994). "The Role of Negative Polarity and Concord Marking in Natural Language Reasoning". In: *Proceedings of Semantics and Linguistic Theory (SALT) IV*.

Feys, Frank, Helle Hansen, and Lawrence S. Moss (2018). "Long-term Values in Markov Decision Processes (Co)Algebraically". In: *Proceedings of CMCS'18*. Ed. by Corina Cirstea. Vol. 11202. Springer LNCS, pp. 78–99.

Fong, Brendan, David I. Spivak, and Rémy Tuyéras (2019). "Backprop as Functor: A Compositional Perspective on Supervised Learning". In: *34th Annual ACM/IEEE Symposium on Logic in Computer Science, LICS 2019, Vancouver, BC, Canada, June 24-27, 2019*. IEEE, pp. 1–13.

Francez, N. (2015). *Proof-theoretic Semantics*. Studies in Logic. College Publications. ISBN: 9781848901834.

Geurts, Bart and Frans van der Slik (2005). "Monotonicity and Processing Load". In: *Journal of Semantics* 22, pp. 97–117.

Goodman, Noah D. and Michael C. Frank (2016). "Pragmatic Language Interpretation as Probabilistic Inference". In: *Trends in Cognitive Sciences* 20.11, pp. 818–829. ISSN: 1364-6613. DOI: `https : / / doi . org / 10 . 1016 / j . tics . 2016 . 08 . 005`. URL: `https : / / www . sciencedirect . com / science / article / pii / S136466131630122X`.

Howard, Ronald A. (1960). *Dynamic Programming and Markov Processes*. The M.I.T. Press.

Hu, Hai, Qi Chen, and Lawrence S Moss (2019). "Natural Language Inference with Monotonicity". In: *Proceedings of IWCS*.

Hu, Hai and Lawrence S. Moss (2018). "Polarity Computations in Flexible Categorial Grammar". In: *Proceedings of The Seventh Joint Conference on Lexical and Computational Semantics, *SEM 2018, New Orleans, Louisiana*. Ed. by M. Nissim (et al).

— (2020). "An Automatic Monotonicity Annotation Tool Based on CCG Trees". Paper presented to the Second Tsinghua Interdisciplinary Workshop on Logic, Language, and Meaning: Monotonicity in Logic and Language (TTLM'20).

Jacobs, Bart and David Sprunger (2019). "Neural Nets via Forward State Transformation and Backward Loss Transformation". In: *Proceedings of the Thirty-Fifth Conference on the Mathematical Foundations of Programming Semantics, MFPS 2019, London, UK, June 4-7, 2019*. Ed. by Barbara König. Vol. 347. Electronic Notes in Theoretical Computer Science. Elsevier, pp. 161–177.

Jacobson, Pauline (2014). *An Introduction to the Syntax/Semantics Interface*. Oxford University Press.

Kalouli, Aikaterini-Lida, Richard S. Crouch, and Valeria de Paiva (2020). "Hy-NLI: a Hybrid system for Natural Language Inference". In: *Proceedings of the 28th International Conference on Computational Linguistics, COLING 2020, Barcelona, Spain (Online), December 8-13, 2020*. Ed. by Donia Scott, Núria Bel, and Chengqing Zong. International Committee on Computational Linguistics, pp. 5235–5249.

Kartsaklis, Dimitri, Ian Fan, Richie Yeung, Anna Pearson, Robin Lorenz, Alexis Toumi, Giovanni de Felice, Konstantinos Meichanetzidis, Stephen Clark, and Bob Coecke (2021). "Lambeq: An Efficient High-Level Python Library for Quantum NLP". In: *CoRR* abs/2110.04236.

Martínez-Gómez, Pascual, Koji Mineshima, Yusuke Miyao, and Daisuke Bekki (Aug. 2016). "ccg2lambda: A Compositional Semantics System". In: *Proceedings of ACL 2016 System Demonstrations*. Berlin, Germany: Association for Computational Linguistics, pp. 85–90. URL: `https://aclweb.org/anthology/P/P16/P16-4015.pdf`.

Moot, Richard and Christian Retoré (2012). *The Logic of Categorial Grammars - A Deductive Account of Natural Language Syntax and Semantics*. Vol. 6850. Lecture Notes in Computer Science. Springer. ISBN: 978-3-642-31554-1. DOI: `10.1007/978-3-642-31555-8`. URL: `https://doi.org/10.1007/978-3-642-31555-8`.

Moss, Lawrence S. (2012). "The Soundness of Internalized Polarity Marking". In: *Studia Logica* 100.4, pp. 683–704.

— (2015). "Natural logic". In: *Handbook of Contemporary Semantic Theory*, Second Edition. Ed. by C. Fox and S. Lappin. Wiley-Blackwell, pp. 646–681.

Moss, Lawrence S. and Hai Hu (2022). "Soundness of Polarity Marking for CCG". unpublished ms., Indiana University.

Moss, Lawrence S. and Alex Kruckman (2017). "All and only". In: *Partiality and Underspecification in Information, Languages, and Knowledge*. Ed. by Henning Christiansen et al. Cambridge Scholars Publishing, pp. 189–218.

Rutten, Jan J. M. M. (2000). "Universal coalgebra: a theory of systems". In: *Theoret. Comput. Sci.* 249.1, pp. 3–80.

Steedman, Mark (2012). *Taking Scope: The Natural Semantics of Quantifiers*. Cambridge, MA: MIT Press.

Vajjha, Koundinya, Avraham Shinnar, Barry Trager, Vasily Pestun, and Nathan Fulton (2021). "CertRL: Formalizing Convergence Proofs for Value and Policy Iteration in Coq". In: *Proceedings of the 10th ACM SIGPLAN International Conference on Certified Programs and Proofs*. CPP 2021. Virtual, Denmark: Association for Computing Machinery, pp. 18–31. ISBN: 9781450382991. DOI: `10.1145/3437992.3439927`. URL: `https://doi.org/10.1145/3437992.3439927`.

Valencia, Victor Sánchez (1991). "Studies on Natural Logic and Categorial Grammar". PhD thesis. Universiteit van Amsterdam.

Moore, Andrew (2002). *Markov Systems, Markov Decision Processes, and Dynamic Programming*. Lecture slides available at https://www.autonlab.org/tutorials.

Yanaka, Hitomi, Koji Mineshima, Pascual Martínez-Gómez, and Daisuke Bekki (2018). "Acquisition of Phrase Correspondences Using Natural Deduction Proofs". In: *Proceedings of NAACL*. URL: `https://www.aclweb.org/anthology/N18-1069/`.

Yin, Wenpeng and Hinrich Schütze (2017). "Task-Specific Attentive Pooling of Phrase Alignments Contributes to Sentence Matching". In: *Proceedings of EACL*, pp. 699–709.

CHAPTER 11

Unitary Recurrent Networks: Algebraic and Linear Structures for Syntax

Jean-Philippe Bernardy

University of Gothenburg

Shalom Lappin

University of Gothenburg, Queen Mary University of London, and King's College London

CONTENTS

DOI: 10.1201/9781003205388-11

ABSTRACT

The emergence of powerful deep learning systems has largely displaced classical symbolic algebraic models of linguistic representation in computational linguistics. While deep neural networks have achieved impressive results across a wide variety of AI and NLP tasks, they have become increasingly opaque and inaccessible to a clear understanding of how they acquire the generalisations that they extract from the data to which they apply. This is particularly true of BERT, and similar non-directional transformers. We study an alternative deep learning system, Unitary-Evolution Recurrent Neural Networks (URNs) (Arjovsky et al., 2016), which are strictly compositional in their combination of state matrices. As a result they are fully transparent. They can be understood entirely in terms of the linear algebraic operations that they apply to each input state matrix to obtain its output successor. We review these operations in some detail, clarifying the compositional nature of URNs. We then present experimental evidence from three NLP tasks to show that these models achieve an encouraging level of precision in handling long distance dependencies. The learning required to solve these tasks involves acquiring and representing complex hierarchical syntactic structures.

11.1 INTRODUCTION

Theoretical linguistics owes two major ideas to the work of Montague (1970a,b). The first is the general hypothesis that semantics is amenable to mathematical formulation. The second is the view that the semantics of a language is a function defined compositionally over its syntax. Realising Montague's program requires that (1) the syntax-semantics interface is expressed as an algebraic structure, and (2) semantic interpretation is achieved through such a structure. We will explore in some detail what these conditions entail.

The emergence of linguistic models based on deep learning have brought considerable improvements in terms of coverage and predictive power, compared to tools based on algebraic theories (Moss, 2022, Chapter 10 of this volume). Unfortunately, using such models has generally means giving up Montague's principles of compositionality. At a surface level, even though the model is expressed as a well-defined function from an input string to a (task-dependent) prediction, this function

$$Q = \tfrac{1}{2} \begin{pmatrix} \sqrt{2} & -\sqrt{2} & 0 \\ \sqrt{2} & \sqrt{2} & 0 \\ 0 & 0 & 1 \end{pmatrix}$$

$$s = \tfrac{1}{2}(0, 1, \sqrt{3})$$

$$Qs = \tfrac{1}{4}(-\sqrt{2}, \sqrt{2}, 2\sqrt{3})$$

Figure 11.1   Example of one step of unitary evolution.

possesses no particular property which conditions its behaviour predictably on various classes of input. Therefore it is arduous, though not impossible, to infer insights about such a model, from a theoretical linguistic perspective. Although it is not impossible that deep-learning models embed a syntactico-semantic interface, in most cases the discrete types of information that the models learn and represent remain opaquely encoded. Concomitantly, the non-linear activation functions that deep learning models apply between the each layer prevent transparent tracking of this information. This is particularly frustrating in light of the fact that prediction functions are specified through the operations of linear algebra, which carry a rich set of tools for structural analysis.

In this chapter, we advocate the Unitary Recurrent Network (URN) as a transparent alternative model of deep learning. This architecture was first proposed by Arjovsky et al. (2016) to solve the problem of exploding and vanishing gradients when applying back propagation in a recurrent neural network, thanks to the norm-preserving properties of unitary matrices (see Figure 11.1 for an example). Its algebraic properties give reason to think that the framework admits of interesting theoretical analysis. The rest of the chapter shows that the URN can be trained to learn syntactic structure, and that the trained models are amenable to white-box analysis.

11.2 TWO FLAVOURS OF ALGEBRAIC STRUCTURES

In general, an algebraic structure is defined by

- a collection of (types of) operations parameterised over a type a –the carrier set, and

- a number of axioms specifying the above operations

For example, as an algebraic structure, a monoid is defined by the two operations $\epsilon : a$ and $(\bullet) : a \to a \to a$, such that

$$\forall x. \, \epsilon \bullet x = x \qquad \text{(left identity)}$$
$$\forall x. \, x \bullet \epsilon = x \qquad \text{(right identity)}$$
$$\forall x \, y \, z. \, x \bullet (y \bullet z) = (x \bullet y) \bullet z \qquad \text{(associativity)}$$

Any given monoid is defined by a *particular* tuple $(a, \epsilon, (\bullet))$. For instance, $(\mathbb{R}, 0, (+))$ is the usual additive monoid over real numbers.

11.2.1 Syntax-semantics Interface

As we have observed, a syntax-semantics interface is defined by an algebraic structure. A simple way to construct such an interface is to encode a context-free grammar, with an indexed carrier set. A rule like $S ::= NP\ VP$ corresponds to the type $a_{NP} \rightarrow a_{VP} \rightarrow a_S$. Among others, Ranta (2004) uses this kind of coding. Any instance of this structure produces a particular semantics. In our example, this involves assigning semantic types to all the syntactic categories (a_{NP}, a_{VP}, a_S, etc.), and defining valid operations for each of the rules. It should be stressed here that the such meaning representations are not limited to the context-free case.

In general, if the algebra $Fa \rightarrow a$ is the syntax-semantic interface, then the initial algebra μF is the set of associated syntactic representations, while any function $\phi : F\alpha \rightarrow \alpha$ is a compositional semantics over such a syntax.[1]

Montague (1974) provides a semantics for quantifiers by means of a continuation monad carrying truth-valued effects. (Barker and Shan, 2004; Groote, 2001). Montague left the type of individuals abstract, but it can be further instantiated to vector spaces, with various interpretations. (Bernardy, Blanck, et al., 2018; Emerson and Copestake, 2016, 2017; Grefenstette et al., 2011; Grove and Bernardy, 2021).

11.2.2 Sequence Algebras and Parsing

On Montague's view, semantics is based on syntactic structure. However, languages do not come with labelled syntactic structures. Rather, basic linguistic data consists of sequences of symbols. In fact, this is assumption already comes with a fair amount of theoretical bias and abstraction, but we will take it as given.

The mapping of raw linguistic data to syntactic structure has been widely studied in the history of parsing. Let's consider an algebraic formulation of the parsing task. The structure of linguistic input, a sequence of symbols, can be captured as a sequence algebra, defined as follows.

Definition 11.1 (Sequence algebra). *A sequence algebra over a set of symbols Σ consists of three operations:*

$$embed : \Sigma \rightarrow a \qquad\qquad embedding\ a\ symbol$$
$$\epsilon : a \qquad\qquad empty\ sequence$$
$$(\bullet) : a \rightarrow a \rightarrow a \qquad\qquad concatenation$$

together with the same laws that define monoids.

(That is, it is a free monoid over the set Σ). The monoid operations and laws express the linear character of a sequence. In particular the laws ensure that the order (and, in general, the structure) of concatenations plays no role in the meaning of a sequence.

The set of sequences is the associated initial algebra. A *parser* is any instance of a sequence algebra with the carrier set a being instantiated to the syntactic structure of interest, for the task at hand.[2] It should be emphasised that this definition entails

---

[1] See Chapter 10 for more algebraic background.

[2] Typically, a parser is also allowed to fail, but we'll ignore that case here.

that the parser is strictly sequence-compositional, in the sense that one can parse any sub-sequence, and compose it with the parse result of any other sub-sequence. This might seem counter-intuitive if one is accustomed to thinking of a parser as an automaton processing the string in a left-to-right order, whose behaviour is described by a state-transition function

$$f : \Sigma \rightarrow s \rightarrow s.$$

However, there is no incompatibility between these two characterisations of parsing. They are functionally equivalent, but they express distinct formal perspectives on the way that parsing operates.

Definition 11.2 (Automaton from sequence algebra). *Assume a sequence algebra* $(a, embed, \epsilon, \bullet)$. *Then we can construct an equivalent parser automaton by letting the internal state be the carrier set:*

$$s = a$$
$$f\, x\, s = s \bullet embed\, x$$

Definition 11.3 (Sequence algebra from automaton). *Assume an automaton internal state* s, *whose behaviour is captured by a state-transition function* $f : \Sigma \rightarrow s \rightarrow s$. *We can define an equivalent sequence algebra by letting the carrier type be the set of state-transition functions:*

$$a = s \rightarrow s$$
$$embed = f$$
$$\epsilon = id$$
$$w_1 \bullet w_2 = w_2 \circ w_1$$

It should however be noted that, for any non-trivial set s, the set $a = s \rightarrow s$ is extremely large.[3] The reformulation of a sequential automaton as a sequence algebra produces a computationally expensive result, unless there happens to be an efficient representation of transition functions over s. There are, then, practical tradeoffs in choosing one approach over the other.

As we see it, the advantages of the automaton approach are that if the set s is small, then it can be implemented by a sequential algorithm in a way that is memory efficient. It also corresponds more closely to psycholinguistic models that rely on sequential processing of inputs.

The sequence-algebraic approach has also advantages. First, it can be implemented as a divide-and-conquer algorithm. The input sequence can be split arbitrarily. Both sub-sequences can be parsed independently, and the results recombined using ($\bullet$). If this recombination operator is efficient, then one obtains an algorithm that is cost effective overall. Valiant (1975) takes advantage of this principle to construct the most time-efficient algorithm for general context-free parsing. The complexity of Valiant's algorithm is sub-cubic. Cubic, or even sub-cubic, complexity is unrealistic for human processing, and so context-free grammars may seem to be a poor

---

[3]if the cardinality of s is $|s|$, then the cardinality of a is $|s \rightarrow s| = |s|^{|s|}$

model for human language syntax. One can, of course, resort to heuristic methods to improve complexity in many situations; but Bernardy and Claessen (2013, 2015) demonstrate a general result in this regard. They show that if the charts are represented by appropriate sparse matrices and input strings are organised hierarchically, then the complexity of Valiant's algorithm becomes linear.

The second advantage of the sequence-algebraic approach for parsing is that one can analyse any value of a out-of-context. In fact, because it can be combined in any context, a value of this type must include, in one form or another, possible interpretations for all the contexts that it can possibly interact with. In practice, such an analysis is possible only if the structure of a is simpler than arbitrary state-transition functions $(s \rightarrow s)$. We will show later how to leverage this theoretical property for URN models. In the case of Valiant's algorithm, the type a is realised by a parse chart. For any sequence of symbols w, the chart $\phi_{valiant}(w)$ contains all the possible syntactic representations of all possible subsequences contained in w. While this sounds expensive, Bernardy and Claessen (2013, 2015) show that this chart is asymptotically (very) sparse for hierarchically organised inputs.

Third, the sequence algebra formulation allows for parallel evaluation. It is possible to compute it at symbols using *embed*, then group those results in adjacent pairs, for each in parallel, then proceed upwards until one has a result for the full input sequence. This can be crucial when using modern parallel hardware for evaluation.

A sequence-algebra need not take the form of a usual parser. It can map a sequence of symbols directly to a semantic value without invoking an intermediate syntactic representation. Such models are now referred to as "end-to-end" systems. They connect one end of a process (sequences of symbols) to the task-specific semantics (the carrier type a). Our focus here is to construct and analyse such systems using an URN architecture.

We have pointed out that an RNN is fully defined by a transition function of the type that we have identified above:

$$f : \Sigma \rightarrow s \rightarrow s.$$

We call such an operation f an evolution function. If the RNN acts as a language model, then it also contains a prediction function whose role is to predict the next symbol given the current state. More precisely, it predicts a probability score for each symbol

$$p : s \rightarrow \Sigma \rightarrow \mathbb{R}$$

The set of these scores is then turned into a probability distribution through a softmax function:

$$\text{softmax} : (\Sigma \rightarrow \mathbb{R}) \rightarrow (\Sigma \rightarrow [0,1])$$

$$\text{softmax}\, q\, x = \frac{e^{q\,x}}{\sum_{x \in \Sigma} e^{q\,x}}$$

While RNNs can be neatly reformulated as sequence-algebras (even if inefficient ones), transformer-like deep learning models cannot be easily expressed in these terms. Indeed, a transformer essentially consists of several layers of attention heads, and the output of each attention head depends on all input positions. This global dependence pattern is incompatible with a sequence algebra. Such algebras require that any input is represented independently of its larger context, in a way that depends solely on its constituents, and its structure.

11.2.3 Linear Algebra

To clarify the structure and interpretation of URNs we will review some of the concepts of linear algebra that we will apply. In fact, linear algebra is central to deep neural networks in general, given that they operate through operations on vectors and matrices. These concepts tend to be suppressed as assumed in much current work on deep learning. It is worth highlighting them here to indicate the differences between URNs and other deep learning networks.

Algebraically, a vector space over a field s is defined by a vector addition $(+)$: $a \to a \to a$, multiplication by a scalar $(*) : s \to a \to a$, and the vector $0 : a$ such that $(+)$ is associative, commutative, invertible, and has 0 as a left and right unit. Additionally, multiplication by a scalar is required to compatible with scalar multiplication; and vector addition must distribute over multiplication by a scalar and *vice versa*. Finally, the scalar unit must be the unit of multiplication by a scalar.

In practice, one seldom works with the algebraic definition. Rather, one uses an array of numbers, say $\mathbb{R}^n$. The reason for doing so is that, given a basis $\vec{e}_i$ of a vector space of dimension n, the set of vectors is isomorphic to the set of representations $\mathbb{R}^n$, with

$$\vec{x} = \sum_i x^i \vec{e}_i$$

But our main object of interest is *linear maps*, which are defined as homomorphisms between two vector spaces (when the source and target spaces are identified, one speaks of a *linear operator*). Again, we do not work with this definition, but rather with representations in the form of matrices of numbers $\mathbb{R}^n_m$, for the same reason that we use arrays of numbers instead of vector spaces as defined above.

Given appropriate bases $\vec{e}_i$ and $\vec{d}_i$ for the source and target spaces, matrix representations are in isomorphic relations with linear maps:

$$F(\vec{x}) = F\left(\sum_i x^i \vec{d}_i\right) = \sum_j \vec{e}_j F_i^j x^i$$

The components of the image of F are obtained by matrix-vector multiplication:

$$F(\vec{x})^j = \sum_j F_i^j x^i$$

These definitions are intended as formal background that is often omitted in discussions of deep neural networks. For a detailed introduction to linear algebra, we recommend consulting standard references (Gantmacher, 1959; Strang, 2016).

To clarify, we are *not* suggesting that vector algebra specifies the syntax-semantics interface for a linguistic theory. It plays an entirely different role in our model.

11.2.4   Linear operators as charts, charts as phrase embeddings

We will be making use of the fact that linear operators (linear maps to and from the same vector space v) form a monoid under composition.

$$a = v \to v$$
$$\epsilon = id$$
$$F \bullet G = G \circ F$$

Notice that the composition of a linear operators is another linear operator. Consequently, one can represent such a composition as a matrix, which is the product of the representations from which it is formed. The corresponding monoid is:

$$a = \mathbb{R}_n^n$$
$$\epsilon = I$$
$$F \bullet G = G \times F$$

By also defining a function $embed : \Sigma \to \mathbb{R}_n^n$ we obtain a matrix-based representation of charts. Because the number of dimensions in such a chart is n^2 (and not infinite as it would be in the general case), it is possible that it is amenable to a *context-independent* analysis. We will use a deep-learning approach to construct *embed* – an appropriate word-embedding – and the methods of linear algebra to analyse the charts. For reasons that will become clear later, we restrict ourselves to *unitary* operators as charts. Such a chart essentially acts as a representation for the input substring that it is built from, and we generally refer to it as the embedding for the substring.

The adjective "unitary" refers to the fact that the norm of the determinant is the unit. It also indicates that the underlying scalar field consists of complex numbers. We will, in fact, restrict the scalar field to real numbers, which permits a more vivid geometrical representation of some of our data. Therefore, the matrices that we employ in URNs are actually orthogonal. We retain the description "unitary" because it now enjoys wide currency in the deep learning literature to refer to URN-like models.[4]

Definition 11.4 (Orthogonal matrix). *A matrix Q is orthogonal iff it is square and $Q^T Q = I$.*

11.3   TWO MODELS

We consider two generative models: an LSTM (Hochreiter and Schmidhuber, 1997) and an URN (Arjovsky et al., 2016). We show them schematically in Figure 11.2.

---

[4]The choice between real and complex fields is not significant for our purposes. In geometric terms (planes, rotations, etc.) the results are the same. A plane can be represented either by two real vectors or by one complex vector. A rotation can be expressed by a unimodular complex number or a real angle, etc. Our results also apply to unitary matrices with complex numbers. Beyond the easier geometric interpretation that it affords, we adopt real matrices for two reasons. First, on the implementational side, we found that the TensorFlow library, which we use in our

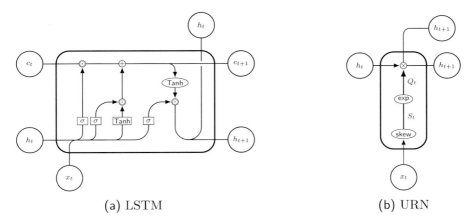

(a) LSTM   (b) URN

Figure 11.2 Schematic representation of RNN cells. In the above, square boxes represent dense layers–with a trainable matrix of weights–followed by an activation function (sigmoid or hyperbolic tangent). Circles and ellipses represent bare functions, with no associated dense layer. Arrows carrying matricial information are drawn thicker. Accordingly, the symbol × corresponds to matrix-vector multiplication, while ⊙ corresponds to the Hadamard product of vectors.

We proceed to describe their evolution functions as mapping from a hidden state h_t to the next state (h_{t+1}):

$$f\, x_t\, h_t = h_{t+1}$$

The expression for h_{t+1} depends on the RNN cell used.

11.3.1   LSTM

To highlight the contrast between LSTMs and URNs, consider, the LSTM (Hochreiter and Schmidhuber, 1997), which is defined as follows:

$$
\begin{aligned}
v_t &= h_t \diamond x_t \\
f_t &= \sigma(W_f v_t + b_f) \\
i_t &= \sigma(W_i v_t + b_i) \\
o_t &= \sigma(W_o v_t + b_i) \\
\tilde{c}_t &= \sigma(W_c v_t + b_c) \\
c_{t+1} &= (f_t \odot c_t) + (i_t \odot \tilde{c}_t) \\
h_{t+1} &= (o_t \odot \tanh(c_{t+1}))
\end{aligned}
$$

Here σ refers to the sigmoid function and ($\diamond$) is vector concatenation.[5]

---

experiments, does not fully support complex numbers. Second, from the theoretical perspective, the description of our models does not require reference to complex numbers. To include them would introduce needless complexity to our account. The precise connection between unitary and orthogonal matrices is explained in, for example, Gantmacher (1959, p. IX.13).

[5] During training we apply dropout to the vectors h_t and x_t for every timestep t.

We observe that the conversion of an LSTM to a sequence algebra (Definition 11.3) would not be interesting or useful. Because it employs non-linear transition functions (sigmoid and hyperbolic tangent), the set of transition functions does not allow a simpler representation than a set of general functions from vectors to vectors.

11.3.2   URN

We define our version of an URN as follows:

$$h_{t+1} = Q_t h_t$$
$$S_t = skew(x_t)$$
$$Q_t = e^{S_t}$$

$skew(x)$ is a function that takes a vector and produces a skew-symmetric (Definition 11.5) matrix by arranging the elements of x in a triangular pattern. For example, with an input vector of size 3, we have:

$$skew(x) = \begin{pmatrix} 0 & x_0 & x_1 \\ -x_0 & 0 & x_2 \\ -x_1 & -x_2 & 0 \end{pmatrix}$$

The upper triangle of S_t is provided by the previous layer (typically the word embedding layer), and its lower triangle is its negated symmetric. This setup ensures that S_t is anti-symmetric. By Theorem 11.2, this entails that Q_t is unitary.

Definition 11.5 (Skew-symmetric matrix). *A square matrix S is skew-symmetric iff $S^T = -S$.*

Lemma 11.1. *Assume that S is a real and skew-symmetric matrix. Then the eigenvalues of S are pure imaginary.*

Proof. Assume u a complex vector, and λ a complex number, such that u is an eigenvector of S with corresponding eigenvalue λ. By definition, $Su = \lambda u$. We have $u^* S u = \lambda u^* u = \lambda \|u\|^2$. Taking the hermitian conjugate of both sides yields $u^* S^* u = \bar{\lambda} \|u\|^2$. Because S is skew-symmetric, we also have $u^*(-S)u = \bar{\lambda} \|u\|^2$, and in turn $u^* S u = -\bar{\lambda} \|u\|^2$. We can then conclude that $\lambda = -\bar{\lambda}$, which is satisfied only when λ is pure imaginary. $\qquad \square$

Theorem 11.2. *If S is skew-symmetric then e^S is orthogonal. Additionally, the rank of S gives the maximum number of eigenvalues of e^S different from 1.*

Proof. By the spectral theorem, S admits a unitary diagonalisation. By Lemma 11.1, the eigenvalues are pure imaginary, and thus we have $S = U^*(i\Theta)U$, with Θ real and diagonal. Let the diagonal elements of Θ be θ_j. We can then compute:

$$e^S = \sum_{n=0}^{\infty} \frac{S^n}{n!}$$

$$= \sum_{n=0}^{\infty} \frac{(U^* i \Theta U)^n}{n!}$$

$$= \sum_{n=0}^{\infty} \frac{U^* (i\Theta)^n U}{n!}$$

$$= U^* \left(\sum_{n=0}^{\infty} \frac{(i\Theta)^n}{n!} \right) U$$

$$= U^* e^{i\Theta} U$$

Thus, the eigenvalues of e^S are $\lambda_j = e^{i\theta_j}$, and each of them is unimodular. Consequently, e^S is unitary. We also know that it is a real matrix, and thus it is orthogonal.

To prove the second part of the theorem, we note that if $\theta_j = 0$ then $\lambda_j = 1$. Because the rank of S gives the number of non-zero elements of Θ, it is also the maximum number of elements of $e^{i\Theta}$ different from 1. These numbers can differ when $\theta_j = 2\pi$ for some j. □

We call Q_t the *orthogonal embedding* of the input symbol at position t.

In contrast to an LSTM, it is useful to specify an URN as a sequence algebra:

$$embed\, x = e^{skew(v(x_t))}$$

$$\epsilon = I$$

$$w_1 \bullet w_2 = w_2 \times w_1$$

Assuming that the hidden state vectors have dimension n, the number of dimensions of the carrier type is $n \times (n-1)/2$, due to the orthogonal restriction. This is a notable improvement over an LSTM. Another consequence of this restriction, which Arjovsky et al. (2016) suggest as a motivation for URNs, is that they are not subject to exploding or vanishing gradients.[6]

In what follows, we let n be the dimension of the state vectors s_i, and N the length of the sequence of inputs. We consider only the case of n even.

11.4   THEORETICAL ANALYSIS OF URN MODELS

We can deduce several properties of the class of URN models from their definition, independently of experimental results. We again highlight the fact that the behaviour of the model for any input string w is entirely characterised by the orthogonal matrix, which is the product of the orthogonal embeddings $embed\, x_i$ of each of the symbols x_i composing it. Studying the model consists in examining these matrices.

---

[6]In fact, this feature is present in all linear models (as defined in Section 11.2.4), but URNs enjoy a stronger property. This property is that the gradients wrt. the hidden state is constant throughout timesteps. Arjovsky et al. (2016) provide a proof for a more general result.

Since the work of Mikolov et al. (2013), vector embeddings have proven to be an extremely successful modelling tool. One of their primary disadvantage in most deep learning systems is that their structure is opaque. The only way of analysing the relationships among word vectors is through geometric distance metrics, such as cosine similarity. The unit vectors u and v are deemed similar if $\langle u, v \rangle$ is close to 1.

For URNs, we use orthogonal matrix embeddings, which exhibit a much richer structure. We apply mathematical analysis to get a clear understanding of this structure and how it relates to vector embeddings.

11.4.1 Compositionality

The product of orthogonal matrices is another orthogonal matrix. Consequently, the results of Section 11.2.4 apply to the URN but to a stronger degree: the carrier set of the sequence algebra can be chosen to that of *orthogonal* matrices, not general matrices. This ensures that the combination of matrices that URNs perform in processing input is strictly compositional at each point in the sequence.

11.4.2 Unit vectors

An orthogonal operator preserves the lengths of vectors that it acts upon. Because composition preserves this property, we can ensure that every phrase embedding is orthogonal by ensuring that $embed(x)$ is orthogonal for every symbol x.

We limit ourselves to state vectors h_i of norm 1 from now on. In all our experiments, we take h_0 to be the vector $[1, 0, \ldots]$ without loss of generality.

11.4.3 Long-distance memory

Cosine similarity is a proximity metric that is commonly used to measure similarity between vectors. A crucial property of orthogonal operators is that they preserve cosine similarities. This is a consequence of the following theorem.

Theorem 11.3 (Orthogonal matrices preserve inner products). *If Q is orthogonal, then for every h, s, $\langle Qh, Qs \rangle = \langle h, s \rangle$.*

Proof. $\langle Qh, Qs \rangle = (Qh)^T Qs = h^T Q^T Qs = h^T s = \langle h, s \rangle$ ☐

This property is one of the primary reasons that we are proposing URNs as a model of deep learning for NLP. It entails that no information is lost through time steps. This formal analysis suggests that an URN will be good at tasks which require long-term memory. We report the results of our experimental work in the latter section of the chapter. They strongly confirm this conjecture.

11.4.4 Distance and Similarity

When working with vectors of unit length only, the cosine similarity is equal to the (euclidean) inner product $\langle u, v \rangle = \sum_i u_i v_i$. It is equivalent to working with euclidean distance squared, because $\|u - v\|^2 = 2(1 - \langle u, v \rangle)$.

Notions of vector similarity and distance can be naturally extended to orthogonal matrices, *via* their effect on the state vector. The Frobenius inner product $\langle P, Q \rangle = \Sigma_{ij} P_{ij} Q_{ij}$ extends cosine similarity, and the Frobenius norm $\|A\|^2 = \Sigma_{ij} A_{ij}^2$ extends euclidean norm. They connect in a way that is similar to their relationship for unit vectors: $\|P - Q\|^2 = 2(n - \langle P, Q \rangle)$.

Lemma 11.4. *For any two orthogonal matrices P and Q of dimension n, $\|P - Q\|^2 = 2(n - \langle P, Q \rangle)$.*

Proof.

$$
\begin{aligned}
\|P - Q\|^2 &= \langle P - Q, P - Q \rangle \\
&= \langle P, P \rangle - \langle P, Q \rangle - \langle P, Q \rangle + \langle Q, Q \rangle \\
&= n - 2\langle P, Q \rangle + n
\end{aligned}
$$

$\square$

Why is the Frobenius norm a natural extension of cosine similarity for vectors? It is not due merely to the similarity of their respective formulas. The relationship is deeper. Crucially, the Frobenius inner product (and its associated norm) measures the average behaviour of matrices on state vectors. More precisely, the following holds: $\mathbb{E}_s[\langle Ps, Qs \rangle] = \frac{1}{n}\langle P, Q \rangle$, and $\mathbb{E}_s[\|Ps - Qs\|^2] = \frac{1}{n}\|P - Q\|^2$.

Theorem 11.5. *For every orthogonal matrix Q of dimension n and a random unit vector s, $\mathbb{E}_s[\langle Qs, s \rangle] = \frac{1}{n}\text{trace}(Q)$.*

Proof. By the spectral theorem, Q admits a diagonalisation of the form $Q = U^*\Lambda U$, with U unitary. Let λ_i be the (diagonal) elements of Λ and let $x = Us$. Remark that because U is unitary, $\|x\| = \|s\| = 1$. Thus $\sum_i |x_i|^2 = 1$.[7] Obviously, $\mathbb{E}\left[\sum_i |x_i|^2 = 1\right]$. By assumption, all dimensions of x have the same distribution (applying Q to s does not change this fact, because multiplying by it conserves densities), and thus $\mathbb{E}[|x_i|^2] = \frac{1}{n}$. We can now compute:

$$
\begin{aligned}
\mathbb{E}_s[\langle Qs, s \rangle] &= \mathbb{E}_s[s^T Q s] \\
&= \mathbb{E}_s[s^T U^* \Lambda U s] \\
&= \mathbb{E}_x[x^* \Lambda x] \\
&= \mathbb{E}_x\left[\sum_i |x_i|^2 \lambda_i\right] && \text{by } \Lambda \text{ diagonal} \\
&= \sum_i \lambda_i \mathbb{E}_x[|x_i|^2] && \text{by linearity of expectation} \\
&= \frac{1}{n}\sum_i \lambda_i \\
&= \frac{1}{n}\text{trace}(\Lambda) && \text{because trace is sum of eigenvalues}
\end{aligned}
$$

---

[7]Here, even if Q is real, U, λ_i, and thus x_i are complex.

$$= \frac{1}{n}\text{trace}(\Lambda U U^*)$$

$$= \frac{1}{n}\text{trace}(U^*\Lambda U) \qquad \text{by trace cyclic property}$$

$\square$

Corollary 11.6. *For any two orthogonal matrices P and Q of dimension n, and a random unit vector s, $\mathbb{E}_s[\langle Ps, Qs \rangle] = \frac{1}{n}\langle P, Q \rangle$.*

Proof. Remark first that $\langle Ps, Qs \rangle = s^T P^T Qs = \langle Q^T P, s \rangle$. Combining this equation with Theorem 11.5 and Lemma 11.4 yields the expected result. $\square$

Theorem 11.7. *For every orthogonal matrices P and Q of dimension n and a random unit vector s, $\mathbb{E}_s[\|Ps - Qs\|^2] = \frac{1}{n}\|P - Q\|^2$.*

Proof. A direct consequence of Corollary 11.6 and Lemma 11.4. $\square$

In sum, as fallback, one can analyse unitary embeddings using the methods developed for plain vector embeddings. Doing so is theoretically sound, even though it would not exploit the richer structure of matrices.

11.4.5 Geometric interpretation of embeddings

The proof of Theorem 11.2 tells us that, in general, every orthogonal embedding Q can be written in the form $U^* e^{i\Theta} U$, with Θ real and diagonal. Remembering that such a Q is real, if $2 \times n$ is the dimension of the hidden state vectors, then Q is interpretable as the combination of n rotations around an n orthogonal hyperplane, with angles given by θ_j. For a real matrix, every such angle will be repeated twice in the matrix Θ. The planes of rotation can be computed by diagonalising Q. Below, we will be comparing embeddings by comparing their rotation planes. Since a plane is given by two vectors, it may be unclear how to actually compare them, since they can themselves be rotated within the plane that they define, without changing the result. We solve this problem by using a measure of similarity based on the solution to the orthogonal procrustes problem, given below. This measure gives a value of 2 when the planes are equal (up to the rotation of the basis vectors), and of 0 when they are orthogonal.

Definition 11.6 (Plane similarity). *Assume two planes in an n-dimensional space, each defined by two orthogonal normal vectors, arranged in an n by 2 matrix. The similarity between A and B is defined by $\text{sim}(A, B) = \max_\Omega \langle B, A\Omega \rangle$ for Ω a 2 by 2 orthogonal matrix.*

By taking the minimum for Ω–any rotation of the 2 base vectors in the plae–we account for equal planes, which might be defined by another basis. $A\Omega$ covers all possible bases of the plane defined by A when varying Ω.

Theorem 11.8. $\text{sim}(A, B)$ *is the sum of singular values of $B^T A$.*

Proof. Let $U\Sigma V^T = B^T A$ be a singular value decomposition of $B^T A$.

$$
\begin{aligned}
\max_{\Omega} \langle B, A\Omega \rangle &= \max_{\Omega} \mathsf{trace}(B^T A\Omega) \\
&= \max_{\Omega} \mathsf{trace}(U\Sigma V^T \Omega) \\
&= \max_{\Omega} \mathsf{trace}(\Sigma V^T \Omega U) \\
&= \mathsf{trace}(\Sigma)
\end{aligned}
$$

The last step follows because $V^T \Omega U$ is orthogonal. The fact that Σ is diagonal entails that the maximum trace for the product is achieved when $V^T \Omega U = I$. $\square$

In general, an orthogonal embedding contains a lot of data, and it can be hard to visualise. How can we obtain a simplified, if abstract, picture of it?

11.4.5.1 Signature of Embeddings

First, we consider only the *angles* of the rotations θ_j, not the planes. While the average effect is a useful measure, it is rather crude. The angles of these rotations define how strongly Q affects the state vectors lying in this plane. We refer to such a list of angles as the *signature* of Q, and we denote it as $\mathsf{sig}(Q)$. We represent any such angle graphically as a dial, with small angles pointing up ⬆, and large angles (close to π) pointing down ⬇.

11.4.6 Average Effect

The squared distance to the identity matrix is a useful metric for unitary embeddings, $\|Q - I\|^2$. Theorem 11.5 entails that this metric is the average squared distance between s and Qs. This is the average effect that Q has, relative to the task for which the URN is trained. Note that this sort of metric is unavailable for the opaque vector embeddings of non-linear deep neural networks. For those systems the norm of a vector embedding is not directly interpretable as a measure of its effect. In an LSTM, for example, vector embeddings first undergo a linear transformation *followed by activation functions*, before producing an output state, in several separate stages.

By Lemma 11.4, the average effect is also equal to $2(n - \langle Q, I \rangle)$. But $\langle Q, I \rangle$ is equal to the trace of Q, which, in turn, is equal to the sum of its eigenvalues ($\sum_j e^{i\theta_j}$). Therefore, the average effect is a measure of how large the angles in the signature are.

11.4.7 Truncation

Another way to simplify the representation is to limit ourselves to matrices $S(x)$ which have non-zero entries only on the first k rows (and consequently k columns). This restricts the total size of the embedding to $(n-1) + (n-2) + \cdots + (n-k+1)$, due to the symmetric constraint. We refer to this setup as *truncated* embeddings.

As an example, the 3×3 skew-symmetric matrix $\begin{pmatrix} 0 & a & b \\ -a & 0 & c \\ -b & -c & 0 \end{pmatrix}$ is 1-truncated if $c =$

0. This truncation reduces its matrix informational content to the single row (and column) $(a\ b)$.

We use the acronym URN to refer to the general class of unitary-evolution networks; k-TURN to refer to our specific model architecture with k-truncation of embeddings; and Full-URN for our model architecture with no truncation. (The letter "T" in TURN stands for "Truncated".)

A property of k-truncated embeddings is that $S(x)$ has at most rank $2k$. It follows from Theorem 11.2 that the corresponding orthogonal embeddings $Q(x)$ can be expressed as rotations around (at most) k planes. The more an embedding is truncated–the smaller k–the simpler its geometric interpretation becomes.

11.4.8 Projection

Finally, to understand an orthogonal embedding Q, it can be enlightening to project Q onto a m-dimensional subspace of the n-dimensional ambient space. We do this by projecting each vector on to the m-dimensional subspace. We will consider the projection of some embeddings onto the space defined by the prediction layer of an URN.

11.5   EXPERIMENTS

We apply the LSTM and the URN to several tasks. In all cases, we employ a standard training regime. We use an Adam optimiser (Kingma and Ba, 2014), with no further adjustment. The learning rate is 0.001, and the batch size is 512. Our implementation is done within the TensorFlow (Abadi et al., 2016) framework (version 2.2), including its treatment of matrix exponential. We apply a dropout function on both inputs of the cell function f at every time step, according to a Bernoulli distribution rate of ρ. This causes some entries of s_i or $Q(x_i)$ for the URN to be zeroed out. No dropout is applied for the LSTM on the linear recurrent vector (c_t).

11.5.1   Cross-Serial dependencies

Shieber (1985) demonstrated the non-context-free nature of interleaved verb-object relations in Dutch and Swiss German. One of Shieber's examples of an embedded verb-object crossing dependency in Swiss German is given in example (A) below.

(A) Jan sät das mer **d'chind** em ***Hans*** es huus **lönd** ***hälfe*** aastriiche
Jan said that we the children-ACC Hans-DAT the house-ACC let help paint
Jan said that we let the children help Hans paint the house.

Similar patterns have been observed in other languages. They can be expressed by indexed grammars (Aho, 1968; Pulman and Ritchie, 1985), as well as a variety of other Mildly Context-Sensitive grammar formalisms (Joshi et al., 1990; Stabler, 2004).

Shieber (1985) identified that cross-serial dependency patterns of case marked nouns and their corresponding verbs can be iterated in this construction. The above pattern can be abstracted as a set of $a^m b^n c^m d^n$ structures, which together form a Mildly Context-Sensitive language.

Formally, we consider the family of languages $\mathcal{C}_k = \{a^m b^n c^m d^n \mid m + n < k\}$. Note that if $k < l$, then $\mathcal{C}_k \subset \mathcal{C}_l$. The training set consists of 51,200 strings picked uniformly from $\mathcal{C}_8$. The test set contains 5,120 strings picked uniformly from $\mathcal{C}_{10}$.

The RNNs are trained as generative language models. Assuming a sample string $w \in \mathcal{C}_{10}$, RNNs are trained to predict the symbol w_{i+1} given w_0 to w_i. Special start and stop symbols are added to the input strings, as is standard.

This is to be contrasted with the testing procedure. At test time, given the prefix $w_0 \ldots w_i$, a prediction of symbol w_{i+1} is deemed correct if it is a possible continuation for $w_0 \ldots w_i$; that is, if $w_0 \ldots w_{i+1}$ is a prefix of some string in $\mathcal{C}_{10}$. A set of predictions for a full string $x_0 \ldots x_k$ is classified as correct, if all predictions are correct up to and including the stop symbol. We report error rates for full strings only. This is because when models make a mistake, it is typically for a single symbol near the end of a string.

11.5.1.1 Results

Both RNNs struggle to generalise these patterns. They can model the training data well, but produce incorrect patterns in some cases on strings of any greater length than the samples in the training corpus.

We report four sets of results. The first set (Figure 11.3a) is the cross-entropy loss for the *test set* obtained by each model across training epochs. Low losses indicate that, on a per-character basis, the models reproduce the *exact* strings in the test set. We see that LSTM models generally make better guesses than URNs, across the board.

The second set (Figure 11.3b) is the error rate over number of epochs for each tested model. The best models can achieve less then ten percent error rate on average on the test set. However, the LSTM models with larger number of units exhibit overfitting.

In the third set we show the error rate for a given training loss in Figure 11.3c. The corresponding ratio is a measure of a model's capacity for correct predictions of a given quality of approximation of the training set. It can be taken as an indication of the model's bias for this task, relatively to generative language modelling. The URN models tend to achieve lower error rates for this task, even though they do less well from a generative language modelling perspective. For instance, the 32-unit URN is able to obtain an error rate below 0.4 with a training loss as high as 1. In general, the URNs provide a smoother decrease in error rate as they learn the language. In contrast, the LSTM models exhibit a sharp drop in error rate around 0.7 training loss.

Finally, we show the error rate broken down by length of pattern (reported as $n + m$). We see here that the LSTMs tend to do better overall than the URNs for lengths unseen in the training data. However, the LSTMs do worse when the number of units increases, while the URNs do better as that number increases, thanks to a lack of overfitting.

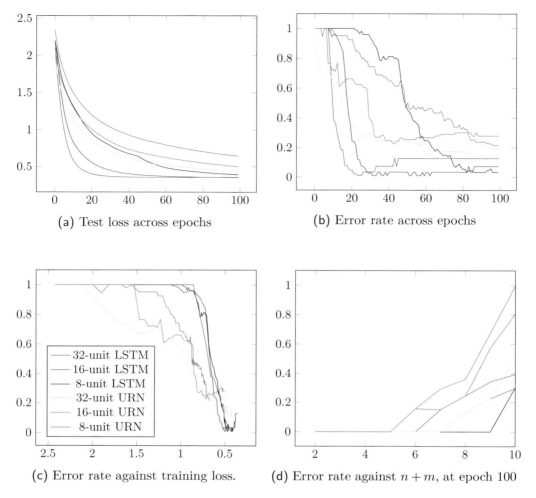

(a) Test loss across epochs

(b) Error rate across epochs

(c) Error rate against training loss.

(d) Error rate against $n + m$, at epoch 100

Figure 11.3   Cross-Serial dependencies results for various models.

11.5.2   Generalised Dyck Languages

In the next experiment, we evaluate the long-distance modelling capabilities of an RNN for a context-free language. As before, we abstract away from the noise of natural language, by constructing synthetic data. Following Bernardy (2018), we use a (generalised) Dyck language. It is composed solely of matching parenthesis pairs. So the strings "{([])}<>" and "{()[<>]}" are part of the language, while "<)" is not.

Formally, we use the language $\mathcal{D}$ defined as the set of strings generated by the following context-free rules: $E ::= \varepsilon; E ::= EE; E ::= oEc$, where (o, c) stands for a pair of matching parenthesis pairs. In all of our tests, we use 5 types of pairs (corresponding, for example, to the pairs () , [], {}, <> and ' '.)

The training phase treats the URN as a generative language model, applying a cross-entropy loss function at each position in the string. At test time, we evaluate the model's ability to predict the right kind of closing parenthesis at each point (this is the equivalent of predicting the number of a verb). We ignore predictions regarding opening parentheses, because they are always acceptable for the language. To generate a string with N matching pairs, we perform a random walk between opposite corners of a square grid of width and height N, such that one is not allowed to cross the diagonal. When not restricted by the boundary, a step can be taken either along the x or y axis with equal probability. A step along the x axis corresponds to opening a parenthesis, and one along the y axis involves closing one. The type of parenthesis pair is chosen randomly and uniformly.

In this task, we use strings with a length of exactly 20 characters. We train on 102,400 randomly generated strings, with maximum depth 3, and test it on 5120 random strings of maximum depth 10. Training is performed with a learning rate of 0.01, and a dropout rate of $\rho = 0.05$, for 100 epochs.

The aim of the task is to predict the correct type of *closing* parenthesis at every point in a string. It should be noted that this experiment is an idealised version of the agreement task proposed by Linzen, Dupoux, et al. (2016).[8] The opening parenthesis plays the role of a word (say a noun) which governs a feature of a subsequent word (like the number of a verb), represented by the closing parenthesis. Matching of parentheses corresponds to agreement. Linzen, Dupoux, et al. (2016) point out that sustaining accuracy over long distances requires that the model have knowledge of hierarchical syntactic structure. If an RNN captures the long-distance dependencies involved in agreement relations, it cannot rely solely on the nearby governing symbols. The measure of distance used by Linzen, Dupoux, et al. (2016) is the number of *attractors*. For our experiment, an attractor is defined as an opening parenthesis occurring within a matching pair, but of the wrong kind. For instance, in "{()}", the parenthesis "(" is an attractor. We complicate the matching task by varying the nesting depth between training and test phases. The *depth* of the string is the maximum nesting level reached within it. For instance "[{}]" has depth 2, while "{([()]<>)}" has depth 4.

11.5.2.1 Results

We report four sets of results. The first set (Figure 11.4a) is the cross-entropy loss for the *test set* achieved by each model across training epochs. Low losses indicate that, on a per-character basis, the models reproduce the *exact* strings in the test set. These losses cannot drop to zero because it is always valid to predict an opening parenthesis. As in the cross-serial task, we observe that LSTM models make better guesses than URN, at least for a similar number of units. However, we see that the training of the URN is uniformly monotonous, while the LSTM can sometimes become worse for a few epochs before converging. In fact, for eight units, the LSTM exhibits overfitting: in this case the test loss increases slowly after epoch 30.

To analyse the performance of each model on the task, we break down the error rate by number of attractors (Figure 11.4b). The URN models are weakest for a

---

[8]We report our experiment for the agreement task for natural language in the next section. Baroni (Chapter 1 of this volume) discusses the deep learning and linguistic aspects of this task in some detail.

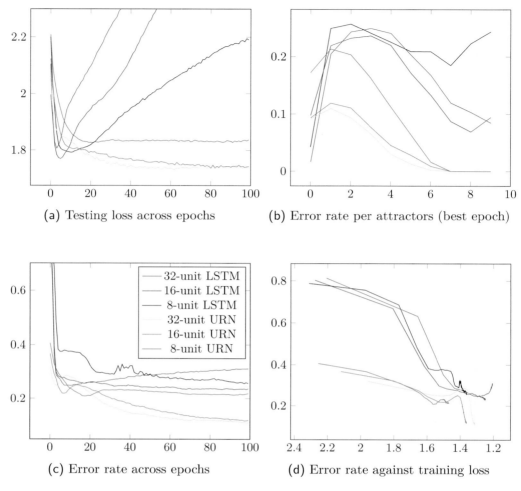

(a) Testing loss across epochs

(b) Error rate per attractors (best epoch)

(c) Error rate across epochs

(d) Error rate against training loss

Figure 11.4 Results for the Dyck language experiment. When reporting error rates as training progresses, we use the maximum error rate across number of attractors.

low number of attractors, and they achieve near perfect accuracy for a large number of attractors. According to Linzen, Dupoux, et al. (2016), this suggests that the models are highly successful in learning hierarchical structure. A high numbers of attractors corresponds to outer pairs, while a low number of attractors corresponds to inner pairs. In sum, in inner positions the URN suffers from some confusion. This confusion decreases as the number of units increases.

The LSTM exhibits good accuracy for adjacent pairs, with zero attractors, such as []. It does worst on pairs with three to four attractors. For larger number of units, the accuracy then increases again, all the way to the longest parenthesis pair. So the LSTM is good at making a prediction which depends only on the previous symbol, and it is also good at making a prediction for a pair which encloses the whole string. This indicates that it is fairly limited in its ability to capture hierarchical structures over long distances, even though it does much better than the majority class baseline, which stands at an 80% error rate.

In what follows, we will consider only the *maximum* error rate for any given number of attractors, over varying epochs. That is, we report on the peak value from the previous graph. Using this metric, the URNs perform consistently better than the LSTMs with the same number of units (and a similar number of parameters). They do so consistently across the training period (Figure 11.4c). However, we note that every model is capable of generalising to deeper nesting levels to some extent, with an accuracy well above a majority class baseline (80% error rate). The URN models beat the majority class baseline within the first epoch, while the LSTMs need a couple of epochs to do so.

Next we report the error rate against training loss (Figure 11.4d), as we did for the cross-serial dependency task. Again, we do not report the average error rate, but rather the *maximum* error rate for any given number of attractors. Here too, the relationship between error rate and training loss corresponds to the bias of the model for the task at hand, compared to a generative language model task. We observe that the URN models outperform the LSTM models across the board.

Finally, we consider variants of the URN model. We report accuracy of the URN model using either truncated embeddings, full embeddings, and for a baseline RNN with full embeddings that are not constrained to be orthogonal (i.e. any matrix). Still, no activation function is applied in any variant. In all three cases, the size of orthogonal matrices is 50 by 50. We report accuracy on the task by number of attractors in Figure 11.5. We see that truncating embeddings does affect performance, but not in a way that qualitatively changes the behaviour of the model. Truncating has an effect similar to using fewer units. The non-orthogonal (arbitrary matrices) model shows steadily decreasing accuracy relative to the number of attractors. We note that even this naive model is not capable of generalising to longer distances. The performance of the full URN is much better overall. This happens despite the fact that the orthogonal system is a special case of the arbitrary linear recurrent network, and so orthogonal embeddings are, in principle, available to the linear RNN without the orthogonal constraint. But it is not able to converge on the preferred solution (even for absolute loss). Our results show that restriction of the model to orthogonal matrices offers a significant benefit in generalisation and tracking power.

11.5.2.2 *Analysis*

Let's analyse the orthogonal embeddings further. We consider the three-truncated embeddings produced in the last variant of the experiment, and we start with the embeddings of individual characters and their signatures (Table 11.2). The average effect, and even the signatures of all embeddings, are strikingly similar. This does not imply that they are *equal*, because they act on different planes. We measure the similarity of planes using Definition 11.6.

We see in Table 11.1 that the planes which undergo rotation by similar angles are far from orthogonal to each other. One pair even exhibits a similarity of 1.73. This corresponds to the fact that the transformations of (and [manipulate a common subset of coordinates. On the other hand, those planes that undergo rotation by different angles tend to be in a closer to orthogonal relationship.

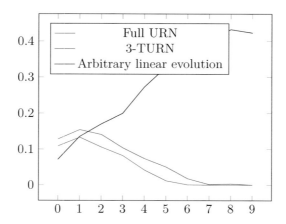

Figure 11.5 Error rate per number of attractors, at epoch 100, with 50 units, for various linear RNN architectures.

TABLE 11.1 Similarity for each pair of rotation planes, for the embeddings of (and [. Headers show the rotation effected on the compared planes.

	⊘	⊖	⊕
⊕	0.33	0.35	1.35
⊖	0.46	1.73	0.2
⊘	1.09	0.2	0.34

TABLE 11.2 Average effect and signatures of parenthesis embeddings and matching pairs.

character	average effect	signature	string	average effect	signature
(	14.79	⊕ ⊘ ⊘	()	0.06	⊕ ⊕ ⊕ ⊕
<	14.34	⊕ ⊘ ⊘	<>	0.06	⊕ ⊕ ⊕ ⊕
{	13.98	⊕ ⊘ ⊘	{}	0.07	⊕ ⊕ ⊕ ⊕
[	14.25	⊕ ⊘ ⊘	[]	0.06	⊕ ⊕ ⊕ ⊕
+	14.20	⊕ ⊘ ⊘	+-	0.06	⊕ ⊕ ⊕ ⊕
)	14.85	⊕ ⊘ ⊘			
>	14.42	⊕ ⊘ ⊘			
}	14.07	⊕ ⊘ ⊘			
]	14.34	⊕ ⊘ ⊘			
–	14.26	⊕ ⊘ ⊘			

11.5.2.3 Composition of Matching Parentheses

To further clarify the formal properties of our model let's look at the embeddings of matching pairs, computed as the product of the respective embeddings of the pairs. Such compositions are close to identity (Table 11.2). This observation explains the extraordinarily accurate long-distance performance of the URN on the matching task. Because a matching pair has essentially no effect on the state, by the time all parentheses have been closed, the state returns to its original condition. The model experiences the highest level of confusion when it is *inside* a deeply nested structure, and *not* when a deep structure is inserted between the governing opening parenthesis and the prediction conditioned on that parenthesis.

11.5.3 Natural Language Long-Distance Agreement Task

Having seen that the URN performs well on synthetic language applications, we turn to a natural language agreement task proposed by Linzen, Dupoux, et al. (2016). This involves predicting the number of third person verbs in English text, through supervised learning. In the phrase "The **keys** to the cabinet **are** on the table", the RNN is trained to predict the plural "**are**" rather than the singular "**is**". This is the natural equivalent of the bracket matching task discussed in the previous section.

The training data is composed of 1.7 million sentences with a selected subject-verb pair, extracted from Wikipedia. The vocabulary size is 50,000, with out-of-vocabulary tokens replaced by their part-of-speech tags. Training is performed for ten epochs, with a learning rate of 0.01, and a dropout rate of $\rho = 0.05$. We use 90% of the data for training, and 10% for validation and testing. A development subset is not required, since no effort was made to tune hyperparameters. Our first experiment proved sufficient to illustrate our main claims. In any case, a TURN has few hyperparameters to optimise.

Figure 11.6 shows the results for a 50-unit TURN with 3-truncated embeddings for the agreement task, for up to twelve attractors. We see that the TURN performs less well than the LSTM of Linzen, Dupoux, et al. (2016). The accuracy drops off for both models, as the number of attractors increases. Statistical uncertainty increases a lot with the number of attractors, due to decreasing numbers of examples.[9]

11.5.3.1 Analysis

Despite the unimpressive accuracy of the model, we can still use our theoretical tools to understand how the learned truncated unitary embeddings work. We first measure the average effect for the embeddings of common words in the dataset (Table 11.3), and other selected words and phrases (Table 11.5) obtained by composition. The table of effects for these words and phrases (ordered from smallest to largest effect) confirms our view concerning the measurement, along a particular plane, of the relations among the unitary embeddings applied to the agreement task. Tokens which are relevant to

---

[9]In earlier work (Bernardy and Lappin, 2022), we have reported that the URN does better on this task than the LSTM. This was due to an error in handling the training set. The current results should be understood as a correction of our earlier reported work.

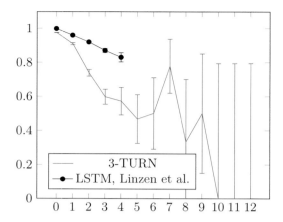

Figure 11.6 Accuracy per number of attractors for the verb number agreement task. Linzen, Dupoux, et al. (2016) do not report performance of their LSTM past four attractors. Error bars represent binomial 95% confidence intervals.

the task (e.g., "is", "which") have a larger effect than those which are not (e.g., the dot, "not").

Unfortunately, the average effect does not yield a sharp distinction among words for the agreement task. It also does not separate some classes of words which have a direct effect on the prediction (nouns, relative pronouns) from words which have only have an indirect effect (object pronouns). We can further refine the analysis by the projection of the word embedding $Q(x)$ onto the subspace generated by the projection layer.

Because we have only two possible predictions for this task, this space is 2-dimensional. The projection is a 2×2 matrix indicating how the word embedding acts on the features determining the prediction of the number of the coming verb.[10] The top left entry in the matrix corresponds to the action on the most relevant feature. Lower values for this entry correlate with a higher direct influence of the associated lexical item on the feature. This matrix is *not*, in general, orthogonal. But the projection of many embeddings is close to the identity matrix. This proximity indicates that the corresponding word has little direct influence on the prediction, although it could have an effect when combined with some other words.

Conversely, words which have a direct effect on the prediction receive a matrix which is far from identity. The pair of words "have" and "in" is particularly noteworthy. They have the same average effect, but different direct effects on the prediction, with "have" showing a much larger direct effect, as expected. The phrase "the keys to the cabinet" has a much larger effect on the agreement task than the phrase "the keys", but they both have a similar influence on the prediction of the next word. Note also that the phrase "the key" and its plural counterpart have a similar average effect, and similar signatures. But the projection on the prediction space shows much less effect for the singular. This can be explained by the fact that number prediction

---

[10]Essentially, we take the average for all other dimensions.

TABLE 11.3   Table of phrase effects for agreement experiment for the most frequent tokens in the corpus, ordered by average effect, from least to greatest. The *projection* column shows the projection of the rotation on the prediction space.

word	average effect	projection	word	average effect	projection
.	0.22	$\begin{pmatrix} 1.00 & -0.01 \\ 0.01 & 1.00 \end{pmatrix}$	from	4.09	$\begin{pmatrix} 0.93 & -0.05 \\ 0.06 & 0.90 \end{pmatrix}$
the	1.44	$\begin{pmatrix} 0.94 & 0.02 \\ -0.03 & 0.99 \end{pmatrix}$	i	4.11	$\begin{pmatrix} 0.91 & -0.07 \\ 0.05 & 0.95 \end{pmatrix}$
his	1.47	$\begin{pmatrix} 0.95 & 0.03 \\ -0.06 & 0.98 \end{pmatrix}$	it	4.14	$\begin{pmatrix} 0.95 & 0.00 \\ -0.04 & 0.91 \end{pmatrix}$
its	2.17	$\begin{pmatrix} 0.97 & 0.01 \\ -0.04 & 0.97 \end{pmatrix}$	and	4.18	$\begin{pmatrix} 0.94 & 0.00 \\ -0.03 & 0.94 \end{pmatrix}$
also	2.27	$\begin{pmatrix} 0.99 & 0.01 \\ -0.03 & 0.95 \end{pmatrix}$	on	4.33	$\begin{pmatrix} 0.94 & -0.08 \\ 0.06 & 0.95 \end{pmatrix}$
their	2.54	$\begin{pmatrix} 0.91 & 0.06 \\ -0.08 & 0.97 \end{pmatrix}$	with	4.36	$\begin{pmatrix} 0.91 & -0.11 \\ 0.05 & 0.95 \end{pmatrix}$
not	2.73	$\begin{pmatrix} 0.96 & 0.04 \\ -0.08 & 0.95 \end{pmatrix}$	has	4.41	$\begin{pmatrix} 0.91 & -0.03 \\ -0.02 & 0.87 \end{pmatrix}$
been	2.82	$\begin{pmatrix} 0.95 & 0.07 \\ -0.05 & 0.94 \end{pmatrix}$	for	4.62	$\begin{pmatrix} 0.93 & -0.06 \\ 0.11 & 0.88 \end{pmatrix}$
at	3.40	$\begin{pmatrix} 0.95 & -0.05 \\ -0.02 & 0.95 \end{pmatrix}$	in	4.62	$\begin{pmatrix} 0.94 & -0.07 \\ -0.02 & 0.93 \end{pmatrix}$
or	3.46	$\begin{pmatrix} 0.97 & -0.05 \\ 0.02 & 0.95 \end{pmatrix}$	have	4.62	$\begin{pmatrix} 0.78 & 0.16 \\ -0.05 & 0.92 \end{pmatrix}$
by	3.50	$\begin{pmatrix} 0.94 & -0.06 \\ 0.02 & 0.93 \end{pmatrix}$	who	4.68	$\begin{pmatrix} 0.84 & -0.10 \\ 0.09 & 0.94 \end{pmatrix}$
one	3.54	$\begin{pmatrix} 0.91 & 0.07 \\ -0.04 & 0.96 \end{pmatrix}$	were	4.88	$\begin{pmatrix} 0.62 & -0.01 \\ 0.08 & 0.95 \end{pmatrix}$
this	3.62	$\begin{pmatrix} 0.92 & 0.01 \\ -0.01 & 0.96 \end{pmatrix}$	that	5.00	$\begin{pmatrix} 0.85 & 0.12 \\ -0.14 & 0.88 \end{pmatrix}$
be	3.65	$\begin{pmatrix} 0.83 & 0.12 \\ -0.14 & 0.93 \end{pmatrix}$	was	5.55	$\begin{pmatrix} 0.72 & -0.03 \\ -0.04 & 0.92 \end{pmatrix}$
an	3.70	$\begin{pmatrix} 0.88 & 0.04 \\ -0.02 & 0.96 \end{pmatrix}$	(	5.68	$\begin{pmatrix} 0.86 & 0.03 \\ -0.13 & 0.91 \end{pmatrix}$
as	3.76	$\begin{pmatrix} 0.93 & 0.03 \\ -0.07 & 0.94 \end{pmatrix}$	)	5.74	$\begin{pmatrix} 0.90 & 0.04 \\ -0.10 & 0.92 \end{pmatrix}$
he	3.95	$\begin{pmatrix} 0.86 & -0.09 \\ 0.09 & 0.94 \end{pmatrix}$	are	6.25	$\begin{pmatrix} 0.53 & 0.02 \\ -0.06 & 0.91 \end{pmatrix}$
had	3.95	$\begin{pmatrix} 0.85 & 0.02 \\ -0.08 & 0.95 \end{pmatrix}$	but	6.27	$\begin{pmatrix} 0.73 & 0.09 \\ -0.22 & 0.89 \end{pmatrix}$
to	3.96	$\begin{pmatrix} 0.97 & -0.05 \\ 0.03 & 0.95 \end{pmatrix}$	is	6.38	$\begin{pmatrix} 0.68 & 0.02 \\ -0.08 & 0.92 \end{pmatrix}$
a	4.06	$\begin{pmatrix} 0.89 & 0.00 \\ -0.04 & 0.95 \end{pmatrix}$	which	7.75	$\begin{pmatrix} 0.71 & 0.01 \\ -0.19 & 0.85 \end{pmatrix}$
of	4.09	$\begin{pmatrix} 0.91 & -0.08 \\ 0.12 & 0.88 \end{pmatrix}$	,	8.35	$\begin{pmatrix} 0.58 & -0.09 \\ -0.26 & 0.77 \end{pmatrix}$

is biased towards the singular in the absence of context. For instance, a lone verb tends to be singular.

We also compute the Frobenius distance between pairs of orthogonal embeddings of the most frequent nouns, with both singular and plural inflections (Table 11.4). As our account predicts, nouns with the same number inflection tend to be grouped together (with a distance of 7.5 or less between them), while nouns with distinct numbers are further apart (with a distance of 7.5 or more).

TABLE 11.4   Distances between embeddings of most frequent nouns and their plural variants. Words which can be both nouns and verbs were excluded.

	article	year	area	world	family	articles	years	areas	worlds	families
article	0.00	7.04	6.51	6.89	5.82	9.26	9.84	10.01	10.87	9.39
year	7.04	0.00	7.62	6.30	5.38	8.22	9.06	9.75	10.14	8.64
area	6.51	7.62	0.00	6.42	6.34	9.57	9.70	10.39	11.63	10.39
world	6.89	6.30	6.42	0.00	5.17	7.32	8.82	9.17	9.13	7.83
family	5.82	5.38	6.34	5.17	0.00	7.71	7.72	8.78	9.49	8.82
articles	9.26	8.22	9.57	7.32	7.71	0.00	5.11	4.79	4.28	4.57
years	9.84	9.06	9.70	8.82	7.72	5.11	0.00	6.42	6.61	7.14
areas	10.01	9.75	10.39	9.17	8.78	4.79	6.42	0.00	5.93	6.09
worlds	10.87	10.14	11.63	9.13	9.49	4.28	6.61	5.93	0.00	7.79
families	9.39	8.64	10.39	7.83	8.82	4.57	7.14	6.09	7.79	0.00

TABLE 11.5   Effect, signature and projection of the embedding of selected phrases.

the key	4.34	◔ ◑ ◓ ◐	$\begin{pmatrix} 0.94 & 0.02 \\ -0.03 & 0.96 \end{pmatrix}$
the keys	5.32	◔ ◑ ◓ ◐	$\begin{pmatrix} 0.46 & 0.10 \\ -0.16 & 0.94 \end{pmatrix}$
the keys to the cabinet	11.85	◔ ◕ ◑ ◓ ◐ ◒ ◐	$\begin{pmatrix} 0.46 & 0.13 \\ -0.08 & 0.91 \end{pmatrix}$

11.6   RELATED WORK

It has frequently been observed that DNNs are complex and opaque in the way in which they operate. It is often unclear how they arrive at their results, or why they identify the patterns that they extract from training data. This has given rise to a concerted effort to render deep learning systems explainable (Linzen, Chrupała, and Alishahi, 2018; Linzen, Chrupała, Belinkov, et al., 2019). This problem has become more acute with the rapid development of very large pre-trained transformer models (Vaswani et al., 2017), like BERT (Devlin et al., 2018), GPT2 (Solaiman et al., 2019), GPT3 (Brown et al., 2020), and XLNet (Yang et al., 2019).

URNs avoid this difficulty through being strictly compositional by design. If they prove robust for a wide variety of NLP tasks, they will go some way to solving the problem of transparency in deep learning.

11.6.1   Learning Agreement

The capacity of Recurrent Neural Networks (RNNs), particularly LSTMs, to identify context-free long distance dependencies has been widely discussed in the NLP and cognitive science literature (Bernardy, 2018; Bernardy and Lappin, 2017; Elman, 1990; Gulordava et al., 2018; Lappin, 2021; Linzen, Dupoux, et al., 2016; Sennhauser and Berwick, 2018). These discussions have considered dependency patterns in both artificial systems, particularly Dyck languages, and in natural languages, with subject-verb agreement providing a paradigm case.

Bernardy (2018) tested the ability of LSTMs to predict closing parenthesis types in a Dyck language. The results are qualitatively similar to those obtained for natural language agreement. In both cases the LSTM makes the least successful predictions for a moderate number of attractors. However, he reports worse overall results than we achieved in our experiments, despite using an LSTM with more units. We attribute the improved performance of our LSTM to a better implementation of the model. A more optimal application of dropouts is a likely factor in getting better results than Bernardy's LSTM (2018).

While LSTMs (and GRUs) exhibit a certain capacity to generalise to deeper nesting, their accuracy declines in relation to nesting depth. This is also the case with their handling of natural language agreement. Other experimental work has illustrated this effect (Hewitt et al., 2020; Sennhauser and Berwick, 2018). Similar conclusions hold for generative self-attention architectures (Yu et al., 2019). Significantly, recent work has indicated that non-generative self-attention architectures, in the mode of BERT, perform poorly on this task (Bernardy, Ek, et al., 2021). Their work suggests that sequential processing is required to solve it.

By contrast URNs achieve excellent results for this task, without any decline in relation to either nesting depth or number of attractors. We have shown that this is because the learned unitary embeddings for matching parentheses are nearly the inverses of each other.

The question of whether generative language models can learn long-distance agreement was proposed by Linzen, Dupoux, et al. (2016). If accuracy is insensitive to the number of attractors, then we know that the model can work on long distances. The results of Linzen, Dupoux, et al. (2016) are inconclusive on this question. Even though the model does better than the majority class baseline for up to four attractors, accuracy declines steadily as the number of attractor increases. This trend is confirmed by Bernardy and Lappin (2017), who ran the same experiment on a larger dataset and explored the space of hyperparameters in detail. It is also confirmed by Gulordava et al. (2018), who analysed languages other than English. Marvin and Linzen (2018) focus on other linguistic phenomena, reaching similar conclusions. Lakretz et al. (2021) recently showed that an LSTM may extract bounded nested tree structures without learning a systematic recursive rule. These results do not hold directly for BERT-style models, because they are not generative language models.[11] For a detailed discussion of these results, see the recent account of Lappin (2021).

Our experiment shows that URNs can surpass state-of-the-art results for this kind of task. This is not surprising. URNs are designed so that they *cannot forget information*. It is expected that they will perform well on tracking long distance relations. The conservation of information in an URN is due to the fact that multiplying by an orthogonal matrix conserves cosine similarities: $\langle Qs_0, Qs_1 \rangle = \langle s_0, s_1 \rangle$. Therefore, any embedding Q, be it of a single word or of a long phrase, maps a change in its input state to an equal change in its output state. Considering all possible states as a distribution, Q conserves the density of states. Hence, contrary to the claims of

---

[11] Goldberg (2019) and Lau et al. (2020) suggest approaches for using them as generative LMs.

Sennhauser and Berwick (2018), URNs demonstrate that a class of RNNs can achieve rule-like accuracy in learning syntactic structure.

11.6.2 Cross-serial patterns

Kirov and Frank (2012) study both nested and cross-serial dependencies with a Simple Recurrent Network (SRN). As far as we are aware, our experiment is the first application of both LSTMs and URNs to cross-serial dependency relations. While both achieve encouraging initial accuracy in recognising the cross-serial patterns, URNs offer significant advantages in simplicity and transparency of architecture. They also displays enhanced stability in learning, and power of structural generalisation, relative to loss in training data.

11.6.3 Quantum-Inspired Systems

Unitary matrices are essential elements of quantum mechanics, and quantum computing. There, too, they ensure that the system does not lose information through time.

Coecke et al. (2010) and Grefenstette et al. (2011) propose what they describe as a quantum inspired model of linguistic representation. It computes vector values for sentences in a category theoretic representation of the types of a pregroup grammar (Lambek, 2008). The category theoretic structure in which this grammar is formulated is isomorphic with the one for quantum logic.

A difficulty of this approach is that it requires the input to be already annotated as parsed data. Another problem is the tensors associated with higher-types are very large, making them hard to learn. By contrast, URNs do not require a syntactic type system. Our experiments indicate that, with the right processing model, it is possible to learn syntactic structure and semantic composition from unannotated input.

Compositionality of phrase and sentence matrices is intrinsic to the formal specification of an URN.

The research that we report here extends and modifies some of the leading ideas in the foundational work of Coecke et al. (2010) and Grefenstette et al. (2011). They provided a system for handling computational semantics compositionally with structures that map onto the matrices of quantum circuits. We offer a model for learning syntactic structure, and for processing in general, that is strictly compositional. It uses some of the same core methods as the earlier work. In future research we will attempt to apply our model to NLP tasks involving semantic interpretation.

11.6.4 Tensor Recurrent Neural Networks

Sutskever et al. (2011) describe what they call a "tensor recurrent neural network" in which the transition matrix is determined by each input symbol. This design appears to be similar to URNs. However, unlike URNs, they use non-linear activation functions, and so they inherit the complications that these functions carry.

11.6.5 Unitary-Evolution Recurrent Networks

Arjovsky et al. (2016) proposed Unitary-Evolution recurrent networks to solve the problem of exploding and vanishing gradients, caused by the presence of non-linear activation functions. Despite this, Arjovsky et al. (2016) suggest the application of ReLU activation between time-steps, unlike URNs. Moreover, we are primarily concerned with the structure of the underlying unitary embeddings. The connection between the two lines work is that, exploding/vanishing gradients prevent an RNN from tracking long-term dependencies. URNs eliminate this problem.

Arjovsky et al. (2016)'s embeddings are computationally cheaper than ours, because they can be multiplied in linear time. Like us, they do not cover the whole space of unitary matrices. Jing et al. (2017) propose another representation which is computationally less expensive than ours, but which has asymptotically the same number of parameters. A third option is allow back-propagation to update the unitary matrices arbitrarily $n \times n$, and project them onto the unitary space periodically (Kiani et al., 2022; Wisdom et al., 2016).

Because we use a fully general matrix exponential implementation, our model is computationally more expensive than all the other options mentioned above. However, we have found that when experimenting with the unitary matrix encodings of Jing et al. (2017) and Arjovsky et al. (2016), we got much worse results for our experiments. This may be due to the fact that we do not use a ReLU activation function, as they do.

To the best of our knowledge, no previous study of URNs has addressed agreement or other NLP tasks. Rather, they have been applied to data-copying tasks, which are of limited linguistic interest. This includes the work of Vorontsov et al. (2017), even though it is ostensibly concerned with long distance dependencies.

11.7 CONCLUSIONS AND FUTURE WORK

Our experiments have shown the following. First, contrary to previous claims (Sennhauser and Berwick, 2018), RNNs can learn to recognise syntactic structures of the sort that characterise natural language syntax, with good accuracy. Furthermore, this can be done both with well-known models, such as an LSTM, and mathematically tractable ones, such as an URN. A particularly attractive result, is that these models achieve such accuracy with less than a couple of thousand parameters. For hierarchical structures, the models can generalise to much deeper depths. For cross-serial patterns, the models can approximate the training data well, but do not generalise well to longer patterns.

Second, we have shown the potential of URNs as devices for tracking and predicting complex dependency relations, over long strings, in a fully compositional way. The fact that URNs achieve good precision in predicting both deeply nested and cross-serial dependencies (up to certain length) suggests that they are able to recognise complex syntactic structures of the sort that are challenging for other neural networks. Furthermore, our experiments indicate that URNs are biased towards predicting the patterns found in context-free and mildly context-sensitive languages, even when trained as generative language models.

Third the fact that URNs satisfy strict compositionality offers an important advance in the search for explainable AI systems in deep learning models. Unlike LSTMs, they are compositional by design. They resolve the question of how to generate the composite values of input arguments in a principled and straightforward way. URNs learn *orthogonal embeddings*, which can be combined to provide representations for any phrase. We have demonstrated that they can be analysed using standard tools from linear algebra.

Fourth, the refined distance, effect, and relatedness metrics that unitary embeddings afford, open up the possibility of more interesting procedures for identifying natural syntactic and semantic word classes. These can be textured and dynamic, rather than static. They can focus on specific dimensions of meaning and structure, and they can be driven by particular NLP tasks. They are not blackbox processing devices that require indirect methods of analysis and assessment, as is the case with most other deep neural systems. Compositionality is realised by eschewing non-linear activation functions, which pervade other architectures, such as LSTMs. The presence of activation functions entail that the combination of two cells cannot be expressed as a single cell.

The move to powerful bidirectional transformers, like BERT, has produced enhanced performance in a variety of NLP and other AI tasks. This has been achieved at the expense of formal grounding and computational transparency. It is even less obvious why such models perform as well as they do on some tasks, and poorly on others, than is the case for LSTMs. By contrast, URNs offer simple, light weight deep neural networks whose operation is fully open to inspection and understanding at each point in the processing regime. They achieve encouraging accuracy in capturing complex hierarchical syntactic structures for both artificial and natural data.

Finally, we observe that the unitary matrices through which URNs compute output values from input arguments are identical to the gates of quantum logic. This suggests the intriguing possibility of implementing these models as quantum circuits. At some point in the future, this may facilitate training these models on large amounts of data, and efficiently generating results for tasks that are currently beyond the resources of conventional computational systems. Of course, quantum systems are still in their infancy, and thus caution is needed here when making claims of efficiency on behalf of quantum computing applied to machine learning.

11.8 ACKNOWLEDGEMENTS

The research reported in this paper was supported by grant 2014-39 from the Swedish Research Council, which funds the Centre for Linguistic Theory and Studies in Probability (CLASP) in the Department of Philosophy, Linguistics, and Theory of Science at the University of Gothenburg. We presented the main ideas of this paper to the CLASP Seminar, in December 2021, and to the Cognitive Science Seminar of the School of Electronic Engineering and Computer Science, Queen Mary University of London, in February 2022. We are grateful to the audiences of these two events for useful discussion and feedback. We thank Stephen Clark for a careful reading of an earlier draft of this chapter. His helpful comments resulted in numerous improvements. We bear sole responsibility for any errors that may remain in the current version.

BIBLIOGRAPHY

Abadi, Martín, Paul Barham, Jianmin Chen, Zhifeng Chen, Andy Davis, Jeffrey Dean, Matthieu Devin, Sanjay Ghemawat, Geoffrey Irving, Michael Isard, Manjunath Kudlur, Josh Levenberg, Rajat Monga, Sherry Moore, Derek G. Murray, Benoit Steiner, Paul Tucker, Vijay Vasudevan, Pete Warden, Martin Wicke, Yuan Yu, and Xiaoqiang Zheng (2016). "TensorFlow: A System for Large-Scale Machine Learning." In: *OSDI*. Vol. 16, pp. 265–283.

Aho, Alfred V. (1968). "Indexed Grammars–An Extension of Context-Free Grammars". In: 15.4, pp. 647–671.

Arjovsky, Martin, Amar Shah, and Yoshua Bengio (2016). "Unitary Evolution Recurrent Neural Networks". In: *Proceedings of the 33rd International Conference on International Conference on Machine Learning - Volume 48*. ICML'16. New York, NY, USA: JMLR.org, pp. 1120–1128.

Barker, Chris and Chung-chieh Shan (2004). "Continuations in natural language". In: *in Proceedings of the Fourth ACM SIGPLAN Workshop on Continuations, Hayo Thielecke*, pp. 55–64.

Baroni, Marco (2022). "On the proper role of linguistically-oriented deep net analysis in linguistic theorizing". In: *Algebraic Structures in Natural Language*. Ed. by Shalom Lappin and Jean-Philippe Bernardy. Taylor and Francis.

Bernardy, Jean-Philippe (2018). "Can RNNs Learn Nested Recursion?" In: *Linguistic Issues in Language Technology* 16 (1).

Bernardy, Jean-Philippe, Rasmus Blanck, Stergios Chatzikyriakidis, and Shalom Lappin (Aug. 2018). "A Compositional Bayesian Semantics for Natural Language". In: *Proceedings of the First International Workshop on Language Cognition and Computational Models*. Santa Fe, New Mexico, USA: Association for Computational Linguistics, pp. 1–10. URL: https://www.aclweb.org/anthology/W18-4101 (visited on 03/01/2021).

Bernardy, Jean-Philippe and Koen Claessen (2013). "Efficient Divide-and-Conquer Parsing of Practical Context-Free Languages". In: *Proceedings of the 18th ACM SIGPLAN international conference on Functional Programming*, pp. 111–122.

— (2015). "Efficient Parallel and Incremental Parsing of Practical Context-Free Languages". In: *Journal of Functional Programming* 25. ISSN: 1469-7653. DOI: 10.1017/S0956796815000131.

Bernardy, Jean-Philippe, Adam Ek, and Vladislav Maraev (2021). "Can the Transformer Learn Nested Recursion with Symbol Masking?" In: *Findings of the ACL 2021*.

Bernardy, Jean-Philippe and Shalom Lappin (2017). "Using Deep Neural Networks to Learn Syntactic Agreement". In: *Linguistic Issues in Language Technology* 15.2, p. 15. ISSN: 1945-3604.

Bernardy, Jean-Philippe and Shalom Lappin (2022). "A Neural Model for Compositional Word Embeddings and Sentence Processing". In: *Proceedings of the Workshop on Cognitive Modeling and Computational Linguistics*. Association for Computational Linguistics.

Brown, T., B. Mann, Nick Ryder, Melanie Subbiah, J. Kaplan, P. Dhariwal, Arvind Neelakantan, Pranav Shyam, Girish Sastry, Amanda Askell, Sandhini Agarwal, Ariel Herbert-Voss, G. Krüger, Tom Henighan, R. Child, Aditya Ramesh, D. Ziegler, Jeffrey Wu, Clemens Winter, Christopher Hesse, Mark Chen, E. Sigler, Mateusz Litwin, Scott Gray, Benjamin Chess, J. Clark, Christopher Berner, Sam McCandlish, A. Radford, Ilya Sutskever, and Dario Amodei (2020). "Language models are few-shot learners". In: *ArXiv* abs/2005.14165.

Coecke, Bob, Mehrnoosh Sadrzadeh, and Stephen Clark (2010). "Mathematical Foundations for a Compositional Distributional Model of Meaning". In: *Lambek Festschrift, Linguistic Analysis* 36.

Devlin, Jacob, Ming-Wei Chang, Kenton Lee, and Kristina Toutanova (2018). "Bert: Pre-training of deep bidirectional transformers for language understanding". In: *arXiv preprint arXiv:1810.04805*.

Elman, Jeffrey L. (1990). "Finding structure in time". In: *Cognitive Science* 14.2, pp. 179–211.

Emerson, Guy and Ann Copestake (2016). "Functional Distributional Semantics". In: *Proceedings of the 1st Workshop on Representation Learning for NLP, Rep4NLP@ACL 2016, Berlin, Germany, August 11, 2016*. Ed. by Phil Blunsom, Kyunghyun Cho, Shay B. Cohen, Edward Grefenstette, Karl Moritz Hermann, Laura Rimell, Jason Weston, and Scott Wen-tau Yih. Association for Computational Linguistics, pp. 40–52. DOI: 10.18653/v1/W16-1605. URL: https://doi.org/10.18653/v1/W16-1605.

— (2017). "Semantic Composition via Probabilistic Model Theory". In: *IWCS 2017 - 12th International Conference on Computational Semantics - Long papers*. URL: http://aclweb.org/anthology/W17-6806.

Gantmacher, Felix Ruvimovich (1959). *The Theory of Matrices*. AMS Chelsea publishing.

Goldberg, Yoav (2019). "Assessing BERT's Syntactic Abilities". In: *ArXiv* abs/1901.05287.

Grefenstette, Edward, Mehrnoosh Sadrzadeh, Stephen Clark, Bob Coecke, and Stephen Pulman (2011). "Concrete Sentence Spaces for Compositional Distributional Models of Meaning". In: *Proceedings of the Ninth International Conference on Computational Semantics (IWCS 2011)*.

Groote, Philippe de (2001). "Type raising, continuations, and classical logic". In: *Proceedings of the Thirteenth Amsterdam Colloquium*, pp. 97–101.

Grove, Julian and Jean-Philippe Bernardy (2021). "Probabilistic compositional semantics, purely". In: *Proceedings of Logic and Engineering of Natural Language Semantics 18*.

Gulordava, Kristina, Piotr Bojanowski, Edouard Grave, Tal Linzen, and Marco Baroni (2018). "Colorless Green Recurrent Networks Dream Hierarchically". In: *Proceedings of the 2018 Conference of the North American Chapter of the As-*

sociation for Computational Linguistics: Human Language Technologies, Volume 1 (Long Papers). New Orleans, Louisiana: Association for Computational Linguistics, pp. 1195–1205.

Hewitt, John, Michael Hahn, Surya Ganguli, Percy Liang, and Christopher D Manning (2020). "RNNs can generate bounded hierarchical languages with optimal memory". In: *arXiv preprint arXiv:2010.07515*. URL: https://arxiv.org/pdf/2010.07515.pdf.

Hochreiter, Sepp and Jürgen Schmidhuber (Nov. 1997). "Long short-term memory". In: *Neural Computation* 9.8, pp. 1735–1780. ISSN: 0899-7667. DOI: 10.1162/neco.1997.9.8.1735.

Jing, Li, Yichen Shen, Tena Dubček, John Peurifoi, Scott Skirlo, Yann LeCun, Max Tegmark, and Marin Soljačić (2017). "Tunable Efficient Unitary Neural Networks (EUNN) and their application to RNN". In: *arXiv*.

Joshi, Aravind K., K. Vijay Shanker, and David Weir (1990). *The Convergence of Mildly Context-Sensitive Grammar Formalisms*. Tech. rep. Philadelphia, PA: Department of Computer and Information Science, University of Pennsylvania.

Kiani, Bobak, Randall Balestriero, Yann Lecun, and Seth Lloyd (2022). *projUNN: efficient method for training deep networks with unitary matrices*. URL: https://arxiv.org/pdf/2203.05483.pdf.

Kingma, Diederik P. and Jimmy Ba (2014). "Adam: A Method for Stochastic Optimization". In: *CoRR* abs/1412.6980. URL: http://arxiv.org/abs/1412.6980.

Kirov, Christo and Robert Frank (2012). "Processing of nested and cross-serial dependencies: an automaton perspective on SRN behaviour". In: *Connection Science* 24.1, pp. 1–24.

Lakretz, Yair, Théo Desbordes, Jean-Rémi King, Benoît Crabbé, Maxime Oquab, and Stanislas Dehaene (2021). "Can RNNs learn Recursive Nested Subject-Verb Agreements?" In: *arXiv preprint arXiv:2101.02258*.

Lambek, Joachim (2008). "Pregroup Grammars and Chomsky's Earliest Examples". In: *Journal of Logic, Language and Information* 17, pp. 141–160.

Lappin, Shalom (2021). *Deep Learning and Linguistic Representation*. Boca Raton, London, New York: CRC Press, Taylor & Francis.

Lau, Jey Han, Carlos Armendariz, Shalom Lappin, Matthew Purver, and Chang Shu (2020). "How Furiously Can Colorless Green Ideas Sleep? Sentence Acceptability in Context". In: *Transactions of the Association for Computational Linguistics* 8, pp. 296–310.

Linzen, Tal, Grzegorz Chrupała, and Afra Alishahi, eds. (2018). *Proceedings of the 2018 EMNLP Workshop BlackboxNLP: Analyzing and Interpreting Neural Networks for NLP*. Brussels, Belgium: Association for Computational Linguistics.

Linzen, Tal, Grzegorz Chrupała, Yonatan Belinkov, and Dieuwke Hupkes, eds. (Aug. 2019). *Proceedings of the 2019 ACL Workshop BlackboxNLP: Analyzing and Interpreting Neural Networks for NLP*. Florence, Italy: Association for Computational Linguistics.

Linzen, Tal, Emmanuel Dupoux, and Yoav Golberg (2016). "Assessing the Ability of LSTMs to Learn Syntax-Sensitive Dependencies". In: *Transactions of the Association of Computational Linguistics* 4, pp. 521–535.

Marvin, Rebecca and Tal Linzen (2018). "Targeted Syntactic Evaluation of Language Models". In: *Proceedings of the 2018 Conference on Empirical Methods in Natural Language Processing*. Brussels, Belgium: Association for Computational Linguistics, pp. 1192–1202.

Mikolov, Tomas, Ilya Sutskever, Kai Chen, Greg Corrado, and Jeffrey Dean (2013). "Distributed Representations of Words and Phrases and Their Compositionality". In: *Proceedings of the 26th International Conference on Neural Information Processing Systems - Volume 2*. NIPS'13. Lake Tahoe, Nevada, pp. 3111–3119.

Montague, Richard (1970a). "English as a formal language". In: *Linguaggi nella Societa e nella Tecnica*. Ed. by B. Visentini et al.

— (1970b). "Universal grammar". en. In: *Theoria* 36.3, pp. 373–398. ISSN: 1755-2567. DOI: 10.1111/j.1755-2567.1970.tb00434.x. URL: https://onlinelibrary.wiley.com/doi/abs/10.1111/j.1755-2567.1970.tb00434.x (visited on 10/26/2020).

— (1974). "The Proper Treatment of Quantification in Ordinary English". In: *Formal Philosophy*. Ed. by Richmond Thomason. New Haven: Yale UP.

Moss, Lawrence S. (2022). "Algebra and Language: Reasons for (Dis)content". In: *Algebraic Structures in Natural Language*. Ed. by Shalom Lappin and Jean-Philippe Bernardy. Taylor & Francis.

Pulman, Stephen and G. D. Ritchie (1985). *Indexed Grammars and Intersecting Dependencies*. Tech. rep. 23. University of East Anglia, pp. 21–38.

Ranta, Aarne (2004). "Grammatical Framework". In: *Journal of Functional Programming* 14.2, pp. 145–189.

Sennhauser, Luzi and Robert Berwick (2018). "Evaluating the Ability of LSTMs to Learn Context-Free Grammars". In: *Proceedings of the 2018 EMNLP Workshop BlackboxNLP: Analyzing and Interpreting Neural Networks for NLP*. Brussels, Belgium: Association for Computational Linguistics, pp. 115–124.

Shieber, Stuart M. (1985). "Evidence against the context-freeness of natural language". In: *Linguistics and Philosophy* 8.3, pp. 333–343.

Solaiman, Irene, Miles Brundage, J. Clark, Amanda Askell, Ariel Herbert-Voss, Jeff Wu, A. Radford, and J. Wang (2019). "Release Strategies and the Social Impacts of Language Models". In: *ArXiv* abs/1908.09203.

Stabler, Edward P. (2004). "Varieties of crossing dependencies: Structure dependence and mild context sensitivity". In: *Cognitive Science* 93.5, pp. 699–720.

Strang, Gilbert (2016). *Introduction to Linear Algebra,* 5th edition. Wellesley-Cambridge Press. ISBN: 978-09802327-7-6.

Sutskever, Ilya, James Martens, and Geoffrey E. Hinton (2011). "Generating Text with Recurrent Neural Networks". In: *Proceedings of the 28th International Conference on Machine Learning, ICML 2011, Bellevue, Washington, USA, June 28 - July 2, 2011*. Ed. by Lise Getoor and Tobias Scheffer. Omnipress, pp. 1017–1024. URL: https://icml.cc/2011/papers/524%5C_icmlpaper.pdf.

Valiant, Leslie Gabriel (1975). "General context-free recognition in less than cubic time". In: *Journal of Computer and System Sciences* 10.2, pp. 308–314.

Vaswani, Ashish, Noam Shazeer, Niki Parmar, Jakob Uszkoreit, Llion Jones, Aidan N. Gomez, Lukasz Kaiser, and Illia Polosukhin (June 2017). "Attention Is All You Need". en. In: *arXiv:1706.03762 [cs]*. arXiv: `1706.03762 [cs]`.

Vorontsov, Eugene, Chiheb Trabelsi, Samuel Kadoury, and Chris Pal (2017). "On Orthogonality and Learning Recurrent Networks with Long Term Dependencies". In: *arXiv*.

Wisdom, Scott, Thomas Powers, John Hershey, Jonathan Le Roux, and Les Atlas (2016). "Full-capacity unitary recurrent neural networks". In: *Advances in Neural Information Processing Systems* 29, pp. 4880–4888.

Yang, Zhilin, Zihang Dai, Yiming Yang, Jaime G. Carbonell, Ruslan Salakhutdinov, and Quoc V. Le (2019). "XLNet: Generalized Autoregressive Pretraining for Language Understanding". In: *ArXiv* abs/1906.08237.

Yu, Xiang, Ngoc Thang Vu, and Jonas Kuhn (2019). "Learning the Dyck language with attention-based Seq2Seq models". In: *Proceedings of the 2019 ACL Workshop BlackboxNLP: Analyzing and Interpreting Neural Networks for NLP*, pp. 138–146.

Index

Italicized and **bold** pages refer to figures and tables respectively, and page numbers followed by "n" refer to notes.